# ISRAEL <sup>AND</sup><sub>THE</sub> DEAD SEA SCROLLS

# ISRAEL AND THE DEAD SEA SCROLLS

## EDMUND WILSON

WITH A FOREWORD BY LEON EDEL AND
A NEW INTRODUCTION BY RAPHAEL ISRAELI

Routledge
Taylor & Francis Group

LONDON AND NEW YORK

Originally published in 1978 by Farrar Straus Giroux

Published 2012 by Transaction Publishers

Published 2017 by Routledge
2 Park Square, Milton Park, Abingdon, Oxon OX14 4RN
711 Third Avenue, New York, NY 10017, USA

*Routledge is an imprint of the Taylor & Francis Group,
an informa business*

Library of Congress Catalog Number: 2011017767

Library of Congress Cataloging-in-Publication Data
Wilson, Edmund, 1895-1972.
  [Israel]
  Israel and the Dead Sea Scrolls / Edmund Wilson ; with a
  foreword by Leon Edel and a new introduction by Raphael
  Israeli.
        p. cm.
  ISBN 978-1-4128-4248-8
    1. Dead Sea scrolls. 2. Israel--Description and travel. 3.
  Bible. O.T. Genesis--Criticism, interpretation, etc. 4. Wilson,
  Edmund, 1895-1972--Travel--Israel. 5. Authors, American-
  -20th century--Biography. I. Wilson, Edmund, 1895-1972.
  Dead Sea scrolls, 1947-1969. II. Title.

BM487.W498 2011
296.1'55--dc23

                                            2011017767

ISBN 13: 978-1-4128-4248-8 (pbk)

# CONTENTS

# INTRODUCTION TO THE TRANSACTION EDITION
by Raphael Israeli

Edmund Wilson (1895-1972), a prolific literary critic and social commentator, published some twenty books in his lifetime, including one on the *Dead Sea Scrolls* (1955), and ten more were published posthumously, mainly based on his diaries. He spent most of his thirty-five years of academic teaching at Princeton, towards the end of which he undertook the study of Hebrew at the Theological Seminary, following his frustration in failing to read Genesis in its original tongue. An intellectually curious and strong-willed scholar of his kind does not yield easily to circumstance, and after his mastery of Greek and Latin, it was only natural for him to venture into the ancient tongue of the Prophets. So, at sixty, with French and Russian also already under his belt, Wilson launched into the conquest of Hebrew.

While involved in his Hebrew grammar, he got wind of the sensational discovery of the Dead Sea Scrolls, in Hebrew and Aramaic, miraculously preserved for two millennia in earthen jars, sheltered in ancient caves, on the northwestern shore of that salt lake. Thereupon, as a reporter for *The New Yorker*, he took a trip to the area to cover that exhilarating event. Wilson pursued his task with enthusiasm and zeal, in an attempt to transmit to his readers an encapsulated history of two millennia plus the contents of the scrolls which gradually revealed themselves as invaluable for understanding the history of the Jewish Second Temple period, the religious divisions among the people of Israel, like the rise of the Essenes, the beginnings of Christianity, and the rule of the Romans. Wilson was not specifically trained in these complex disciplines, neither in the Aramaic language, Jewish *Halacha,* nor in Semitic linguistics, all of which would have been needed as basic tools of serious research into these domains. But his acute flair for history and for ancient lore largely filled that void.

The end result was, that though more of a journalistic report than a field study in anthropology, or a historical analysis of documents, or a series of interviews with great scholars, this elegantly and humorously written volume, first serialized by *The New Yorker,* became one of the most highly regarded narratives of his time, for he artfully wove all the threads of folklore, history, intrigue and jealousies between scholars into a powerful fabric of fluent narration that reads like a thriller. Thus, unlike the Christian and Jewish clergy who regarded Wilson as a trespasser into a field full of pitfalls, scholars looked down upon him as someone who had no clue, and certainly not the prerequisites that were the *sine qua non* for understanding the immense topic at hand.

However, though Wilson was indeed unable to write as a specialist about the Scrolls, which he never claimed to be, he was destined to lend them their world fame precisely by turning their story into a well-written tale, making them familiar to the general public and for which they retained their fascination thereafter. He was preceded in this paradoxical task by non-expert Bedouin herdsmen who accidentally discovered them, and brought them to the scrutiny of antiquarians, who recognized their worth and, while making their own fortunes, transmitted them to scholars and interested institutions of knowledge. But the same trend continued: After Wilson died in 1972, the executrix of his estate, Elana Wilson, turned to yet another non-expert, Leon Edel (1907-1997), also a renowned literary critic and old friend and colleague of Wilson's, to write a foreword for the newly revised edition of 1978. That introduction provided many of the details revealed of the genesis of the book in its original form.

The thread of this tradition was not severed when I took upon myself to write this new foreword to this renewed edition, more than half a century after the book first saw the light of day. I won this honor simply because a couple of years ago, I published with the same publisher, Transaction, yet another non-specialist book on the Dead Sea Scrolls, entitled *Piracy in Qumran: The Battle over the Scrolls of the Pre-Christ Era.* Once again, this volume did not concern the core of the Scrolls and the stories they had to tell, but an external matter that turned out to be of the utmost complexity in our era of endless legal battles, contentions and conflicts, which are often crowned, but never resolved, with ambiguous judgments and verdicts that generate more debates and more dissenting legal opinions. In fact, that volume focused on the legal battles between Israeli Professor Qimron, a genuine expert in deciphering and reconstructing the Scrolls, and the American archaeological editor M. Shanks, who was charged with plagiarizing Qimron's work and who eventually lost his case in both the District and the Supreme courts in Israel.

The legal debate, which lasted years, and at a great cost to the losing defendants, drew considerable attention in the world, especially as regards to the question of copyright. The question was of great weight: Was anyone who reconstructed a text written 2000 years ago by an ancient author, able in his own right to claim authorship of the deciphered and reconstructed texts, where many lacunae had to be filled in through educated guess and scholarly erudition, as the plaintiff claimed; or, did the copyright for authorship remain squarely with the original author indefinitely, exonerating *a-priori* anyone from any charge of plagiarism or usurpation, as the defendant maintained? Two schools of law crystallized worldwide around those verdicts, the one by Justice Dalia Dorner of Israel who decided for the first option, the other around a group of prominent American lawyers who continue to maintain the second, as expressed in the Winter 1995 issue of the *Michigan Journal of International Law*. So, the debate continues.

One of the major issues under debate, which generated much bitterness and many international and interpersonal accusations, was the exclusivity of research with the Scrolls, which was confined to a restricted group of international scholars, who had the sole discretion to decide who researched what, something that seriously crippled the process of publishing the original documents and bringing their findings to the public. Those shackles were largely removed after Israel took possession at the Rockefeller Museum in East Jerusalem (1967), which later consigned the Scrolls to the care of the Israeli Antiquities Authority. Its researchers were more qualified, skilled, trained, and eager to research those parchments, which touched upon the very foundations of their own history and faith, than were the Arab authorities of the Jordanian rule in Jerusalem prior to 1967. But now that the Israel Antiquities Authority has announced that it is partnering with Google to digitize all the Scrolls, in high resolution, and make them available to everybody on Internet, with the push of a button, the question of universal and easy access will be resolved *ipso facto*.

But the controversies are far from settled. One of the instigators has been Professor Norman Golb, from the University of Chicago, an old hand in Judaica, who had issued a stupefying theory that struck at the foundations of the Dead Sea Scrolls research, and which puzzled all researchers in the field. He stunningly put into question the existence of the Dead Sea Sect (which some identified as the Essenes), also known as the Qumran Community, and raised doubts about the link between them and the Scrolls. He contended that the Scrolls had been taken from the library of the Temple and smuggled into the desert for safekeeping from the approaching disaster in the Roman campaign of destruction. If that were true, that would prove that they belonged to the mainstream rather than to dissenting sects. He claimed that Qumran was no place fit for habitation, only a military fort like Massada, where the Scrolls could be preserved. He also theorized, that while Rabbinic Judaism derived from the minority Pharisees, which mounted a coup and imposed themselves on Judaism, Christianity was the direct offspring of the mainstream represented by the Scrolls, arguably the Sadducees. In his view, the fact that there exists a 300-year black hole subsequent to destruction (in AD 70) only shows that the Pharisees obliterated the ancient writings in order to sever the link between the previously predominant Sadducee tradition and their contemporaneous Judaism, which they wished to cast in their new mold.

Golb has been bitterly opposed by Lawrence Schiffman of New York University's Skirball Department of Hebrew and Judaic Studies, who charged that Golb and his family were harassing him. Some of those controversies were upheld by two Israeli archaeologists, Yuval Peleg and Itzhak Magen, who have exploded the Qumran myth by claiming that the place lacked anything unique, thus implicitly supporting Golb's theories. Their digs have revealed findings that included jewelry, imported pieces of glassware and expensive stone cosmetics containers, something that runs fundamentally counter to the earlier assumption that the inhabitants of the place were poor and ascetic. The belief among some scholars that John the Baptist was under the influence of the Essenes makes the entire issue captivating both for the history of Jewish sectarianism as well as for the history of early Christianity. If these revolutionary findings are confirmed, they might alter in many ways the traditional interpretations of the Scrolls. Thus, the tradition-treading book of Wilson, which came out prior to all these debates, is a fresh return of the story of the Scrolls to its original peaceful mystery where everything seemed to be falling neatly into place.

In the meantime, Raphael Golb, the son of Norman the controversial scholar, was convicted in a Manhattan court of law in October 2010 for using online aliases to harass and discredit his father's detractors in the heated academic debate, including Schiffman. As the appeal of that verdict is to be heard in the coming months, it does not seem that the argument will die down any time soon. Golb, the son, is a linguistic scholar and lawyer in his own right, who appears far from having exhausted his capacities for litigation. He is determined to defend his father's reputation from the online smears against it, and to claim a court verdict against Schiffman for having allegedly plagiarized his father's work. Whether the republication of Edmund Wilson's now classic 50-year-old pioneering volume, which cultivated no controversies on this scale, can cool the mood, only time will tell.

# FOREWORD
## by Leon Edel

At Princeton in 1952, during an autumn of much sunshine, I found myself taking long walks with Edmund Wilson. We were both giving the recently established Christian Gauss Seminars in criticism at the university. These brought together professional writers and critics for peer discussions. It is curious to look back, to remember the faces around the seminar table, in the light of subsequent reputations—John Berryman, still beardless; Saul Bellow, about to bring forth Augie March; the unpredictable Delmore Schwartz; the untried Irving Howe and R. W. B. Lewis. We listened closely to Edmund as he talked of the literature of the Civil War (later to become *Patriotic Gore*). He was our senior and to most of us an oracle. I had met him sometime earlier in New York and one day he suggested that I join him on his daily wanderings around the campus and in the older streets of Princeton. "It will be the Edmund Wilson seminar on Princeton for Edel," he said. He was eager to show me what was left of *his* Princeton—thirty-five years after he had been a student. And so we would set out, around 4 p.m. in the diffused light of late autumn, mufflered against chill, rotund Edmund carrying his walking stick, followed by his rotund dilatory cocker spaniel. We were dilatory, too: Edmund liked to linger in front of the old buildings and old houses where he had

once dined with Scott Fitzgerald or John Peale Bishop;
every place had its associations and memories, and his
talk had much vividness and appeal for a literary historian like myself.

One day we inspected the Theological Seminary. I
offered my scrap of knowledge: Henry James's father had
studied there. "I'm studying there right now," said
Edmund. I wanted to say that I hadn't known of his
clerical interests, but he forestalled speculation by adding, "I'm studying Hebrew." And he described how a few
months earlier he had come on his Presbyterian grandfather's Hebrew Bible and how frustrating he found it
not to be able to read Genesis. It was the announcement
of a man who had his Latin and his Greek; who spoke
French fluently and had learned Russian in the 1930's.
Now approaching sixty, he had decided to learn the
archaic language whose ornate letters must be read from
right to left. The Hebrew alphabet and the Hebrew
language had the kind of intellectual and spiritual
mystery Edmund Wilson always found a challenge.

A few days after this he invited me to come to tea at
his house with his theological classmates. When I protested I could be of little help discussing ancient languages, he gave me one of his conspiratorial looks. He
lowered his voice. He explained that his classmates, being
future clergy, were teetotalers. In all politeness he couldn't
pour himself whiskey while offering them tea. "Now, if
you were there, you could be of enormous help." He
would fill my glass with whiskey and then pour some
for himself; and all the amenities would be observed.
"You are using me," I said. But I agreed to be used and
I am glad I did. For I still remember the hushed respectful semicircle around Edmund, the soft tones of the
Hebrew professor, the young future clergy with their

crew cuts and clean turned-down collars and their well-brushed suits, sipping their tea, while Edmund filled my glass (and his own) as promised. It was like a *cheder*, a Hebrew parochial school, and I listened to a whole hour of the *Aleph Beth*. I wished Max Beerbohm could have been present to draw one of his cartoons, like the one of Robert Browning taking tea with the Browning Society. "Mr. Wilson as seminarist learning to read Genesis." This would have been my caption. But what he learned above all is told in the pages of the book he later wrote, now reissued in this new form.

*The Dead Sea Scrolls* had its origin in that winter of Hebrew studies at Princeton when, to the experience of being an elderly seminarist, Edmund Wilson added the wonders of an archaeological and journalistic flight into the very heart of old Palestine. In his mounting enthusiasm for his Hebrew grammar and the spelling out of Genesis, Edmund came on the news of the discovery of certain obscure Hebrew and Aramaic manuscripts in caves near the northwest corner of the Dead Sea. There followed his trip to the Holy Land, as reporter for *The New Yorker*, to see the ancient landscapes for himself and to interrogate the experts. The Dead Sea, as a piece of geography, belonged to the dreams of Edmund's childhood. He has described how his father had a favorite phrase about "weltering around in a Dead Sea of mediocrity." Edmund must have remembered this when he found himself "weltering" around a desolate landscape, seeing here and there some old Bedouin woman attending a flock of black goats. He was living an archaeological drama. Hidden away, like Tutankhamen's tomb, had been these precious writings, old and seemingly indecipherable scrolls, which had sat out their time in deep caves as centuries rolled by—from the time of the Roman

Empire to modern wars in Israel. Reading him, it is not difficult to imagine the ardor with which Edmund Wilson pursued his complex subject; it was the kind of subject he had always liked best, involving as it did history, politics, ancient lore, and all his faculties for imaginative reconstruction and historical analysis.

There has been much brilliant journalism in our century, but most journalists deal with the actual and the immediate; they have time neither to read history nor to equip themselves linguistically. Edmund Wilson's reportage linked a popular narrative to high erudition. For his task, he read or reread Josephus, Pliny the Elder, Philo, and also Gibbon. He had read Renan long before and now returned with enthusiasm to him. He pored over the learned journals with that leisurely absorption he had cultivated in all his researches. The result was an extraordinary coup for *The New Yorker*: a modern Sherlock Holmes story, in which Edmund unveiled for us the accidental discovery by some Bedouin boys of the scrolls while tossing stones into caves near the Dead Sea; the intricate dealings with Near Eastern political and religious figures, in that mixture of obsequiousness and malice we find in the writings of Lawrence of Arabia; and then the advent of the archaeologist and the scholar. Within all this was the delicate fabric of churchly fears and jealousies lest old myths and old beliefs be overthrown. Edmund Wilson was embracing a grandly historic subject which scholars and clergy considered sacred ground. Small wonder that he was treated as a trespasser, if not an interloper. The Christian clergy, possessing the Word, found it hard to entertain the danger of some possible new Word. The Hebrews felt, with their ancient Talmudic saturation, that they alone could interpret old writings; and that no amateur could possess what they had laboriously acquired as the gift, so to speak, of the centuries. Other scholars felt the exact opposite—there was a danger that learned Jews might read too much into texts that required scientific explication.

All this is told by Edmund in his narrative with good humor and a play of irony—the commerce in antiquities, the rivalries, the courtesies of old Eastern manners, the subterfuges of truth and deceit. The general opinion now, some two decades since Wilson published his first account, and one decade since he brought out his extensive updating of it—both reproduced in this edition—is that he performed an unusual function, aside from writing a fascinating research story. General Yigael Yadin, the Israeli archaeologist, has expressed this with great simplicity in what may be regarded as an ultimate tribute. The scrolls, Yadin remarked, were discovered, not by expert archaeologists, but by stray Bedouins, "and their importance was brought to the knowledge of the world at large, again not by an archaeologist, but by a very scholarly amateur, Edmund Wilson."

Today there is agreement that the Dead Sea scrolls, preserved out of antiquity as few such manuscripts have been, shed considerable light on forms of Judaism never known before; these forms contained within them hints of Christianity, or as one of the authorities puts it, "it was the Judaism amid which Christ and his first followers lived, thought and wrote." But even if still later some of these views may be altered by further discoveries. Wilson's book will remain as a record of a great scholarly "find" in our century. It is a methodical interrogation of the available expertise. The book gains added drama in that it was researched and written against a background of the crucial life-and-death struggle in the Middle East— almost as if *Biblical times were being reenacted in the*

clinging of the Jews to their epical books while engaged
in their historic survival and reclamation of a homeland.

What struck me as I read these pages once again is
how much of Edmund Wilson's curiosity and probing
intelligence they reveal. Wilson said at the time he was
"heavily enmeshed in 3,000 years of Jewish literature
and history." He added that once you really got into it,
"there is no easy way of getting out again." This was the
spirit in which he worked. "I am no Semitic scholar,"
Wilson said. "I can only give my own account of what
others have established or conjectured." But it is exactly
this kind of account which the scholars themselves—involved in the intricacies and the politics of discovery—
could never have given. Wilson amusedly likened his
position to that of Ernest Hemingway amid the bull-
fighters and the bulls. Hemingway's enthusiasm had not
included an ability to perform as toreador.

Wilson is never better than when he describes the ter-
rain itself, that Dead Sea geography to which he had heard
his father allude. "Monotonous, subduing and dreadful"
were the words he used, a country impersonal and without
physiognomy, the mounds resembling the humps of the
camels grazing on them. And then the dark dry caves
where the ancient scriptors stored their scrolls for safekeeping, and the texts themselves with their mysterious allusions to Sons of Light and Sons of Darkness. We feel all
the excitement of a quest illuminated by history and learning. When I again looked at "On First Reading Genesis,"
the first part of the essay which has been added to this
edition, I found myself remembering the semicircle of
youthful seminarists, gathered round their elderly and inquiring fellow student, the late Princeton afternoon, the
gathering dusk, when the great adventure still lay ahead—
a journey into fabled times amid fabled peoples. No book
quite like this has been written in our century.

# ISRAEL
## 1954

# I

## ON FIRST READING GENESIS

I DISCOVERED a few years ago, in going through the attic of my mother's house, an old Hebrew Bible that had belonged to my grandfather, a Presbyterian minister, as well as a Hebrew dictionary and a Hebrew grammar. I had always had a certain curiosity about Hebrew, and I was perhaps piqued a little at the thought that my grandfather could read something that I couldn't, so, finding myself one autumn in Princeton, with the prospect of spending the winter, I enrolled in a Hebrew course at the Theological Seminary, from which my grandfather had graduated in 1846. I have thus acquired a smattering that has enabled me to work through Genesis, with constant reference to the English translation and the notes of the Westminster Commentaries, and this first acquaintance with the Hebrew text has, in several ways, been to me a revelation. In the first place, the study of a Semitic language gives one insights into a whole point of view, a system of mental habits, that differs radically from those of the West. But, besides this, I had never read Genesis before. In college I had taken the second half year of a course in Old Testament literature, so I did have some familiarity with the prophets and the later phases of Biblical history, but the Pentateuch and the earlier historical books were known to me only in patches or through simplified versions of Bible stories that had been

3

read to me when I was a child. I came to them in the
original for the first time rather late in life, when I had
already read many other books, and since such an experience is probably rare—Hebrew being studied mainly
by Christian seminarists and orthodox Jews, both of
whom come to it early and with definite religious pre-
dispositions—I am going to give a report on it. I am
myself neither a Jew nor a Christian, and I propose to
disregard, in doing so, the little I know of the tons of
theological commentary that have been written by the
various churches. I do not propose to take for granted—as,
from recent conversations on this subject with even well-
educated people, I conclude I am warranted in not doing
—that the reader is any better acquainted with even the
most famous Bible stories than I was when I recently
began to explore them.

First of all, the surprises of the language. The Bible in
Hebrew is far more a different thing from the Bible in
any translation than the original Homer, say, is from the
best of the translations of Homer, because the language
in which it is written is more different from English than
Greek is. To speak merely from the point of view of style,
the writing of the earliest books is a good deal tighter and
tougher—Renan calls it a twisted cable—than is easy to
imitate with the relatively loose weave of English. It is
also much more poetic, or, rather, perhaps—since the
King James Version does partly take care of this with its
seventeenth-century rhythms—poetic in a more primitive
way. Certain passages are composed in a kind of verse, and
even the prose has a metrical basis. The first verse of
Genesis, for instance, almost corresponds to a classical
hexameter, and we soon feel we are reading an epic or a
saga or something of the sort. The progress of the chronicle is interspersed with old prophecies and fragments of
ballads that have evidently been handed down by word

of mouth and that stand out from the background of the narrative by reason of their oracular obscurity and their "parallelistic" form. There are many plays on words and jingles that disappear in our solemn translations, and the language itself is extremely expressive, full of onomatopoetic effects. The word for "to laugh" is *tsakháq* ("kh" as in "Chekhov"), and thus Isaac is called Isaac (*Yitskháq*) because Sarah, in her delightful scene with God, cannot refrain from laughing when He tells her she shall yet bear a child; a light rain is called *matár*, a heavier downpour *géshem* (it was a *géshem* that caused the Deluge). The words for the emotions are likely to come from the physical states that accompany them. The verbs for "to love" and "to hate" are both based on heavy breathing: *aháv* and *ayáv*. Patience and impatience are rendered as the taking of long or short breaths.

The Hebrew language is also emphatic to a degree with which our language can hardly compete. The device for affirming something strongly is to repeat the important word, and God's warning to Adam that he will "dying, die," if he disobeys His orders, seems weakened in our version—"thou shalt surely die"—as does Joseph's assertion that "stolen, I was stolen out of the land of the Hebrews" by "indeed I was stolen." Nor can we match the vehement expression of the violent Hebrew emotions. When Jehovah, about to invoke the Flood, has become disgusted with man, it is not adequate to say that the thoughts of man's heart were "only evil continually"; in the *"raq ra kol hayyóm"* of the text, we seem to hear the Creator actually spitting on his unworthy creation. "And Isaac trembled very exceedingly" is the rendering of the King James Version of the passage in which Isaac discovers that Jacob has deceived him, which falls short of "Isaac trembled mightily a great trembling," and in the next verse we read that Esau "cried mightily a great

and bitter cry." This violence and vehemence of the
Hebrews is implicit in the structure of the language itself. They did not conjugate their verbs for tenses, as the
modern Western languages do, since our modern conception of time was something at which they had not yet
arrived—a significant feature of the language that I want,
in a later section of this essay, to discuss by itself at
length. What the Hebrews had instead of tenses were two
fundamental conjugations for perfect and imperfect—
that is, for action completed and action uncompleted.
And both of these two "aspects" theoretically exist in
seven variations for every verb (though actually the
complete set is rare) that have nothing to do with time.
The primary form of the verb is known as the "light" or
simple form, and the second is the passive of this. So
much seems plain enough sailing, but what follow are
three intensive forms—active, passive and reflexive—and
two causatives—active and passive.

These verbs, which take little account of time, are the
instruments, then, of a people who, at the period
when this language was formed, must have been both
passionate and energetic. It is not a question of *when*
something happens, but whether the thing is completed
or certain to be completed. There are special forms, the
causatives, for getting things done: "I will multiply your
descendants," "They made Joseph take off his coat." The
intensives are unexpected to the non-Semitic reader, who
has difficulty in getting the hang of them, but feels a
dynamic element in the very bone of the language, and
soon begins to find them fascinating. The translator of
these strange verb forms, which double the middle consonant and vary the pattern of vowels, is obliged to resort
to an adverb or a stronger verb. The intensive form of
one of the words for "to kill," the paradigm verb that the
student learns, is given in the grammars as "kill bru-

tally." So you have "break" and "break to pieces," "grow" and "grow luxuriantly." A curious example, which occurs in Genesis 24:21, illustrates the problems of translators. When the emissary of Abraham meets Rebecca at the well and watches her attentively in silence, to see whether she will behave in the way by which he has proposed to God that the wife appointed for Isaac may be made to reveal herself, a verb that means "to look at" is put in the intensive form. The old Revised Version made it "And the man looked steadfastly on her"; the new Revised Version has it "gazed at her"—the first of these, that is, adds an adverb, the second tries to find an appropriate verb, and the nuances conveyed are different.

These intensives are sometimes baffling. It is not always easy to see what is implied in a given context. The forms may, in certain cases, turn intransitive into transitive verbs; the intensive of "to learn" may mean "to teach," or indicate multiplicity or frequency. The student soon finds himself groping amid modes of being and acting that cannot be accommodated to our Western categories, and of which the simplified descriptions supplied by his beginner's grammar do not really give him much grasp. The intensive reflexive, for example, has uses that are puzzling to render or even to understand. It seems to imply behavior that ranges from what Henry James, borrowing from the French, meant by "abounding in one's own sense" to what we mean by "throwing one's weight around." When Enoch or Noah "walks with God," he does so in this form of the verb "to walk," and nobody has ever known how to render it. Yet one gets from the Hebrew original the impression that the walking of these patriarchs was of a very special kind, that it had the effect of making them both more important and more highly charged. This expression, in the Old Testament, says Dr. John Skinner, the author of the volume on

Genesis in the International Critical Commentary series, in general "signifies intimate companionship, and here denotes a fellowship with God morally and religiously perfect. . . . We shall see, however, that originally it included the idea of initiation into divine mysteries." I have looked Enoch up in a number of translations, and the only attempts I have found to give the verb form its special force are in the independent modern translations by James Moffatt and Monsignor Knox, the former of whom says that Enoch "lived close to God," the latter that he was "the close friend of God." The flaming sword set by God at the gate of the Garden of Eden is made to "turn" in the intensive reflexive, and the English translations, from the King James Version to the Revised Standard Version, render this as "turned every way." I imagine something a little more spectacular. Gesenius's standard lexicon seems to bear me out in suggesting "brandished, glittering." Yet as soon as you are beginning to pride yourself on seizing the force of the intensive reflexive, you are pulled up by finding that this variation of the verb that means "to shave" implies, in the hygienic prescriptions of Leviticus, nothing more interesting than "to shave oneself" or "to get oneself shaved."

When Abraham, foreseeing that the beauty of Sarah will cause Pharaoh to want her for his harem, has passed her off as his sister, in order that Pharaoh may not be impelled to put him out of the way, and when Pharaoh, afflicted by God for a sin he has committed unknowingly, learns at last what is causing the trouble and sends Abraham about his business, he says, "Here is your wife. Take her and go!" We are amused, when we first read this incident, to find "send" in the intensive form and to hear the brusque snap of "qakh valékh!" Yet we later on find that these words are more or less a conventional formula that does not necessarily imply irritation and that "send" in the intensive occurs when the sending is not necessarily ejective. There is something, we become aware, peremptory in the language itself. You have drawn-out "cohortative" forms that express, for the first person, exhortation, strong intention or earnest entreaty, along with clipped jussive forms for other people or things, as when God says, "Let this or that happen." The whole language is intensely purposeful, full of the determination to survive by force or by wit, to accomplish certain objectives, to lay down laws that will stabilize life and ensure its perpetuation, to fix the future by positive prophecies.

As this will of the ancient Hebrew finds expression in the dynamic verb forms, so the perdurability of the people is manifested in what may be called the physical aspects of the language. The prime unit of Hebrew is a group of three consonants. Nearly every verb consists of such a trinity. The values may be modified—the consonant may be doubled or be altered to a kindred sound, as "f" to "p," "v" to "b"—by a dot written inside the letter, and the intervening vowels may be indicated by a system of dots and dashes written above and below, but they were not so originally written and are not—except in poetry and in a single daily paper—so written today in Israel. The Hebrew alphabet thus differs from our alphabet in not including characters for the vowels, or even, in every case, different characters for kindred consonantal sounds. It is a system of twenty-two integers, a set of unsupplantable blocks, and each Hebrew word makes a shell into which a varying content of vowel sounds may be poured. The verbs are modified by prefixes and endings, and some of the conjugations take prefixes, but, to a Westerner, the most striking feature of the Hebrew conjugations is the way in which a shift of meaning (from active to passive, for example) is effected by a vowel change inside this consonantal shell—the kind of thing that we do on a lesser scale in inflecting our so-called strong verbs: e.g., "sing, sang, sung." We may put in an "o" for the noun and get "song," and the Jews, too, can use the same shell, with a different vowel content, for a noun. What impresses is the hardness of this shell.

Our first look at the text of the Bible, when we have mastered the alphabet, is likely to give us the feeling that this sytem is extremely impractical. It requires what must seem to the beginner an annoying and easily avoidable effort to coördinate with the heavy consonants the elusive little dashes and dots that hover about them like midges, especially since two of the former are not consonants in our sense at all but gutturals, no longer pronounced, which have to be regarded as blanks and read with the sounds of the vowels that are indicated above or below them. Even the printing of these signs is difficult, impossible for a linotype machine, since they appear in innumerable combinations. The result is that, even in learned books, the consonants are, if possible, written without "pointings," and what you get is a kind of shorthand. You must already know the words extremely well in order to be able to recognize them. Yet some further acquaintance induces respect, and a perception that this method is appropriate, an inalienable element of the Jewish tradition. The characters themselves are impressive—not so fluent as the Roman and Greek, and retaining even more than these the look of having been once cut in stone.* To write out Hebrew vocabulary, with black ink and a stub pen, affords a satisfaction that may give one a faint idea of the pleasures of Chinese

---

* The movement from right to left is supposed to have been determined by the engraver's having held the chisel in his left hand and the hammer in his right, and thus naturally having worked from the right.

calligraphy, as well as a feeling of vicarious authority as one traces the portentous syllables. One remembers the hand of Jehovah writing on Belshazzar's wall (though He had to write Aramaic in order to be understood by that alien and uninstructed king). These twenty-two signs that Moses was believed to have brought back from Egypt graven on the Tables of the Law, and from which, in their early Phoenician form, all our European alphabets have been derived, have, austere in their vowel-less terseness, been steadily proceeding from right to left, over a period of two thousand years, among people that read from left to right; and in the Bible they take on an aspect exalted and somewhat mysterious: the square letters holding their course, with no capitals for proper names and no punctuation save the firm double diamond that marks the end of a verse, compact in form as in meaning, stamped on the page like a woodcut, solid verse linked to solid verse with the ever recurrent "and," the sound of which is modulated by changes of vowel, while above and below them a dance of accents shows the pattern of the metrical structure and the rise and fall of the chanting, and, above and below, inside and out, the vowel pointings hang like motes, as if they were the mole-cules the consonants breathed. Difficult for the foreigner to penetrate and completely indifferent to this, they have withstood even the drive toward assimilation—to their Spanish and Germanic neighbors—of the Jews of the Middle Ages; and in the dialect of German that is Yid-dish, in newspapers spread in the subway, they still march in the direction opposite to that of all the other subway newspapers, English or Spanish or Italian, Hun-garian or Russian or Greek, with only a light sprinkling of points to indicate Germanic vowels. And we have seen them reassemble in Israel, reconstituting their proper language—not embarrassed in the least by the fear that

the newspaper reader of our century, even knowing Hebrew perfectly, may have difficulty in distinguishing, in
the British reports, a vowelless Bevan from a vowelless
Bevin. They march on through our modern events as if
they were invulnerable, eternal.

But in the meantime, the Bible confronts us, in the dignity and beauty of its close-packed page.

The opening of Genesis is wonderful: the spirit of God
in the darkness that hovers or broods on the waters, the
sudden decree of light, the teeming of earth, sea and sky.
The story of the Garden of Eden and the episode of Cain
and Abel are imperfectly disengaged from some very ancient matrix of folklore, and parts of them are blotted in
obscurity. What is the explanation of the phrase that so
strangely recurs? "Your desire shall be for your husband," says God to Eve, "and he shall dominate you."
"If you do not do well," He tells Cain, "sin is lurking at
the door. His desire is for you, but you will dominate
him." Is the second the mistake of a copyist, whose eye
has slipped back to the earlier passage, or an obsessive
idea of the author's? The serpent here is not the Devil,
as the Jews later thought him to have been, but simply
"the wiliest of all the beasts of the field." The Fall here
has not the importance that it was later to take on for
the Christians. Except for one reference to Adam in Job,
the Old Testament does not mention it again. It was
Paul who set up Original Sin, with the dreadful results
we know for Catholic and Calvinist doctrine. The Creator
here is all too human—we should nowadays say He was
manic-depressive or something of the sort. He immediately becomes jealous of the man He has molded, angry at Adam for eating the fruit that has made him "like
one of us" by imparting to him the knowledge of good
and evil, and fearful lest he eat of the tree of life and so

become immortal, too—as He is later, out of jealousy of human success, to frustrate the building of the city in which everyone speaks the same language and to impose the confusion of the Tower of Babel. What we do find in the story of Adam and his family are those living and salient traits—the relations of Adam and Eve, the sullen personality of Cain—that give these fragmentary legends a human truth and have caused them to haunt our imaginations; and you have, also, the earliest examples of that specialty of the Jewish genius—the development of the moral consciousness, of man's relations with God. This dawning of the moral sense brings with it, for Adam and Eve, an immediate awareness of their animal nature and the impulse to clothe themselves.

After Adam, the chronicle is almost lost in a cloudy domain of myth. Methuselah lives nine hundred and sixty-nine years; Enoch walks with God, then vanishes, "for God took him." The formidable race that the Septuagint calls "giants" and the Masoretic Bible "Nephilim" (fallen ones?) are dwelling on the earth. The sons of God interbreed with the daughters of men. Something in all this has gone wrong, though it is not clear precisely what. The Creator, at an earlier stage so nervously suspicious of man, so anxious lest man try to compete with Him, now decides he has gone to the bad and regrets He has ever made him. He decides to wipe mankind out, but relents in favor of the family of Noah. There follows the account of a flood which, according to Sir Leonard Woolley, must actually have occurred locally some three thousand years before Christ, in the region between the Tigris and the Euphrates—an account that seems less poetic as well as less realistic than the similar record preserved in the Babylonian epic *Gilgamesh*. It is curious to compare the two stories. The Babylonian one mentions reed huts, the remnants of which Woolley found below a thick layer of river silt, and the adventures of the Ark are "lived," described here in much more detail than in the Biblical tale of the Flood. One is struck by the behavior of these earlier gods. "The gods were frightened by the deluge, and, shrinking back, they ascended to the heaven of Anu. The gods cowered like dogs crouched against the outer wall." Later, when the waters are going down and a sacrifice is offered, "The gods smelled the savor, the gods smelled the sweet savor, the gods crowded like flies about the sacrificer." * This was not the way of Jehovah, who has absolute authority and absolute power, and could not behave so abjectly.

It should be said at this point that the text of Genesis is regarded as a patching together of texts by two different hands, combined, perhaps, with passages from still older sources. One sees clearly in the Hebrew the reasons that certain points seem confused in translation—though actually they have partially been ironed out—for the original is still more confused. In the two recensions that have been here brought together, it is evident that one of the scribes had referred to God as "Elohím," the other by the name that we call "Jehovah." The first of these words is a plural—most commonly used with a singular, but occasionally with a plural verb—which seems to designate spirits or powers that preside over the phenomena of the universe. It will be noticed that the Creator in the Eden story expresses his displeasure that Adam has "become like one of *us*," and this plurality of Elohím, the indeterminateness of his or their identity, lends mystery to certain incidents—the wrestling of Jacob with the "angel," the destruction of Sodom and Gomorrah—in which a "man" or several "messengers" turn out to be what

---

* I quote from the translation by E. A. Speiser, so excellent in its literary quality, included in *Ancient Near Eastern Texts*, Princeton University Press, 1950.

we translate as "God," though the names of Elohím and
Jehovah, sometimes alternating, sometimes appearing together, make the ancient conception of deity rather difficult, at this early stage, to grasp. Jehovah is a definitely
singular God, the pillar of monotheism. He figures in
the Bible at first as the national divinity of the Hebrews,
competing with neighboring divinities, but He is later,
without ever losing His special relation to the Hebrews,
to become a universal God; and one of the things that
make Genesis interesting is to see how this universal
Deity develops out of primitive conceptions, incompletely
fused, of a personal Hebrew patron and a host of primeval
spirits. The Jehovah who is to figure for the Christian as
an omniscient Heavenly Father, brought closer to humanity by sending them a Son, for the Jew as a transcendent
principle that cannot be given a name—"Jehovah" is itself
a substitute for the unpronounceable name of God, and
the Jew, in his religious services, substitutes for this
"Adonái" (my Lord)—this soaring and awful conception is only trying here its first brief flights. Nor are
there here any Christian angels, with flowing white robes
and great wings, only divine "messengers," easily mistaken for human beings. The Hebrew word for "messen-
ger" was translated by the Greek word "ἄγγελος" and
this later gave rise to "angel," which has come to connote
a being that does not exist in the Hebrew text. Nor is
there as yet a Devil; even the Satan who appears in Job
but is otherwise scarcely mentioned is merely "the Ad-
versary," an antagonist opposing Jehovah. There are only
the men of a nomad tribe groping after some understanding with a superhuman power or powers. The scribe
himself is groping for their history, and his narrative
is blurred not only by an undetermined conception of
God but also by other discrepancies that result from his
pious unwillingness to deal boldly with his differing

sources. In comparison with this unknown editor, the unknown writer or writers who turned out the Homeric
poems did a smooth and harmonious job on the ancient
materials that he or they worked with. But that was not
the Oriental way. The Semitic peoples, it seems, liked to
preserve all the versions, with the result, in the text of
Genesis, that the factual elements are rarely consistent:
the chronologies do not come out right, the enumerations
do not add up correctly. In the case of the episode mentioned above, of the imposture practiced by Abraham
on Pharaoh in passing off Sarah as his sister, you are
given the same story three times—told the second time of
Abraham and Abimelech, the third time of Isaac and
Abimelech. The men of the passing caravan to whom
Joseph is sold by his brothers are designated first as Mid-
ianites, and then, in succession, as Ishmaelites, Midian-
ites and Ishmaelities. The wonder is, with all this untidi-
ness, these absurdities and incongruities, that the dialogue
should be so telling, the situations presented with so sure
a stroke, that the personalities of the principal characters
should remain so convincing and so interesting. Abraham,
Jacob and Joseph are created as living figures in a way
that makes relatively trifling the imprecisions of the different versions; it is even perhaps true that their outlines
are thrown into a kind of relief by the factual uncertainty
of the legend. Renan tells us of one of his teachers at the
seminary of St. Sulpice that, in expounding this episode
of Abraham in Egypt, he had difficulty in explaining how
Sarah, who is apparently supposed to be nearly seventy,
was capable of exciting the desire of Pharaoh. He "would
call our attention," says Renan, "to the fact that, after all,
such things had been known, and that 'Mlle. de Lenclos,'
at seventy, had inspired passions and precipitated duels."
The extraordinary thing is that, in the course of all the
centuries during which these stories have been read

and pondered, such outrageous anomalies as this have not bothered people more.

With the emergence of the patriarch Abraham, there begins that remarkable narrative which also includes the careers of his descendants, Isaac, Jacob and Joseph. We may wonder that these personages should run so true to familiar Jewish types till we realize that Jewish children, for more than three thousand years, have been brought up with these Biblical figures before them.

The relations of Abraham with Jehovah strike a note that today sounds feudal. He is respectful toward Him, even obsequious, yet their intercourse exhibits at the same time an element of what may almost be called homely intimacy. Abraham may argue with Jehovah, and Jehovah, who has made with him a covenant and chosen him as "father of many nations," never thunders against him as the Jehovahs of the prophets do. It is natural for this Jehovah to visit His earthly agent, in the guise of a human traveler and in the company of two other travelers (throughout this visit called "men," but later described as "messengers"), at noon, by the oaks of Mamre, as Abraham is sitting in front of his tent. The travelers ask him where his wife is, and he tells them that she is inside the tent. The visitor who is Jehovah explains to Abraham that He will come that way again in the spring, and that Sarah shall then have a son. She has been barren, and she and Abraham have already been through the episode, so painful for everyone concerned, of Hagar, the Egyptian maid, to whom Abraham has given a child and whom Sarah has driven away. Sarah has been listening inside the tent door, and when she hears this prediction, she laughs to herself. "Now that I am worn out," she says, "how should I have pleasure, and my husband an old man?" "Why did Sarah laugh?" asks the visitor. "Does she think that God cannot do it?" "I didn't laugh," says Sarah, frightened. "No, but you did laugh," says God.

In the meantime, Jehovah reflects that He had better take Abraham into His confidence and explain to him that recent reports as to what is going on in Sodom and Gomorrah make the situation sound so serious that He has decided to have it looked into: He may be obliged to destroy these cities. When He broaches this subject to Abraham, the latter thinks at once of his nephew Lot, who at the moment is living in Sodom. There ensues a significant dialogue, in which Abraham, playing on Jehovah's sense of justice, gradually beats Him down in such a way as to insure Lot's survival. Is it right that the good men in Sodom, Abraham puts it up to Him, should be punished along with the vicious? "The Judge of the whole earth will surely not commit an injustice! Suppose there are fifty good men: would it not be unjust that these should perish?" Jehovah feels the force of this; very well, He will spare the city if He finds in it fifty good men. "Behold, I have dared to speak to my Lord," Abraham is quick to add, relapsing into abysmal humility now that he has won his point—"I who am dust and ashes!" But he persists: "Suppose five of the fifty are lacking?" Jehovah is obliged to admit that this would not be fair either, and gradually, step by step, begging God not to be annoyed and protesting his own unworthiness, he persuades Him to agree that for ten good men He will refrain from exterminating the Sodomites. (Nothing is said of Gomorrah, where Abraham has no relations.)

The messengers of Jehovah arrive at the city, where they find Lot sitting at the gate. He cordially invites them to his house, where he gives them an excellent dinner, but before they have gone to bed, the whole male population of Sodom—to a man, the narrator says—gather outside the house and demand that the visitors be sur-

rendered to them. They have seen the divine messengers
and found them all too attractive. In this scene, there is a
real terror (echoed with less effect in the similar episode
of Judges 19, though the latter is more brutal and more
gruesome). Lot goes out and shuts the door behind him.
He offers the Sodomites his daughters, if they want them
(knowing, perhaps, that he is perfectly safe), but he cannot betray the guests whom he has taken under his roof.
"You are not one of us!" shout the Sodomites, with the
jeer that was so often to be made to the Jew. "You're all
by yourself here—you're only a sojourner! You can't tell
us what to do! We'll see that you get it worse than they
do!" They yell at him to stand aside, mob him, are about
to break down the door, but the messengers pull Lot inside, strike the invaders with blindness, and shut the door
in their faces. "Now gather all your family together," the
messengers order Lot, "and get them away from here.
This place has become such a scandal that Jehovah has
sent us to wipe it out." But the Sodomite husbands of
Lot's two daughters imagine that the visitors are joking,
and Lot himself is reluctant to go. When they have not
left at dawn the next morning, the messengers drag Lot
and his family out—the sons-in-law are left behind—and
tell them to flee for their lives before the brimstone begins.

The insistence all through these episodes of the earlier
part of Genesis is on family—i.e., race survival, the importance, by measures however extreme, of perpetuating
the consecrated seed. One feels in the story of Sodom,
coming after the promise that Sarah shall still bear a
child in old age, that the horror for the Jews of the
Sodomites is the menace of "genocide." When Lot's
daughters, deprived of their husbands, are living miser-
ably with their father in a cave, they have no way of saving this seed except by getting him drunk and inducing

him to make them pregnant. We are made to feel not that
the daughters of Lot have here committed a sin, but
rather that their action is justified by the desperateness
of the situation. With this fierceness of the will to persist
goes a sense, which redeems the sternness of the patriarchal relations, of the pathos of parental feelings. When
Hagar is about to bear Abraham's child, she cannot help
being insolent to Sarah, and Sarah retaliates by treating
her so harshly that she runs away. She is met by a mes-
senger of God, who reassures her and makes her return;
but later, after Isaac has been born, when Sarah has fears
lest Ishmael, Hagar's child, may come to share with him
Abraham's heritage, she drives her away again. Abraham
gets up early and gives Hagar some bread and a skin of
water. With the child, she goes into the wilderness, and
when all her water is gone, she puts Ishmael under a
bush and sits down some distance away, saying, "Let me
not look on the death of the child!" Then the little boy
begins to cry, and God hears him and shows Hagar a well
of water. So later, God, testing Abraham, orders him to
sacrifice Isaac. When they are going up together to the
mountaintop, the boy speaks up: "My father!" "Here am
I, my son." "We've got the wood and the fire, but where
is the lamb for the offering?" The father is obliged to
reply, "God, my son, will provide the lamb." These
strokes of human feeling, of insight, are so trenchant and
so authentic, and they so surely awake a response in all
kinds and conditions of people, that there are moments
when the gods and heroes of the so much more expertly
handled, the so much more sophisticated Homeric poems
seem less real than the nomads of Genesis when the finger of the unknown scribe, tracing the ancient story,
flashes across the page the verses that make them live.
This finger also makes the contact, momentous in its day
and place, between God and the humblest life, and the

God of the patriarchal chronicle is a much more attractive deity than the God of the Garden of Eden, the Flood and the Tower of Babel. The mind that created Hagar, dying of thirst with her baby, had also to create the God who would pity them and allow them their role in the world. The composer of the conversation between Abraham and Isaac on their way to the sacrifice could not admit of a God who would compel His chosen agent to go through with this cruel ordeal. In these fumbling and awkward old stories, we can see man becoming aware of the conscience that begins to dignify him, that seems to tower above him.

The adventures of Abraham's grandson Jacob are distinguished by no such tenor of submissive and patient piety. His life has a strange discontinuity, for his ultimately successful career is characterized, on the one hand, by exploits of outrageous cunning and, on the other, as it were, broken into by visitations of Jehovah that strike a note quite different from Abraham's intercourse with a deity who treats him as a trusted servant. Jacob, described as a quiet boy, is his mother's favorite son, but his father prefers his twin brother, the more virile and active Esau. The young Jacob first induces his brother, who has come back hungry from hunting, to trade his birthright for a supper of lentils, the smell of which is driving him crazy; then later, when their father is dying, incited by his partial mother, he tricks the old half-blind Isaac into mistaking him for his brother, in order to make sure of receiving his father's special blessing that will establish him as the head of the family. Esau, learning of this, swears to kill Jacob, and their mother sends Jacob away to live with his uncle Laban. On his journey, Jacob sleeps out-of-doors, and in a dream sees the messengers of God ascending and descending by a ladder between Heaven and earth. At the top of the ladder is Jehovah,

who tells Jacob that He is the God of his grandfather and
his father, and that Jacob can count on his backing; that
his family shall multiply and that through them the peoples of the earth shall be blessed. When Jacob wakes up,
he is frightened: "What a fearful place this is!" he says.
"It must be God's house and the gate of Heaven!"

We now have a long account of Jacob's sojourn with
his uncle Laban. He falls in love with Laban's daughter
Rachel, but Laban will not let him marry her till he has
worked for Laban seven years—a period that, so great is
Jacob's love for her, seems to pass, the narrator tells us,
like only a few days. But at the end of this time, when
Jacob has earned her, Laban fails to keep his promise;
in the darkness of the marriage night, he succeeds in passing off on Jacob his older daughter Leah, whom he wishes
to get married off first, but then offers Jacob Rachel,
too—the marriage to take place at once—if the young
man will agree to work for him seven years longer. While
Jacob is serving this second term, the relations between
him and his wives are subjected to a good deal of strain,
because Rachel, whom he loves, has no children while
Leah is producing four. Because she is not beloved—because she is "hated," the narrative says—God has taken
pity on Leah and is trying in this way to console her. But
Rachel makes her maid sleep with Jacob and then claims
the resulting two sons as her own. Leah, who has now
stopped bearing, makes Jacob give *her* maid, too, two
sons. During the wheat harvest, an incident occurs. One
of Leah's sons finds some mandrakes and brings them to
his mother. The Hebrew word for mandrake has the same
connotation as our "love apple"; it was supposed to be
an aphrodisiac and also to promote conception. Rachel
asks Leah for some of these, but the bitter Leah replies
that Rachel has taken her husband's love; will she rob

her of even her mandrakes? If Leah will give her the mandrakes, says Rachel, she will let her sleep with Jacob. The
result is that Leah again conceives, while poor Rachel
has no luck with the mandrakes. But at last God remembers Rachel and allows her to give birth to Joseph. Jacob
decides, at this point, that he has had enough of working
for Laban, but Laban has come to realize that Jacob is
under divine protection, that he has prospered because of
his nephew's presence. He offers to pay Jacob whatever
he asks, and a duel of cunning commences.

This conflict has its comic aspect. Jacob offers to stay
on awhile if Laban will allow him to take for his own all
the spotted goats and sheep and all the black lambs.
Laban agrees, but then removes these from the flocks
and has his sons keep them apart from the rest. Jacob,
encouraged by God, as he afterwards tells his wives, se-
cures a mixed-colored breed simply by setting up striped
sticks at the water troughs where the animals mate. He
also sees to it that the spotted breed is produced from
the most vigorous specimens. This makes Jacob extremely
rich, and he finally decides to leave Laban. Without fore-
warning his uncle, he goes off with his wives and his children, his camels, his sheep, goats and asses, his male and
his female servants. Rachel, without Jacob's knowing it,
carries away her father's household gods, the Hebrew
equivalents of lares and penates. Laban comes after them
and makes a scene. Why has Jacob left his uncle in this
furtive way instead of allowing him to kiss his daughters
good-by and to send them away with music? He searches
the tents for the household gods, which Rachel hides in
her camel's saddle. Jacob, not knowing she has them,
becomes angry and denounces Laban. "If I hadn't had
God with me," he says, "I should never have got away
from you with anything to show for my work!" Laban is

obliged to back down. They make a covenant, and Laban goes home. Jacob proceeds on his way and encounters divine messengers. "This is God's army," he says.

But the thought of reunion with Esau now begins to worry Jacob. He devises a strategy for propitiating his brother or keeping out of his reach, in case Esau still wants to kill him. First of all, he sends out men to announce his return, and they report that Esau is coming to meet him, accompanied by four hundred followers. Jacob is apprehensive. He divides his company in two in order that, if one part should get massacred, the other should have a chance to escape. He then prays, reminding God that He has promised to stand behind him and to see to it that his children survive. After this, he instructs his servants to go ahead of him with a present for Esau consisting of over five hundred animals. They are to drive them in procession, drove by drove, with intervals between the droves, so as to make the strongest possible impression. They must wait until Esau has seen the first drove and demands to know whose they are, then they will tell him it is a present for him, sent by his servant Jacob, who is following close behind. Each new drove will come as a fresh surprise. Soon Jacob himself will appear, and perhaps this will do the trick. Yet Jacob is evidently anxious and tense. He sends his wives and his children to the farther side of the Jabbok River. Now he is all alone, and he passes through a strange experience, a crisis and test of the spirit that accompanies this critical moment of his meeting his brother again and perhaps predetermines its upshot. This is the episode that has come to be known as the struggle of Jacob with the angel—perhaps out of euphemism, since the editors of the sacred text had a tendency to play down passages that appeared disrespectful to God. Actually, no angel is ever mentioned. Jacob wrestles all night with a "man." That they all but liter-

ally went to the mat is shown by the Hebrew verb, found
only here, which is made from one of the nouns for
"dust" (which is similar in sound to the name of the
Jabbok). They are "dusting" one another. The mysterious opponent realizes that he cannot get Jacob down, so he
strikes him on the socket of the thigh and puts his thigh
out of joint. "Let me go," he bids Jacob, "for the day is
breaking." But Jacob is still able to hold his own: "I
shall not let you go till you bless me." The being asks
Jacob's name, and when Jacob tells him, he says, "Your
name shall no longer be Jacob, but Israel"—meaning
"striver with God"—"for you have striven with both God
and men, and prevailed." Jacob asks his opponent's
name; the other refuses to answer, but blesses him before
he departs. Jacob knows that he has wrestled with God,
that he has seen Him face to face, yet still lives. The
sun rises, and he goes away limping. Thereafter, he is
sometimes called Israel. It is the first time the name occurs. Is there some implication here of a rivalry of God
with His creation? What is striking for us today in this
passage is that even the chosen leader, who identifies himself with the spirits that preside over man's destiny and
the forces of nature, must pit himself against them, like
Prometheus, in order to win something from them; that
this name the Jews gave themselves contained, or was
afterwards made to contain, the idea that they had conquered, at a maiming cost, some share in the power of
God.

The meeting with Esau goes off very well, though Jacob
is plainly nervous. There follows a hideous episode of the
kind that even devout readers of the Bible have not often
cared to remember. Such stories are in themselves far
from elevating; they do not provide texts for sermons or
suggest subjects for paintings, yet, in the narrative of the
Bible, their savagery has the effect of setting off the

strong purposes, the flashes of revelation, that represent
the emergence of the moral sense, of the nobler human
ambitions—those principles and aspirations that seemed
to the ancient Jew so much on a different level from the
ferocity and the duplicity which were also a part of his
history that he regarded them as promises and precepts
handed down to him by a higher being. Jacob now buys
some land in Canaan, and Shechem, the son of the local
prince, seduces Jacob's only daughter, Dinah—"and hum-
bled her," the narrative adds, which seems to imply rape.
But Shechem's "soul was attached to Dinah; he loved
her, and he spoke to the heart of the girl." Schechem goes
to his father and asks him to arrange for him to marry
Dinah. The father takes it up with Jacob and proposes
that his people and Jacob's should live on good terms together, intermarry and trade with one another, that Jacob
should settle among them. Schechem, whose soul longs
for Dinah, offers Jacob and her brothers any gift they
ask, if they will let him make her his wife. But Jacob's
sons have just come in from the cattle, and, still furious at
the wrong done Dinah but not betraying their feelings,
they make the objection to Jacob that they cannot allow
their sister to be married to a man who has not been
circumcised, and insist that if there is to be intermar-
riage between Shechem's people and theirs, all the
former must undergo this operation. Young Shechem at
once consents, and his father, who has always humored
him, goes to the gate of the city and announces that this
drastic measure is forthwith to be carried out. Every man
who goes out of the gate must be stopped and subjected
to circumcision. When this has been going on three days
and the male inhabitants of the city are all suffering from
the effects of the operation and unprepared to defend
themselves, two of Jacob's sons, Simeon and Levi,
descend on them and slaughter them all, including, of

course, Shechem and his father, and they carry away Dinah, who has been kept in Shechem's house. They also plunder the city and devastate the countryside, driving off all the animals and enslaving the women and children. When Jacob finds out what has happened, he rebukes his revengeful sons; he shows them what a mess they have made, that his name is now a stink to the people there. He has only a handful of followers, and his neighbors will combine against him and kill them all. The stupid young men reply, "Could we let him treat our sister like a harlot?"

God tells Jacob to go to Bethel, and Jacob makes his household purify themselves and hand over to him all their images of the false local gods. He reaches Bethel without interference, because God has restrained his enemies, and he builds an altar there. God now repeats his promises, and Jacob moves on to another place. But Rachel has conceived again, and on the way she falls into labor. "Don't be afraid," says the midwife, when her pains become agonizing. "You will bear another son." But Rachel dies in giving birth to this son, and, dying, names him Ben-oni, Son of My Suffering. Jacob, however, changes this to Ben-yamin, Son of the Right Hand. He marks Rachel's grave and journeys on. The last thing we hear of him in this section is that one of his sons, Reuben, has gone to bed with Rachel's former maid, his father's concubine, by whom Jacob has had two sons. "And Israel," the narrator says, "heard about this"— Israel, the striver with God.

There follows the story of Joseph, which I shall not attempt to retell. It is, of course, a success story, the prototype of all success stories. Joseph is the able Jew who makes good in a foreign land. In his function as Pharaoh's governor, he reminds us of Disraeli Prime Minister and of the powerful Jewish viziers of the tenth and eleventh centuries in Spain. He scores off his envious brothers, who have sold him into Egypt, first by putting them to a great deal of inconvenience, then by forgiving them and setting them up in Egypt; and he gratifies his father Jacob and arranges for him a serene old age. There are moments when we feel about Joseph that he is a little what is meant by the Yiddish word *allrightnik,* when we are tempted to sympathize with the brothers in their resentment at his reading of dreams that is always to his own advantage. Except for this gift of interpreting dreams, he has little communication with the Deity, and we may easily find Jacob more interesting, with his trickery, his love for Rachel, his victimization by Laban and his finally sending his father-in-law about his business, his difficult domestic relations and his uncontrollable children, his sporadic contacts with God that jolt him into consciousness of his destiny. But Joseph, with his solid character, his career of worldly advancement, makes a necessary intermittence—or, rather, an intermittence that convinces us we are dealing with a human world—in this chronicle of intercourse with the Deity, so that the next advance in this intercourse will come with a peculiar impressiveness: the Moses of Exodus, who will talk to God, face to face, on a loftier level than Abraham, who will derive from Him authority and leadership of a more compelling kind than Jacob's.

All these incidents take place in a world in which the time values are always vague, because Hebrew verbs have no real tenses. This whole question of time is so interesting, the time-sense of a people is so fundamental, so important for understanding its mentality, that I want to discuss it in a more general way, and not merely in connection with the Bible.

"What was perhaps most astonishing to the modern

European," a former governor of Kenya, Sir Philip Mitchell (quoted in the issue of August 1953 of the German magazine *Der Monat*), has reported of the natives of that region, "was their not having any calendar or way of telling time, the fact that they oriented themselves solely by the moon and the seasons, the rising and the setting of the sun. Before the modern Europeans took over, there did not, except for the Swahili spoken on the coast, exist in any language from Abyssinia to the Transvaal any way of saying 'on January 1, 1890,' or 'at two-thirty in the afternoon,' or of expressing any other such idea."

Now, the Jews of the Old Testament were not, of course, quite in this primitive state, but their time-sense was so little developed that they did not even have a word for "hour," and, as we have seen, they took no interest in accurate chronology. The Babylonians evidently had sundials three hundred years before Christ, but the only possible reference in the Bible to any such time-telling device is a dubious one in Isaiah 38:8, where the "grades" that have been interpreted as the degrees of a dial might mean also a flight of steps. We so much take for granted, in our part of the world, our schedules of clock and calendar time that it is difficult to adjust ourselves to the mental habits of peoples who do not share our conventions.

This is certainly one difference that throws us off in our attempts to deal with the Russians. The visitor to Moscow may at first be misled by the fact that he and the Muscovites make use of similar clocks, and that the Russians, since the Revolution, have adjusted their calendar to ours; he may assume that appointments will be kept, that meetings will begin on time, and he is likely to become impatient when he discovers that *seichás* (this hour) is often equivalent to "never." Yet if he studies the language, he should realize that the Russians are living in an older, a much less closely scheduled world.* The tenses of the verbs in any language are the key to a people's idea of time, and the tenses of the Russians are different from ours and different from those, I believe, of any of the Romance or Teutonic languages. The basic thing to grasp here is that the Slavs lack the Western conception of a definite moment in the present, of the present as a definite moment. You cannot say in Russian, "I tell you 'No!,'" or, like John Burroughs in his well-known poem, "Serene, I fold my hands and wait." The Russians, like the ancient Jews, make their fundamental distinction between action completed and action going on. You can only say in Russian, "I am telling you 'No!'" —that is, put the verb in the "imperfective." In the "perfective," there is no present tense; you can have an action completed only in the future or in the past. The line from John Burroughs would have to be rendered in Russian either "I am folding my hands and shall wait" or "I have folded my hands and am waiting." The language does not allow for an action completed in the present, and the past is also lacking in precisions that our Western languages make. The Russian past is an old past participle that is inflected (quite uselessly, from our point of view) for gender as well as number, but the use of which is otherwise exactly like the illiterate use of the past participle that is current in the American South: "I taken her out for a walk." In Russian there is no pluperfect; you cannot, by a change of the tense, make it clear that some action or event has taken place before some other. Nor is there any distinction such as we make between a perfect and a simple past; though I have written, "I have

* Old Slavonic, a literary language, had a fuller equipment of tenses, but—except for a few survivals among the southern tongues—these were lost by the Slavic languages when they developed in a colloquial way.

folded my hands" above, for the sake of natural English, the Russians would be simply "I folded." When something is past, it is past, and the antiquated Russian language does not worry about the chronology of past events in relation to one another. Nor does it have any grammatical machinery for adjusting events in the past to the point of view of the present—that is, to the point of view of the moment when the speaker is speaking.* Thus, it could not be said in Russian of Chekhov's three sisters that they thought they would go to Moscow. A neighbor of theirs would have said, "They thought they *will* go to Moscow." The difference between us and the Russians is that, here again, we are equipped with the conception of the present as a definite point. This point, for us, stands as a limit to the past, and the past, as seen from this moment, falls into an ordered perspective. With us, the conditional "would" relegates the intention of the sisters to a moment when it was not yet possible to know whether or not their intention would be carried out; they might or might not have gone. Chekhov knows, of course, that they will never get off, but if he told you about it in Russian, the language would not provide him with any way of even hinting that there was anything problematic about it. It sets no limit and adjusts no perspective. In telling of the sisters' hopes, the language must transport the speaker to the period when these hopes were being entertained, and at that period, as I have earlier pointed out, there was no way in Russian for the sisters to say, "Today we shake the dust of this place from our feet and

* There is a Russian conditional mode, but it is only used for the past in connection with definitely negative ideas, or when, speaking from the point of view of the present, one is quite sure that something has not occurred. It may be mentioned that the same form of the conditional is used for the past and the future. *I should have done something* and *I should do something* are said in the same way.

definitely clear out for Moscow!" It is easier in Russian than it is for us indefinitely to put things off, as Chekhov knows his three sisters will do; so far as their grammar goes, the time of departure may never come, and from the moment when this ceases to be future, it is bound to be conceived as continuous: action still uncompleted. It will take them a long time to prepare, it will take them a long time to travel.

What cannot be grasped by your Russian friend who keeps you waiting an hour and a half is that for you a moment of the present will come when you stand with your watch in your hand and the hands of the watch at, say, two-forty-five (the times for which appointments are made in Russia often seem to us incomprehensible and soon cease to carry conviction, as when someone says, "Two, or perhaps half past two, or perhaps better a quarter to three").* If you make sure to arrive at a meeting a little in advance of the hour set and find that you must wait some time before the doors will be opened, it is because the time for beginning is understood differently by the Russians and the hour officially mentioned has nothing whatever to do with it. Eventually they will drift in, and the moment to start will come; they will feel it, not check it on their watches. Nor will their watches tell them when to stop. Once a meeting, a performance at the theater, a banquet, an interview, a lecture, a lesson has got itself under way, it will go on till the subject has been covered, till the drama has run its course, till everyone has had enough. And, as a result of this willingness to squander time, the theatrical entertainment or the novel or the serious discussion, with Russians, is likely to flourish more richly and to develop in a way more organic

---

* Turgenev—in other ways, a scrupulous man—used to tax Henry James's patience and sometimes offend Flaubert by never turning up at the appointed time.

than enterprises of this kind usually do with us. As the performance will not be cramped, so the preparation will not have been hurried. Rehearsal, rewriting, preliminary study will not have been menaced by a deadline, by the last train to Montclair or Stamford, by an engagement to meet somebody at six o'clock and talk about something else till you dine with somebody else at seven. And this lack of our sense of clock-time is also one reason the Russians—excelling at research and pure science—have proved themselves, since the Revolution, so ill suited for industrial operations, which depend on close timing and deadlines, the kind of thing perfected by our Taylor system. The programs of the Five-Year Plans were attempts to impose on the Russians the conception of clock and calendar time, to stampede them into the Western frame. In our mechanized part of the world, such a device is neither needed nor conceivable. Our industrial time runs on—the seconds clicking by like cogs—as steadily as the conveyor belt that carries the parts of the car that must always be the model of a particular calendar year. If some step in the process jams, it is soon got going again; our factories do not stop for lunch, as the Russian ones do, or as they did when I visited them in 1935. The accurate continuous functioning of the American industrial machine involves, more or less, our whole lives. But the Five-Year Plans of the Russians were like unaccustomed blocks of Western time set down in the Eastern eternity, as their plants were set down on the steppes; and though their front ends were squarely presented, a triumph of theatrical décor, they would tend to melt away on the other side, to succumb to the Russian continuous present. The planners themselves, in the meantime, instead of starting work with the workers and keeping in touch with the plant, would have been coming to their offices late in the morning and escaping from the discipline of the clock by getting together for interminable conferences that would go on for most of the night. The recent order that Soviet officials must be at their desks from nine to six is one of the ever recurring, the almost Sisyphean attempts on the part of the governing group to synchronize Russia with the schedule of the West.

Now, the Jews of the Old Testament were living in a world of time that, from our modern Western point of view, was even less advanced than the Russian. In their language, as in Russian, the primary distinction was made between completed and incomplete action, but there were no definite tenses at all. The beginner is usually told, as the best rule of thumb to start out with, to translate the perfects as pasts and the imperfects as futures. But he soon finds out that this will not do. It is true that the ancient Jew usually thought of future action as uncompleted and completed action as past, but our categories of future and past can hardly be said to have existed for him. In my old grammar of 1838, the author, a Professor Isaac Nordheimer of the University of the City of New York, begins his discussion of the Hebrew tenses by explaining that the efforts of Europeans to work out a system of tenses has been "hitherto attended with very incomplete success," because of the fact that "Occidental scholars" cannot help proceeding on assumptions "derived . . . from the manner in which the various points of time are indicated in the Indo-European languages, rather than from the nature of the subject itself." He goes on to try to grapple with the nature of the Hebrew idea of time, and he presents us with a diagram. Let the straight line AB, he says, represent the sequence of time. Let us assume that for the Jews this sequence extended beyond A into an infinite past and beyond B into an infinite future. Let us take, upon this line, a point C somewhere between A and B, which will represent the present, *our* conception of the present. But here the trouble begins. The Jews even more than the Russians lacked our Western conception of the present moment—a feature that, it seems, marks a very advanced state in the history of language development. For them, no point C could exist. When the narrator of a Biblical story tells of something that has happened in the past, he does not keep it in a definite relation to a fixed point of reference in the present, the point at which the story is supposed to be told. He puts himself back into the time of the story, and by a logic not unlike that which is exemplified by the Russian sisters who thought they *will* go to Moscow, he may put in the imperfect ("future")—since the action has not yet been completed at the time of which he is telling—some event which, from our point of view, is already completed and belongs to the past. If we should try to proceed by our rule of thumb in translating Genesis 41:50, we should find ourselves putting it that Joseph "begat two sons before the years of famine will come." Dr. Nordheimer's diagram elucidates this by showing that the moment the storyteller puts himself back to a point D, between A and C, the happenings between D and C will be shifted from the past to the future; but he tries also to make it account for a feature of Hebrew grammar that must be one of the strangest in the history of language—the principle that when a verb-form follows the conjunction "and," the imperfect is written for the perfect and the perfect for the imperfect. That is, if you relied on the rule of thumb, you would find yourself translating, "And God *will say,* 'Let there be light,' " instead of, "And God *said.*" It seems to me that this phenomenon eludes Dr. Nordheimer's argument, and that the Hebrew line of eternity ends by slipping away from all his alphabetical points and retaining only the property of extending indefinitely in either direction; nor have I seen any other explanation that appeared to me satisfactory. I shall not discuss this problem except to point out that it illustrates how difficult it is for us today to grasp the old Hebrew idea of time.

The points on Dr. Nordheimer's line cannot even be used to demonstrate other features of the Hebrew verbs more accessible than the "*and* conversive." A striking example of this, and a very significant one, is the so-called "prophetic" use of the perfect. If Jehovah or a prophet declares with the utmost conviction of certainty that something is going to happen, the action or event is put— since its eventual completion is not to be doubted—in the form of the verb that denotes completion. The implication is "It's as good as done." If you translate, as everybody has had to do, these prophetic perfects as futures, you miss an important nuance. When Jehovah says to Moses, "I am what I am," we are faced with the converse problem. Both verbs are in the imperfect, so, if we followed our rule of thumb, it would give us "I shall be what I shall be"—which again would be incorrect, since what the author of Exodus means to say is that God's existence has never ceased, that it is still going on and will never end. (This passage seems to be echoed in John 8:58: "Before Abraham was, I am.") Both these instances of usage are much to the point, for they both imply the conception of a single and eternal God, which was fundamental to Hebrew thought. For this Deity, the point C, the present moment, is a matter of little importance. Hence the carelessness of chronology in the Bible, the long shadows cast by the patriarchs, the habit of feeling that the prophets are still, like Jehovah, in being (the verb that means "to prophesy" has no "light" active but is always in the light passive, which indicates that God is speaking *through* the prophet, or in the intensive reflexive, which indicates raving or exaltation), so that it shocked no one's sense of reality to attribute to them writings that dealt with events occurring years after their deaths or to read back into them predictions of happenings—the coming of the Messiah, for example—that in their lifetimes had not even been imagined. "Instead of narrating, Israel predicts, that is to say, systematizes," says Renan in this connection. "That is why it has prophets, not historians. The invasion of the Scythians, for example, is not narrated anywhere. The episode of Gog, in Ezekiel, is a description of it, transformed into a symbol for the future. In this curious state of mind, everything becomes a type and a general formula. The thing that has actually happened counts for almost nothing." The Book of Daniel, which is written in terms of Belshazzar and Nebuchadnezzar and the Babylonian captivity, was intended to apply to a situation four hundred years later, when the Jews, then returned to Jerusalem, were being persecuted by Antiochus Epiphanes.

Renan believed also that this vagueness of the time-sense, this lack of an equipment of tenses, which is common, it seems, to the Semitic languages, had been one of the factors that contributed to preventing the Semitic peoples from acquiring techniques and "progressing" along the same lines as the European world. They had never been geared into our time-system. Though modern clocks were not used in Europe till some time in the thirteenth century, it seems to have been the Romans who established our clock and our calendar. The Greeks, of course, had water clocks and sundials and an elaborate system of tenses that indicated with precision, as the Semitic languages could not do, the relation of happenings to one another. But the Romans, with their conquests, imposed their system wherever their armies came; they left the construction of their language along with their other constructions. The Romance languages inherited them, and the Teutonic ones took their stamp. We live today in a Roman structure of present, past, pluperfect, future and future perfect. (The current tendency to drop this last tense, to slur the relations of events in the future, is probably due to our desperate rush to pull future events into the present.) And we live not merely, as the Romans did, in a world of years, months, weeks and days, but in a world of minutes, seconds and infinitesimally split seconds.

Does the Westernized modernized Jew not live in this structure, too? He has mastered it; in a practical way, he lives by it. Yet his Bible and the language in which it was written seem never to be quite absent from the background of his mind. The Talmud has kept them alive as immediate inalienable realities that have annihilated time and space through fifteen centuries of exile and dispersion. Most Jews have a dimension of eternity, and this is one thing that sets them off from, and to some extent makes them seem strange to, the people whose view of the world is conditioned by self-limiting historical units: the development of civilizations, the births and the deaths of nations. Our myths are the temporal myths of Caesar and Pericles, of Charlemagne, Washington, Hitler; but the myths of the Jews are timeless—the patriarchs and prophets who never die, the Messiah who never comes. The legend of the Wandering Jew is an attempt by the Gentiles to synchronize the Jewish eternalness with the vicissitudes of their own intensely temporal history. The sense of persistent values that survive and transcend our historical epochs, as it has always been inherent in Jewish religion, is also implied in their language; and some acquaintance with the Hebrew Bible may be useful in making us realize how much our conception of time is an artificial contrivance; that tonight at eight-thirty, when we hope for a new revelation afforded by some popular drama, the night of August 9th, when we did or did not commit the crime, the point C that fixes the moment of the present, have an importance that is purely conventional. I do not mean that we ought to go back to the world of the Hebrew prophets or that the Jews as a people still live in this world, though one sometimes gets the impression that there are rabbis and scholars who do; but today one begins to be dubious of our passion for historicity, which seems at moments to become maniacal. I have lately been typing old notebooks of mine that go back to 1914, and I find that, for every year, I have recorded the current slang and the favorite popular songs. Is this valuable? I thought it was, and I expect to make some use of this data. Like everyone else in our part of the world, I am incurably history-minded. But what about all the issues of all the innumerable newspapers recorded on microfilm, all the minutes of all the meetings carefully filed away? We are shocked and indignant when the Russians, with their less highly developed historical sense, do not hesitate to sponge out the record of a decade or of half a century and to substitute something simpler, which will be more advantageous to the party in power (remember that the Russian verb does not indicate the relations of events in the past; when an action is past, it is simply past). We are amused by the rabbinical mind, which occupies itself with the moral situation of Jonah inside the whale as if it were a permanently important problem. But how long can our civilization go on storing up and stuffing our heads with so much minute historical information?

M. André Malraux, in his novel *The Walnut Trees of Altenburg*, written in the midst of the last World War, presents an international group of thinkers in various departments of knowledge discussing those basic conceptions that underlie the mentality of every civilization without ever being subjected to criticism, because they are so taken for granted that people are not aware of them. And one of these, a great anthropologist, arrives at the conclusion that, for us, the uncriticized conception is not "the nation," as somebody else has suggested, but the historical point of view itself. We live, he insists, in history "as the religious civilizations lived in God," and behind our conception of history is our special conception of time.

Shall we someday come to reckon differently—to abridge historical processes, to range over longer periods, to see events in different relations, to have a different conception of events themselves? Our present conception of time, which has till recently dominated our imaginative writing and is still extremely strong, seems essential to our mechanics, to our science, which has merged with our study of morals. Now, the critical study of the Bible that has been one of the features of our scientific period has shown that the Jewish ideas about morals, the principles ascribed to Jehovah, were modified from prophet to prophet—and hence, from era to era, under pressure of varying situations, economic, political, social. And yet there is something there that is less affected than one might expect by these changes in time and locale: the principles of rectitude and justice, represented by the permanent Jewish God (as later, with Christianity, the claims of human fellow-feeling). When the resolute Western grammarian makes an effort to introduce our time sequence into the timeless Hebrew verbs, they continue to remain something else. "Many have concluded," says Dr. Kyle M. Yates, the author of an excellent beginner's grammar, *The Essentials of Biblical Hebrew,* "that uniformity in the determination and translation of these points [the nuances of mood and tense] is impossible," but he insists that they must exist, and he draws up a table of them. The weakness of such systems is that they are bound to wear the aspect of gratuitous creations, since the meanings assigned by their formulators cannot, except in a very few instances, be shown to have any connection with the actual mechanism of the verb-forms. And so, when the garbled events of the Bible are subjected to an exact rearrangement that satisfies our Western chronology, we see that they still remain something else—something that is scarcely impaired by the extreme improbability that Methuselah lived almost a thousand years, that Sarah was nearly seventy when she proved irresistible to Pharaoh, that Jacob's great love for Rachel kept him working for Laban seven years. It is something that has done a good deal to sustain the morale of the Gentile as well as that of the Jew through the strictly historical happenings—the wars, the persecutions, the conquests, the migrations and the natural disasters of the last three thousand years.

Yet the Biblical "aspect of eternity" has its disadvantages, too. It is the Jews who have given to the Western world all four of its great religions—Judaism, Christianity, Mohammedanism and the half-religion Marxism—and they all of them have in common a compelling and delusive utopianism. The Jew expected the Messiah, who was to lead him out of captivity; the Mohammedan looked forward to his paradise; the medieval Christian expected the Judgment Day and the reign of Christ for infinity. Karl Marx, who liked to bait the utopian socialists and believed himself free from their errors, actually derived his appeal in great part from his vision of a socialist Armageddon and a socialist Judgment Day, when the sheep would be separated from the goats and the reign of Justice begin, as his "History" was also an omnipotent God that guided a chosen group. All these visions were solemn promises that gave people the courage to live, and in which they believed so vividly that it was almost as if the visions were already fulfilled. They belong to the "prophetic perfect," that phase of the Hebrew verb which indicates that something is as good as accomplished. And the escape from historical time—from the compromise, the modification, the incomplete satisfaction, the accepted misunderstanding, the complicated adjustments of every day—may bring with it something obsessive, as all four of these religions have shown, that easily produces intolerance. Now, intolerance is suicidal, for it stimulates intolerance on the other side. To believe in a word of God unchangeable and eternal (as promulgated by any of these prophets) is to stop human self-improvement, human self-creation dead—in the literal, as it always turns out, as well as in the "spiritual" way. This sense of transcendent principle has always had to be corrected by the realistic observation, the practical worldliness, of the Graeco-Roman tradition. It is the reciprocal relation of the two that has made what there is of our civilization.

# II

# ÉRETZ YISRAÉL

SAMARITAN PASSOVER:   A vertiginous trip up the mountain that commands, astoundingly, stage by stage, a more and more immense view of Palestine. This, in the Biblical sense, is a High Place of worship indeed. At the top, we get out of the car and are struck by a prodigious wind that did not reach us in the valley below but that now seems about to sweep us off. A crowd of Arab children, who have come for the show, follow the foreign visitors and laugh noisily as we struggle against the gale and stumble among the rocks. There is nothing to be seen on this summit but a small Mohammedan shrine and the buried foundations of a Byzantine church that makes, in the grass, an octagon.

But farther down, out of range of the wind, the Samaritans are celebrating their Passover. Their High Priest, since early morning, has been reading the Samaritan Pentateuch and has now nearly got through Deuteronomy. This High Priest and two of his elders are garbed in long gowns of green; other elders are gowned in white. All wear hieratic beards and white turbans with red tops. The Samaritans are extremely inbred; there are now only three hundred and four of them—two hundred and seventeen here in Jordan, and the rest over the line in Israel. The elders, in their robes of ceremony, can hardly be told apart. They are tall and well grown, but their bones look frail. Their faces a little lack character, and yet give the impression of exceptional purity. They do not resemble the Arabs, among whom they have now so long lived; they are paler and like Jews of the classical stamp, whose aquiline profiles have been bred away till their noses are almost straight. In a circle about these *Cohaním* (priests) sits an audience partly made up of other Samaritan men, in red tarbooshes and business suits. The women seem all to be lurking in the tents that the Samaritans have put up on the mountain and to which, for the period of the Passover, they have come from the town of Nablús on the plain. There is an outer ring of alien visitors, whose presence reminds one a little of one of those Indian dances of the American Southwest which sightseers are allowed to attend. The American vice-consul from Jerusalem is there to represent the Consulate, to which an invitation has been sent, and the director of the American School of Oriental Research is also present.

The reading of the Pentateuch ended, the High Priest makes a short speech in Arabic, in which the word "Arabia" comes out in a climactic way and is enthusiastically applauded. Then he leads the *Cohaním* in praying, repeating over and over again, "There is only one God," but steadily increasing, step by step, the tempo and the volume. Just below stands another assembly, a group of the younger men, robed in white and with sleeves rolled up for the sacrifice, wearing red tarbooshes and sandals tied with strings. They, too, are determinedly praying. Beside them, in the angle of a stone fence, wait seven fat brown-faced sheep—one for each of the seven Samaritan families—which have been recently purchased with careful selection and scrupulously washed every day. They conform to the prescription of Exodus, on which the Passover service is based, that "your lamb shall be without blemish, a male a year old." And now the sun is just setting; the moment for the sacrifice arrives. The High Priest gets up on a stone and recites the first six verses of Exodus 12, Jehovah's instructions to Moses and Aaron for commemorating their flight from Egypt, which culminate with the words "And the whole assembly of the congregation of Israel shall kill it in the evening." The young men have carried the squirming sheep to a ditch which contains a stone altar, and they now hold the animals' heads over this and saw through their throats with large knives. This releases a demonstration, not an outburst but a reverential acknowledgment. You hear whistles, cries, clapping of hands. The fathers of families now at once smear the blood on the foreheads of their first-born children, and in earlier days they dashed away to smear it on the lintels and posts of their doors. Inquiries as to why this was not being done brought only evasive answers, and it has been only from *Life* magazine that I have learned—there was a *Life* photographer present—that the Samaritans are now so poor that they have to borrow tents from the Arabs, who object to having them bloodied. On the sheep, now mere fat woolly lumps, they pour boiling water from pots, and begin plucking off the wool, to establish that the bodies are unblemished. The High Priest withdraws to his tent to entertain the invited guests.

By this time the sun has disappeared, and an all-but-full bright moon is shining, but suddenly, as we walk through sharp stones in the direction of the High Priest's tent, the whole world is blotted out by a darkness of a kind that I have never seen elsewhere and that summons to my mind impressively that opaque word *"arafél,"* which is supposed to be compounded of "darkness" and "cloud" and which in Exodus is applied to the obscurity out of which the Ten Commandments were uttered: "And

the people stood afar off, and Moses drew near to the
thick darkness where God was." This darkness is not
black, but a sort of dull and dense brown, and seems almost of the consistency of soft-coal smoke. Invisible to
one another and hoping we are not getting lost, we try to
hold our way on the rocky road that hardly differs from
the stony hillside, till at last we see a group of parked
cars, with the lights of the tents behind them. Received
by Amrán Ishák, the High Priest, cordially but rather
remotely, we sit down on benches and beds and are offered arrack and wine, biscuits of unleavened bread and a
dish of a paste called khúmas, that you scoop up with
pieces of matzah. While the ceremony was going on, the
Arabs, it seems, were not idle. One of the ladies has just
managed to rescue a ring which she felt being slipped off
her finger, and a young theological student from Union
Seminary, in New York, has lost his fountain pen and his
watch. The High Priest assures him with dignity that he
will see that these things are restored. Amrán Ishák has
written a book on his people, their history, beliefs and customs, and parts of it, in English translation, are sold to
the visitors in the form of pamphlets. Up to this year, I
am told, they have been given away, and the visitors have
made small contributions, but this year a set price has
been put on them, and one of the white-gowned young
men snatches a pamphlet away when, in consequence of
a misunderstanding, something less than this price has
been offered. Amrán Ishák draws back from the scene
with a look of controlled indignation. One feels that he
is deeply embarrassed, but one cannot tell whether he is
angry at the visitor's trying to cheapen the sale or at the
young Samaritan's bad manners. It is evident, in any case,
that he does not know how to deal with this situation.
Though the members of his community are, many of
them, small businessmen in Nablús, he still lives in the

world of the Bible, and his book is a résumé of history
from the minority Samaritan point of view. There is something about his aspect at once austere and anxious.

The Samaritans originally, of course, were as much a
part of the Children of Israel as were the ancestors of the
Jews. Their kingdom in the north was, in fact, called
Israel, in contradistinction to Judah, the kingdom of the
south. But in 721 B.C. this northern kingdom of Israel
was wiped out by the descent of the Assyrians, and its
people never recovered from this. All the more important
elements of the population were taken away to Assyria,
but the poorer people were left behind, and these inter-
bred with the conquerors and corrupted their Jehovah
worship with that of the Assyrian gods. These were the
ancestors of the modern Samaritans. Later on, they were
to feud with the people of Judah, who, once the northern
kingdom had been destroyed, were in a position to make
of their own city, Jerusalem, the unchallenged religious
center of the Israelite world. Jerusalem fell to Nebuchadnezzar in 586, and the Judahites were carried off to Babylon, but when, fifty years later, the Persian king Cyrus,
in his turn, conquered Babylon, he allowed them to return to Jerusalem, where they set about rebuilding their
temple. The Samaritans at this point approached them and
offered to collaborate with them, but the Judahites regarded them now as a people of doubtful blood, contami-
nated by heathen religion, and refused to allow them to
participate. The breach was made final when a brother of
the High Priest, who had been sharing in the priestly
functions, married a Samaritan wife, and was exiled by
the elders of Jerusalem, where a very strong policy against
mixed marriages had been laid down by Nehemiah. This
man, with the backing of his father-in-law and reinforced
by other Israelites who had been persecuted for similar
reasons but backed by the Persian king, well content

to see the Jews divided, withdrew to Mount Gerízim and built a temple there; he seems to have been the founder of the present Samaritan sect of independent worshippers of Jehovah. The Samaritans, in any case, possessed their own text of the Pentateuch, and refused to recognize the prophets, whom they treated as the spokesmen of a rival faction. They rejected the whole version of Israelite history composed by the dominant Judahites; they have never regarded themselves as Jews, but always refer to the Jews as a race of successful impostors, very much as the Trotskyites did with the Stalinist regime in Russia. The Samaritan variants from the orthodox text of the five books supposed to have been written by Moses are relatively slight in extent, but the Samaritans consider them of crucial importance, for they indicate firmly and consistently that Mount Gerízim, at the foot of which they live and on which they celebrate their Passover, is the spot designated by Jehovah as the headquarters of his cult; not Jerusalem, which, at the time when the commands of the Pentateuch were given— that is, at the time when the Children of Israel had just arrived at the Promised Land—was not yet in Israelite hands. The Samaritans assert that the Jews, and not they, have doctored the holy writings—that the selection by God of Jerusalem as the center of Israelite religion could hardly have been made before Solomon's Temple was actually in existence. They deny the contention of the Jews that this designation was really a prophecy, and they point out that the form of the verb "to choose" that occurs in the Samaritan version precludes the possibility of this. The truth is, it seems, that the Pentateuch, in the general version accepted by both Orthodox Jews and Samaritans, was put together during the Babylonian exile—so, on the one hand, the Samaritans are perfectly right in insisting that the mention of Jerusalem was made after the building of Solomon's Temple, while, on the other hand, the inference must be that the Samaritans accepted this version from the Judahites, who had composed it, and that they added to it some references to Mount Gerízim.

Yet actually, from the point of view of history, the Samaritans have a pretty good case. Gerízim and its neighbor Ébal are the mountains named in Deuteronomy as the places for proclaiming, respectively, the blessings and the cursings of God. Nablús is certainly the ancient Shechem, the place in which Jacob is supposed to have settled when he came back from serving Laban, and the Samaritans claim that it is also the place where he had previously had his dream of the angels on the heavenly ladder. They are able to adduce the authority of Joshua 24 that the bones of Joseph were eventually brought from Egypt in order to be buried at Shechem, that it was at Shechem that Joshua set up a great stone "in the sanctuary of the Lord." Here, too, according to them, between the two mountains, was Moreh, the meadow where Abraham pitched his tent, and they believe that it was on Mount Gerízim, and not on the rock in Jerusalem which the Mosque of Omar now shelters, that the sacrifice of Isaac was averted. In any case, they built their own temple on Gerízim. This was later destroyed by the Jews in the period of Hasmonean ascendancy, in the second pre-Christian century; rebuilt, under Hadrian, when, at the time of the Jewish revolt of the second post-Christian century, the Samaritans had aided the Romans; then destroyed again by the Romans, in 484, at the instigation of the Christians. A rebellion under Justinian, in the following century, brought down on the Samaritans total suppression.

That is, political suppression. Their cult, as we have seen, still survives, and we visitors, leaving Amrán Ishák's

tent, go back to the sacrifices. The directions set forth in
Exodus are being exactly followed. There is, to be sure,
one modern innovation. A bicycle pump has been used to
blow up the dead sheep and facilitate the removal of the
skin from the carcass, but this, of course, has not been
prohibited, since no such devices were known to Moses.
And now, in the red light of fires—the darkness has
passed, and the moon is out—the naked remains are hanging, identifiable only by their dangling heads and their
hairy legs and hoofs, each from a horizontal pole supported by two uprights, which are held by a pair of
young men. These stand before the butcher, who cuts the
carcasses open and removes first the slimy intestines, then
the complicated mass of the other organs, from which the
liver is hanging. There is a warm smell of raw flesh and
excrement. These tripes are washed, salted and burned,
according to the Biblical prescription. Then the bodies
are salted and roasted—since God has forbidden boiling:
"Eat not of it . . . sodden at all with water"—in an oven
made of plaster and earth that has been heated over a fire
built in a pit in the ground. They will be cooked for three
hours, then eaten at midnight, the moment when, relent-
ing at last to release the Children of Israel, "The Lord
smote all the first-born in the land of Egypt." They will
be eaten to the chanting of hymns, with the ordained
bitter herbs and unleavened bread, and hastily—it is part
of the ceremony that the celebrants must tear the meat
apart with their hands—since God has said specifically,
"Ye shall eat in haste," as they had eaten when they were
leaving Egypt.

We did not wait for this final rite, but the wife of the
director of the American School wanted, she said, to stay
long enough to see a sheep actually roasted. A very feminine reaction, I thought: her interest had been excited in
a culinary operation, and she wanted to see the meat in

the oven. With the director himself I talked of the Samaritans' pious conviction that they are still being punished by Jehovah for their dalliance with the heathen deities, and of their touching resignation to the inevitable dying-out of their clan. They believe themselves to be fulfilling the prophecy of Deuteronomy 28:62, that "Ye shall be left few in number, whereas ye were as the stars of heaven for multitude." "They were guilty of syncretism," the scholar replied, and reminded me, by this humorously meant remark, of the distance between their point of view and ours. What is strange to us in this ceremony is the performance of a barbaric butchery with restraint and a complete sobriety; and, coming from the modern world, it is difficult for us to realize that the problem that most occupies the minds of the Samaritans is how to avoid marriages that will involve a too close consanguinity. In the Samaritan community in Israel, the elders have so far relaxed their law as to permit a few marriages with Jewish women, and I was told by someone who had visited it that he had been startled there to hear German spoken; yet, in general, the Samaritans expect to die out, and, in the meantime, the High Priest writes, "This nation carries out the ancient customs according to the Mosaic law as well as they can, and have always offered the proper prayers to the God of all creation, that He might keep them from all harm, misfortune and all violence."

While I was standing there in the dark, a long-gowned and bearded elder came up quietly from behind me and begged in a low voice, "Baksheesh for the Samaritans!"

*The Guardians of the City:* It is absurd, no doubt, as well as pathetic that, from principles of religious purity, the Samaritans, after living among Arabs for something like thirteen centuries without intermarrying with them, should be dooming themselves today to extinction. It is a *reductio ad absurdum* of the Hebraic tradition of exclusiveness. But one finds in the Jewish community, on the other side of the line, in the Meá Shearím (Hundred Gates) quarter of the new city of Jerusalem, a minority no less intransigent—the ultra-orthodox group that calls itself N'tureí Kartá, Guardians of the City. Just as the Samaritans exclude the Jews, and the Orthodox Jews exclude the Christians, so the Guardians of the City exclude, by their rigorous Judaism, not merely non-orthodox Jews but also the majority of the orthodox, and, together with other residents of more or less their way of thinking, have actually established in Meá Shearím, in this modern all-Jewish city, a community much like a ghetto.

This group derives from all over Europe—Poland, the Baltic Provinces, Rumania, Hungary, Germany—as well as from the United States. For hundreds of years, special scholars were sent by the Jewish communities of Europe —and, since the later nineteenth century, of America—to study in Old Jerusalem. They were subsidized for life from a fund supplied by free contributions from the congregations of countless synagogues, and they were expected to devote themselves to the study of Torah—that is, of the Pentateuch and its infinitely elaborated commentaries. The families of these students eventually "increased and multiplied" to a community of some five thousand. They had the comfort, in the Old City, of living close to the Wailing Wall, but, at the time of the war with the Arabs of 1948-49, they were driven to take refuge outside the old walls, where they gave themselves their present title of Guardians of the City. The city they guard is not that which the Israelis have made their capital. The Guardians of the City will not recognize the Israeli state, for they believe that it is only the Messiah who can found a state of Israel on earth, and that the

profane impostures of the Zionists are preventing the
Messiah from coming. Insisting that Hebrew is a sacred
tongue that cannot be used for everyday purposes, they
refuse to speak this national language and adhere to
their native Yiddish. They will not share in the general
life; they have managed to remain more or less autono-
mous; and though they have come from so many countries, they give an impression of all but complete uniformity. As in the case of the Samaritans, they are very
inbred, and there is a dominant influence—Polish. They
are said to reproduce in their costume the fashions of
well-to-do Poles of two hundred years ago. On a Sabbath,
when the people are walking out, all in their best clothes,
they strike, in the Middle East, a note strangely inappropriate. Even in the hottest weather, when such costumes
must be almost intolerable, the men wear large round fur
hats (called streimels) and long straight coats (kaftans)
of dull or of glossy black that come down just below their
calves, under which they have knee breeches as often as
trousers and white, black or yellow stockings. In obedi-
ence to Leviticus 19:27—"You shall not round off the
hair on your temples or mar the edges of your beard"—
they have allowed beards and hair to grow, and have cultivated, in front of their ears, the long locks that are
the sign of the most literal orthodoxy. The women must
walk behind the men. Their heads were shaved when they
were married, and they wear unattractive wigs. The men
are not allowed to shake hands with the women, and even
their husbands, I was told, are not supposed to look them
in the face; there is prescribed for sexual intercourse—
which cannot take place in the light or unless the parties
are dressed—a method that obviates this. Rabbinical law
provides that a husband may divorce his wife for letting
the dinner burn. The walls of the Meá Shearím quarter
are covered with posters that warn the men not to let their

women listen to radio—"You will hear a woman sing, but will it be a clean woman?"—and they are rallied to resist the Israeli law that conscripts women for military service.

The lives of these people, their conviction of merit, their prestige in the eyes of their neighbors, are all made up of observances or of casuistical substitutes for observances. Thus they are not supposed to carry handkerchiefs, and they wind them around their belts. The reason for this is as follows. The prohibition against work on the Sabbath occurs in the chapter of Exodus (35) which orders the building of the Tabernacle. This led to the later conclusion that only work connected with this building was meant, and this work was discriminated into thirty-nine classes, of which one was the carrying of an object from one place to another. The significant types of place were specified, in turn, as four, and the most severe prohibition was that against transferring private property to any public place. The Tractate *Sabbath* of the Talmud discusses, in this connection, the problem of clothing and adornment. It becomes a very nice question which articles may be classed under these categories, and how they shall be worn so as not to be carried and not to be subject to the defilement Leviticus warns against. The handkerchief does not appear in the Talmud, but is later dealt with in the *Shulkhán Arúkh,* a code of religious practice completed in the sixteenth century, which explains that it must be worn "below the outer garment," that it must not be knotted on anything (tying knots on the Sabbath is one of the thirty-nine prohibitions), and that it ought to be "wound on the trousers," so that it will not be directly carried. I was told that if they indulge themselves in trimming their beards, they do it with blunt scissors, since the prohibition of Leviticus 19:27 against "marring" the edges of the beard is thought to be limited by 21:5: "They

. . . shall not *shave* off the edges of their beards"—so that, according to a Talmudic interpretation, it is permissible to use anything but a razor, and having the scissors blunt removes them, presumably, as far as possible from the category of razor.

There are children of all ages in the street, the little boys all with skullcaps and sidelocks, which ought to be worn with dignity and do not suit the scrambling young. A crazy man squats by the wall and prophesies or airs his grievances—it may well be the same thing; an old man of solemn aspect, with white beard and black skullcap, sits out on his little porch reading what must be a holy book. A deformed and cross-eyed man—typical idiot of a Central European village—limps along the pavement. I was told by an American Jew that a visit to Meá Shearím reminded him of nothing so much as *The Cabinet of Dr. Caligari*, but I did not find it quite so macabre. The people seem mostly healthy and rather remarkably tall, but—what is not characteristic of Israeli Jerusalem—they do live in a certain squalor.

I persuaded a newspaperman to take me to the synagogue, which, though its actual congregation is not more than four or five hundred, is the N'tureí Kartá headquarters and the core of the orthodox resistance. He warned me that it would be dirty, but the atmosphere of rigorous devotion did much to redeem this. We arrived during Afternoon Prayers, and a pleasant, stout, white-bearded man offered us seats on a bench; a dingy and much-thumbed prayer book lay on the desk before us. The more pious of the members, in flat-brimmed black hats, were praying against the wall, bobbing their heads at the name of God, which provoked an echoed response even from those who were not actively participating. For people were coming and going and walking around the room. Some showed a touch of dandyism in their well-curled and well-oiled brown earlocks and their long yel-low-and-brown-striped coats; others, with sallow com-plexions, who nibbled their fingers and picked at their beards, had intellectual faces that seemed capable of ex-altation. One lean young man, with a thin pointed beard, looked a little mad. A small boy, with skullcap, cropped head, red side curls and a torn yellow sweater, was no doubt filled with dreams of distinction—dreams the real-ization of which might seem to the outside visitor to be bounded by this plain, shabby room, at the same time his school and his field of ambition, yet which actually know no bounds, since they must occupy themselves entirely with a realm of divine law that would always and every-where remain the same. Above, on one side, loomed the gallery for women, blankly, inexorably boarded off, in which they cannot be seen and from which they cannot see anything.

Prayers over, the black-hatted men sat down at long tables, on benches along the wall, and stuck their noses in volumes of the Talmud. You have to study Talmud, my companion explained, by night as well as by day. Yet the synagogue is also a social center, and people hang around to gossip. We go to talk to the rabbi, about whom a circle has gathered. His name, Amrám, is, I take it, the same as that of the Samaritan priest, and he makes upon me a lit-tle the same impression: of a purity that approaches the insipid yet is backed by an official firmness. He is pale, and his eyes and his beard are pale. One eye is half-closed, as if from too much reading. One would say that his face is a good face if it were not that it so plainly looks out from a world that is different from ours that we know it would not be possible for the Rabbi and us to agree as to what constitutes goodness. The saintliness of Rabbi Am-rám is accompanied—as it were, protected—by a quality that is not perhaps shrewdness but rather a habit of cal-

culating in his dealings with the people of an alien
world which it is impossible for him at all to take seriously. From that world he wants no publicity; he has
never allowed himself to be photographed. I feel as if I
were peering at something that is hardly meant to be seen.
The Rabbi Amrám's family have been living in Jerusalem from five generations back. When he is asked what
the aims of the Guardians are, he replies that they just
want to be simple Jews who live as their forefathers did.
They cannot accept Israel, because it is not the true
Israel; the Messiah alone can establish that. At this point,
the jolly old man, who had offered us seats and who was
now standing by, said something with great emphasis that
was relayed to me as "They eat pig!" The Rabbi has
never sent a letter since the beginning of the present ré-
gime: if he should do so, he would have to buy a stamp,
and this would imply recognition. He has refused, for the
same reason, to acquire a ration card, but his congregation keeps him fed. He does not think it right to contend
with the Arabs, and he adduces a Talmudic teaching that
one must not revolt against the Goyím, but he denies
that a man named Laibala Weissfisch, a fanatical maker
of Torah scrolls, who has recently visited the United
States, allegedly to make proposals prejudicial to the interests of Israel to the Arabs in the United Nations, is in
any sense a spokesman for the Guardians. When, however, we ask Rabbi Amrám whether or not the story is
true that, at the time of the Arab war, the Guardians had
flouted the nationalists by going to the enemy with a white
flag, prepared to make a separate peace, he answers that
actually it is not true, but that he has never made a point
of denying it, since he regards it as a good idea, perfectly
consistent with their principles, which they probably
ought to have thought of and carried out. I asked him
whether he hoped ever to get back to the Old City, and he

replied, "That would be God's blessing!" When we had left, I said to my guide that I was sorry I had not inquired what he thought of the state of the world. "I can give you his answer," my friend replied, "exactly as if you had asked him: he would have told you that he leaves all that to God."

Yet this mild-appearing patriarch—he has seventeen children—so venerable at forty-eight, has made himself a formidable nuisance. If Meá Shearím is a ghetto, it is a ghetto that persecutes its neighbors as much as they persecute it. The Guardians of the City have constantly to be haled into court and are often sent to prison. They and others of their way of thinking bar off public roads on the Sabbath to make them impassable for cars, which, when stopped, are surrounded by children dangling earlocks and shouting, "Shabbas! Shabbas!" The Guardians take down the numbers of cars that are out between Friday and Saturday evenings, watch to find them parked and smash them up. This has made the police apprehensive. Last Purim, a frivolous young man attended a costume party in the costume of a denizen of Meá Shearím, with streimel, kaftan and sidelocks. After arriving, he went back to get something from his car. It had been raining, and he lifted the hood to see whether the engine was wet. It was Friday evening, Sabbath. A policeman immediately seized him. The young man explained his costume, but the policeman refused to believe him. "Pull my sidelocks and see," said the reveller. But the policeman thought this was a ruse, that the fanatic wanted to frame him and would have questions asked in parliament. The masquerader had to take them off himself. On the issue of female conscription, the struggle has reached a point— with the Guardians and their sympathizers flatly refusing to yield—where, in order to avoid the necessity of trying to use force and creating martyrs, the government may have to back down. The power that the Rabbi wields within his own sphere of influence seems to be all but absolute. The movies are strictly forbidden, and if a man is known to have gone to one, he is sure to have his subsidy cut off or find himself put out of his flat. Since the Guardians of the City do not recognize the Chief Rabbinate, anyone who is known to have stood in the presence of the top-hatted Chief Rabbi (let alone have entered his synagogue), even in connection with a funeral, is immediately ostracized. They have several times burned a newsstand, not far from Rabbi Amrám's synagogue, that persisted in selling the novels that the women are forbidden to read, and the illustrated weeklies, which are considered pornographic. To almost everybody else in Jerusalem, the Guardians of the City are a headache, a constant source of embarrassment. The worst of it is that, unlike the Samaritans, they are militant proselytizers, with methods not unlike those of the Communists. They spy on their own people and spy on their own spies; they organize demonstrations and infiltrate Talmudic schools. What the Israelis are to the Arabs—not that they use these methods—the Guardians of the City are to Israel.

*The Fiction of S. Y. Agnón:*  This obsolete Galician world, preserved in Meá Shearím, has been brilliantly presented in literature by a man of unquestionable genius, Shmuél Yoséf Agnón, who today resides in Jerusalem and occupies, at sixty-six, the undisputed position of foremost living Hebrew writer. I do not hesitate to speak of his genius, though I am unable to read him in Hebrew and have had access only to those of his works that have been translated into English—the novel called *The Bridal Canopy,* out of print but obtainable through Behrman House, New York; a long short story called *In the Heart of the Seas,* which is one of the volumes of the Schocken

Library; and a shorter piece called *Chemdat,* in the autumn, 1952, issue of the Jerusalem periodical *Israel Ar-
gosy.* (A book called *Days of Awe,* a treasury of legends
and traditions connected with the Jewish high holidays,
also published by Schocken, is of less interest to non-
Jewish readers.) In Israel, people complain that these
versions do nothing like justice to Agnón's remarkable
style, but the two books, at any rate, that have been translated by I. M. Lask certainly read very well, and even in
the alien medium it is evident that the texture of the writing is distinguished, poetic and strongly personal.

   Since I know nothing save at second-hand of the very
considerable literature in Hebrew that has come out of
Central Europe, Russia and Palestine in the course of the
last century and this, I cannot speak of Agnón's relation to
other Hebrew writers. But one is struck at once, in reading him, by similarities to two other Jewish artists—Marc
Chagall and Franz Kafka, both born, like Agnón, in
the eighties. The picture of Jewish life in Agnón is, as in
their cases, completely different from any kind of "genre"
work that is derived from nineteenth-century natural-
ism. Involved in this picture, to be sure, is a definite local
setting of domestic interiors and taverns, poultry yards
and village crafts—long journeys in wagons on country
roads, with the landlords looming remotely as menaces
more often than patrons, the Gentiles, in general ("forgive me for mentioning them"), present only, as it were,
offstage, to be shunned when they parade their "images"
out-of-doors in religious processions. (The religion of the
Gentiles is so little understood even by the masters of
Talmudic learning that the symbolic Christian fishes on
tombstones are taken as indicating the graves of Jewish
descendants of Jonah.) But far more important than any
of this are the rituals of the Jewish holidays, the marriage and funeral ceremonies, the devotions of the syna-

gogue and the pursuits of the yeshiva, House of Study, where young and old pore over the Talmud, memorizing pages, disputing in form. It is these that make the frame on which everything rests—a life of the spirit that requires concentration and is always more or less intellectual, a constant solicitude as to the attitude toward one of God, who is usually called the Name and remains rather impersonal as well as invisible, since He does not, as in Christianity, figure as the Heavenly Father of a part-human intercessor, yet is somehow, in His infinite wisdom, arranging and projecting everything.

The humor and the pathos of Agnón—and he is truly a master of both—result from the spectacle of men and women *living* in a homely environment, which has been searchingly observed by the author but is only implied by his delicate art, yet *imagining* in terms of a universe that has no real locale or date except possibly in the hoped-for return to that distant idealized Israel toward which the most pious among them have never ceased to yearn. The whole content of Agnón's work—at least, in those of his stories I know—is the poetry and irony of this situation. It is, I fear, not very impressive merely to read *about* Agnón; the mixture of Galician village life with esoteric rabbinical learning may well not appear enchanting. And yet Agnón makes it so. He has partly the same sort of charm as Chagall, the charm of a peasant world —though these Jews are not really peasants—both enlivened and veiled by folklore, in which the domestic animals become almost the equals of men, and visions of husbands or brides seem, in broad day, to float in the heavens. The dream of the boy in *Chemdat,* in which he sees his unloving stepmother sitting in the top of a tree and whistling like a bee-eater, is very much in the vein of Chagall, as is such an animal parable as that in *The Bridal Canopy* by which one of the wagoner's horses,

Ivory, demonstrates to his companion, Peacock, that it
would be wise not to kick at the yelping dogs of the un-
friendly Gentile foresters: "There was a cock that lived
with a Jew" and who became very much depressed from
brooding on the Eve of Atonement, which requires, as he
has learned from the prayer book, the taking of a cock
by the worshipper and whirling it about his head, with
the words "This cock shall go to death," and then hand-
ing it over to the slaughterer. He communicates his anxiety to a mouse, and, as the upshot of a conversation in
which a good deal of Scripture has been quoted by both,
the mouse makes an offer to help him. "Choicest of
Poultry," he says, "the days of the Night Prayers of
Penitence that precede the New Year do approach, when
men arise betimes to the synagogues; I shall go to eat up
the prayer book so that not so much as a single letter
shall be left." Says the cock, "For thy salvation have I
hoped, O Lord!" When the family of his owner have left
the house, the mouse is as good as his word and comes
out to eat the prayer book, but "thereupon the cat on the
watch fell upon him and consumed him." And when Peacock heard this story, "he kept his legs out of the argument and never interfered with what wasn't his own
affair."

But in Agnón you have also the moral, the theological
element that is characteristic of Kafka. Kafka, born in
Prague in the eighties and the son of a wholesale merchant, was one generation removed from the villages to
which his father sold his wares, and he did not study
Hebrew until late in life, but he derived from his mother's
family a tradition of piety and learning. Though five
years older than Agnón, he represents a later, more "assimilated" phase of the same Judaic culture, and it is
only by reading Agnón that you come to see how deeply
Judaic the work of Kafka is. (I am told that the most re-

cent work of Agnón is even closer to Kafka.) Though in
Kafka you do not get explicitly the background of Talmud and ghetto, the typical hero of Kafka, like the typical hero of Agnón, is a man who is trying to survive in an
alien, often unsympathetic and only partly comprehensi-
ble world, and who is bent on maintaining or discovering
a technique that will make it possible for him to live in it
on good terms with the Name.

The difference between Agnón and Kafka is that Reb
Judel of *The Bridal Canopy*, though equally at cross-pur-
poses with the larger social community and even with
the common conditions of life, is diverted only momen-
tarily from the path to salvation he has taken, the path of
study and prayer, whereas Kafka's all but anonymous
"K.," who is never given a Jewish origin, cannot be sure
of anything, and confuses, as Reb Judel would never do,
his duty to an imperfectly accessible God with his duty to
established society. In Kafka, the situation of the Jew in
Central Europe makes connections, as Agnón does not,
with a more general social situation, and he becomes the
moralist and poet—or, better, perhaps the poet of moral
uncertainty—of a baffling historical moment. It is difficult to see how Agnón can ever have Kafka's audience.
Yet, inside his traditional Jewish world, the human interest of Agnón's fiction is much wider and warmer than
Kafka's. You have not only Reb Judel's relation to the
Name; you have also the importunate problems of his
family and his neighbors—the good-for-nothing and morally callous cantor who gets drunk on the Day of Atonement yet can make the congregation weep; the poor young
man who has slept for years on a bench of the synagogue,
using his pants for a pillow, and who, finally becoming
betrothed to the daughter of a well-to-do tax collector,
looks forward with painful longing to the comforts of
the bridal bed, but who, lifting his foot to get into it, on

a prenuptial visit to his father-in-law's house, hears the
crack of the whip of the coach in which his prospective
bride is running away with a Gentile. You have the ar-
rogant and choleric official the whole structure of whose
life is shaken by losing his pet cat; the sterile wife,
loved by her husband, whom the persistent campaign of
his relatives compels him at last to divorce; the gentle
daughters of the Hassid Reb Judel himself, who, dow-
ryless, pay the price for their father's relentless piety.
These personal situations—by which the ideals of Judaism are shown as implicated with human nature, if not
quite, perhaps, tied down to earth—are always treated
by Agnón with sympathy. In Kafka, the irony of the
French Flaubert has tinctured with a certain contempt the
abstraction of Jewish analysis. The irony of Agnón is all-
pervasive, too; he is never sentimental, still less melodramatic. But—it may be a manifestation of the spirit of
the Hassidic sect, who particularly cultivated cheerfulness
and whose exploits Agnón loves to celebrate—Agnón
never blights his characters, and he cannot resist a miracle. Reb Israel Solomon's cat will be found; the wife
whom her husband is divorcing will faint, in the first sign
of pregnancy, when he has taken her before the rabbi;
the daughters of Reb Judel will discover a buried treasure in the moment when all seems lost. In the story called
*In the Heart of the Seas*, in which a group of Hassidím
actually sail to Palestine, the element of the miraculous
is carried even further, yet it never offends as incongruous, since it passes into the narrative as something it
is perfectly natural to add to the memory, the legend—
something, indeed, that is necessary in order to justify the
Jews and the ways of the most Holy and Blessed to His
People. So a precise and poetic notation—"The day
gradually faded. The East turned silver and a rising mist
chilled the ground"—may merge in the smoothest way

with a vision that is apocalyptic, and episodes built up solidly may finish with the suddenness of a folk tale—Agnón is an accomplished storyteller with a technique of his own of suspense and surprise—and slip without transition to something else.

Agnón is a classic; he is taught in schools; he has been mentioned for the Nobel Prize. One is quite ready to accept him as a true representative of that great line of Jewish writers that begins with the authors of Genesis. But one feels that he comes at the end of a culture. He himself is evidently as saturated with the learning of the Bible, the Talmud, the Cabala, and all the rest as one of his own Hassidim, yet—so far as I have read it, again—there is always an element of pastiche in his work. The larding of literature with ancient quotations has long been a feature of Hebrew writing, and the poetry of the eleventh-century Jehúda Halévi seems almost as much put together from the Bible as a medieval cento from Virgil; but isn't there, after all, a great difference between the attitudes toward the passages they quote of Agnón and of Jehúda Halévi? It was said to me in Israel by an admirer of Agnón that he is marvelously noncommittal—that he never gives it away that he does not see his people in their own terms, that he does not believe as they do. And this made me aware that his public must apprehend Agnón somewhat differently from the reader with no Jewish background. It may be possible for such a reader to misunderstand Agnón's humor. These stories seem at first to belong to the category of the false-naïve. One assumes that they could not have been written by a man who took Judaism seriously in the sense that his Hassidic heroes do. Yet even a slight acquaintance with the Talmud will make us realize from how far back the elements of fantasy and irony have been intimately associated, in literature, with the strictest Jewish religion. Mr. Michael L. Rodkin-

son, the translator of the Talmud into English, speaks of
"the vein of satire or humor that runs through" this variegated work, so difficult for the Gentile to get the hang
of. And one remembers Renan's theory that the Book of
Jonah was a work of humor, a satire on the prophets of
the Exile, so much in love with their predicted dooms that
they were furious when these were averted. It may be
that this Jewish self-mockery, tragic in its implications,
this drollery that is also moral, goes back to the first
great defeat at the hands of the Babylonians, and the im-
potence for action, the minority status, that this for a
time imposed. It is, in any case, very old, the irony
which still gives its accent to Agnón and to the Yiddish
humorists. For the Jew, the fundamental irony is that
God should have made him promises of special protection and favor, and then have allowed him to suffer a
succession of crushing disasters. There is a story of a
medieval rabbi who, at a time of savage persecution, made
a public confession of sins that he would have been quite
incapable of committing, in order to save face for God.
Is he a comic or a tragic figure? The non-Jew must be on
his guard against failing to appreciate how deep the Jewish irony goes, and not merely in terms, thus, of Jewish
tradition, but also—since our ideals at moments, must
seem to fail us all—in experience of human life.

Yet, even allowing for this, is not Agnón's work a monument to a culture that has lost much of its reality, that
can no longer be accepted as valid? One of his other two
long novels, I understand, deals with the Polish-Jewish
world in the period after the First World War, when it was
already disintegrating, and the other with the second immigration to Palestine, at the beginning of the present
century. It all sounds rather elegiac, and I learn from
Mr. Simon Halkin's book, *Modern Hebrew Literature*,
that a nostalgia for the life of the ghetto has become an

important motif in the writing of Agnón's generation. On the other hand, not quite all Israelis share the general taste for Agnón. I met a few who did not approve of him. These were young people, impatient of the synagogue, who desired to get as far away as possible from Reb Judel, with his drug of study, in his closed-in precarious world.

I encountered a postcript to Agnón's world as I was coming from Meá Shearím one Sabbath. I had not been there before, and, although, consulting a map, I had identified the Abyssinian Church House by a colored nun who was gardening, I presently became confused by the convents and churches and schools of the many nationalities and religions, so uglily and grimly entangled in the great barricades of barbed wire that have not been removed since the Arab war. My objective, as a landmark, was Barclay's Bank. Stopping to examine my map, I caught the eye of a black-hatted, black-bearded, bespectacled little man standing all by himself in the sun on the other side of the street. He came over and addressed me in German. I asked him the way in English, and he walked along to show me. I noticed that he omitted the articles in English and asked him whether he was Russian. "Away back, perhaps," he said. "I don't know." He made a remark or two in clumsy Russian, and then explained that he came from Poland. I asked how he had learned English. "I took ten lessons," he said. How long had he been in Israel? "A year and three-quarters," he answered, "but it only seems a few months." I saw that he was happy to be there. He practiced some craft—I don't remember what. As we went on, I got the impression that he was perhaps a bit off his head. At one point, he slipped into Yiddish—"Do you speak a little Yiddish?" he asked. There were stories I did not understand: a tennis match,

and then someone fell dead. But I got an impression of
a dreadful experience that he had now at last put behind
him and from which he had now ascended into a realm of
freedom and peace. "I never had a quiet day in Poland,"
he said, in concluding these memoirs. When he had
brought me to Barclay's Bank, we shook hands, and he
beamed and went back.

*Theocracy*: The Guardians of the City are an extreme and fanatical group. But what is the importance in
Israel of the Orthodox Synagogue in its normal official
form? The word I heard most often when I asked about
this—and uttered with apprehension—was "theocracy."
All the most intelligent Israelis I talked with were opposed to allowing the Rabbinate to dominate Israeli life.
The principal issues here seem to be the observance of
the Sabbath, kosher food and the licensing of civil marriage. On Friday afternoon, at sundown, almost everything shuts down in Israel, and remains so till the following sundown. It is just as complete and frustrating as
the old-fashioned Puritan Sunday. The buses do not run,
and even the non-religious Jew may not care to be seen
in a taxi. The prohibition against working on the Sabbath
may, in the case of the more scrupulous orthodox, inter-
fere with the public services, and has sometimes given
rise to absurdities of casuistical dispensation, as when a
wireless operator was authorized by his rabbi to continue
sending messages on condition that he use his left hand
and write only in the Roman alphabet. In regard to the
kosher problem, though most Israeli restaurants are non-
kosher—in the Swiss-run King David Hotel, even bacon
occasionally turns up—the importation of non-kosher
meat is forbidden by the government under pressure from
the Rabbinate, and kosher meat is expensive. The problems—to an outsider, so odd—to which the old dietary

laws give rise was illustrated for me one day when I visited the children's barnyard on one of the communal farms (*kvutzót*). Here the children themselves took care of the animals and poultry (which latter included a peacock), and they all were immensely plump and had the look of beloved pets. I mistook some little turkeys for guinea fowl and was told by the doctor who showed me around that they were hoping to eventually raise guinea fowl, but that, for reasons of which he was not quite sure—because guinea fowl did not have spurs, he thought—they had not yet got it cleared by the Rabbinate. He inquired of a boy who was standing by, but he did not know either; "There are better rabbis than I," the boy added. The doctor went on to explain to me that they had got around the prohibition against rabbits and guinea pigs by the plea that these animals were bred not for eating but for laboratory experiments.

The difficulties and incongruities of rabbinical rule in a modern state were several times brought out for me in connection with the marriage question. The insistence on rabbinical marriage makes it impossible for those who, by conviction, are non-religious or anti-religious to get legally married at all—with the result that in the communal farms, as one person delicately put it to me, "there is a good deal of non-marriage." The anachronistic character of these marriage laws was illustrated in a curious way by a story that was told me in Israel by an American businessman, himself a Jew, who had been living in New Hampshire. He made periodical trips to Israel, and had been asked by a lady, whom he had known in the States but who had gone to live in Israel, to appear as a witness for her at some religious formality in connection with her coming marriage. He was surprised and a little horrified to find himself taking part in a ceremony based on Deuteronomy 25:7-9, which decrees that if one of two brothers shall die without male issue, his widow must marry his surviving brother unless it is agreed between them that he will publicly repudiate her. If the parties do so agree, the man, in the presence of "the elders of his city," must announce, "I do not wish to take her," and the widow must then "pull his sandal off his foot," spit in her brother-in-law's face, and answer, "So shall it be done to the man who does not build up his brother's house." It was the carrying out of this that startled my friend from the States. In the course of another conversation—this time with scholars and writers of the generation still in its thirties—I inquired about an anti-clerical organization about which I had heard from someone. Two of the people present did not know that this existed, but it turned out that the third belonged to it. He went on to explain, however, that he could not support one of its principal aims: to get civil marriage and civil divorce legalized. His reason for this was based on Deuteronomy 23:2: "No bastard shall enter the assembly of the Lord; even to the tenth generation none of his descendants shall enter the assembly of the Lord." By "bastard," he meant the child of civilly divorced parents or the child of a married woman by a man who is not her husband in rabbinical law; but it had occurred to him that the child of a civil marriage, as well as his descendants to the tenth generation, would suffer from the disability of remaining, for the orthodox, bastards and excluded from divine service. To the other young people present, this point seemed unexpected, as it did to me. They told him he read the Talmud too much.

Yet, as the conversation went on, these dissenters from Talmudic scruples developed a point of view which, to me, was equally unexpected. I had been talking to a man of about their own age, born in the United States, who had been ordained as a rabbi and who at home had moved

further and further in the direction of the Reformed Synagogue. He had finally given up the priesthood and come
to settle in Israel, where he was now doing secular work.
He had told me that he hoped to see there a complete rewriting of the prayer book and a substitution for the
orthodox ritual of a kind of Biblical cult along the
lines of the ceremonies sometimes performed in the
*kibbutzím,* in which the reading of passages from Scripture was accompanied by singing and dances. This
idea, when I probed my young friends with it, awakened immediate derision. They guessed at once that
it came from an American and declared that, however
little orthodox they were, they considered the Reformed
Synagogue entirely inappropriate for Israel. They themselves had come, as children, from Poland, Lithuania
and Russia, and they regarded the Reformed Synagogue as an essentially non-Judaistic product of the
pressure upon the Jews of Protestantism in Germany
and the United States. It was a form of adaptation
to alien societies that would be quite out of place for
them. And, in talking to other Israelis, I found a pre-
ponderant loyalty to the Orthodox Jewish faith as against
any substitute. It is difficult to get statistics on Orthodoxy or even on synagogue attendance. The sole figure
as to which it was possible to get anybody to hazard an estimate was that twenty per cent of the Israelis wore earlocks. But it is plain that the Orthodox Synagogue, even
for many who are not very pious, has its importance as a social center; and the holidays seem to be celebrated by
practically everybody. They take them perhaps more
seriously, enjoy them perhaps more, than Christians do
any of their holy days except Christmas. Rosh Ha-Shanah
is a religious occasion, as New Year's is not for Christians,
and the latter have nothing like the Day of Atonement,
which seems always to impose for the Jew the duty of

setting himself right with his conscience by repairing, or
at least acknowledging, his trespasses against his fellows.
These holidays give its structure to the Jewish year; and
without an established religion, it would hardly be possible to keep them up. Besides this, it is the Jewish religion that has sustained the Jews in their exile, that has
preserved their coherence as a people and that has led
them, at the end of centuries, to return to Palestine. Their
secular state is quite new; it is, after all, the orthodox
"theocracy" that has provided their internal government
for the last two thousand years, and it will not be so easy
to get rid of it or even to do without it. In the meantime,
it becomes a political force, sits in the Knésset, the Israeli
parliament, and enters into expedient alliances. Yet, in
spite of this intervention, the Israeli Rabbinate seems to
tend, as churches are likely to do, to regard its own wel-
fare as inevitably at variance with the purposes of the
secular state. "The anti-religious movement," said a government official to me, "has restrained itself in the interests of the national unity; the religious elements haven't."

*Tanách:* But, aside from rabbinical influence, the Bible—which the Jews call Tanách, putting together the
initials of its three main divisions: the Law, the Prophets
and the Writings—figures in the life of Israel in a more
striking way than one might expect. Every evening, at
what is called the "peak listening hour," just before the
eight-thirty broadcast, the music for the chanting of the
classic announcement from Isaiah 2:3—"For from Zion
will go forth the Law, and the word of the Lord from Jerusalem"—is sounded on the Jerusalem radio, and a
chapter of the Bible is read. This reading is a remarkable
performance. It is done by Mr. Shlómoh Bertónov, the
son of a well-known actor and himself formerly an actor.
Now, it is natural, in reading the Bible, to reflect that the

narrative and poetic parts would lend themselves to such
recitation as has long been practiced in Italy by the professional reciters of Dante, and it is something of the
kind, on a very high level, that Mr. Bertónov has been
giving his audience. In the course of my visit, I was able to
hear only parts of Jonah and Zechariah, but these seemed
to me among the best readings that I had ever heard of
anything. Mr. Bertónov enunciates so clearly that every
syllable tells, and by pronouncing the aleph and the ayin,
the two Semitic gutturals that have dropped out of use in
Hebrew, he adds to the effect of authenticity. He dramatizes his readings just enough, brings to them just enough
of the Russian actor's gift of impersonation, to make you
feel you are really listening to God admonishing Jonah
or Zechariah foretelling the rebirth of Jerusalem. This,
you say to yourself, is how the Prophets must have
sounded—at the same time august and astringent, with
strong rhythms that seem so natural to the language that
this might be indeed the language of God. How positive and vibrant that word "Adonái" that is read for
the unutterable name of God and that has now become
inseparable from the rhythmical context! But it is not
merely the high spots of eloquence and drama that
Mr. Bertónov has been broadcasting; he has been reading the Bible straight through, and I was told that
he was never more impressive than in handling such un-
promising passages as the repetitive rites of Leviticus, the
enumerations of Numbers and the ever-recurring genealo-
gies—in which last the importance of every name for the
conservers of the old chronicle was brought out in such a
way as to make one feel a sense of triumph in the persistence of the Twelve Chosen Tribes through the otherwise
anonymous ages. When these readings had gone on for
over a year, the audience, I was told, began to grow
rather restive, since they had just been taken through

these more tedious books, and weren't sure that they hadn't had enough; but when at last Mr. Bertónov took a few weeks off and they had to hear a substitute at eight-twenty, they soon felt that something was lacking and began writing letters of protest. At the time of my visit to Israel, Mr. Bertónov was still only a little more than two-thirds of his way through. (The Hebrew Tanách is arranged somewhat differently from the Christian Bible.) I was sorry not to hear him do the Psalms, on which he was beginning the day I left.

Another and more curious evidence of the vigorous survival of the Bible in the consciousness of this modern state is a fortnightly newspaper called *Chronicles*, which puzzled me when it first caught my eye on the newsstand, and which continued to seem to me odd even after I had bought and read it. The headlines announced, "JACOB'S SONS ARRESTED IN EGYPT ON SPY CHARGE," and a story lower down ran as follows:

### JACOB PROTESTS: "MY SONS ARE INNOCENT!"
#### BY OUR CORRESPONDENT

HEBRON, 21 Nisan—"It's all a terrible mistake!" said Jacob (also known as Israel), when he heard that his sons had been arrested in Egypt as spies. . . . Your correspondent found the venerable old Hebrew (he is getting on for 130) lying down in his tent, with difficulty holding back the tears that came to his eyes. . . .

On the inside page, I found a picture of "seven scrawny cows"—"TWO DOWN, FIVE TO GO. With each crop failure, another cow is rubbed out"—and a department called "Learn Egyptian," which contained an easy lesson in hieroglyphics, with the reminder that "Egyptian, like Akkadian, is read from left to right." An editorial brought out the fact that Zaphnat-Paneach (the name given Joseph by Pharaoh) "comes himself of Hebrew stock. But this very fact seems to cause him to bend over backwards in an effort to be 'more Egyptian than the Egyptians themselves.' Not only has he failed to lift a finger to clear the suspects, but, on the contrary, he was the first to accuse them of being spies and of having entered the country with hostile intentions. It is he who is fanning the fires of racial hatred, with his baseless charges against ten innocent men." The next number of *Chronicles* was devoted to the death of Joseph and contained an editorial beginning, "A great Hebrew and a great human being has passed away," a black-bordered mourning notice inserted by "The Bereaved Family," and an ad by a Theban embalmer announcing, "For the Man of Distinction, there is our 40-day de luxe method—Plan 3: Extraction of brain by special new process, via the nostrils. Removal and special embalmment of all internal organs except the heart," etc., etc.

The whole thing was well sustained, and I assumed that it was meant to be humorous till I learned that this singular paper, which is subsidized by a wealthy Dutch lady, is intended to be educational. It is printed in three editions—Hebrew, German and English—and distributed widely for use in schools. There can be no question, however, that an element of satire has got into it—as, for example, when an editorial mentions that Egypt, "the greatest, nay, the only military power on earth today, the nation on whose good will hinges the fate of a starving world, is in a state of high hysteria and deadly fear over the harmless activities of ten brothers who came to Egypt to buy food for their hungry wives and children." But the paper, in this respect, also, furnishes another exam-

ple of the confusion of past with present that has always
been characteristic of the Jewish point of view.

These Biblical analogies, one feels, are often at the
back of Israeli minds. General Yigaél Yadín, the son of
the late Professor Sukénik of the Hebrew University, is a
scholar as well as a soldier. At the time of the Arab war,
when he was acting as Chief of Operations, he concluded, from his knowledge of the Bible, that the Syrians, in their attempt at invasion, would inevitably take the
same route as the ancient armies of Assyria two thousand eight hundred years before. He read his officers the
relevant passages from Kings before the fighting began,
and consulted them in posting his modern troops. The result was entirely successful, and this story, which is often
told, has suggested to me other parallels, which I did not,
in fact, hear mentioned. It was said to me by a humane
Tel-Avivan, not long ago from the States, apropos of the
murderous raids by which the Israelis retaliate for the
murderous raids of the Arabs, that he feared that his
fellow-countrymen were a little losing respect for the Sixth
Commandment, and the justice-loving side of the Biblical
tradition leads this kind of Jew to worry as to whether
the Israelis have a right to their land; they would feel
better if the Arabs got their compensation. Yet whoever
has been responsible for such incidents as Kíbya and
Nahhalín might have cited plenty of texts, such as Exodus 23:28-30—"And I will send hornets before you,
which shall drive out Hivite, Canaanite and Hittite from
before you. I will not drive them out before you in one
year, lest the land become desolate and the wild beasts
multiply against you. Little by little I will drive them out
before you, until you are increased and possess the land"
—and Deuteronomy 6:10-11, in which Jehovah promises
the Israelites to give them "great and goodly cities, which
you did not build, and houses full of all good things,

which you did not fill, and cisterns hewn out, which you
did not hew, and vineyards and olive trees, which you did
not plant." Do such memories confirm the minds of the
occupants of Arab houses, of the cultivators of Arab
farms, whose original owners can still see their old
homes, just across the frontier, and occasionally give way
to the impulse to revisit them and seize a few sheep? The
terrorism of modern Israel was the result of the Nazi
persecutions and of the policy of the British, who refused
to let those who were fleeing from them even land in a
country which the British themselves had set aside as a
Jewish refuge, and who finally left the Jews to the mercy
of seven Arab states ("seven nations mightier than yourselves," Deuteronomy 7:1). It was in those days as justi-
fiable as anything of the kind can be. But, though many
people disapprove of it, the terrorist habit has been established, and the element of moral fanaticism that stimulates and sustains it seems something of a reversion to
Biblical times, when the Twelve Tribes, returning from
Egypt, invaded and conquered Canaan. The terrorist Me-
náchem Beígin, who has been described by Arthur Koest-
ler as giving the impression of a gentle young school-
master, but who once, in an anti-British gesture, blew up
a whole wing of the King David Hotel, destroying ninety-
one people, British, Arabs, and Jews indiscriminately, is
at present a member of the Knésset. The reprisals against
the Arabs are evidently carefully planned (I do not
mean to imply that Beígin is necessarily involved in
them). The day after the Nahhalín incident—I had heard
the explosions at midnight, sitting in my hotel room—
the telephone boy said to me, "That was a good operation
last night!" As I was later to learn from the New York
Times, but not from the Jerusalem Post, six Arab homes
had been bombed and a village mosque had been sacked;
nine people had been killed, including a woman, and

nineteen wounded. True, the Arabs had massacred the
passengers in a bus—killing nine men and two women
and wounding a couple of children—in the Négev a few
weeks before, and had been long making themselves a
nuisance with their continual shootings and thefts.

I am, however, not interested here in examining this
situation. I want to suggest, simply, that the Israelis, in
relation to the Arabs, have shown certain signs of returning to the callous intolerance of the Israelites in relation to
the people they dispossessed. I was sometimes reminded of
the tone of Jehovah, in His final speech to Jonah, in regard to the hundred and twenty thousand Ninevans,
"who do not know their right hand from their left." Jehovah is scolding Jonah for his indifference to the fate
of these Ninevans, but His opinion of their cultural level
is undisguisedly low. So the position of the Arabs in Israel
—especially as one sees them in the country—is rather
like that of the Navahos in the American Southwest:
a once fierce but still picturesque, pathetically retarded
people, cut off from the main community but presenting a
recurrent problem. In a large Arab town like Acre, the
squalor of the swarming streets inspires in an Israeli the
same distaste that it does in the visiting Westerner. For
the Jew, who takes family relations so seriously and who,
in Israel, has labored so carefully with the orphans from
Poland and Germany and the children of the illiterate
Yemenites, the spectacle of flocks of urchins, dirty, un-
taught, diseased, bawling and shrieking and begging,
in the narrow and dirty streets, inspires even moral horror. If the restrictions imposed on marriage by the ancient rabbinical law are considered by many too rigid,
the facility of divorce for the Arabs, which, together with
their nomadic habits, encourages the father of a family
simply to abandon his offspring and move on to take a
wife in another place, must be felt to be an evil far worse.

It is not that a certain contempt for the Arabs is not natural for anyone trained in the West, nor is it that any ruthlessness of Israel is not matched by the infantile spite of the Arabs and the rather stupid obstinacy of the Arab refugees in Jordan, who have refused the offers of U.N.R.-W.A. to accommodate them in other localities and continue to insist on returning to their villages and farms in Israel. I am occupied here solely with bringing out the operation in Israel of a certain Jewish tendency toward exclusiveness—I shall deal later on with the converse of this, the life-giving elements of the Jewish tradition—as a limiting and sometimes a destructive influence.

One feels this exclusiveness, also, in the attitude toward the literature and the language. If you arrive with the notion that the revival of Hebrew is an artificial chauvinistic absurdity, like the official use in Ireland of Irish, you will realize the difference between them when you find that all Israelis speak Hebrew and hear how natural the language—so quick and staccato, made up mostly of short words—sounds on Israeli lips. But, though many people in Israel speak English, and though the signs on the principal streets are in English as well as in Hebrew, even the foreigner who knows the alphabet will often be baffled or lose his way. The Israeli will tell you with perfect truth that his children, who have been talking Hebrew from birth, read the ordinary vowelless printing more easily than the exceptional "pointed" text, but for the foreigner it is all a shorthand, to decipher which you have to know the language well even to make out the signs on the shops. It is as if you arrived in an English-speaking country and found everything printed in abbreviations like "blvd.," "bldg." and "Ltd."

This impression of cultural exclusiveness is borne out by a reading of the admirable book—indispensable for the understanding of Israel—called *Modern Hebrew Litera-*

*ture: Trends and Values,* by Mr. Simon Halkin. Mr.
Halkin, who teaches this subject in the Hebrew University in Jerusalem, is a man of the great intellectual world
and far from indifferent, himself, to the literatures of
other traditions and tongues, but the story he has to tell
is that of the turning-away of a certain school of Jewish writers from the German-Jewish enlightenment of the
early nineteenth century to a rigorous preoccupation with
Hebrew language and thought—a movement which was
to concentrate more and more on the Zionist return to
Palestine, and then, when the country was won, on the
building of the state of Israel. One feels the doors shut
behind one. Here is a book which discusses at length the
literary activity of the Jews in the Germany of the early
nineteenth century, yet which never mentions Marx or
Heine; that deals with Moses Mendelssohn almost exclusively from the point of view of his failure in pure devotion to the perpetuation of Hebrew letters; a book for
which Kafka and Proust—Europeans, though so deeply
Jewish—are completely beyond the horizon. One is guided
through a narrow corridor at the far-distant end of which
the gleam of the sanctum sanctorum only makes one the
more aware of an all-enveloping darkness. In this corridor, we cannot catch sight of any of those outstanding
Jews who have made themselves places in the modern
world, contributed to the general light: Bergson and
Einstein, Trotsky and Freud, Disraeli and Brandeis and
Brandes—one would almost say Weizmann himself, who
was, after all, a great chemist. There is something of this
narrowness, also, in the tendency of even the most alert
and the best-educated Israelis to be occupied with the
problems of Israel at the expense of awareness of or interest in what is happening in the world at large. In the
Jerusalem *Post,* certainly, the quarrel of the Israelis with
the Arabs throws everything else into the background, till

you are almost ready to believe that more serious hostilities between them would amount to or imply a world war, and the Israeli side of the controversy is presented with such mass and vehemence that you can get no idea from the press of what is really going on in the Arab states only a few miles away.

Even the movement against this narrowness has taken on the characteristic accent of intransigence and Biblical reference. The group of young people that calls itself Aleph and that publishes a paper of that name but is usually known as the Canaanite movement has been interestingly accounted for, in terms of the social forces behind it, by Mr. Robert L. Lindsey in the July, 1954, issue of *Commentary*. Mr. Lindsey explains that, for many young Israelis, the various forms of the Jewish faith have ceased to have any validity. The theocracy of Orthodox Judaism is in process of being got rid of. Zionism has lost its force —since the goad of anti-Semitism that stimulated it has never been felt by the new generation and the return to Palestine from exile is, of course, no longer an objective for the young men and women who were born there. The Socialism that blended with Zionism in one of its early phases has lost credit through the anti-Israel policy of the Labour Government in England and the persecution of Zionism by the Soviets. And if one finds oneself neither a Zionist nor a member of an Orthodox congregation, in what sense is one still a Jew? Let the conception, then, of Jewishness be dropped. Why perpetuate unnecessarily the quarrels of the Israelis with their neighbors? Let them cut off their connections with the Diaspora, let them cease to accept money from abroad. Let them make common cause with the Christians, the Moslems, the Kurds, the Circassians, the ancient Syrian Druses (who are supposed still to worship the Golden Calf) and all the other Middle Eastern groups, who are as much ingrown as the

Jews and equally handicapped by being so, but who are all forced to live together and ought really to call themselves Canaanites, since Canaan is what their country was originally called. But the Canaanite movement, it seems, has also a theological aspect, which Mr. Lindsey does not explain. The Canaanites propose to repudiate not merely the whole Diaspora but also that part of Jewish history —a part which is almost the whole—that is based on the worship of Jehovah. For the Canaanites, not only is Moses a foreign heresiarch, who brought the Israelites from Egypt to Canaan and sent them over to sack its cities, to dispossess its inhabitants and to impose on it the cult of an alien God, but Father Abraham himself is an interloper. They have returned to the worship of Astarte "in groves and high places"—which is jollier, certainly, than the synagogue, since Astarte was the goddess of love. (Let us hope they do not revive Moloch.) But, even in trying to establish a solidarity with the other Middle Easterners, they are behaving with a Jehovan exclusiveness in turning the principle of exclusion against all the rest of the Jews.

I read the Hebrew Bible every afternoon with a young teacher from the University, a man who had been born in Jerusalem and had never been in any other country. From the French windows of the King David Hotel, that opened on a little balcony, one looked over, across the valley of Gihon, to the walls of the Old City, and, pointing to the Jaffa Gate, my instructor was able to explain to me how the "inns" at which travellers slept and such lodgings as the "house" of Rahab the harlot were more or less a part of the gate, which was still—as I was later to find when I visited the Old City—a market place and center of gossip, like the square in a Latin town. One turned from the dark heavy text to the bareness of present-day Jerusalem, with

its pale buildings, ancient and modern, below the immense bright sky. The Pentateuch, under these circumstances, came to seem to me so purely, so profoundly Jewish that it became for me a matter of wonder that so
many non-Jewish peoples had been able to take it over and
adapt it to serve their needs. It began to seem quite gro-
tesque that the chapters and chapters of observances—
which would seem to be of serious interest only to anthro-
pologists, historians and Orthodox Jews—should have
been studied with reverence by the Christian Church, that
the incidents of Israelite conquest should for centuries
have furnished texts for the sermons of Anglican and
Puritan divines. The reading back of Christianity into the
books of the Jewish scriptures, the turning to Christian
purpose of the "Yet I know that my redeemer liveth" of
Job, and of the "man of sorrows" of Isaiah 53—once the
"sea of faith" has ebbed, what a curious exploit it seems!
My young instructor was in a constant state of astonishment, verging on indignation, at the renderings of the
King James Version, the only English text I had with me,
which he had never examined before. I had been told
by another young Israeli scholar that it had one day occurred to him to wonder how the Christian authorities
interpreted that roundly erotic rhapsody called *The Song
of Solomon* or *The Song of Songs*, the rabbinical view
of which makes Jehovah the bridegroom and Israel the
bride. He had been charmed to discover such chapter
headings as "The mutual love of Christ and His church,"
"Christ awaketh the Church with His calling," "A further
description of the Church's grace" ("How beautiful are
thy feet with shoes, O prince's daughter . . . Thy two
breasts are like two young roses that are twins," etc.).
Yet if Israel and Jehovah, why not Christ and the Church?
It was, after all, the Hebrews themselves who set the example for the Christians of describing the recent in terms

of the ancient, of regarding the careers of contemporaries as fulfilments of inspired prophecies, of showing that the new meaning was there all the time in the old text.

*Jerusalem the Golden:*    Waked up every morning early by the bright, firm and even light, looking out on translucent clouds that hung in a pellucid heaven, far below which Mount Zion, a modest mound in the bosom of the high barren hills, just outside the walls of the ancient city, was crowned with the diadem of its monastery, I grew to be fond of Jerusalem, of which much of the attraction resides in its combining luminosity with bareness. This is said to be the best time of the year—late March and early April: the steep and yet rounded hills, studded with little gray boulders, striated with narrow ledges, are now freshened for a brief time with green, and in the country, where the mixed flocks of goats and sheep graze on the fenceless slopes, there is a sprinkling of wild red poppies and little yellow daisies. In a few weeks, they tell me, the landscape becomes parched, with only the deep-green oases created by irrigation. It is a mild and monotonous country, and this is what is unexpected. Did the Prophets, in their gloom of foreboding, flash their lightning of conviction from these quiet hills, where everything is open to the sky? Were the savage wars of Scripture fought here? Did its paeans first sound from these pastures? The prejudice of the Jews against images may be partly explained by these contours which do not suggest shapes, by these colors which do not compose pictures. The little old villages of the Arabs were almost like boulders themselves; Stephen Spender has truly said of them that they fit into the mountainsides like teeth in a jawbone. The new settlements of the Israelis are equally unostentatious—neat groupings of low white houses that give an effect of ease; I saw one with pale pink roofs that was charming. Modern Israel, on the whole, has kept to the old Jewish severity. There are no pictures in orthodox homes, and the pictures in other houses, even where the books are good, are likely to be not well chosen. It is strange to reflect that from here came those legends that inspired so much of the art of the Renaissance, all that blazing of color, that teeming of flesh—Pharaoh's daughter in her gorgeous silks, surrounded by the ladies of an Italian court, as she comes upon Moses in the bulrushes; the rippling and wistful Botticellian Judith, exhaling a delicate charm after cutting off the head of Holofernes; the beautiful blue madonnas, the heaven-cracking crucifixions; Michelangelo's romantic Moses, his full-bodied Adams and Davids; all the coffers of the Roman churches overflowing with jewels and fabrics, all the Florentine miles of paint. How very unlikely it seems that they sprouted from the history of these calm little hills, dotted with stones and flocks, under pale and transparent skies.

The emotion and the drama of the Bible not only no longer seem present in Palestine; they have left no real monuments behind them. The Acropolis and the Forum are still there to see, but Solomon's Temple and Palace are not. It is only that the site of Jerusalem has in itself an arresting grandeur. No great city of Europe stands so high, and it is wonderful and almost terrifying to look out on the valley of Kidron and across at the opposite hillside littered with the tombs attributed to Absalom and other ancients as well as with the stones of a cemetery of modern Jewish graves which the Arabs have thrown on their faces, or to gaze up the precipitous slope at the wall that still circles the city. But of Jewish pre-Christian Jerusalem, little today survives: the fragment of wall to which the Jews used to come to weep for their lost kingdom, the tombs of the Sanhedrin in the hillside, with their high and imposing façades and their narrow rectangular doors, designed to make looting difficult, that give glimpses of large square chambers, plundered long ago and empty now. The foundations of the present old wall are supposed to have been laid by Herod, but the rest of it was probably built by the Byzantines and Suleiman the Magnificent. If the wide paved expanse of the sanctuary in which the Mosque of Omar stands on what has always been accepted as the site of the Temple was actually laid out by Herod, it was done under the influence of the Romans. Below it lies the only construction that impresses like those of Rome: the great pillared subterranean vaults that are known as Solomon's Stables. Here the Jews took refuge from Titus, come to destroy their Temple; here, more than a thousand years later, come to rescue the Holy Sepulcher, the Knights Templar put up their horses. One can see their hitching holes in the columns. These grim and enormous piers that stretch away in endless long rows, lit only by one set of windows, on the side that forms part of the precipice, make a kind of gray underground forest that is dreadful and troubling today, with its air of an abode of power that no power has permanently possessed or has stamped with its peculiar identity, neither Herod nor Rome nor Christendom. But, for the rest, what could be less suggestive than those dreary grottoes and caves and rocks, sheltered mostly by rubbishy churches, that are shown you as Calvary, the Sepulcher, the place of the Annunciation, the house of Jesus at Nazareth, the Fountain of the Virgin, the Tomb of the Virgin, the place where the Virgin died. They are none of them considered authentic, and would not be any better if they were. Only Galilee, the Lake of Tiberias, as you come down to it from the mountains above —softly misted, with its blues and greens, the far bank a wall of wrinkled yellow rock, and its waters blue, still and dull—has something of idyllic mystery. At Caper-

naum, on the far bank, is a synagogue in which Jesus is
supposed to have taught, and one passes a church on a little hill that is said to mark the setting of the Sermon
on the Mount. Yet, even discounting the miracles, it is
hard to imagine what happened here in any very lively or
concrete way. I found it easier, when I was traveling
through Italy and passing the Lago di Garda, on which I
could see from the train the little peninsula of Sirmio, to
imagine the poet Catullus coming back from his Bithyn-
ian exile and, as he puts off the cares of his journey,
finding peace in his longed-for bed. For Garda was concrete to Catullus, it was solidly and pleasantly a part of
his life. He has left a description of it, by which we can
recognize it. But the Gospels do not describe Galilee.
Sirmio is still there in Italy, but in a sense the Holy
Places are not there.

What you find in Palestine instead is a kind of debris
of the three great religions that have sprung from and
flourished there. Side by side and mutually exclusive,
you have the synagogue, the church and the mosque, as
well as the many varieties of the Christian church in
both its Eastern and Western, its Catholic and its Protestant forms. They have for so long been practicing dissen-
sion in the name of the single God whom they all derive
from the ancient Jews that one has almost forgotten the
irony of their bitterness or contempt for one another.
But the non-religious visitor, in entering these places of
worship, bewildered by the constant necessity of remembering whether to keep on his hat, take off his hat or take
off his shoes at the door, may become a little impatient
with the outward forms of religion. On Mount Zion—
which has given its name to Heaven—he discovers a
state of affairs, a squalor, confusion and strife, at the
same time disgusting and comic. I climbed up there
with a guide, by a long flight of steps, to inspect the

so-called tomb of David. You see, first, inscribed on a
wall in bold and clear Hebrew lettering, the familiar quotation from Isaiah—"For from Zion will go forth the
Law, and the word of the Lord from Jerusalem." But
Mount Zion, just outside the old wall, is a corner of the
Old City that has remained in Jewish hands. The frontier,
with its barbed-wire spite-fence, runs right between it and
the wall, and you are obliged to enter the tomb by a narrow path lined with barbed wire and hung with signs in
Hebrew and English that warn you, "Danger Mines."
Beyond the barbed wire are an empty Arab house and
little fields that must once have been lawns but are all
grown up now with long grass. The red poppies and yellow
daisies remind you of that passage from Edgar Quinet
that Joyce likes to play with in *Finnegans Wake:* the wild
flowers that go on blooming through the wreckage of
civilizations and come down to us through the ages,
*"fraîches et riantes comme aux jours des batailles."*

Inside the supposed tomb, you find a Jewish house of
prayer, dedicated to David, with a display of silver vessels and sacred red cloths, presided over by pale bearded
custodians. This a few years ago was a Moslem house
of prayer, before the Jews captured it from the Arabs. Up
against it is a Benedictine monastery, the Church and
Convent of the Dormition, which is supposed to mark the
spot where the Virgin died, or rather, where she fell
asleep just before her ascension to Heaven. I succeeded
in persuading this man to come with me to see the
monastery, though he showed a certain reluctance—I do
not know whether because he was hesitant about getting
too close to the Arabs or because he was afraid that the
monks might not want him in their Christian cathedral;
and another Jewish visitor, who heard us talking, hooked
on to us and decided to go with us. He said that he ought
not to go—an Orthodox Jew, it seems, is forbidden to

enter a Christian church—but that he didn't want to miss
the opportunity. Most of the monks had been withdrawn
since the war, but we found a German brother who took
us around. It was not a very beautiful place; it had been
built fifty years before, under the patronage of the late
Kaiser, on the foundations of a Crusaders' church.
There was an altar contributed by German Catholics for
somebody murdered by the Nazis, and Hungarian chapels
with frescoes in horned-toad Hungarian style. The monk
took us down to the crypt and lit candles to show us
the monument over the spot where the Virgin is supposed,
not to have died, but to have made her departure from
earth: she lies rigid, with an ivory face and mantled in
dried-blood marble. The two Jews were quiet, a little shy.
Emerging, we explored apprehensively the deserted stone
paths of the monastery that led us between high walls and
ended in barbed-wire cul-de-sacs. There is no neutral
ground here, and where the two sides are close together,
the inhabitants of the two cities like sometimes to take pot-
shots at one another. We returned to the valley, keeping
carefully to the path that makes the right-of-way to Zion
and crosses the neutral strip which separates Israel from
Jordan. This is mined and fenced off with barbed wire.
Occasionally a dog or a child strays over and steps on a
mine. Not far off, an extension of this valley was the ill-
famed ancient Gehenna, where the Hebrews relapsed into
the primitive cult of sacrificing their children to Moloch.
On your way to and from Zion, you pass the Jerusalem
Animal Hospital, which is just over the line on the Israeli
side. The barking of the dogs in this hospital had been
keeping me awake at night, and, before I found out what
it was, I had almost imagined that the dogs on both sides
took up at night the quarrel of their masters and yapped
at each other till morning. (At the time of certain shootings in this part of the city that have taken place since

I left, the veterinary hospital, I learn from the *Times*, was isolated from food supplies, but the "matron" stood by her charges and has received a citation from the S.P.C.A., with a bronze medal of the kind "usually awarded to an animal for bravery," as well as one from the American Feline Society.)

The presence of this valley of hatred, though rarely referred to in Israel, is constantly felt and inflicts constraint. For the Eastertide pilgrims who cross the line on their way to the Mount of Olives and the other places associated with Jesus, it should heighten their respect for his teaching. The passage from Israeli to Jordanian Jerusalem has been made by the Arabs, in their fear of the Israelis and their somewhat childish desire to behave as unpleasantly as possible, to seem almost as difficult and perilous as gaining admission to Lhasa. If you come with an Israeli passport, they do their best to make it impossible, and travelers are driven to such farcical devices as double passports and detachable visas. One visitor who had been in Israel and who, just as he was leaving Jordan, inadvertently thanked the authorities in Hebrew was held up for several hours. I had found this same atmosphere of suspicion when I applied for a visa in London: the doorman at the Jordan Legation had held the door open on a crack and directed me to the rear of the building, where I climbed up a kind of fire-escape to some rooms on the top floor, apparently closed off from the rest, in which an anxious official, alarmed at my having written "None" after the question about my "Religion"—I had previously been questioned as to whether I was Jewish —suggested in a feeble way that he might forward my request to his capital and convinced me that my case was hopeless. When I did succeed finally, through the efforts of our consul—who functions in both the Jerusalems— in crossing the inflamed frontier, I happened to arrive in

Old Jerusalem at the moment when the Israelis were changing the guard at the Hebrew University on Mount Scopus. This institution was founded by Weizmann in 1925 and has a library of a million volumes, but it is an enclave now in Arab territory, under the protection of the United Nations and not available for use by the Israelis, who have thus lost their scholarly equipment and are obliged to house their college where they can. There is also a Mount Scopus hospital which the Israelis had also to abandon when the Arabs, shooting into their convoys, killed several doctors and nurses. The Israeli guard on these buildings is changed every two weeks, and there at the Mandelbaum Gate, in front of the gashed and gutted houses that have been left as they were at the armistice, with their gaping arched Arab windows that so much suggest a life of ease, stood a squad of Arab soldiers at attention, while the gray Israeli trucks, which were blinded so that the inmates could not see out, had their oil drums and food supplies searched.

The medley of sects and religions is seen at its most fantastic in the shrines of the Old City. The so-called Mosque of Omar is a pretty little Moslem rotunda, gracefully arched and domed, and covered with charming blue tiles contributed by Suleiman the Magnificent, that shelters a large yellowish old bumpy rock believed by the Jews to have been, first, the rude altar to which Abraham came with Isaac, then the threshing floor of Araunah the Jebusite, on which David was ordered by God to build the altar that later became that of the Temple. It is surrounded by an iron grille contributed by the Crusaders. This monument is now in the hands of the Arabs, and it is the Moslems who worship there at the consecrated rock of the Jews. The Church of the Holy Sepulcher, which shelters two other rocks, supposedly Calvary and Jesus' Tomb, is guarded by a Mohammeda

doorman, who always has charge of the keys, but it is
otherwise occupied by Christians. This confused and un-
comforting building—on the site of which, according to
legend, Hadrian erected a Temple of Venus, in order to
keep Christians away from it—now houses five Christian
churches, cathedrals within a cathedral: the Greek Orthodox, the Roman Catholic, the Syrian, the Armenian and
the Coptic, the services of which overlap, interrupting
and blurring one another.

The Church of the Holy Sepulcher is badly in need of
repairs—is, in fact, on the point of collapse and only
propped by a precarious scaffolding—but the five cults
responsible for it can never agree as to what is to be
done. When I inquired what was going to happen to it,
I was given the cynical answer that the very next earthquake would shake it down and that no one then would
have to worry. It is a macabre claustrophobic place, and
probably contains more bad taste, certainly more kinds
of bad taste, than any other church in the world. You
enter the imprisoned parvis through the wall of the Arab
street by apertures inconveniently narrow, and are confronted by a great cage of braces that almost conceals
the façade: a metal structure trimmed with barbed wire,
which makes it resemble a station of the old New York ele-
vated railway. Going in, you see first, on your left, an
Oriental bed in an alcove, on which, when he is not on
his feet, the Mohammedan caretaker reclines. (There
are services that take place at night, when visitors are
locked in the church.) Before you, flanked by monstrous
candles that almost reach to the ceiling, that look as if
they were made of celluloid and are painted like postcards or greeting cards with miniature views of Jerusalem
and little bows of blue ribbon, lies the smooth flat red
Unction Stone, where the body of Jesus is supposed to
have lain and which the pilgrims get down on their

knees to kiss, the more fastidious ladies wiping it first with a handkerchief. Exploring the cramped and cluttered, the labyrinthine and closetlike interior, among blue and red balls, tinsel stars and bulbous brass lamps and thuribles that hang from the ceiling like Christmas-tree ornaments, you come upon the Sepulcher itself, which stands like a kind of tower in the center of a gloomy rotunda, the paint of whose dome was peeled off by a fire in 1808 (caused by a drunken Greek monk) and whose paintings are masked by the scaffolds that hold the pillars erect. On the bases of these pillars are fixed strips of glass that will break if a crack occurs. In your efforts to get the hang of this dark and disorganized interior, you may look in on a kind of exhibition room where reliquaries of gold and silver are lit up in a long glass showcase, and where little old women in black are circulating and kissing the part of the glass that is opposite each of the relics. In a chamber of the Russian Church, hung with embroidered pictures that are heavy with Byzantine gold, and portraits of the prelates of the Orthodox Church, half fancy, half photographic, you come upon a bearded old priest, sitting behind a table and competently answering in various languages the questions of a crowd of visitors, who are writing their names in a book. Climbing narrow and high stone stairs, you arrive at a giddying gallery, one corner of which is scribbled with names and addresses from all over the world, among the scrawled scripts of which the word "DUBLIN" stands out, printed. Here you find dreadful modern mosaics—of Abraham and Isaac, and other Old Testament subjects—the gift of the presiding Franciscans. Descending to the crypt by a broad flight of steps, you are handed a candle and penetrate, in the darkness, to the spot where the True Cross is supposed to have been found, in Constantine's time, by the Empress Helena. Above it looms a

faceless statue, bulky and spooky in the darkness, that the
flame of the candle falls short of.

At the Tenebræ services of Holy Week, the Church of
the Holy Sepulcher is jammed by what is, I suppose, one
of the most international congregations and one of the
most variegated to be seen anywhere in the world. There
are excursions of nuns from all over Europe, accompanied by shepherding and ciceroning priests. The white-
gowned choristers, the brown-robed Franciscans, the
Greek priests in their flat-topped black hats are all in
their best clothes. The Latin Patriarch, in a little red
cap and a richly embroidered coat, is conducting the
Tenebræ office from a throne that faces the Sepulcher.
Christianized Arab women, with white headdresses and
Arab robes, kneel on the floor with their children. A black
nun in a big starched white cap with corners that stick
out like wings is praying by herself in a niche so dark
that only the bonnet is visible above the huddled figure.
Catholic priests and Anglican clergymen stand about in
black clothes and British boots. There are whiffs of urine
and incense. What if the whole stale and rickety place,
fissured by some piercing note, should come down on our
heads and bury us! There is also a claustrophobia
brought on by the vulgarity and the scrambled cults. One
recalls that, at the ceremony of the Holy Fire in 1834,
the tension, the heat, and the crowding produced a terrible panic. When the moment has come for this yearly
miracle, a specialty of the Eastern rite, the Greek Patriarch passes into the Sepulcher, in which, the day before,
Good Friday, the holy flame has been extinguished, and
hands out a bunch of candles, bound together in a cage-
topped torch, which are supposed to have been ignited
without human intervention. The pilgrims and other worshippers, who have often been standing there all night,
now press forward to light their own candles—for the

fire, rekindled by a miracle, is supposed to ensure salvation. This results in a mad and remorseless scramble.

At the ceremony on Holy Saturday, 1834, the candle smoke became so stifling that three people fell out of the galleries and were killed on the heads of the crowd below. "One poor Armenian lady, seventeen years of age," writes the Honorable Robert Curzon,* who was present, "died where she sat, of heat, thirst and fatigue." On his way out of the church, he continues, "I got as far as the place where the Virgin is said to have stood during the crucifixion, when I saw a number of people one on another . . . [stretching] as far as I could see towards the door. I made my way between them as well as I could, till they were so thick that there was actually a great heap of bodies on which I trod. It then suddenly struck me they were all dead! . . . I . . . saw that sharp hard appearance of the face that is never to be mistaken. Many of them were quite black with suffocation, and further on were others all bloody and covered with the brains and entrails of those who had been trodden to pieces by the crowd." Farther on, he found the crowd trying to get out the great door. "The guards outside [Mohammedans], frightened at the rush from within, thought that the Christians wished to attack them, and the confusion soon grew into a battle. The soldiers with their bayonets killed numbers of fainting wretches, and the walls were spattered with blood and brains of men who had been felled, like oxen, with the butt-ends of the soldiers' muskets. Everyone struggled to defend himself or to get away, and in the mêlée all who fell were immediately trampled to death by the rest. So desperate and savage did the fight become that even the panic-struck and frightened pilgrims appeared at last to have been more intent upon the destruction of each other than

* *Visits to the Monasteries of the Levant*, London, 1849.

desirous to save themselves." Curzon himself escaped only by fighting his way back into the body of the church across the dead and dying. He noticed that the Unction Stone was piled with corpses. At least five hundred people were killed. And even in 1918, Sir Ronald Storrs was forced, at this ceremony, to protect from the blows of the jealous Armenians a visiting Greek archbishop, "as he passed in glittering tiara from the Tomb to the 'Golgotha Chamber.'"* Not many years before, the Franciscans and Greeks had come to blows over the right to sweep certain stairs, and bystanders were hurt by the flying stones.

It is a relief to get out of the place and catch a glimpse of a courtly kaváss—one of those red-fezzed and bright-jacketed attendants who walk before important personages, pounding the pave with their staffs—engaged in exchanging amenities with a lady who had just left the church.

Yet the lasting significance of Jerusalem is not in the least diminished by the scandal and grotesquerie of the Holy Sepulcher, by the fact that the Temple has been destroyed and that its site is in the hands of the Moslems, who will not let a Jew come near it, that the city is now split across by the quarrel of the Israelis and Arabs. It has been always of the essence of the Jewish genius that it works through the spirit and the intellect, that, in spite of the importance to the Jews of such names as Jerusalem and Zion, it does not need a habitation other than the souls of men. It is a paradox of Jewish history that a moral force, an inspiration, which has leapt geographical boundaries and been felt by so many minds, regardless of race or class, should have been generated and transmitted by a people who have carried exclusiveness to fantastic lengths, who have manifested the extremes of

* *Orientations*, London, 1937.

intolerance and who have suffered from equal intolerance on the part of the champions of other religions which
have taken their cue from the Scriptures. (It is strange to
think that even the Feeneyites, shrieking against the Jews
on Boston Common—the disciples of a heretic priest,
who has taught them that only Catholics can be saved—
should be doing it in the name of a God whom they owe
to the Jewish Bible.) One cannot, of course, blame the
Jews for all the horrors of Mohammedan and Christian
history; bigotry and cruelty are universal. Yet the Bible,
on one of its sides, does tend to encourage both. Julius
Caesar, who dispassionately and ruthlessly cut off the
hands of the Gauls, who slaughtered them and sold them
into slavery, did not do so in the name of God; and the
Greeks, who looked down on the "barbarians" and who
fought them when the necessity arose, did not preach
their extermination on account of their worship of alien
gods. This has been the regrettable side of the influence
of the religious ideas of the Jews: the impulse to fanaticism. The life-giving positive side—often involved with
the other, though certain of the great Jewish teachers
have embodied it in its purest form—is the faith in, the
affirmation of, the power of the human spirit, in touch
with its divine source and independent of place or condition. This paradox, this contradiction, is illustrated in a
striking way by Jesus' conversation with the woman of
Samaria. On my trip to Mount Gerízim to attend the Samaritan Passover, I stopped off at Jacob's Well, at which
this conversation is supposed to have taken place and
which is apparently one of the very few Holy Places that
have any chance of being real, and I reread the scene in
John 4. The purely sectarian issue between the Samaritans and the Jews is brought up in the most typical way.
(Jesus himself—to the Jews a heretic—was accused by
them of being a Samaritan.) "Our fathers," says

the woman to Jesus, "worshipped on this mountain [Gerízim], and you say that in Jerusalem is the place where men ought to worship." The reply that Jesus is reported to have made is a curious combination of the old point of view of the Jews, and the claim to an exclusive and literal correctness, with the intense religious instinct that accompanies this and transcends it. "Woman, believe me," He answers, "the hour is coming when neither on this mountain nor in Jerusalem will you worship the Father. You worship what you do not know; we worship what we know, for salvation is from the Jews. But the hour is coming, and now is, when the true worshippers will worship the Father in spirit and truth, for such the Father seeks to worship Him. God is spirit, and those who worship Him must worship in spirit and truth."

For the Christian, the center of worship was no longer to be Jerusalem, and the second destruction of the Temple was to compel even the most orthodox Jews (if not the Samaritans) to dissociate the spirit of God from any particular place. Even the later Zionists, returning to the earthly Jerusalem, were loyal to a vision that was hardly of earth. How implausible it seems that Protestants in Britain and the United States should be singing their hymns about Israel, Zion and Jerusalem the Golden, without—for the most part, certainly—attaching to them very much meaning of an historical or geographical kind! How implausible that English poets should have written of the "Traffic of Jacob's ladder/Pitched betwixt Heaven and Charing Cross," and of fighting to "build Jerusalem/In England's green and pleasant land"!

I thought, when I returned to the modern Jerusalem, that the bright light, the high bare hills, were more surely the Jerusalem of the Psalms and the Prophets than even the best-documented relics of the Temple and the ancient wall. This was the Jerusalem of which Jesus said that not

one stone should be left upon another, that it was destined
to be "trodden down of the Gentiles." The substantial
tomb built by Herod for the family that he murdered and
for whose murder he tried thus to atone is still standing,
just behind my hotel. It was right on the firing line during the war and is still snarled about with barbed wire.
During the period of hardship that followed the war, it
was lived in by a destitute family and is full of tin cans
and turds; it has never been cleaned out for tourists.
Nation has risen against nation, as Jesus predicted they
would, and kingdom against kingdom; there is little now
to be read of in the papers save "wars and rumors of
wars." Through this city, among these mountains, have
passed, in the course of some twenty-five centuries, the
Hebrews, the Babylonians, the Greeks, the Persians, the
Romans, the Byzantines, the Arabs, the Turkomans,
the Franks, the Moslems, the Crusaders, the Mongolians,
the Mamelukes, the Turks, the British, the Israelis. Jerusalem has been ruled or governed by—to name only a few,
the most notable—David, Solomon, Nebuchadnezzar,
Nehemiah, Antiochus Epiphanes, the Maccabees, Pompey, the Herods, Pontius Pilate, Bar-Kochba, Chosroes
II, Godefroy de Bouillon, Saladin, Suleiman the Magnificent, El-Jazzar, Sir Ronald Storrs and Ben-Gurion. One
can hardly grasp all these vicissitudes—the peoples and
nations and causes, the policies and personalities. Their
history becomes unimaginable, and they all seem to re-
compose, like the sequence of colors of the spectrum, in
this tranquil luminous sky. The Jews made Jerusalem the
high place of God and thus gave it to the whole human
race.

*Degániya:* Something of this strange disparity between Palestine's baldness and meagerness and the visions it has always evoked was felt even by the Zionist

leader Aaron David Gordon, when he first came in 1904
to what he called, what was called in the Bible, and what
is still called today Éretz Yisraél, the Land of Israel.
"There was born in me a curious emotion," he writes in
one of his letters, "or, rather, a mingling of two conflicting emotions, which is difficult to explain. On the one
hand, it seemed as if this great wide expanse frightened
me and shocked me. It stood naked in the powerful light
that flooded it, revealing all things with cruel brilliancy
as far as the eye could reach and seeming to say, 'Nothing
is hidden from my eyes.' " And he could not look into the
distance, for the mountains shut off his view, "barriers
against my sight." "Many days passed in this frame of
mind before I began to struggle against myself and to
think deeply of the characteristics of Éretz Yisraél: small
and narrow is the land; just back of those mountains it
all but ends—'For the bed is too short for a man to
stretch himself.' . . . What the mind, however, cannot
succeed in doing, life, nature and work achieve. While
the hands learn to work, the ears to hear, the eyes to see,
the heart to feel and to realize what is here, the soul
learns to soar over mountains, to skip over hills, to exalt
itself, to stretch itself to infinite distance, to embrace the
land around, the world and its inhabitants, and to see itself embraced in the arms of the whole world."

He goes on to speak of Russia, with its pogroms and its
trumped-up ritual-murder case, and of the persecution of
the Jews in Poland—in the lofty Biblical manner, never
naming any country or person: "A great and mighty nation storms against you in an outburst of rage, hurls itself
against you like a ravenous beast. . . . I see a different
nation. This nation, too, is unable to stand on its own feet,
and it, too, wishes to swallow you." He goes on, in the
same high prophetic strain, to the problem of assimilation, of the Jews that want other Jews to build a home "in

a land that neither you nor your ancestors have known.
You are ready to go wherever they lead you. They teach
you to talk the language that their captors have taught
them. You say it is your language, and you repeat all
that they say; you sing the songs they sing. There is nothing too difficult for you to do; there is no road too narrow
for you to follow, no life too insignificant for you to desire. All is small, poor, weak, wretched, wretched—all is
in ruins. . . . Desolate, bewildered, I stand and observe
you, my people! I observe you with glazed eyes; I do not
understand you, and I do not understand myself." Then,
"suddenly a spirit touched and wakened me: 'Son of
Man!,' and I was among the mountains, high on the summit of a mountain peak. . . . 'Son of Man!' There will
yet come a day . . . when your sons and daughters will
dream a dream," and they "will come to seek the interpretation of the dream in the land of their fathers. They
will seek it with all the power of their hands, with all the
strength of their hearts. They will dig it out of hidden
places; they will carry on every kind of work in the field
and in the vineyard in seeking for it. They will renew the
earth and their lives in the search. . . . In the end, they
will become great, greater than the mountain peaks on
the face of the earth; they will see what no man saw before them, and they will become mighty on the earth.
Then will the Jewish people blossom again; then will
they stand upright and live; then will they become a nation."

Gordon, who had spent most of his adult life as an
official on a baronial estate in Podolia, in southern Russia, came to Palestine in 1904 and died there in 1922.
He did not live to see his prophecy fulfilled. But he spent
the last ten years of his life in the pioneer community of
Degániya (the name means Corn of the Lord), founded
in 1909. He had in Poland been rather well off, and he

now had the prestige of a sage and saint, but he worked on the land with the rest and shared a room with three other men. Degániya was the first of the movement of self-supporting Jewish collectives, the *kvutzót* and *kibbutzím*. The members of these in the early days must have been all more or less intellectuals, but Tolstóy as well as Zionism had led them to manual labor.

I had been given a letter by a friend at home to a married couple in Degániya, and when I was visiting Galilee, I looked them up. The wife had been a schoolteacher in Prague, who, as a young woman, had interested herself in the refugee Jewish children from Galicia that had been brought to Prague by their parents when their country, at the time of the First World War, had been overrun by the Russian Army. She had told them little stories that proved such a success that she finally published them in a book, which became the first of a popular series. After the war, she emigrated to Palestine. At the time, 1920, the Degániya community had produced a daughter *kvutzáh*, Degániya B, of which she became one of the charter members. She learned Hebrew, taught in the school. Degániya was still more or less a desert, and they endured a good deal of hardship. She is proud of having been one of the pioneers in what was then a daring experiment. The old group had been quite conservative, but the new one set out to practise socialism. "They said we were subversive and crazy, and now the communities are an institution. It was we who launched the whole movement: *Achtung!*" She is a small brown woman with spectacles, who has injured her foot and has to limp but gets along briskly. She is lively, energetic, enthusiastic. Her apartment—by right of seniority, she and her husband are allowed two rooms instead of the usual one—is full of German literature and books on child psychology, and there is a shelf of prehistoric artifacts, picked up in the neighborhood, for

she is an amateur archeologist; but I found her in the
mending room, where the clothing of the *kvutzáh* is put
to rights, busy at the sewing machine. She showed me the
school, which the teachers and children were getting ready
for Passover, and the building where those children were
housed who were not the sons and daughters of community members. A number of these young boys and girls had
been among the victims of Hitler. They were orphaned
and neurotic and hard to handle. Some of them had had
the experience of seeing their parents murdered and finding themselves totally abandoned. The community had
taken them in. We visited the chicken house, with its perspective of caged compartments, all full of snow-white
fowls, and its enormous mechanical incubators that turned
thousands of eggs around. On the grounds stood an old
army tank. At the time of the Arab war, the Syrians attacked Degániya, and a battle was fought on the grounds
themselves. The enemy was finally driven out, but not before many members had been killed, including several
children. There is a monument now to the dead, but the
tank has been left as a souvenir, as well as a bit of the
trench from which they had fired on the enemy.

These grounds of the collectives, with their flowers
and paths, their oases of shady trees, seemed to me peaceful and pleasant, and though I had heard that the communities were sometimes rent by factional disagreements,
I did not get an impression of strain. On the contrary, it
seemed to me that things were done in a quiet and leisurely way. Everybody is very soft-spoken. The *kvutzáh*
is completely self-governing, and every member is responsible for something. They do not pay for food or
clothes, schooling or medical service—they even get an
allowance of cigarettes. They also accumulate credits,
which they draw in money and spend as they please.
One thinks at first of the Russian collectives, but the

*kvutzáh* is something quite distinct from those. It is voluntary; the members are well educated; they do not hesitate
to say what they think. This is rather the old Russian
idealism of the beginning of the present century. Tolstóy
is mingled with Zionism—one of the principal buildings
is named for him—and Socialism of the old, still innocent brand has been made easily to blend with Tolstóy.
And there is also a psychology of pioneers that sometimes recalls America. These Zionists, in earlier days, had
to contend with malarial swamps, which they have now
filled in and made fertile, and with murderous bands of
Bedouins, who now would not dare to come near them.
When I mentioned that I felt the atmosphere to be one of
security and ease, I was reminded at once that all this had
been won only by decades of labor, anxious effort and
austere living.

The Zionists, I came to realize, have constituted a kind
of élite. I have never seen anyone else quite like some of
the children of Zionists, who have been born in or come
young to Palestine. The wonder is that, growing up there
and sometimes having never traveled, they should be so
well bred and so well-informed. They reminded me of
young modern Greeks. But to have emigrated to Palestine at all, to have made for oneself a life there, implies,
of course, on the parents' part, self-confidence and dedicated purpose, a high level of thinking and feeling; and
the children have not known at first-hand the humilia-
tions and horrors from which the parents escaped.

*Éretz Yisraél:* And now what about the Israel that
you read about in the papers? If the reader has expected
a survey, this chapter is likely to have sounded like
one of those tales of Agnón's in which the narrator, in
recounting an anecdote of something that happened to
his uncle, finds it necessary not only to explain how his

grandparents came to get married but also to involve in
his story Moses, Aaron and Jeremiah, Akiba, Rashi,
Maimonides and the Rabbi Baal Shem Tov. But, as in
Agnón's case, so in this—that is, I think, the right way to
tell the story. I have already tried to suggest the perspective of three thousand years in which Israel ought to be
seen—though the happenings of these millennia, which
to the Western mind present a perspective, are somehow,
apparently, for the Jewish mind, all contemporary and
real at once, and easily identified with one another.

But what about immediate problems? What about the
balance of trade, which seems so overwhelmingly against
the Israelis? What about the guaranteed profits, the arti-
ficially kept-up wages, that are subsidized by foreign phi-
lanthropy? The unemployment, the inadequate housing?
The obstructions to arranging with their neighbors for
the development of the water power of the Jordan River?
What of compensating the Arabs for their losses and
eliminating border incidents? What about the danger of
war? What about Histadrút, that unique yet typical product of twentieth-century industry—a labor organization
which is also itself in business and the biggest employer
of labor in Israel, and which is sometimes a little ambiguous on the subject of the right to strike—whose imposing new headquarters, outside Tel Aviv, are sometimes referred to as the Kremlin? What about the color
problem, since in Israel the black Jews and the white
Jews are obliged now to live together, and the two do not
care to mix? What of the problem of educating the Yemenites, who have been transported en masse from the
south of Arabia—in what was called Operation Magic
Carpet—by planes, which did not surprise them, since
they took them for the giant birds that an old tradition
had promised would rescue them and carry them back
to Palestine, but who found themselves, once disem-

barked, in a terrifying modern world of which they could not make head or tail? How about the Moroccans and Algerians who had to be brought to Israel to save them from the reprisals of the vanquished Arabs, but who seem to have turned out to be riffraff, the only Jews in the world who are not willing to work? I have suggested, I believe, the one answer to this tangle of questions, too. It is the faith that keeps Israel going and that has allowed her to take all these problems on, the faith of the Jewish prophets from Moses to Aaron David Gordon, and the loyalty of contemporary Israelis to this. "When I first came here from Germany," said the doctor from Berlin I have already mentioned, the physician for a large *kvutzáh,* "I didn't feel at all at home—I could easily have gone to America. But after three years I wanted to stay." The visitor soon comes to see why. The Jerusalem that Israelis adore is not the group of mainly modern buildings, the truncated system of streets, neither colorful nor very bustling, on the bristling edge of hostile territory, but the Jerusalem that lives in their hearts.

It is a relief to come here from Europe, from the European discouragement and cultural staleness, the running down and falling apart. Here the people have something to hope for, a survival that is not yet all achieved; and, though bitterly at odds with their neighbors, they are occupied within their own borders with a work of reintegration among their own so diverse elements. One feels at moments that they have even got used to their nasty feud with the Arabs, and do not think much about it. I felt far less tension in Israel when these incidents were going on—though, of course, I was not so much involved —than I did when I returned to the States, to the atmosphere of the McCarthy hearings, Indo-China and the hydrogen bomb, and, as soon as I stepped on the dock, found the task of getting out my baggage through a

porter system stupidly organized—with passengers ex-
asperated and apprehensive, and porters and officials
surly—so much more difficult than in any other country.
I found no such confusion in Israel, no such ordeal for
the nerves (the whole official side of Israeli life has bene-
fited by British training)—not even in Tel Aviv, which
Jerusalem regards as a beehive but which seemed to me,
so far as I saw it, with its cafés, its coffeehouses, its
entertainments and its boulevard along the sea, to have
something of both Athens and Vienna. Fanaticism you
find, yes. Fanaticism, as was said to me by one Israeli, is
always at home in this land. It grows there like cactus
and citrus fruit, fed by the divine light. And yet the Children of Israel are genuinely at ease in Zion. It is remarkable how soon you forget, as they seem almost to have
forgotten, from how far and from how many places they
have come back to live in Palestine.

The Jews, in the nineteenth century, began for the first
time, systematically, to try to explain themselves—their
literature, their history, their customs—to an "enlightened" outside world that was prepared for the first time
to study them—their language, their religion, their morality—in a serious and sympathetic way. Jewish scholars, for example, wrote popular essays—such as those of
Darmesteter and Deutsch, published in France in the six-
ties—describing the Talmud to Gentiles, and the Christian scholar Calvin Stowe tried to perform the same service, from the Gentile side, for this hitherto mysterious
work—though the first full translation of the Talmud
into English only appeared in the first years of this century. Instead of Marlowe's Barabas and Shakespeare's
Shylock, you had Lessing's Nathan the Wise and George
Eliot's Daniel Deronda. The process of "assimilation"
was rapidly going on, and in some cases went so far that
the Teutonized or Gallicized or Anglicized Jew quite lost

touch with his own tradition; yet there were always re-
crudescences on the part of the "Christians" of the super-
stitious barbarism of the Middle Ages, and the relations
between Gentiles and Jews were always liable to a certain
amount of strain. Now, the return of the Jews to their
country of origin, the reversion to their ancient language
and, with these, a certain relaxation—in the sense that
a steel spring may be said to relax from bending—into
their habits of self-sufficiency, has made it possible for
them to stand alone and not to worry about pleasing some
dominant "race"; digging themselves in has set them free,
with the result—but superficially a paradox—that the
Jews seem in Israel less different instead of more different from other people. This has had its moral effect on
Jews all over the world, and it is the great thing to grasp
about Israel.

# THE DEAD SEA SCROLLS
## 1947–1969

This volume contains, first, a slightly revised reprinting of my book *The Scrolls from the Dead Sea*, published in 1955. This was originally preceded by the following note:

This essay, in a somewhat abridged form, first appeared in the *New Yorker* magazine. I am indebted to that periodical for making possible my trip to Palestine, and to its editors and checking department for the careful attention they gave the text. I should also thank the Metropolitan Mar Athanasius Yeshue Samuel, Père Roland de Vaux of the École Biblique in Old Jerusalem, Dr. James Muilenberg of the Union Theological Seminary, and Dr. W. F. Albright of Johns Hopkins for reading all or part of the manuscript and giving me the benefit of their criticisms and corrections, as well as for assistance of other kinds. I also owe a special debt to Mr. Stewart Perowne of Jerusalem, who arranged my expedition to the Dead Sea.

There follows here an account of the work that has been done in connection with the scrolls since 1955 and of my trip to the Middle East—also financed by the *New Yorker* —undertaken in 1967 for the purpose of bringing my earlier report up to date. Most of this latter material originally appeared in the *New Yorker*. Other acknowledgments in connection with it appear in the Introduction. I have not hesitated, in the second part, to repeat information from the first, because the subject is so complicated and so unfamiliar to most readers that they may well not remember accurately the names and events from the earlier chapters.

# THE SCROLLS FROM
# THE DEAD SEA
## 1955

# I

## THE METROPOLITAN SAMUEL

AT SOME POINT rather early in the spring of 1947, a Bedouin boy called Muhammed the Wolf was minding some goats near a cliff on the western shore of the Dead Sea. Climbing up after one that had strayed, he noticed a cave that he had not seen before, and he idly threw a stone into it. There was an unfamiliar sound of breakage. The boy was frightened and ran away. But he later came back with another boy, and together they explored the cave. Inside were several tall clay jars, among fragments of other jars. When they took off the bowl-like lids, a very bad smell arose, which came from dark oblong lumps that were found inside all the jars. When they got these lumps out of the cave, they saw that they were wrapped up in lengths of linen and coated with a black layer of what seemed to be pitch or wax. They unrolled them and found long manuscripts, inscribed in parallel columns on thin sheets that had been sewn together. Though these manuscripts had faded and crumbled in places, they were in general remarkably clear. The character, they saw, was not Arabic. They wondered at the scrolls and kept them, carrying them along when they moved.

These Bedouin boys belonged to a party of contrabanders, who had been smuggling their goats and other goods out of Transjordan into Palestine. They had detoured so far to the south in order to circumvent the Jordan bridge, which the customs officers guarded with guns, and had floated their commodities across the stream. They were now on their way to Bethlehem to sell their stuff in the black market, and they had come to the Dead Sea in order to stock up with water at the spring of Ain Feshkha, the only fresh water to be found for miles in that dry, hot and desolate region. They were quite safe from discovery there: it was a locality that had no attractions, to which nobody ever came. In Bethlehem, they sold their contraband, and showed their scrolls to the merchant who was buying it. He did not know what they were and refused to pay the twenty pounds they asked for them; so they took them to another merchant, from whom they always bought their supplies. Being a Syrian, he thought that the language might be ancient Syriac, and he sent word by another Syrian to the Syrian Metropolitan at the Monastery of St. Mark in Old Jerusalem.

The Metropolitan, Mar Athanasius Yeshue Samuel, expressed a decided interest. He knew that nobody since the first Christian centuries had lived anywhere near Ain Feshkha, and he had been struck by the visitors' telling him that the scrolls were "wrapped up like mummies." When one was brought to him at the monastery, he broke off a bit and burned it, and could smell that it was leather or parchment. He recognized the language as Hebrew, but was not a Hebrew scholar and could not make out what the manuscript was. He sent word that he would buy the scrolls, but in the meantime the Bedouins were off again on another expedition. Several weeks passed. It was July before one of the Syrians called up to tell the Metropolitan that he and the Bedouins would bring him the scrolls. The Metropolitan expected them all morning. He finally went to lunch, and it was then that the visitors arrived. They were turned away at the door, and the priest who had refused to receive them came to the Metropolitan and told him that some tough-looking Arabs had appeared with some dirty old rolls, and that, seeing that these were written not in Syriac but in Hebrew, he had sent the Arabs to a Jewish school. The Metropolitan at once got in touch with the Syrian who had brought the Bedouins and learned with annoyance that these latter, turned away, had shown the scrolls to a Jewish merchant, whom they met at the Jaffa Gate. This merchant had offered them what they thought a good price, but explained that, in order to collect it, they must come to his office in the Jaffa Road in the predominantly Jewish New City.

Now, Jerusalem, by the summer of '47, was already sharply divided between the Arabs and the Jews. The British, in their effort to propitiate the Arabs and to keep them out of the hands of Russia, had prevented refugees from Europe from landing in Palestinian ports, and this had imposed on the emigrants much hardship and even caused a large number of deaths. The Jews, in reprisal for this, had organized a terrorist group, which had been murdering British soldiers, and the British had been hanging these terrorists. The Jews had retaliated with bombs and mines, leaving a hangman's noose on the scene of each assassination. The British had then kidnapped a sixteen-year-old boy, who was supposed to be a member of the Stern group. The Jews believed him to have been tortured and killed: his body was never found; and the terrorists blew a hole in the jail where the British had been locking up political prisoners. Some of the men who had done this were caught and hanged, and the Jews hanged two British sergeants and wired one of the bodies with a booby-trap. At the time when the scrolls were thus offered for sale, the Jewish parts of Jerusalem had been put under martial law; and, in consequence, the Syrian merchant, who sold the scrolls to the monastery, had no difficulty in convincing the Bedouins that the Jewish merchant was planning to trap them—that, once off base in the Jaffa Road, they would be robbed of their property and put in jail; and he mentioned the Palestinian law that newly discovered antiquities must immediately be reported to the government. He even induced the Bedouins to leave five of the scrolls in his shop, and eventually to take them to the monastery, where the Metropolitan purchased them, along with a few fragments, for a price which has never been made public but which is rumored to have been fifty pounds.

The Metropolitan Samuel has sometimes been charged with slyness in his handling of the Dead Sea scrolls; but if occasionally he has exercised guile, I believe that it has been only such wariness in the matter of not showing one's hand as is quite conventional in the Middle East—a minimum routine requirement in a land where all business transactions are based on a convention of bargaining. I should say, in fact, that, far from making trouble for himself by trying to be too clever, the Metropolitan has been handicapped by innocence. Not knowing the Western world, it was long, as will later appear, before he was able to profit in any degree proportionate to the value of his unique acquisitions; and he deserves immense credit, one cannot but feel—especially if one takes into account the chapter of ineptitude that follows—for having had the good sense to recognize that hitherto unknown manuscripts from the uninhabited region of the Dead Sea would be likely to prove of interest, and for persisting, in the teeth of discouragement, in sticking by this conviction. With his black and abundant beard, his large round liquid brown eyes, in his onion-shaped black satin mitre, his black robes with their big sleeves and the great cross of gold and the ikon of the Virgin that hang about his neck on chains, the Metropolitan—with not too much priestly fleshiness and pallor—is a notably handsome man, who would recall an Assyrian bas-relief if his expression were not gentle instead of fierce. In demeanor, he is dignified, simple and calm, with a touch perhaps of something child-like. He is not at all an "intellectual," has no special schol-arly interests, but is assiduous in his role as priest of the Syrian Jacobite Church, which long antedates the Greek and boasts that its line comes direct from the Holy See of Antioch founded by Peter, and that it ruled at one time the whole Christian East. This is one of the five churches permanently represented in the Church of the Holy Sep-ulcher, and the Monastery of St. Mark is supposed to stand on the site of the house where the Last Supper took place.

The first thing the Metropolitan Samuel did when he had bought the Hebrew manuscripts was to send one of his priests with the merchant to check up on the story of the cave. The cave was found in the place that the Bed-ouins had indicated, and in it were found the jars, frag-ments of the linen wrappings and scraps of the scrolls themselves. The two men spent a night in the cavern, stifling in the terrible heat—it was now the second week of August—and, having brought no provisions but melons, they decided they could not stay longer. They did not even manage to bring away, as at first they had hoped to do, a specimen of the big clay jars. (The Bedouins, how-ever, had taken two and had been using them to carry water.) The problem was now to find out what the manu-scripts were and how old they were. The Metropolitan Samuel consulted a Syrian he knew in the Palestine De-partment of Antiquities, and a French priest at the Do-minican École Biblique, a center of archaeological re-search in Old Jerusalem.

The outsider cannot help being struck by the frequent reluctance of the learned world to recognize important discoveries. In connection with the failure of scholars first

to recognize, then to acknowledge, the antiquity of the
Dead Sea scrolls, Professor W. F. Albright of Johns Hopkins has pointed out that "the discovery of Pompeii and
Herculaneum was in its time relegated to the realm of fiction by outstanding personages, that some archaeologists
and many more philologians refused to accept the strati-
graphical results of Schliemann and Dörpfeld for decades
after the beginning of the excavations of Hissarlik [an-
cient Troy], and that the decipherment of cuneiform was
not accepted by all informed students of antiquity until
well after the end of the nineteenth century." There have
been forgeries and hoaxes, of course: the false books of
Livy, the supplement to Petronius; and the scholar must
be on his guard against innocently swallowing such products. Yet there is also at work here the natural instinct to
simplify one's scholarly problems by establishing a closed
field. One likes to feel that one has seen all the evidence.
One has mastered it and worked out one's theories; and it
is very upsetting—especially, if one suffers from imaginative limitations—to have to be obliged to deal with new
material. There are still doubts expressed in some quarters
as to the genuineness of the great Russian medieval poem,
*The Expedition of Igor*. The only manuscript of this was
discovered in the eighteenth century, and this original,
although it had been copied, was burned in the Moscow
fire of 1812 Yet the case against it is really based on the
argument that there is nothing else like it, and the argument for its authenticity was definitively put by Pushkin
when he declared that, in the eighteenth century, there
existed no known Russian writer who was gifted and
learned enough to have perpetrated so brilliant a hoax.
How much stronger, then, both for and against, are the
arguments in respect to the scrolls! How much more improbable, on the one hand, the finding of Biblical manuscripts which antedated those that were previously known!

How even more improbable that anyone should attempt so elaborate a fraud!

In order to understand the importance of the Dead Sea manuscripts and the stubborn incredulity of scholars, one has to realize that, except for a fragment or two, our earliest text of the Hebrew Bible—the so-called Masoretic text —though it had probably been established as early as the beginning of the second pre-Christian century, is no more ancient than the ninth Christian century; and that, before that, our main versions of Scripture are the Alexandrian Septuagint, a translation into Greek which is supposed to have been begun somewhere in the third pre-Christian century and not finished till two hundred years later, and St. Jerome's Latin Vulgate, made in the fourth century. All our literary knowledge of the world of the Bible has been based on this early Christian text and these two later translations, together with a Samaritan Pentateuch, some excerpts in early Aramaic versions and the Greek quotations of Justin Martyr in his dialogue with the Rabbi Trypho. All of these have been much debated, since they differ from one another in ways which seem to indicate that they were made from Hebrew versions other than the Masoretic text. But it took a certain courage to face new Hebrew materials where none had been imagined to exist. "In none of the similar episodes of the past two centuries . . ." continues Professor Albright, "has there been such a wide refusal on the part of scholars to accept clear-cut evidence." The first experts consulted by the Metropolitan Samuel gave him no encouragement whatever. The two ablest archaeologists then in that part of the world were apparently Mr. G. Lankester Harding of the Department of Antiquities of Transjordan and Père Roland de Vaux of the École Biblique; but the latter at the moment was away in Paris, and to the former the Metropolitan did not succeed in gaining access. The people whom he did see at these institutions told him that the thing was unheard of: the manuscripts could not be old. No effort seems even to have been made to read them till the Metropolitan showed them to a Father J. van der Ploeg, a visiting Dutch scholar at the École Biblique, who identified one of the scrolls as Isaiah, but was discouraged by the scholars of the school from pursuing the matter further.

The Metropolitan now took the scrolls to the Syrian Patriarch of Antioch, who thought they could not be more than three centuries old, but suggested his consulting the professor of Hebrew at the American University in Beirut. The Metropolitan went to Beirut but found that the professor was away on vacation. He decided to study the problem himself, and, coming back to Jerusalem, he got his friend from the Department of Antiquities to supply him with some books on the Hebrew alphabet. The Syrian archaeologist assured him that he was wasting his time, that the scrolls were "not worth a shilling"; but the Syrian brought to the monastery a Jew from the New City, a Mr. Tovia Wechsler, who was something of a Hebrew scholar. This visit of Mr. Wechsler, according to the Metropolitan's account, occurred toward the end of September. Mr. Wechsler, however, remembers it as having taken place already—in July—and his statement about it is also at variance with what was later known definitely about the scrolls. He, too, was unable to believe they were as old as the Metropolitan hoped. Mr. Wechsler pointed at the table on which the manuscript had been laid—about this he and Samuel are agreed—and declared, "If that table were a box, and you filled it with pound notes, you couldn't even manage the value of the scrolls, if they are two thousand years old, as you say." He did not credit the story of their having been found in a cave by the Dead Sea. He noticed, in examining one of them, that corrections written in the margins and fillings-out of the columns at the bottoms, where the text was becoming obliterated, had been made in an ink that contrasted by its clearness with the ink of the original copyist, and he drew the inference from this that the scroll "had been in use by a very poor community for a considerable time and had only recently been abandoned." He jumped to the conclusion that the manuscripts had been stolen from a Palestine synagogue at the time of the anti-Jewish Arab riots of 1929. He recognized a text of Isaiah and observed that it differed slightly from the Masoretic text. The second of the documents he looked at he believed to be a Haftaroth scroll—that is, a selection from the Prophets of lessons to be read in synagogues. But no Haftaroth have ever turned up among the known Dead Sea scrolls, and the Metropolitan says that what Wechsler must have taken for a Haftaroth scroll was a manuscript of the Torah (the Pentateuch) which was shown him on the same visit but which had nothing to do with the Dead Sea lot. Among these, as was afterwards found, were three non-Biblical books which had never been seen before, and others think that Mr. Wechsler must hastily have taken one of these for a modern synagogue scroll. To this theory Wechsler replies that it reminds him "of the story about the man who related that he had seen a camel, and after having circumstantially described the animal, was asked by someone in his audience, 'Maybe you saw a cat?'" The incident remains rather obscure. When the matter was later looked into by the American School of Oriental Research, the only Hebrew manuscript the searchers found in the library of the monastery was a relatively modern Torah.

"Needless to say I felt discouraged," the Metropolitan writes, "but somehow I still felt they were wrong." One may at first find it surprising that a man of such importance in Jerusalem—the equivalent of a Western archbishop—should have taken so long a time to discover the competent authorities, who were right there ready to hand; but one is often surprised in Jerusalem at the lack of knowledge and interest shown by the various groups in one another's affairs. In the published discussion of the scrolls one finds, for example, that the Metropolitan Samuel is sometimes referred to as "the Patriarch"; and, in talking with scholars in the New City, on a recent visit to Israel, I was astonished by their vagueness about him: some imagined him to be still in his monastery, though he had left it in 1948. It will be noticed that the Metropolitan, in his efforts to deal with the scrolls, almost always has recourse to other Syrians. In the Middle East, it seems, your church is your social world, and you know little, apparently, of any other. Even in the United States, the congregations of the four different Syrian churches mix little with one another; and an American is sometimes puzzled, in crossing some frontier in the Middle East, to be asked for his "nationality" when he has already registered his American citizenship: "nationality," he learns, means "religion." At any rate, it seems to have been only by chance that the Metropolitan Samuel did finally get in touch with an institution which could help him, and, even then, the contact had no results. It happened that a Jewish doctor called at the monastery to inquire about renting a building that was a part of the church's property. The Metropolitan took the opportunity to ask him about the scrolls. This visitor did the obvious thing: he called up President Magnes of the Hebrew University. Dr. Magnes, a few weeks later, sent two men from the University library. They said that they would have to consult an authority on these subjects and asked to photograph a few columns of one of the manuscripts. The Metropolitan gave his consent, but the librarians never came back. On the same afternoon, also summoned by the doctor, a Jewish antiquity dealer arrived at the monastery. He recommended that pieces of the scrolls be sent to certain dealers in Europe and the United States. "This," says Samuel, "I declined to do."

It is not clear whether the failure of the men from the library to come back, as they promised, to the monastery was due to the troubled conditions or to the absence of E. L. Sukenik, the University's head archaeologist. In any case, Professor Sukenik returned at the end of November, and was told by a Jerusalem antiquity dealer (not the one who had visited the monastery) that some manuscripts from a cave on the Dead Sea were in the hands of a dealer in Bethlehem. This dealer was the buyer of contraband to whom the Bedouins had first brought the scrolls. He had got wind of their having some value and had bought up the remaining manuscripts. These were the three other scrolls that the Metropolitan Samuel had not had a chance to buy.

What followed was recorded by Sukenik in his diary:

"November 25, 1947: Today I met X [antiquity dealer]. A Hebrew book has been discovered in a jar. He showed me a fragment written on parchment. *Genizah?!* [A *genizah* is a room in a synagogue in which old discarded manuscripts are stowed away. All the manuscripts of the synagogue are sacred and may not be destroyed. Sukenik assumed that the Dead Sea cave had been used for this purpose.]

"November 27, 1947: At X's [the dealer's] I saw four pieces of leather with Hebrew writing. The script seems ancient to me, very much like the writing in the Uzziah inscription. Is it possible? He says there are also jars. I looked a bit and found good Biblical Hebrew, a text unknown to me. He says a Bedouin of the Ta'âmireh tribe brought it to him.

"November 29, 1947: This morning I was at X's. Again I looked at the parchments, they suggest odd thoughts. In the afternoon I went with X to Bethlehem. I saw the jars, and it's difficult for me to say anything about their date. I took them.

"This evening we heard that the partition proposal had been accepted by more than a two-thirds majority. Congratulations!"

This was the partition of Palestine, which had been voted that day by the United Nations. The atmosphere was now very tense. Sukenik had consulted his son, an officer in Haganah, the underground Jewish defense group, as to whether the roads were safe enough for him to make the journey to Bethlehem. "As a military man," says the younger Sukenik (now General Yigael Yadin), "I answered that he ought not to make the journey; as an archaeologist, that he ought to go; as his son—that my opinion had to be reserved." The father had got through to Bethlehem and brought back all but one of the second lot of scrolls—which turned out to consist of three manuscripts (one of them in three pieces) and a handful of fragments. Open and savage hostilities broke out the next day. The Arabs tried to isolate the Jews by cutting off their communications with Tel-Aviv: they ambushed the Jewish buses, burning them and shooting them up.

Sukenik's diary continues:

"December 1, 1947: X says that we shan't see one another in the near future because of the Arab strike, proclaimed for the next three days.

"I read a little more in the 'parchments.' I'm afraid of going too far in thinking about them. It may be that this is one of the greatest finds ever made in Palestine, a find we never so much as hoped for.

"December 5, 1947: More killings. The strike was over today, but not the violence. The find leaves me no peace. I'm bursting to know what will come of it all. It might turn out that the neighborhood has many things of this sort. Who knows what surprises still await us.

"December 6, 1947: Night. I sit and think and think about the scrolls. When will I see more of them? Patience, patience.

"December 21, 1947: Days of awe. I contacted X. We're to meet tomorrow at noon near the gate [to the Security Zone].

"I came. I bought another scroll in very bad condition.

"January 13, 1948: I went to the main Post Office (near the border). X came. He promised to get in touch with Bethlehem. I said the *Hagomel* blessing as I left [a blessing to be said on occasions of escaping from mortal danger].

"December 31, 1948: An historic year in our people's history has concluded. A painful year—Matti died, God bless him! [the author's youngest son, lost in action as a fighter-pilot].

"Were it not for the *genizah*, the year would have been intolerable for me."

The excitement of discovering the scrolls had enabled him partly to forget the war. At a time when the Arab Legion had, between three and five every afternoon, been shelling the offices of the Jewish Agency in the middle of New Jerusalem, he had not hesitated to call a press conference at this dangerous place and hour, promising important news. To attend it required strong nerves. An American correspondent fainted in the street on the way, and had to be carried in by his colleagues. The reporters were flabbergasted when Sukenik, who appeared to be quite unperturbed by the flashing and banging about him, announced the discovery of the Dead Sea scrolls: except for a few scraps in the past, the first ancient Hebrew manuscripts known. He thought they must be as old as the first or second century B.C. They heard the name of Isaiah, and something about a hitherto unknown work to which Sukenik had given the title, *The War of the Chil-*

*dren of Light against the Children of Darkness.* At the moment this was mentioned, a shell burst. The reporters had at first been rather peevish at having been asked to risk their skins for old manuscripts, but they ended with being impressed by the scholar's overmastering enthusiasm.

It was, however, not till the February of 1948 that the Metropolitan Samuel succeeded in making contact with someone who could tell him about the scrolls. It was remembered by one of his monks, Brother Butros Sowmy, that he had been well received, ten years earlier, when he had had occasion to visit the American School of Oriental Research, and he suggested calling them up. This was done, and Brother Butros Sowmy took the scrolls there on February 18 and showed them to the then Acting Director, Dr. John C. Trever. The Director, Dr. Millar Burrows of the Yale Divinity School, was away on a trip to Iraq. Dr. Trever, a younger less experienced man, was not able at once to estimate, as Professor Sukenik had done, the probable age of the manuscripts, but when he began to suspect what they were, he, too, became much excited. "Remembering the box of slides in my desk," he writes in the *Biblical Archaeologist,* "on *What Lies Back of Our English Bible?,* I thumbed through them for the section on early Hebrew manuscripts. One glimpse at the picture of the British Museum Codex from the ninth century assured me that these scrolls were far older. The next slide was of the Nash Papyrus, a small fragment in the University Library at Cambridge containing the *Shema* and the Ten Commandments." Now, the so-called Nash Papyrus, which was bought about fifty years ago from an Egyptian dealer by an Englishman, is written in an archaic script which at that time was otherwise hardly known, and it had usually been regarded as the oldest Hebrew manuscript in existence. It has been dated by various authorities from sometime early in the second pre-Christian century to sometime toward the end of the first century A.D. So it was natural that Dr. Trever should also have become exhilarated when he saw that "the similarity of the script in the papyrus and the scrolls was striking." But, he adds, "the picture was too small to help much." He had no camera there, so he copied out a passage from one of the scrolls and eventually identified it as a part of Isaiah. Later on, he persuaded the Metropolitan to allow him to photograph all the scrolls, convincing him that their value would be much increased if they were published and an interest in them stimulated. This decision, as we shall later see, was in some ways a very fortunate, and in other ways, a rather unfortunate one.

But nothing could be done at once. In the course of the battle for Jerusalem, the current had been cut off, and it was doubtful whether it would be possible to get light to photograph the manuscripts. While they were waiting— Dr. Trever and his colleague Dr. William H. Brownlee— they looked up, by kerosene lamps, everything they could find in the library that might throw light on the Nash Papyrus. By midnight they felt quite certain that the new Isaiah scroll was as old as, if not older than, this. "Sleep," writes Dr. Trever, "came with greater difficulty. The added evidence kept racing through my mind. It all seemed incredible. How could we be right?" The next morning the current came on; but there were fifty-four columns of Isaiah alone, and they were far from having got through them by noon, so the Syrians from the monastery stayed to lunch. "The hour of fellowship around the table we shall long cherish," Trever writes, "for it gave us a feeling for ecumenical Christianity, and it brought us closer in our friendship and understanding of the Syrians." The Metropolitan, of course, was delighted that his faith in the antiquity of the scrolls had finally been justified. Not wanting to give away the cache to anyone who chose to go there, he had at first told the people at the school that the scrolls were uncatalogued manuscripts which had turned up in the monastery library; but later, when his confidence had been gained, he gave them the whole story. Dr. Trever, thereupon, explained to him that the antiquity laws of Palestine required that all such discoveries should immediately be reported, and the Metropolitan assured them that in future he would scrupulously coöperate with the Department of Antiquities and the School. After lunch, they returned to their task. Parts of the scrolls were in pieces, and they had to fit them together. They fastened them with Scotch Tape, but presently the tape gave out. They had been able to get through only two when the Syrians in the afternoon had to return to their monastery, but the Metropolitan left them two more, which turned out to be two sections of a single document. The smallest of the scrolls was so stuck together that they decided it constituted a problem which would have to be carefully studied, and the Metropolitan took it away.

Dr. Trever at once sent off prints of columns of the Isaiah scroll to Dr. W. F. Albright of Johns Hopkins, one of the ablest living Biblical archaeologists and an authority on the Nash Papyrus, which he had studied intensively over a period of years. They heard from him by air mail on March 15. He had written the same day he received the letter: "My heartiest congratulations on the greatest manuscript discovery of modern times! There is no doubt in my mind that the script is more archaic than that of the Nash Papyrus . . . I should prefer a date around 100 B.C. . . . What an absolutely incredible find! And there can happily not be the slightest doubt in the world about the genuineness of the manuscript."

In the meantime, Professor Sukenik had heard—but not till after he had bought the three manuscripts—from one of the University librarians who had been to the monastery, of the existence of the other five scrolls. Yet another Syrian merchant, having learned of Sukenik's interest, seems to have offered, without the Metropolitan's knowledge, to arrange to sell them to Sukenik. Late in February, he came to the monastery and asked for permission to show them to him. The Metropolitan produced the photographs, but the go-between objected that these were too small. At a time when the fighting was fierce and the current again cut off, Sukenik met the Syrian merchant at night on the neutral ground of the Y.M.C.A., and with a flashlight examined the manuscripts. He persuaded the man to let him take them home, and kept them for two days, copying out several columns of Isaiah, which, to the owner's annoyance, he published. (There was a second Isaiah scroll—but in a very fragmentary state—among those that Sukenik had purchased.) He was eager to buy this other lot of manuscripts, and repeatedly sent emissaries to the monastery, but the Metropolitan Samuel had already signed an agreement with the Americans of the School, according to the terms of which he allowed them to publish the texts they had photographed, if they did so within three years. The Metropolitan, in return, was to receive fifty per cent of the profits from such publication.

The Americans at the school were eager to visit the cave, but the state of war made this impossible. The Mandate was to end at midnight of May 14, when it was plain that the Jews and the Arabs would finally be left to fight it out, and for the scholars, the most pressing problem was to get out of the way in time. Before this had been arranged, the Metropolitan one day, without warning, sent a taxi, accompanied by a bodyguard, to bring Dr. Trever to the monastery. The American was apprehensive, but as soon as he arrived at St. Mark's, he was reassured to see its master standing at the top of the stairs and greeting him with a smile. "He took me into his office and handed me a folded sheet of paper. Within the fold was a piece of one of the scrolls! Instantly I recognized it as a portion of the Habakkuk scroll, for the color of the leather on which it was written, the script, the size and the shape all coincided. The edges were eaten away by worms, as was the beginning of that scroll, and it looked exactly like the missing right-hand part of the first column, the absence of which had been such a disappointment to Dr. Brownlee when he was studying it. Half of a previous column was on it, also, proving that the scroll had originally had at least one more column at the beginning. . . . Needless to say, I lost little time in getting this new fragment photographed also." Dr. Trever was made even happier when "the Metropolitan informed me that Brother Butros had left that morning with all the manuscripts, to take them to a place of safety outside Palestine." This was what the Americans had recommended. They themselves got away a few days later.

The Mandate came to an end. The British simply departed. They had refused to allow their control to be transferred to any other body or to legalize a local militia. They were leaving the Jews and the Arabs already at one another's throats, and were counting on the seven Arab states arrayed against the small Jewish colony to fall upon it and destroy it or drive it out. The Arabs, under Brigadier Glubb, formerly of the British Army but now ranking as an officer of the Arab Legion, immediately began to shell the ancient Jewish quarter, which was isolated in the Old City. The monastery stood close to this and caught the fire from both sides. Brother Butros Sowmy was killed, and the monastery suffered damage which the Metropolitan estimated at £30,000. He did not, however, leave Jerusalem till the autumn, when the conflict had still not been settled. After sojourns in Transjordan and Syria, he sailed for the United States and arrived at the end of January, 1949, bringing the scrolls with him. Dr. Burrows, now back at Yale, had encouraged him to come to this country. The American School had arranged to publish the text of the scrolls, and the Metropolitan hoped that this would help him to sell the originals. But we must drop at this point his adventures with these, for here a new chapter begins.

# II

# THE ESSENE ORDER

Père Roland de Vaux of the École Biblique and Mr. G. Lankester Harding of the Department of Antiquities, now Jordanian, not Transjordanian, lost no time, when the war was over and the time of year was favorable—February, 1949—in visiting the cave where the scrolls had been found. They worked there for nearly a month, and collected many smaller fragments and a good deal of broken pottery. This was thought to be mostly late Hellenistic, but there were also some pieces of a Roman lamp and a Roman cooking pot, and these latter gave rise to a theory—for which there was no real evidence—that they had been left in the cave by Origen, the early Church Father and editor of the Biblical texts, who fled from persecution to Palestine in the first half of the third century and who says that he found near Jericho some Biblical manuscripts in a jar. The predominantly Greek pottery seemed to show that the manuscripts could not have been written later than the first Christian century. From the shards of the jars they calculated that the cave must once have contained a collection of at least two hundred scrolls.

When the word got around to the Bedouins that the manuscripts from the caves were valuable, they began to look in other caves, and in the latter part of 1951 they turned up at the École Biblique with handfuls of crumbled papyrus and parchment that were obviously the

remnants of similar scrolls. De Vaux at once called up
Harding and told him that they must move to take over
the search. They descended on the Dead Sea (January
21, 1952), with the Bethlehem Chief of Police and two
soldiers from the Arab Legion, and were guided by the
Bedouins to a group of four caves, about fifteen miles
south of the original cave, very high in the steep cliffs.
Other Bedouins, upon their arrival, came swarming out of
these holes like chipmunks. They sent a few to jail with
light sentences, and the Department of Antiquities hired
the rest to carry on the search. Harding and de Vaux now
officially took over the exploration of all this region. There
were four of these caves—very large ones, about a hundred and fifty feet long and fifteen feet high and wide.
They had been lived in at various periods. The earliest
traces of human habitation went back to the fourth mil-
lennium before the Christian era. There were objects
from the Bronze Age and the Iron Age; and many relics
from the Roman period, a whole equipment for living:
lamps, picks, javelin points, nails, needles, combs, buttons,
spoons, bowls and plates made of wood, a chisel, a scythe
and a trowel. There were also twenty Roman coins dating
from Nero to Hadrian. Nine of these belonged to the
years—132-135 A.D.—of the Second Revolt of the Jews
against the domination of the Romans. There were many
fragments of manuscripts and potsherds that had been
used for writing: Greek, Latin, Hebrew and Aramaic.
There were several letters in Hebrew—one of them most
amazing: a note written evidently in the midst of the war
by the Jewish leader Bar-Kochba, in which he bawls out
one of his captains. He speaks of "the Galileans," but
without making it plain whom he means or what sort of
role they are playing. (If these Galileans are Christians,
we know that they had refused to support Bar-Kochba,
in loyalty to Jesus, who had said, "My kingdom is not of

this world.") Père de Vaux, from all this, has concluded
that the cave was a stronghold of the Jewish resistance,
and was eventually raided by the Romans. In its debris
were found shreds of Torah scrolls, which look as if the
enemy had torn these scrolls up.

Among the fragments of manuscript from these and
other caves in the South, at least one important document
has already come to light. We know that the Jews of the
second century, at the time when Christianity was having
its first great success, became very much annoyed by the
Christian exploitation of the Septuagint for the purpose
of showing, by quotations from it, that the advent of Jesus
as Messiah had been predicted by the Prophets, and that
they, the Jews, had a version designed to discredit this interpretation by bringing the Greek text, as they claimed,
closer to the meaning of the official Hebrew. This problem is discussed at length in one of the writings of Justin
Martyr, the second-century Christian convert and apol-
ogist—a dialogue which is supposed to take place between
Justin and the Rabbi Trypho. Justin quotes several passages from this Jewish translation and declares that, compared to the Septuagint, they are obviously flat and inadequate. No such Jewish translation has hitherto been
known; but, by a great piece of luck for scholars, some
fragments of precisely these passages from the Prophets
that Justin cited to Trypho have turned up among those
found in these caves. This discovery was made by Père
D. Barthélemy of the École Biblique in Jerusalem, who
has tracked down also in other texts quotations from a
Greek translation that does not correspond with the Septuagint and that is evidently from a Hebrew hand.

But these documents—though, of course, of great interest—are not relevant to our main subject and have apparently no connection with the discoveries of Qumrân (as

the Arabs called the wadi or ravine near which the first scrolls were found). These were now to be sensationally added to. The French monk and the English official had hardly finished with these other caves when new fragments of manuscripts were brought them from a cave near the first one explored. They set out now to examine systematically all the caves in the Qumrân neighborhood. They entered two hundred and sixty-seven, and in thirty-seven of them found pottery and other relics of human occupancy. In twenty-five of these, the pottery was identical with the jars from the original cave. Several of the caves contained scrolls, which, unprotected by jars, were in a state of disintegration, often buried under layers of dirt. The fragments of these collected ran into the tens of thousands. It was becoming more and more apparent that a library had been hidden here—a library which seems to have included almost all the books of the Bible, a number of apocryphal works and the literature of an early religious sect. The Essene sect had been thought of—for reasons I shall presently explain—as soon as the first scrolls were read. Mr. Harding and Père de Vaux had already, before finding these new manuscripts, had the notion of investigating a hitherto neglected old ruin not far from the original cave, and, in November and December of 1951, had started digging it out. This ruin was buried on the shore between the cliffs and the sea, a little to the south of the cave, with only a bit of stone wall protruding above the ground. It has been known to the Arabs as the Khirbet Qumrân (*Khirbet* meaning *ruin*). A French traveller in 1851 believed it to be a remnant of the ruins of the Biblical Gomorrah. Later archaeologists have thought it a small Roman fort. It had never, up to that time, attracted very much attention; but it has been now almost completely excavated by Mr. Harding and Père de

Vaux. What has been made to emerge is astounding: a very ancient stone building, containing from twenty to thirty rooms and thirteen cisterns for water, and with much of its equipment intact. On one side of it, between it and the sea, lies a cemetery with more than a thousand graves. The building has the look of a monastery, and a convergence of evidence seems not merely to suggest but almost beyond question to establish that it was one of the habitations—if not, actually, the headquarters—of what has previously been known as the Essene sect. But before we describe it further, we must explain who the Essenes were.

A good deal has already been known about this sect from three writers of the first century A.D.: Pliny the Elder, Josephus and Philo. Pliny's description is brief but very important in the present connection, for it locates the Essene community exactly where this building and the library were found. "On the western shore of the Dead Sea, the Essenes have withdrawn to a sufficient distance to avoid its noxious effects—a solitary people, and extraordinary beyond all others in the whole world, who live without women and have renounced all commerce with Venus, and also without money, having the palms for their only companions. They constantly renew themselves from the steady stream of refugees that resort to them in large numbers, men who, weary of life, have been driven by the vicissitudes of fortune to adopt their manner of living. Thus through thousands of centuries, incredible though it seems, a people has perpetuated itself in which no one is ever born. So useful for recruiting their number is the disgust of other men with life. Below them the town of Engadda [En-Gedi] once stood—in its palm groves and general fertility second only to Jerusalem, but now a heap of ashes like it. Beyond this is Masada, a fortress on a rock, and itself not far from the Dead Sea. To this point Judea extends."*

This seems definitely to identify the monastery; but it is all that Pliny tells us. He is summarily and tersely Roman; his point of view is alien and rather ironic. But Philo and Josephus, both Jews, have a good deal more interest in this Jewish order. The thousands of centuries with which Pliny credits it must either refer to the future or simply be due to his vagueness. It seems probable, from

---

* Since the above was written, a French scholar, Charles Burchard of Göttingen, has called attention, in the *Revue Biblique* of July 1967, to another description of the Essenes in the *Collectanea Rerum Memorabilium* of C. Julius Solinus, who lived probably in the third A.D. century. This description appears at first to be borrowed, like so much of Solinus, from Pliny, but there are interesting divergences which seem to show that they must both have been derived from the same Greek source in distinctly different versions. There is a curious passage in Solinus which explains—a feature of the Essene community which is not mentioned by other writers—that only those who are chaste and innocent can be admitted to the order, because anyone else, "though he may try with all his might to obtain an entrance, is divinely rejected, *divinitus submovetur.*" Exactly what *divinitus* (divinely) means it is impossible to tell. Mr. Burchard comes to the conclusion that this echoes some local legend that the habitat of the Essenes itself, through some mysterious agency, repulses unsuitable applicants. Dr. W. F. Albright, in a paper on *The Archaeology and Identity of the Sect,* in *The Scrolls and Christianity,* Society for the Propagation of Christian Knowledge, regards as "absurd" a Loeb Library translation of Pliny which is based, like the one I have given above, on the assumption that *"ab occidente litora Esseni fugiunt usque qua nocent"* means that they went as far from the shore as possible in order to get away from the noxious effects of the waters of the Dead Sea. He believes the text defective, as it certainly seems to be, and proposes emending it to read, *"Ab occidentali litore Esseni fugiunt usque adhuc ea quae nocent,* On the western shore the Essenes have up to the present got away from those things that are injurious"—that is, the ills of society. He says that "there is nothing about the Dead Sea which is harmful to the people who live on its shores. Quite to the contrary, the northwestern shore was lined with winter resorts before 1948." 1969.

Josephus' acccount, that the Essenes had had their rise in
the middle of the previous century. For Philo, the Alexandrian scholar, who had something himself of the monastic temperament, the Essenes supplied an example to illus-
trate the thesis of his *Treatise to Prove that Every Good
Man Is Also Free*. In this and in another passage, quoted
by the historian Eusebius, he gives us accounts of the
manners of the Essenes that are appropriate to his purpose
and congenial to his own personality. But since Philo's
accounts are partly duplicated by the fuller account in
Josephus, it is easier to base one's description on this,
noting Philo's divergences from it and his amplifications
of Josephus' points. An historian and man of affairs, Josephus portrays the Essenes somewhat more realistically
than Philo; and since he was once a member of the order
himself, his account of it must stand as authoritative.
During his lifetime, Josephus tells us, the three principal
sects of the Jews have been the Pharisees, the Sadducees
and the Essenes. He himself, by the age of nineteen, had,
he says, been through all three of them, and had also
spent three years in the desert, mortifying his flesh, with a
holy hermit named Bannus, who clothed himself only
with what grew on trees, ate only such food as grew wild,
and disciplined himself to chastity by constant cold-
water baths. From these various religious experiments,
Josephus had emerged as a Pharisee. He later took an active part in the wars of the Jews with the Romans; but the
struggle for Jewish independence was already becoming
desperate, and the drive toward asceticism, retreat from
the world, had evidently been strongly felt by him. He
deals with the Essenes at much greater length than with
either of the other sects.

The Essenes, says Josephus, are bound together more
closely than these other sects: they constitute, in fact, a
brotherhood, which has something in common with the

Pythagoreans. They have quite renounced pleasure, identifying it with vice, and school themselves in temperance and self-control. "Marriage they disdain, but they adopt other men's children, while yet pliable and docile, accepting them as their kin and molding them in accordance with their own principles." (Philo differs from this: he says that there are no youths or children among them, that only the mature are admitted.) "They do not, indeed," Josephus continues, "on principle, condemn wedlock—the propagation thereby of the race, but they wish to protect themselves against women's wantonness, being persuaded that none of the sex keeps her plighted troth to one man." This is supplemented by Philo, who says that the Essenes repudiate marriage, "because they clearly discern it to be the sole or the principal danger to the maintenance of the communal life, as well as because they particularly practice continence. For no Essene takes a wife, because a wife is a selfish creature excessively jealous and an adept at beguiling the morals of her husband and seducing him by her continued impostures. For by the fawning talk which she practises and the other ways in which she plays her part like an actress on the stage she first ensnares the sight and hearing and then, when these victims have, as it were, been duped, she cajoles the sovereign mind. And if children come, filled with the spirit of arrogance and bold speaking, she gives utterance with more audacious hardihood to things which before she hinted covertly and under disguise, and casting off all shame she compels her husband to commit actions which are hostile to the life of fellowship. For he who is either fast bound in the love-lures of his wife, or under the stress of nature makes his children his first care, ceases to be the same to others and unconsciously has become a different man and has passed from freedom into slavery." The Essenes have renounced riches, also: they eat only the simplest fare, and they wear their clothes and their shoes to shreds before they will provide themselves with new ones.

Philo says that there are more than four thousand Essenes; Josephus that there are about four thousand (a large number for Palestine in those days). "They occupy no one city," says Josephus, "but settle in large numbers in every town." Philo, too, describes them as "dwelling in many towns of Judea," but says that they avoid the large cities and prefer to "live in villages." The great point that is made by both is that the Essenes have organized communities which are grouped around a center, where they come together for meals and to which they are always responsible. They hold all their goods in common. New members must surrender their property to the order, and all must contribute to it their earnings. In return, they are provided with everything they need. A steward or manager does all the buying and handles all the money. Keeping anything back is severely punished. Even the clothing is common property. They are supplied, says Philo, with thick cloaks for winter and light mantles for summer. There is no buying or selling among them, and anyone can take anything for nothing from his "brother"; but they cannot give presents to relatives except with the permission of their superiors. When they travel, they carry nothing along with them, except arms to defend themselves against bandits, for an Essene will be cordially received by any Essene community. There is, in fact, in every town where the Essenes have established a community, a member of the sect appointed to welcome arrivals from elsewhere and to see that they are taken care of. The sick are supported, if they cannot work; the old people are cared for, says Philo, even if they are childless, as if they had many children. Most of them, says Josephus, live to be over a hundred.

They cultivate the earth or devote themselves to peaceful arts (Philo). They are farmers, shepherds, cowherds, bee-keepers, artisans and craftsmen. They will not make instruments of war. They will not engage in commerce; they know nothing of navigation. There are among them no slaves and no masters. They maintain a fraternal equality, believing that human brotherhood is the natural relationship of men, which has only been destroyed in society by the competition of the covetous. They read much in the writings of the ancients, says Josephus, (hence, no doubt, the many scrolls in the caves); yet (Philo) they do not cultivate the logical side of philosophy, do not expend "any superfluous care on examining Greek terms," but occupy themselves only with the moral side. They study medicinal roots and the properties of stones (these were probably charms); they are inspired in foretelling the future (several instances are given of this). They pay scrupulous attention to cleanliness and are always washing themselves. Their habits of defecation, for the Middle East of those days, were remarkably sanitary. They considered it defiling to rub oil on themselves—which must have exposed them painfully to the brutalities of the Mediterranean sun. They were compelled to keep a dry skin, and they always dressed in white. "In their costume and deportment," says Josephus, "they resemble children under rigorous discipline."

Their whole day is subjected to this discipline. They do not converse before the rising of the sun; they only recite traditional prayers, in which they entreat the sun to show himself. After this, they go out to their work, at which they continue till the fifth hour (about 11 o'clock). They pay no attention to weather, says Philo, and never use it as an excuse for not working; and they return from their work rejoicing, as if from an athletic contest. They then wash themselves with cold water, put on their linen raiment, and proceed to their refectory as if to a shrine. Here they sit down in silence, and are served by the baker with loaves, and by the cook with a plate of a single course. The presiding priest says grace and prays again at the end of the meal, after which they lay aside their linen clothes, treating them as holy vestments, and go back to their work in the fields or shops. At evening, they dine again, with any guests who may happen to be with them. No chatter or uproar: they speak in turn. "To persons from the outside," Josephus says, "the silence of those within gives the impression of some awful mystery." Silence for the Essenes is very important. When ten are sitting together (a Jewish quorum), one of them will refrain from speaking if the other nine desire to be silent. They are stricter in observance of the Sabbath than any of the other sects; but they do not, like them, offer animal sacrifices: they do not believe in this practice, asserting they have purer lustrations of their own.* The Essenes are, in consequence, excluded from the court of the Temple in Jerusalem, and apparently they never go near this center of Jewish worship. In doctrine—whereas the Sadducees do not believe in immortality and think the soul dies with the body—the Essenes regard the body as corruptible but hold that the soul is imperishable. Emanating from the finest ether but dragged down by a natural spell, the spirit becomes caught in the prison of the body; but, once set at liberty by death, it rejoices and is borne aloft. Like the Greeks, the Essenes believe that the more vir-

* There have, however, been found jars of animal bones, buried inside the community enclosure—which seems to indicate that the animals had been eaten at sacred feasts. Mr. Frank Moore Cross, Jr., suggests that, though the Essenes did not sacrifice in the Temple, they may have carried on a private sacrificial cult. The War Scroll, also, speaks of burnt offerings. But Professor Yadin points out that everything in that scroll refers to what is to happen in "the Time to Come." 1969.

tuous souls have reserved for them, somewhere beyond
the sea, a final place of retirement, where there is no snow
or rain or heat, and which is always refreshed by a gentle
breeze, while the baser ones will be committed to a murky
and turbulent dungeon, where they will suffer eternal
torment.

Josephus and Philo are agreed in emphasizing the general respect in which the Essenes are held. They surpass,
the former declares, both the Greeks and the barbarians
in virtue, and they have succeeded for many years in
keeping up their high level of discipline. Both writers
bring home to us the horror of the world from which the
Essenes have withdrawn but which, morally, they have
been able to stand up to. The Jews had had the Seleucid
king Antiochus Epiphanes (inheritor of the Near Eastern section of the empire of Alexander the Great) setting up his statue of Zeus, "the abomination of desolation," to be worshipped by them in their Temple. They
had successfully, under the Maccabees, revolted against
the Seleucid tyranny—but only, before very long, to see
their own rulers, among them the Herods, become as corrupt and as cruel as the foreigners they had displaced, and
they had later, in 70 A.D., been defeated by the armies of
the Roman Titus, who, like those of Nebuchadnezzar,
had destroyed their Temple. "Though at different times,"
says Philo, "a great number of potentates of every variety
of disposition and character have occupied their country;
some of whom have endeavored in cruelty to surpass even
ferocious wild beasts, leaving no sort of inhumanity un-
practised, and have never ceased to murder their subjects
in whole troops, and have even torn them to pieces while
living, like cooks cutting them limb from limb—till they
themselves, being overtaken by the vengeance of divine
justice, have at last experienced the same miseries in their
turn; others again, having converted their barbarous

frenzy into another kind of wickedness, practising an ineffable degree of savagery, talking with the people quietly, but, through the hypocrisy of a more gentle voice, betraying the ferocity of their real disposition, fawning upon their victims like treacherous dogs, and becoming for them the causes of irremediable miseries, have left in all their cities monuments of their impiety and hatred of all mankind, in the never to be forgotten sufferings endured by those they oppressed; and yet no one, not even of those immoderately cruel tyrants, nor of the more treacherous and hypocritical oppressors, was ever able to bring any real accusation against the multitude of those called Essenes or Holy Ones. But everyone, being subdued by the virtue of these men, looked up to them as free by nature, and not subject to the frown of any human being, and have celebrated their manner of messing together and their fellowship with one another—their mutual good faith is beyond description—which constitutes sufficient proof of a perfect and supremely happy life." Josephus, also, speaks of this fortitude and of the admiration it compels: "They make light of danger, and triumph over pain by their resolute will; death, if it comes with honor, they consider better than immortality. The war with the Romans tried their souls through and through by every variety of test. Racked and twisted, broken and burnt, and made to pass through every instrument of torture, in order to induce them to blaspheme their Lawgiver or to eat some forbidden thing, they refused to yield to either demand, nor ever once did they cringe to their persecutors or ever shed a tear. Smiling in their agonies and mildly deriding their tormentors, they cheerfully resigned their souls, confident that they would receive them back again." Except for what Josephus calls the "terrible oaths" exacted from an initiate joining the order, they refuse to swear any oath, saying that "one who is not believed without an appeal to God stands condemned already"; and "any word of theirs," says Josephus, "had more force than an oath." He tells us that Herod the Great excused the members of the sect from taking an oath of loyalty; but makes it clear that this was due to the recollection that one of them, happening to see him in the street at a time when his political position was dubious, had "slapped him on the backside" and predicted that he would one day be king. This Essene had also predicted that Herod would later go bad; but the non-Jewish Herod, who was hated by the Jews, could afford, by the time he was reigning, to forget the unfavorable part of the prophecy and to show himself magnanimous by indulging the Essenes.

In reading these contemporary accounts of the Essenes, we are struck by two kinds of resemblances. For one thing, the modern traveller is often reminded of the Zionist and Israeli collective farms that are known as *kvutzot* and *kibbutzim*. Here the property is held in common, as that of the Essenes was; the purchasing is done by a manager or a management. The members of these communities have in some cases even shared their wardrobe, putting on any clothes that would fit them, as the Essenes did their winter and summer cloaks. Like the Essenes, they bring up adopted children—in the case of the Israeli communities, orphans and refugees. They have had to face tyrants as terrible as any that the Essenes fled from, and it has given them the same sort of impulse toward natural brotherhood that inspired the monasteries of the Essenes.

But the thing that we are immediately struck by is the resemblance of the Essenes to the Christians. You have the doctrine of human brotherhood; you have the practice of ritual washing, of which baptism was a prominent feature; you have communism, which the early Christians practiced among themselves (Acts 2.44-45: "And all who believed were together, and had all things common; and they sold their possessions and goods, and distributed them to all, as any had need"). You have phrases that bring Christian echoes. One finds Philo, for example, saying that the Essenes did not "store up treasures of silver and gold," nor "acquire vast sections of the earth out of a desire for ample revenues," and one remembers Matthew 6: "Lay not up for yourself treasures on earth," etc. When Josephus tells us that the Essenes held the body to be corruptible, but the soul immortal and imperishable, we think of First Corinthians 15.53: "For this corruptible must put on incorruption, and this mortal must put on immortality." You have the courage to defy the Romans, the "making light of danger" and the "triumph over pain." And—what is very important—you have the fact, which both Philo and Josephus make clear, that the Essenes, though of Jewish birth, have not come together on a basis of race, "for one does not speak of race when it is a question of voluntary acts." The Essenes have been brought together by their "zeal for virtue and by the passion of their love for mankind" (Philo). It seems obvious that the monastic tradition of the Christians must ultimately have derived from the Essenes, and there has always been a theory that Jesus was originally an Essene. This problem we must leave till later, when we discuss the unexpected revelations in connection with the origins of Christianity that have resulted from the Dead Sea scrolls. We should also remark, at this stage, that there were elements in Essenism that sound as if they had come from Persia or Babylonia: the non-Jewish rite of baptism and the early morning practice of sun-worship.

Now, the manuscript pieced out by Trever from two of the Metropolitan's scrolls turned out to be the Manual of Discipline of an early monastic order, and a compari-

son of this new document with the descriptions of the
Essenes quoted above has left very little doubt as to what
this order was. If the passage from Pliny identifies the
monastery, the detailed account by Josephus identifies the
Manual of Discipline, which was found in the cave near
the monastery. Josephus must have studied this handbook,
or one very much like it. His summary of Essene procedure tallies almost exactly with the Manual. We learn
from both of these documents, for example, that the Essene principle of human brotherhood was combined with
a stringent hierarchy. The candidate for membership, Josephus tells us, is not admitted the first year. He is given
his white clothing, his loin cloth and a small mattock for
digging his own latrines. "He is brought into closer touch
with the rule and is allowed to share the purer kind of
holy water, but is not yet received into the meetings of
the community." He has then to be tested for two years
more, and if he qualifies at the end of that period, he is
allowed to share the common food, but he must first swear
"terrible oaths—first that he will practice piety toward the
Deity, next that he will observe justice toward men: that
he will wrong none, whether of his own mind or under
another's orders; that he will forever hate the unjust and
fight the battle of the just; that he will forever keep faith
with all men, especially with the powers that be, since no
ruler attains his office save by the will of God; that, should
he himself bear rule, he will never abuse his authority,
nor, by his dress or by any other external mark of rank,
allow himself to outshine his subjects; to be forever a lover
of truth and to expose liars; to keep his hands from steal-
ing and his soul pure from unholy gain; to conceal nothing from the members of the sect and to report none of
their secrets to others, even though tortured to death. He
swears, moreover, to transmit their rules exactly as he himself received them; to abstain from robbery; and in like

manner carefully to preserve the books of the sect and the names of the angels. Such are the oaths by which they secure their proselytes." The humility imposed on the Essene, the commitment not to "abuse his authority" or to display "outward marks of rank" may remind us of the "Let not yourselves be called masters, for Christ is your only master" of Matthew 23.10. Yet with the Essenes the grades of seniority were maintained in the strictest fashion at the community meals and elsewhere. "So far," says Josephus, "are the junior members inferior to the senior that a senior, if but touched by a junior, must take a bath, as if after contact with an alien."

The injunction to keep faith with the powers that be may remind us of the "Render therefore unto Caesar the things that are Caesar's; and unto God the things that are God's" of Matthew 22.21. So inevitably does it seem to be true that definitive political defeat, the disappointment of practical hopes, gives rise to an intensive development of the more unworldly kind of religion. An obvious recent example is the efflorescence of mysticism in Russia after the failure of the Revolution of 1905. We are today going through something similar, at a time when disillusion with socialism, following close on a loss of confidence in the traditional competitive system, has been driving the bewildered idealists to look for comfort in the various churches. Now, the Jews, in the days of the Essenes, had succeeded in reviving their state under the leadership of the Maccabees, but had later taken a terrible beating at the hands of the more organized and "modern" Romans. The Essenes, who, though they possessed certain doctrines and followed certain practices of their own, were still basically Judaistic, had to assume, like the Old Testament prophets, that their miseries had been willed by God. The Jesus of the Christian Gospels seems to belong to a later stage, when God has been dissociated from Caesar; but once this break has been made, the Christian is in some ways in a stronger position than the priests who drew up the Essene oath. The Essenes are smarting and sullen—we find their attitude toward their enemies stated bitterly and in most un-Christian terms in the Manual and other writings; the Gospels have a heartening ring of audacity and spiritual freedom.* Yet it was also, as it now appears, the sectarians that had framed this oath who were preparing, by their precept and discipline—"to report none of their secrets, even though tortured to death"—the resounding moral triumph of the Crucifixion.

Our main interest at this point, however, is to check the Manual of Discipline with the accounts of Josephus and Philo. You find here the property held in common and entrusted to a "custodian of property" (the phrase is that of the Manual); the devotion to the Lawgiver (presumably Moses), qualified by the substitution of "a fragrant offering of righteousness and perfection" for the traditional sacrifices in the Temple; the lustrations in holy water; the insistence on self-control: one is fined for giving way to anger; the subordination, within the order, of "the lesser" to "the greater, in regard to goods and means"; the common table and the sacred repasts; the rule about speaking in turn; the prerogatives of the majority, who can even keep someone from talking if the sentiment of the company is against it; the prohibition—also mentioned by Josephus—against "spitting into the midst of the session of the many." You have the probationary period—of a year, says Josephus; the Manual does not specify exactly—at the end of which the neophyte is permitted (similar phrases are used) to "draw close" to the order; then two more years of novitiate, in the course of which he is allowed to share in the "purification" (Manual), "purer kind of holy water" (Josephus), but not yet admitted to the meetings; if he succesfully completes

* Yet see pp. 245-46, Mr. Yigael Yadin's view of this. 1969.

this novitiate, he swears the "terrible oaths" and thereafter
partakes of the common meals. You find, also, in the Manual of Discipline, a good many other details that are not in
Josephus or Philo. There is the whole code of censure and
punishment, by which the discipline of the sect was en-
forced, that is omitted from Philo's idyllic picture. This system is rigorous and drastic enough, but Josephus explains
that the Essenes were "just and scrupulously careful in
their trial of cases, never passing sentence in a court of less
than a hundred members." But the decision, once reached,
is irrevocable. Those who are expelled from the order find
themselves in a difficult situation, for the oaths they have
taken forbid them any food not prepared by the order, and
they may try to live on grass and "waste away." But the order will then sometimes take pity on them, believing they
have been punished enough, and has actually received a
good many back. "One shall not speak to his brother," says
the Manual, "in anger or in complaint . . . ; nor shall he
hate him [in the uncircumcision] of his heart—though he
shall reprove him on the very day so as not to incur guilt
because of him. Indeed, a man shall not bring accusation
against his fellow in the presence of the many who has not
been subject to [previous] reproof before witnesses." Professor Brownlee, in a note to his translation of the Manual, points out that Matthew 18.15-17 "gives us the clue
for interpreting the passage. Jesus specifies three stages for
dealing with an erring brother: (1) personal reproof; (2)
reproof before witnesses; (3) reproof before the Church."

One very important aspect of the teaching of the sect is
indicated by Josephus, without special emphasis, when
he is summarizing the oath: the new member is made to
swear "that he will forever hate the unjust and fight the
battle of the just." In the Manual we find this theme
elaborated at length in a section which describes the divi-
sion of all mankind into two antithetical groups, dom-

inated, respectively, by a spirit of Darkness and a Spirit of Light. The Children of Darkness are angrily denounced. Though it was wrong to hate a brother in the faith, or even to lose one's temper, it was a duty to loathe and to curse that alien and wicked people who were dominated by the Spirit of Darkness. We shall later, when we come to the other scrolls, return to this feature of the literature of the sect. It is enough for the present to say that the Children of Darkness were probably the Romans, at the hands of whom the Jews had suffered so much.

# III

# THE MONASTERY

THE LANDSCAPE of the Dead Sea wilderness is monotonous, subduing and dreadful. This country is completely impersonal. It is a landscape without physiognomy: no faces of gods or men, no bodies of recumbent animals, are suggested by the shapes of the hills. "Nothing but monotheism could possibly come out of this," said one of my companions, who knew Palestine. "There's not a crevice for a nymph anywhere." The already fading grass of spring—my visit was in early April—had the look of greenish mold on enormous loaves. Tawny without warmth, of a dun not enriched by shadow, these mounds also somewhat resembled—it was the only living image one could think of—the humps of the camels that grazed them, dull yellow and gawkily bending, with their dusty white calves beside them. One hillside was flecked by a herd of black goats. Here and there, all alone in the emptiness, squats motionless a Bedouin woman, who, though she seems as unperceptive as a boulder, is keeping an eye on a camel or goat; and we pass a few torn and black Bedouin shelters that might be the old tents of Abraham. A watchtower, now deserted, is still standing at a spot where, before the war, a plant run by Jews made potash, and there are ruins of a little inn that was fought over and wrecked by the Jews and Arabs, and finally plundered by Bedouins. As the road begins to drop below sea-level—at the bottom, almost thirteen hundred feet—you feel pressure increasing on your eardrums, as you do coming down in a plane.

Arriving at the Sea itself, you find two or three simple buildings, where a British officer of the Arab Legion presides over the "Dead Sea Fleet." This consists of a few small motor-boats that are kept here to patrol the frontier, since Israel begins just south of here, not far from where Pliny said Judea stopped. He has two little mongrel dogs, and he is able to invite us to tea. The Dead Sea is a dull pale blue that reminds one of the Great Salt Lake, and the hills across the water that wall it in are of yellows and purples and blues and browns so dull that such words for color are almost too vivid to refer to them. One of them is Mount Nebo, from which Moses, when he had rescued his people from Egypt and wandered for years in the wilderness, looked across at the Promised Land.

We jolt in our jeep over backbreaking rocks, where the tracks of an ancient road have lately been just made out. The all but bare ground is rusted with streaks of some reddish plant, and dabbed here and there with statice, a dreary little white everlasting. The palms that were noted by Pliny as the only companions of the Essenes must have disappeared centuries ago. The only forms of vertebrate life that we see as we drive in toward the monastery are a hawk and a crow contending for some small animal that the crow has caught but that the hawk has forced him to drop. The crow is reluctant to leave his prey, but the hawk keeps on circling, incisively and slowly, and the crow has to keep a sharp watch on him. There are scorpions and vipers here, several of the latter of which the excavators have had to kill. It recalls that "great and terrible wilderness" of which Moses speaks in Deuteronomy 8.15, with its "fiery serpents and scorpions and thirsty ground, where there was no water." There are no fish in the heavy sea, but only microscopic animalcula. The land-

scape has something, perhaps, of Greece, yet there is nothing of the exquisite spectrum of violet, mauve and blue
that is a function of the fluid Greek light. One is aware of
neither light nor darkness. It is as if one were sunk below
them; to live here seems a sort of self-burial. The visitor
from the modern world, confronted by the blank of this
region, is forced to make an effort of imagination to convince himself that anything interesting can ever have happened in it. Yet one finds oneself here in the "wilderness"
of First Samuel, where David fled from Saul at En-gedi
on "the rocks of the wild goats" and where Saul, to relieve
himself, entered one of the caves in which David and his
men were already hidden, yet in which David spared Saul's
life; where, later, the word of God came to John the Baptist; and where, not far to the north, at the point where the
Jordan flows into the Dead Sea, is the place to which
Jesus came in order to be baptized by John. This arid de-
pression in the earth is also that wilderness where Jesus is
supposed to have fasted for forty days. On our way here,
we have passed the mountain upon which, according to
tradition, Jesus was tempted by Satan, who showed him
from it the kingdoms of the world. Further south is the
mesa of Masada, where Herod the Great built a palace in
order to put himself beyond danger and where a thousand
Jews fled from the Romans and, when the Roman engineers had built a ramp to the top, chose to cut their own
throats rather than fall into Roman hands; on the equally
desolate opposite shore are the ruins of another Herodian
palace, Machaerus, the stronghold described by Josephus,
where John the Baptist was imprisoned and beheaded by
the younger Herod. This fortress was built on a very high
rock with deep ravines on all sides, and enclosed by a great
wall that had hundred-foot towers at the corners. Near it
were many springs, some bitter and some sweet, of a variety of temperatures, including two that flowed from two

rocks like breasts, one hot and the other cold; and inside
the magnificent palace, there was said to have grown an
enormous plant that was the colour of flame by day and
at twilight was seen to shine—a plant which eluded the
grasp of persons who tried to pluck it and poisoned them
if they succeeded, which could only be paralyzed by pour-
ing on it the urine or the menstrual fluid of a woman.
This plant had the valuable property of expelling the
devils from people possessed; but the only safe way to get
hold of it was to first have it pulled up by the roots. To
accomplish this, one dug away the earth and tied a dog to
these roots; the dog's master would then go away, and the
dog would run after him and jerk up the plant. As a result of this operation, the dog would at once fall dead, but
it would now become possible to handle the plant. When
Judea fell finally to Titus, Machaerus was all but the last
fortress taken: the Romans caught an insubmissive youth
called Eleazar and scourged him in sight of the citadel, then
erected a cross in plain view and threatened to crucify him.
This caused the Jews to surrender, and the garrison, as
promised, were allowed to go free; but the Romans made a
point of murdering, at the foot of the cliff, the seventeen
hundred men in the town, and enslaved their women and
children. And across the lake from Machaerus, to the
place to which our jeep has now brought us, the Essenes
once resorted to worship God and to save their souls from
these infamies; to turn away from the Way of Darkness
and follow the Way of Light.

Their monastery, built crudely of gray blocks of stone,
still stands, as was noted by Pliny, some distance away
from the shore. The cliff rises steep behind it, and one
catches sight, here and there, of the dark cracks of natural
caves such as the one in which the scrolls were found.
Between the Dead Sea and the monastery spreads the
cemetery of a thousand graves. Père de Vaux has opened

nineteen of these, and they are all more or less the same.
The skeletons lie on their backs, with their heads in the
direction of the south, and their hands crossed on the
pelvis or stretched straight along the sides. What is singular about these graves is that there is almost nothing in
them but bones. Only one of those opened contained a
coffin. It is unusual to find ancient graves without some
sort of funeral objects: ornaments or weapons or recepta-
cles for food, signs of rank or distinction or equipment for
the journey to the other world. The absence of such objects in these graves would seem to be perfectly appropriate to the reported austerity of the Essenes, but it makes
them rather uninteresting to excavate. There have, however, been found in them, among the fragments of jars
that seem to have got there accidentally, a few that belong
to a type which has not hitherto been known except for
a single specimen. This specimen, dug up from the citadel
of Jerusalem, has been dated in the first B.C. century, before the constructions of Herod the Great. Père de Vaux
has now ceased to explore the graves, but he has pretty
well established one important point. The bones are very
fragile and were sometimes found crushed, but a careful
examination shows that one of the skeletons is certainly
a woman's, and that two or three others may be. To have
women connected with the order at all was, in general, as
we have seen, contrary to the practice of the Essenes; but
Josephus—in a postscript to his main account—explains
that one branch of the sect does allow its members to
marry: "They think that those who decline to marry cut
off their chief function of life, the propagation of the race,
and, what is more, that, were all to adopt the same view,
the whole race would very quickly die out. They give their
wives, however, a three years' probation." Pliny, it will be
remembered, says specifically of this community that they

did not admit women; but, in this case, his information may have been out of date or inaccurate.*

Before going on to the monastery itself, I must give some account of Père Roland de Vaux, who does not in the least resemble any of the conventional conceptions of a typical French priest. It may be that the French character is today to be seen at its best, not in the literary men, the politicians and the antiquated generals about whom we mostly hear, but in persons who have been lucky enough not to share in the decay of France, who have had some overmastering interest that kept them out of the country or sustained them through the years of demoralization. One felt, in reading *The Silent World*, by the deep-sea diver Cousteau that here, rather unexpectedly, was to be seen something of true French greatness: good sense combined with daring, the capacity under all conditions—in this case, the resistance to inhuman pressures, breathing from a tank at the bottom of the sea—for realistic and accurate observation, for exercising a cool intelligence. Such figures, it seems to me, are more satisfactory than most of the people one reads about in, say, André Gide's journal, or even than Gide himself. I had of Père de Vaux, in his different department, an impression somewhat similar to that made by his countryman Cousteau: of intellect, expertness, fortitude, tenacity, an element of daring and—what now seems so rare in France—effectiveness. He has brown eyes of the high powered headlight kind that seem magnified by his glasses' thick lenses, and long white regular teeth that are always dis-

* Père de Vaux, in *L'Archéologie et les Manuscrits de la Mer Morte* of 1961, says that the first female skeleton was found in a grave of an abnormal kind outside the limits of the official cemetery, and that a few further feminine skeletons and some skeletons of young children have been found in what he calls *"cimetières secondaires"* further away from the monastery. 1969.

played in talking. His sharp nose is of a salience and aquilinity that strongly suggest the Old Testament, as does his coarse bristling brown beard. With his belted white-flannel Dominican robe, the hood of which falls back on his shoulders and at the belt of which hang his beads, he wears a beret, heavy shoes and what look like substantial blue golf stockings. He tells stories extremely well, continually smokes cigarettes and altogether has style, even dash. In the archaeological world, there persists a curious legend that, before becoming a Dominican, Père de Vaux was an actor in the Comédie Française. This is evidently a gratuitous inference—drawn from his eloquence as a speaker and from something that suggests a stage presence—on the part of the scholars of the American School, who do not perhaps appreciate how much time and work it takes to qualify as an actor at the Comédie. The story has, in any case, been denied, with amazement, by de Vaux himself, who explains that his education has been "wholly classical and clerical." I did not find him theatrical: he seemed to me quite unselfconscious, and intent on his work with a gusto that almost amounts to voracity. I was struck by his vigor one day when I happened to see him striding out of the Tenebræ service at the Church of the Holy Sepulcher, quickly outdistancing the rest of the crowd—in what I suppose was a dark robe of ceremony, his face burnt a brown brick-red, his boarlike nostrils and beard pressing on to their next destination. On the site of his excavations, among the ruins and rocks, he climbs on short legs like a goat. He evidently loves the rough side of it; discards his clerical costume and puts on working clothes. He has camped out on the "dig" for days. Once they shot a hyena, he tells us. They ate it: it was "very good," something like wild boar. They hung it a long time, then boiled it, spicing it well. I could imagine him proceeding intrepidly along the almost razorback top of a nar-

row and wall-like formation, in the steep prow of which
is a cave where one of the biggest caches of scrolls was
found. This cave had been spotted by a Bedouin when a
partridge he had been hunting flew into it. It is situated
high in the rock, and at first they had used ropes to climb
into it; but they later made a hole in the top of the ridge
and thus opened another entrance which made possible
an approach from the top. This looked almost like tight-
rope walking, but Père de Vaux said that it had not taken
him long to come to feel as much at ease with it as if it
had been merely a question of going up and down stairs.

He was delighted to take people there, but the very idea
made me giddy. It even made me giddy to climb with him
to the top of the monastery's highest wall—fifteen feet
above the ground—and to perch there, clinging to the
stones, while Père de Vaux expounded the building to us.
He was giving us a bird's-eye view. The main structure
presents a large rectangle, ninety-eight by a hundred and
twenty feet, made of rudely cut blocks of stone joined
with earthen mortar. There are windows, and the walls
inside are plastered. The floor has been paved with peb-
bles. Layers of ashes seem to show that the roofing, probably made out of the Dead Sea reeds, had eventually been
burned, and the empty mold left by the trunk of a palm
suggests that it was used as a beam or for some kind of
central support. In the northwestern angle stood a two-
story tower, evidently used for defence, the basement of
which was a storehouse. Inside the monastery proper,
there are a kitchen which has been identified by the oven
and the hole in the wall for a flue; and what was presumably the refectory of the sacred repasts, close to which
were found neatly stacked about a thousand bowls and
jars. Another chamber, seventy-two feet long, has the
look of an assembly room, with a platform of stone at one
end that may perhaps have served as a pulpit from which

the sacred books were read. A room with tables and benches constructed of plaster and brick was evidently a *scriptorium*, where the scrolls were copied out. Three ink-wells were also found here—one of bronze, which has turned green, and two of terra cotta, turned black—in which there is still some dried ink. The brotherhood presumably made their pens from the reeds that grew by the lake-shore. There is a pottery, with a kind of round nest of stones, which may have held the potter's wheel; and a mill for grinding grain, of which the two parts, for some reason not known, turned up in different rooms. Lying about in various places were nails, locks and keys, hoes, scythes and pruning knives. There was a jar which resembles exactly the jars in which the first lot of scrolls were preserved, as both resemble the fragments found in 1952 in the newly discovered caverns; and there are lamps which match those in the caves.

Among the most striking features of the monastery are the six large cisterns, with steps leading down into them, upon which the inmates depended for water. Into these cisterns they evidently canalized the rains that descended by a trough from the hills and of which the supply was undoubtedly scant. Père de Vaux says that only twice in all the months of the three years he has worked here has he seen any water come down from these hills. The Essenes must have had to store, in the relatively rainy season, all their water for the rest of the year. And they had, also on the surface level, seven smaller cisterns—of which some of the piping can still be seen—which must have been used for the "lustrations" and the baptisms of which so much is said in the literature of the sect (seven, for the Jews, was a mystical number). There are even two little cupped hollows in the room where the scrolls were copied, which must have been basins for washing in connection with this holy work. Another basin is probably a cesspool.

Unaccountably, one finds here and there the traces of some more pretentious building: square stones and sections of column that must once have been the parts of a portico or colonnade, and two queerly placed bases of columns set close together in the ground, as if they had been stands for something. Scattered about the building were about four hundred coins. No coins have been found in the Qumrân caves; and this perfectly fits in with what we are told by Philo and Josephus: that the finances of the Essene brotherhood were entirely handled by a manager. De Vaux has concluded that the members of the community lived in the near-by caves, and also in huts or tents— since pottery and large forked poles have been found stuck away in crevices or sheltered by overhanging rocks in a way which would seem to indicate that they had been concealed or stored by people who were living outside the caves. The building would have been their center, to which they would have been fully admitted only after they had completed their probation.

To trace the conclusions to which Père de Vaux has been led by the evidence supplied at this site and by the known facts of history enables one to feel some of the beauty and experience some of the excitement of the methods of modern archaeology, which have now been developed so far past the stage when the excavator plundered the "dig" for objects of conspicuous interest, leaving the various layers—which might represent whole cities, whole periods—in chaos. The procedures in use at present aim at something like scientific accuracy, and record every stratum successively before digging on to the next. From the pottery, the coins and the stonework, and from various other indications, Père de Vaux and the men working with him have arrived at the following chronology of the history of the Qumrân building. There have been found, first of all, some remnants of a very ancient Israelite wall,

which de Vaux dates about 700 B.C., and which he believes to have had no connection with the later develop-
ments of the site. The later construction, he thinks, was
begun in the late second century B.C. The first close sequence of coins commences with Antiochus VII in 136
B.C. and runs through the Hasmonean period to 37 B.C.—
that is, it covers the period of Jewish independence and
extends to the accession of Herod the Great. The next
group begins with the reign of his son, Herod Archelaus
(4 B.C.-6 A.D.), and extends to 68 A.D. There would seem
to have been an interval, then, when the building was left
unoccupied. (Two coins from this interval between the
two sequences may be easily accounted for by their happening to have been still in circulation when the building
was eventually reoccupied.) Another big gap occurs between 68 and 132 A.D., but there are thirteen coins that
belong to the period of Bar-Kochba's final revolt against
the Romans in 132-135, and all of these later coins were
found on the same level of soil.

In view of the fact that there are many coins from the
reigns of the late Jewish kings, John Hyrcanus and Alexander Jannaeus, Père de Vaux thinks it probable that the
monastery was built in the reign of the former (136-106
B.C.) and occupied during that of the latter (104-78 B.C.).
The whole period of the occupancy of the Essenes would
have extended from the end of the second century B.C.
up to the year 68 A.D. But how to explain the hiatus between 37 and 4 B.C.? Certain signs seem to show that the
monastery was damaged at some point by an earthquake.
There is a fissure that runs all through the steps to one
of the big cisterns and which can be traced in the rest of
the building; the tower has been reinforced with stones
that are banked about the base; and there is a room with
a propped-up wall that seems to have been closed and condemned. Now, the date of this upheaval would seem to be

determined, again by the invaluable Josephus, who tells us that in the seventh year of the reign of Herod the Great, not long before the Battle of Actium—which would put it in the spring of 31—Judea was shaken by an earthquake, in which thirty thousand people were killed. The building would not have been reoccupied—as the coins of Archelaus show—till somewhere near the beginning of the Christian era. But why did the community wait thirty years before moving back into the monastery? De Vaux has suggested that there is documentary evidence which may throw some light on this problem, and this I shall explain in a moment, when we arrive at the document in question. It may be noted, in the meantime, that loads of debris, apparently left by the earthquake, were removed from the building and piled outside, where they are still to be recognized.

But the Romans in the end got the Essenes—either killed them or caused them to flee. In the second year of the first Jewish revolt—67-68 A.D., when the second sequence of coins ends—the building must have been destroyed. There are broken-down walls, signs of burning, and iron arrowheads lying about. After the Roman operations of 67—we return to Josephus' narrative—the Tenth Legion was encamped at Caesarea on the Mediterranean, and in June of the following year, Vespasian paid a visit to Jericho and the Dead Sea. He was curious to find out for himself whether the latter was as heavy as people said, and he had some of his men who could not swim thrown into the water with their hands tied behind them, and noted that they rose to the surface. The Romans must have remained at Qumrân at least well into the reign of Titus—sometime after 79 A.D.—as is shown by three coins stamped *Judæa Capta*. This Roman post is explained by the special facilities of the monastery site for keeping a watch on the shore from the mouth of the Jordan to Râs

Feshkha, and overlooking the whole northern half of the sea. The Romans had also to deal with the precipitous fortress of Masada, already mentioned above, not far south of the monastery. This had been captured in 66 by the Jews, who had slaughtered the Roman garrison and who succeeded in holding it till April of 73, three years after the fall of Jerusalem. There was only one point that was vulnerable, and this the Romans finally breached with a battering ram, but then found themselves confronted with a bulwark, which the occupants had just put up; this the besiegers eventually burned. Inside, they found alive only two women and five children. All the rest of this stubborn remnant of nine hundred and sixty Jews had been induced by their leader to kill themselves. He had reminded them, according to Josephus, that they had "long ago resolved never to be servants to the Romans, nor to any other than God Himself."

That the ruin at Qumrân was used again during the second Jewish revolt is indicated by the coins from that period. Ten of these coins were found in the dugout at the bottom of the tower. Whoever now occupied the building had shut off the whole southeastern end of it. "The building has changed its function," says de Vaux. "It no longer shelters the general services of an organized community. It serves only as habitation for a limited group of persons, who lodge in the little rooms, cook their bread in the oven . . . protect themselves from attacks . . . and keep a lookout in the tower." When the Romans had subdued this second revolt, the building was abandoned forever. Two Arab and three Byzantine coins that were found at the surface level must have been left by travellers who camped there. We do not know what became of the Essenes.

# IV

# THE TEACHER OF RIGHTEOUSNESS

WE DO NOT know what became of the Essenes; but we do know a good deal more now—since the discovery of the Dead Sea library—about what had been happening to them, how they lived and what they believed. It ought to be said at this point that the evidence of the ancient coins —which seems to show that the occupancy of the sect, preceded no doubt by their presence in the region, must have extended from about the last third of the second pre-Christian century (with a thirty-year interruption) at least to 68 A.D., the eve of the victory of the Romans—appears definitely to settle, in a general way, the dating of the manuscripts, about which, before the excavation of the ruin, there had been much rather violent controversy. We can form no idea, of course, except from internal evidence, as to when the works copied were written, but it seems clear that the copies could not have been made any later than the descent of the Romans, at which moment the manuscripts were hidden in caves—like the one which de Vaux risked his neck to reach—that were as hard to get at as possible. This fits in with the date assigned by Albright, who, arguing from the palaeographical evidence, immediately put the Isaiah scroll at about 100 B.C.; with the conclusions of the pottery experts, who said that the jars were pre-Herodian and dated them not later than the end of the last century B.C.; and with radio-carbon tests, which, applied to the linen wrappings, gave a range of possibility between 168 B.C. and 233 A.D.

Not only did the documents found combine with the passages in ancient writers and the discovery of the monastery itself to make it possible to form some conception of a remarkable religious movement of which little hitherto had been known; but, in relation to certain other late Hebrew writings, known but not fully understood, which had already been assigned to this same general period, the new manuscripts at once set up what may be likened both to a chain reaction and to the clustering of iron filings around a magnet.

First of all, there were the so-called Zadokite fragments. These are parts of a document or documents that were discovered at Cairo in 1896, in excavating the *genizah* of a medieval synagogue. The manuscripts are supposed to date from sometime between the tenth and the twelfth centuries A.D.; but the original writings themselves must derive from the same source, and hence date from the same period, as those of the Dead Sea monastery. This seemed obvious from the first lot of scrolls, since the Zadokite document expounds the same doctrines, deals with the same events, and even makes use of the same language, as the Manual of Discipline and others of the scrolls; but the matter has now been put beyond doubt by the finding in one of the other caves of several fragments of the "Zadokite" text. I shall not, therefore, list the close resemblances between these and the other documents; I shall simply count them in with the others when I come to describe, in a moment, the history and doctrine contained in this whole body of writing. Two points should, however, be mentioned. Neither these fragments nor the Manual of Discipline nor any other of the writings yet read ever refers to the members of the sect as Essenes. In the Manual, as in the fragments, its priests are always the "sons of Zadok"; and its laity is not given any special name. Now, we do not know for certain who this Zadok was. It is believed, however, by nearly all scholars that the Zadok of the Bible is meant: the priest who anointed Solomon—since it is said, in one of the fragments, in connection with the polygamy of David, that when David had forgotten the Law, it was rediscovered by Zadok. The Essenes, as appears from the ancient descriptions, regarded themselves as reformers, and these fragments describe a conflict with the official priests of Jerusalem which resulted—the second fact to note—in a migration of the sect to Damascus. This migration, Père de Vaux suggests, may account for the abandonment of the monastery over the unexplained period of thirty years. The discrepancy between the name that was given the dissident group by the authors who have written about it and the name that they gave themselves has been accounted for by the theory that the order were called Essenes, "Holy Ones," only by outsiders. In future, I shall follow the example of other writers on the subject in referring to them simply as "the sect," "the brotherhood" or "the order."

But, besides the so-called Zadokite work (sometimes known as the Damascus Document), there are at least four apocryphal* Old Testament books that evidently have close connections with the literature of the sect: *The Book of Jubilees, The Book of Enoch, The Testaments of the Twelve Patriarchs* and *The Assumption of Moses.* These works have been dated somewhat differently by

* There is, of course, a distinction between apocrypha and pseudepigrapha, and these writings belong to the latter class. The apocrypha, though the word is sometimes used to cover both, are properly texts that occur in the Greek translations of the Bible which were carried into the Catholic translations but which do not occur in the Masoretic canon and were excluded from the Protestant one. 1969.

two of the leading scholars in this field of Old Testament apocrypha—R. H. Charles and C. C. Torrey—but the divergences are not very great, and Charles and Torrey are agreed that these writings were produced, in their present form—chronologically in the order named—between the second half of the second century B.C. and the early years of the first century A.D. Though they had hitherto been known only in translation—Greek, Latin or Ethiopic—it had already been assumed that the originals were in Hebrew or Aramaic. This assumption and the dating are now confirmed by the tie-up with the Dead Sea scrolls. Aside from the internal evidence of subject and phraseology, we have a reference to *The Book of Jubilees* in a passage of the Zadokite fragments, in connection with the novel calendar which the dissident sect adopted and which cut them off—since their holy days now came on different dates—from orthodox Jewish worship; and a fragment of *Jubilees* itself as well as fragments of *Enoch* and *The Testaments of the Twelve Patriarchs*, in what are evidently the original Hebrew and Aramaic texts, have turned up among the Qumrân writings.

A tie-up with the literature of the Christians is shown by the direct quotation in the New Testament Epistle of Jude (14) of a passage from *The Book of Enoch;* by an obvious reference in Jude 9 to an episode in *The Assumption of Moses*—the struggle, over the body of Moses, of the Archangel Michael with Satan; and by passages in the *Twelve Patriarchs*, to which we shall come in a moment. And there are also unmistakable resemblances between all these pre-Christian or non-Christian writings and certain works that were once accepted as part of the Christian canon but later rejected from it.

An extra dramatic touch was given the whole situation when Professor Otto Eissfeldt of Halle called the attention of scholars to a document—first published in 1901—

that must date from somewhere near the beginning of the ninth Christian century. This was a letter from a Patriarch of Seleucia to a Metropolitan of Elam. "We have learned," the Patriarch writes, "from trustworthy Jews who were then being instructed as catechumens in the Christian religion, that some books were found ten years ago in a rock-dwelling near Jericho. The story was that the dog of an Arab out hunting went into a cave in pursuit of game and did not come out again; its owner went in after it and found a chamber in the rock, in which there were many books. The hunter went off to Jerusalem and told his story to the Jews, who came out in great numbers and found books of the Old Testament and others in the Hebrew script; and, since there was a scholar well read in literature among them, I asked him about many passages which are quoted in our New Testament [as] from the Old Testament but are not found anywhere in it, either in copies in the hands of the Jews or in those in the hands of the Christians. He said [that] they are there and can be found in the books discovered there. When I heard this from the catechumen and had also interrogated the others without his being present, and heard the same story without variations, I wrote about it" to friends in that part of the world and asked them to look up these manuscripts and check "whether the passage 'He shall be called a Nazarene' [Matthew 2.23], and other passages quoted in the New Testament as from the Old Testament but not found in the text which we have, could be discovered anywhere in the Prophets." He asked also about the passage: "Have pity upon me, O God, according to Thy mercy . . . sprinkle me with the hyssop of the blood of Thy cross and cleanse me" (which does not occur in our New Testament, but is evidently a Christianized version of Psalm 51.) "This expression," the Patriarch continues, "does not appear in the Septuagint nor in those other [translations] nor in the Hebrew [text]; but that Hebrew said to me: 'We have here found more than two hundred Psalms of David among our books' . . . I have, however, received from them no answer to my letter on these points, and I have no suitable person whom I can send. This is as fire in my heart, burning and blazing in my bones." The passages the Patriarch inquired about can hardly be expected to turn up among the Dead Sea documents. They are obviously of Christian origin, and the literature of Christianity probably did not begin to be written down till after the destruction of the monastery. But the ninth-century searchers of the caves might well have found in *The Book of Enoch* the already mentioned prophecy invoked by Jude as well as—in a work that, as we shall later see, turned up among the first lot of scrolls—a good many unknown psalms.

The letter of the ninth-century Patriarch, taken in conjunction with the recent finds, throws light on another mystery. There was founded at Baghdad, in the eighth Christian century, an heretical Jewish sect, who rejected the authority of the Talmud and renewed the direct contact with the Bible. This sect, who called themselves Karaites, still exists in the East, and, before the Revolution, survived in Russia. Now, the literature of the Karaites is full of references to the Zadokite sect, and one of the Karaite authors says that the Zadokite writings were circulated among them widely. The Zadokite fragments from Cairo, the *manuscript* of which has been assigned to some date in the Middle Ages, was actually found among Karaite books. The Karaites invoked these writings, says J. L. Teicher of Cambridge, who has especially studied this aspect of the subject, "to demonstrate the lineage of their creed by reference to the documents of an ancient opposition to Talmudic Judaism." And he believes that their peculiar calendar, their dietary rules and some

other customs were inspired by the literature of the sect.
But why does the characteristic language of the sect turn
up suddenly in the ninth century without having played
any part in earlier post-Christian Jewish literature? Because, Dr. Teicher answers, the Zadokite writings had
just been discovered in the cave that the Patriarch heard
about. His letter must, of course, have been written before
either he or his correspondent died—that is, sometime in
the last half of the eighth or very early in the ninth century. Teicher says that the peculiar forms of the script of
the Dead Sea manuscripts also suddenly begin to appear
in Hebrew documents of the tenth century. It has further
been noticed by De Vaux that one of the Karaite authors,
writing about 937 A.D., tells of an ancient sect, which he
seems to assign to the same general period as the Sadducees and Jesus, who are called the Magharites because
their books have been found in a cave (*magharah* in
Arabic means *cave*); and the same sect is also mentioned
by two later Muslim writers, one of whom says that it
flourished in the middle of the first century B.C.

Thus today a whole set of documents, never before understood in relation to one another, seem perfectly to fall
into place and acquire a new significance as belonging to
the literature of the Dead Sea sect or representing, in
some earlier or later phase, the tendencies it represents.
There takes shape a whole missing chapter for the history
of the growth of religious ideas between Judaism and
Christianity—a chapter which, as Albright has said in his
Postscript of 1951 to Brownlee's translation of the Manual
of Discipline, "bids fair to revolutionize our approach to
the beginnings of Christianity." "Rabbinical studies," he
adds, "are even more directly affected, and it is safe to say
that nothing written on the sectarian movements of the
last three centuries of the Second Temple can escape
thorough revision in the light of the evidence now avail-

able and still to be published." More recently, in a review in the *Herald Tribune* book supplement of July 18, 1954, he has said that it will now "be necessary to rewrite all our New Testament background material, since the new sources fill an almost total blank in Jewish literature between the latest apocrypha and the earliest rabbinical sources." One may cite here, also, the opinion of one of the leading French Hebrew scholars, M. André Dupont-Sommer of the Sorbonne, who has published two books on the scrolls. Of the hitherto so puzzling literature of the pre-Christian apocrypha, he writes in the first of these books: "All questions of literary and historical criticism relative to this literature must be entirely reconsidered. We are confronted with a whole mass of documents the historical study of which presented extreme difficulties, since so many of the allusions they contained remained for the most part indecipherable. But now the religious history of the last two centuries before our era has been illuminated by new light; a thousand details in the writings of this period now become intelligible, emerging at last from chaos."

I have mentioned the apocryphal documents of the "intertestamental" period which were already known in translations before the discovery of the Dead Sea scrolls. In connection with these scattered writings, it was long ago fully realized that they belonged to a transitional literature between Judaism and Christianity. The invocation of the Savior-Messiah becomes more important and pressing than it has been in the canonical books; and the new writings more and more take the form of apocalypses—that is, of supernatural visions which reveal past, present and future under the guise of a phantasmagoria of symbolic persons and animals, divine and diabolical beings, celestial and infernal phenomena. The situation is summed up by Charles in his introduction to the second volume of his great edition of the apocrypha. The Judaic Law of the Pentateuch had come, he says, by the third pre-Christian century to be conceived "as the final and supreme revelation of God . . . there was now no longer room for independent representatives of God appearing before men, such as the pre-Exilic prophets." According to Zechariah (13.1-5), writing about 300 B.C. from the conservative priestly point of view, a man could be, or ought to be, put to death for setting himself up as a prophet. The result of this was that a writer who had had a new revelation was forced to ascribe his account of it either to one of the canonical prophets or to one of the pentateuchal patriarchs. The late apocryphal writings are put forth, in many cases, as the utterances of Enoch or Moses, Jeremiah, Baruch or Isaiah. One such work, the Book of Daniel, got into the regular canon, though—in the Hebrew Bible, not the Christian one—it was not admitted to the company of the Prophets but relegated to the section of miscellaneous Sacred Writings. This work, which purports to deal with events of the Babylonian Captivity, is actually meant to apply to the struggles of the Jews of the Hellenic period against their Seleucid king, Antiochus Epiphanes, and it contains, in Daniel's visions and Nebuchadnezzar's dreams, the first extensive examples of the apocalypse in its characteristic form. The problem for the scholar or historian was to work out the correspondences between the fantastic happenings described in this apocalyptic literature and actual recorded events; and this task is made rather difficult by the tendency of Jewish writers to see everything from the standpoint of God: lacking our Western historical sense, they mix up past, present and future and refer to contemporary persons under the names of legendary figures.

Now, two of the first lot of scrolls belong to this apocalyptic type. One of these—the one that Professor Sukenik described to the correspondents in the midst of the Arab shellfire—was called by him *The War of the Children of Light against the Children of Darkness*. (This has hitherto been known only in passages to the authorities I here rely on, since Professor Sukenik died before he had finished editing it. The whole of the Hebrew text has only just been brought out by his son, General Yigael Yadin.) The other of these unknown works represents a special variation, itself hitherto unknown, on the familiar apocalyptic form. Ostensibly a commentary, verse by verse, on the canonical prophet Habakkuk, it is in reality a history of happenings that were recent at the time it was written but that are chronicled here in terms of the assumption that Habakkuk was prophesying them. (This was a genre which had not been known when the first lot of scrolls was found, but among the more recently found manuscripts, some fragments have now been identified as belonging to a similar interpretation of Micah.) Both these documents deal with a war, and in both cases the enemy are called the Kittim. Kittim is a name which originally and properly meant the people of Kition, a city in Cyprus, but it was later applied by the Jews, with their still rather dim ideas of their Mediterranean neighbors, to the Eastern islands in general, to Macedonia, and even to Italy. In *The War of the Children of Light*, we hear of the "Kittim of Asshur," evidently the Syrians, the Seleucids, and the "Kittim of Egypt," evidently the followers of the Ptolemies. In the Habakkuk Commentary, they are simply the Kittim, but their practices and methods are described with a certain amount of particularity: we are told that they are "swift and valiant in battle," that they are "a source of terror . . . to all the nations," that they are "insolent toward the mighty" and "mock at kings and chiefs," that they "scorn the fortresses of the people" and "surround them" and "lay them in ruins," that their captains "take

command" and then "disappear one after the other," that
they plunder the people they conquer and afterwards saddle them with taxes, and that they "put many to the
sword, young men, adults, old men, women and children,
and have no pity for the fruit of the womb." All this
would appear to apply to the Romans better than to anyone else. The disappearance of the leaders one after the
other might well describe the situation that prevailed during the Civil Wars when consuls and generals were always being changed. The fact that the Kittim are also said
to "devour all the nations like an eagle" would be equally
appropriate for the Romans, whose standards had eagles
on them; and the identification would seem to be clinched
by the custom attributed to this enemy of "sacrificing to
their standards." "Their arms," says the author of the
Commentary, "are themselves the object of their religion."
The cult of the battle *signa* among the Roman legions is
attested by a number of ancient writers. Though all scholars do not agree in identifying the Kittim with the Romans, the conclusions of General Yadin, in a study of
*The War of the Children of Light*, would seem to confirm
this hypothesis. He believes that certain weapons assigned
to the enemy are to be recognized as Roman short swords,
and that many of the military details of the conflict described in this scroll can only apply, or would best apply,
to the period of Julius Caesar. The Kittim of Asshur and
the Kittim of Egypt would be Syrians and Egyptians
allied with them.

M. Dupont-Sommer, whose arguments I have summarized above, believes that the Commentary was most probably written in the year 41 B.C.—that is, three years after
Julius Caesar's death. He has also attempted to identify
in it two figures who are never named but who are evidently of great importance in the history of the Dead Sea
sect. One of these is a Teacher of Righteousness, a priest

who has been favored with divine revelations and who is
the leader of a community, a party, the members of which
are poor and who call themselves "the New Covenant."
The teacher is referred to as the Elect of God. He insists
on the strictest observance of the Law, yet is at odds with
the priests of Jerusalem. He has been persecuted by a
Wicked Priest, sometimes, apparently, referred to as the
Prophet of Untruth or the Man of Untruth, who has
"swallowed him up in the heat of his anger," has "dared
to strip him of his clothing," and has struck him "in the
execution of iniquitous judgments," when "odious profaners have committed horrors on him and vengeance on
the body of flesh." (I am following Dupont-Sommers'
rendering. Other scholars translate these passages differently. I shall return to this problem later.) But the persecutors are to be punished: "so, at the end of the festival,
on the resting of the Day of Atonement, he [the Teacher
of Righteousness] appeared in splendor unto them for the
purpose of swallowing them up, and that they might stumble on that fast day, the sabbath of their resting." (This
rendering is Brownlee's, as are those that follow.) And we
are told that the Wicked Priest, "in the sight of the
Teacher of Righteousness and the men of his counsel,"
has been given by God "into the hands of his enemies to
abuse with smiting that he might be consumed with bitterness of soul, because he has done evil against His elect."

Who is this Teacher of Righteousness, and who is this
Wicked Priest? I have spoken of the close similarities between the Manual of Discipline and the Zadokite fragments. A new link in the chain of evidence was supplied
when it was noted that the Teacher of Righteousness also
figured in the Zadokite work (the phrase is exactly the
same save for the omission in the latter of the article), and
that in both cases his followers are said to be bound by a
Covenant or New Covenant. The word "covenant," fur-

thermore, is used throughout the Manual of Discipline in referring to the members of the order. It will also be seen from the description above of the followers of the Teacher of Righteousness that this, too, coincides with the picture put together from Josephus and Philo. The Prophet of Untruth and the Man of Untruth both appear in the Zadokite fragments, and the Prophet of Untruth is mentioned in the fragments of the Micah commentary. M. Dupont-Sommer assumes that both these are names for the Wicked Priest, and he finds in Josephus a figure whose role seems to correspond with what we are told about this hated man. This is Aristobulus II, one of the Jewish Hasmonean dynasty, high priest of Jerusalem as well as king, who ruled over the Jewish state for three and a half years (between 67 and 63); who was arrested in 63 and imprisoned by Pompey at Rome; who escaped and returned to Palestine but was caught and sent back in irons—so that he must have been forced, "in bitterness of soul," to take part in Pompey's triumph; and who was finally, in 49, poisoned in prison by Pompey's supporters. There is one striking piece of evidence in favor of this identification. The Commentary speaks of "the house of Absalom and the men of their counsel, who were silent at the reproof of the Teacher of Righteousness and did not help him against the Man of Untruth, who had rejected the Law among all peoples." Now, we know from Josephus that Aristobulus had an uncle named Absalom and had married his daughter.

As for the Teacher of Righteousness, this may have been a general title that was given to a succession of Messiahs. Before the discovery of the Dead Sea scrolls, the earliest references known to the Messiah as "The Elect One" and "The Righteous One" occurred in *The Book of Enoch*—which Charles assigned to the early years of the first B.C. century; and not only do these names appear in the literature of the Dead Sea sect, they are applied in the Gospels to Jesus—as is the phrase "the Son of Man," which, though common in the Old Testament prophets, is first applied to the Messiah in *Enoch*. There were certainly several persons accepted as Messiahs by various writers in various situations; yet these documents from the Dead Sea cave do seem to refer to a specific man. A number of suggestions have been advanced, and Josephus has again been consulted, together with Second Maccabees, in both of which is found the story of a high priest of Jerusalem called Onias, exemplary in his "godliness" and "hatred of wickeness," who was first supplanted by his brother, then murdered by the successor of that brother. But this was under the Seleucids; Onias was put to death in 171 B.C. In this event, the Dead Sea monastery would first have been occupied (136?) some twenty-five years later than the murder of the Teacher of Righteousness, and the sect would have had time to abandon the custom of animal sacrifices (or to practice it apart from the Temple), which Onias, as High Priest, would of course have had to observe, as he would have had to adopt their peculiar calendar (first described in *The Book of Jubilees,* which has been dated by R. H. Charles between 153 and 105 B.C.). In this case, the Wicked Priest would be the High Priest Menelaus, of whom we are told in Second Maccabees that "he came to Jerusalem, bringing nothing worthy the high priesthood, but having the passion of a cruel tyrant and the rage of a savage beast." He is also, like the Wicked Priest, described as a monster of rapacity. It is evident that Onias' murder much shocked the Jewish world, and it has long been supposed that the reference in the ninth chapter of Daniel (165 B.C.?) to a Messiah of whom it is prophesied that he shall "be cut off" and "have nothing," applies to the murder of Onias. But then what becomes of the theory nailed down by Dupont-Sommer with the reference to the House of Absalom and the worship of the Roman standards? Since no other personal name is mentioned, this Absalom may be merely the Absalom of the Bible, invoked in a symbolic sense for Joseph, a nephew of Onias, who robbed him of much of his authority; and how do we know that the Seleucid armies did not worship their standards, too? It was one of Dupont-Sommer's points that the Kittim of the Commentary cannot be the Syrians, since the Syrians would not be said to come from the "isles" of the sea, but it has been objected to this that the word translated *isles* is a vague one, which may be used for any maritime region, and that if it is possible that the Kittim were Macedonians, it is possible also that they might have been Syrians—especially in view of the fact that in *The War of the Children of Light* it is quite plain that the Kittim are Seleucids. And if the Wicked Priest was Menelaus, may not the Man of Untruth have been a different person?—Antiochus Epiphanes perhaps. M. Dupont-Sommer himself entertains an inverse hypothesis: that the names, although interchangeable, may both apply to two people: Aristobulus II and his brother who succeeded him, Hyrcanus II. The situation has been complicated further by certain scholars' calling attention to the possibility that, from the point where a shift is made in the verb-forms of the Habakkuk Commentary, the events alluded to may belong to the domain of prophecy —that is, may be merely predicted because they are strongly desired. (In his account of *The War of the Children of Light against the Children of Darkness*, the editor, General Yadin, describes it as an ideal vision of a triumph which was still in the future, but one which was presented in terms of actual Hebrew weapons, strategy and ritual tactics.)

Dr. W. H. Brownlee believes that the whole story involved in the Habakkuk Commentary is supposed to be

told by the Teacher of Righteousness, and that he is made
to predict for the future the events that followed his
death. Dr. Brownlee also believes that *three* Wicked
Priests are referred to—Alexander Jannaeus, Aristobulus
II and Hyrcanus II; and he discovers a succession of clues
for identifying them in this chronological order. He suggests that the Teacher of Righteousness may be a certain
Judah mentioned in the Talmud, who is said to have re-
buked Hyrcanus I. He explains that when he published
his translation of the Habakkuk Commentary (quoted
above), he had assumed that it was the Wicked Priest
who "reproved" the Teacher of Righteousness, but that the
text may be read also the other way; he finds in Josephus
an Essene named Judas (the Hellenized form of Judah),
who instructed his disciples in the art of prophecy and
who was evidently opposed to the official priesthood.
Now, among the three scrolls from the original cave that
were acquired by Professor Sukenik is a collection of
thirty-five psalms—hitherto completely unknown—which
have been called the "Thanksgiving Hymns." (The complete text of these hymns has now at last been published
by the Hebrew University in Jerusalem; only five of them
up to this time were generally available to scholars.)
These are thought to have been composed either by the
Teacher of Righteousness himself or, in honor of him, by
a disciple who acts as the prophet's mouthpiece. Dr.
Brownlee points out that each one of them begins with
the phrase, "I will praise thee, O Lord," and that these
were the words of Leah when Judah, her fourth son, was
born. The author of these psalms, says Yadin, "speaks
eloquently of his persecution and of the persecution of his
people, and then, for more than twenty pages, gives
thanks, in majestic language, for his deliverance from his
enemies." But we do not know whether this deliverance
has actually taken place or is merely being predicted with

certainty. Although you have, here again, descriptions of weapons and tactics of war, you have no clear historical data.

I have indicated here, in the most simplified form, only three of the lines of theory that have been worked out by various scholars to elucidate the Habakkuk Commentary. The literature of the subject is enormous, and it is impossible to summarize it briefly. I have tried merely to give some idea of the difficulty of determining the actual events—and one cannot always be sure they *are* actual—that are dealt with in these late Hebrew writings; of accommodating apocalyptic visions to the more realistic chronicles of such Hellenized-Romanized Jews as Josephus and the author of Second Maccabees. But if definite events and the actors in them are hard to pin down as history, the doctrines and the mystical symbols are not so easily to be mistaken. These are not in all cases consistent —they must belong to a religious movement that extended through some two and a half centuries; but it is obvious that a certain theology not only runs through all this group of late apocryphal documents and the literature of the Dead Sea sect, but extends to the New Testament, also. It will not be possible here to trace the whole intricate web of cross-references and interrelations that threads these writings together. I shall have to confine myself to describing the principal elements of this school of Messianic thought.

One of its most important doctrines, then, is the morality of the Two Ways, quite unknown to the ancient Hebrews, that appears in so many of these documents. One finds in this literature again and again the Way of Darkness and the Way of Light, the Spirit of Darkness and the Spirit of Light, the Children of Darkness and the Children of Light. The Light is Truth, and the Darkness

Falsehood. The Messiah, the Teacher of Righteousness, is opposed to a Demon of Evil, most frequently known as Belial or Beliar. The Way of Good leads to salvation; the Way of Evil to torment. There is to be a Last Judgment at the end of time—equally unknown to ancestral Judaism —when the Messiah shall divide the world. He, the Elect One, shall save the Elect, the people of the New Covenant. The wrongs they have suffered at the hands of their enemies will finally be avenged. But, in the meantime, they must keep themselves holy by means of the sacred repasts presided over by a priest, purgation by baptism and constant washings. There are three references in the Zadokite fragments to the "well of living water" that saves, which seem to anticipate the conversation of Jesus with the woman of Samaria at the well, when he speaks of the "spring of water welling up to eternal life," and the several New Testament passages that associate baptism both with such Old Testament references as those of Jeremiah to God as a "fountain of living waters" and with spiritual regeneration through Christ. The living waters of Jeremiah are a metaphor, but it seems clear that the water of the Zadokite fragments, taken in conjunction with what we know of the ceremonies of the sect, is something more than a metaphor. We find, for example, in the Manual of Discipline the following significant passage: "And then God will purge by His truth all the deeds of man, refining for himself some of mankind in order to abolish every evil spirit from the midst of his flesh, and to cleanse him through a Holy Spirit from all wicked practices, sprinkling upon him a Spirit of truth as purifying water to cleanse him from all untrue abominations and from wallowing in [or, being defiled by] the spirit of impurity— so as to give the upright insight into the knowledge of the Most High and into the wisdom of the sons of Heaven, to give the perfect way of understanding." It may be, as I have mentioned above, that baptism as well as sun-worship, had already reached Palestine from the East—as the doctrine of the Two Ways, with their spirits of Light and Darkness, recalls the Two Spirits of Zarathustra, and the later Persian theology of Manichaeism that regarded the world as the object of a struggle between two spirits of Light-Good and Darkness-Evil, which existed independently of one another, instead of as the work of an omnipotent God who had created both Good and Evil—a religion which, originating in the third A.D. century, for a time gave Christianity some fairly severe competition.

The doctrine of the Two Ways is found, however, in a document that has become a part of Christian literature yet has always remained rather mysterious. Before this document was actually discovered, it had been known, from the ancient lists of canonical and non-canonical writings, that there had once existed a work called the *Didachē* or *Teaching of the Twelve Apostles*. It had also been suspected that some work, referred to by scholars as *The Two Ways*, had been used and partly incorporated into a number of early church manuals and writings of the apostolic fathers. In 1882, the German Catholic scholar Adam Krawutzcky attempted a reconstruction of *The Two Ways*, and it is one of the dramatic accidents of scholarship that in the very next year, 1883, a newly found Greek text of the *Didachē* should have been published by a Greek Metropolitan of Constantinople—a text that began "There are two ways . . ." and the first section of which was obviously the unknown work that Krawutzcky had been trying to reconstruct. His guesses were confirmed to an astonishing extent. The next year, a fragment of a Latin version of what was clearly the same document was also brought to light, and it was seen that this did not contain the specifically Christian references that were a feature of the Greek *Didachē*. It was now thought by certain scholars that *The Two Ways*—I quote from the eleventh edition of the Encyclopædia Britannica (1910-1911)—"had the appearance of being a Jewish manual which had been carried over into the use of the Christian Church." "But this," the Britannica adds, "is of course only a probable inference; there is no prototype extant in Jewish literature." There can be now, however, little doubt as to the source not only of *The Two Ways* but also of the second part of the *Didachē*, which is a manual of church ordinances. You have here, just as you have in the Manual of Discipline of the Dead Sea monastery, the two ways of light and of darkness that lead respectively to life and to death, and that are presided over each by its angel, and you have, also, the similar language of the "strife" that goes on between them and the "crown" that the good man may win. You have the baptism (in the *Didachē*, preceded by fasting), which we know to have been fundamental to the ritual of the sect, and you have a sacred repast, which involves broken bread and a cup of wine, but at which the wine represents "the Holy Vine of Thy [God's] son David," and the bread the "life and knowledge which Thou didst make known to us through Jesus, Thy child." Note that, though Jesus is mentioned here, there is nothing about the Christian atonement. It had sometimes been believed hitherto that the ceremony of the bread and the wine in the Gospel accounts of the Last Supper was based on the blessing of the bread and wine in the Jewish celebration of the Passover; but Professor Karl Georg Kuhn, of Göttingen, has pointed out, in a study of the development of the Eucharist, that the Passover ceremony is a family affair, at which both men and women are present and at which the father presides, whereas the primitive Christian Communion, in the tradition of the Last Supper, had for participants only men, who were the members of a limited circle, and was presided over by the head of a congregation. We have seen that the banquets of the sect were sacred and a very important part of its ritual. Professor Kuhn believes that the Christian Communion derives from these, and that the atonement was introduced into it by Jesus himself. But this is not, as we have seen, in the *Didache*, and others believe that it was introduced later.

The discovery, among the fragments found in the first Qumrân cave, of two missing columns of the Manual of Discipline which had not been published when Dr. Kuhn wrote, increases the plausibility of this theory that the ritual of the Last Supper ultimately derives from the sect. A procedure is here prescribed which has even more striking resemblances to that of the Christian Communion. Whenever as many as ten shall gather together for a banquet, they shall take their seats in order of precedence, and the priest and the Messiah shall preside. The company may not touch the bread and the wine till the priest has blessed them and taken some—after which the Messiah first takes some, then the others in order of rank. It may be that the ceremony here described is a liturgical anticipation of a banquet expected in Heaven, that the Messiah is not actually present but that the priest is acting in his name, as the Christian priest does for Christ. It has also been suggested that an incident in Luke's description of the Last Supper has a significance which can only be understood in connection with the ritual of the Manual: "A dispute arose among them as to which of them should be regarded as the greatest. And he [Jesus] said to them, 'The kings of the Gentiles exercise lordship over them; and those in authority over them are called benefactors. But not so with you; rather let the greatest among you become as the youngest, and the leader as one who serves.'" We do not know what the relation of Jesus to the Essene order was, but it sounds as if, on this occasion, he were deliberately upsetting its protocol. We have learned from Josephus how rigid, among the members of the sect, was the hierarchy based on seniority, and the language of "greatest" and "youngest" is very much what we get in the Manual, which talks about "greater" and "lesser."

The resemblances between the Manual and the *Didachē* have been carefully traced by a Canadian priest, Père Jean-Paul Audet,* who has also published in *La Revue Biblique* a study, from the same point of view, of another once supposedly Christian work, the *Shepherd* of Hermas (both subjects are covered in the papers that have appeared under the general title *Affinités Littéraires et Doctrinales du 'Manuel de Discipline'*). This is a book of "Visions, Mandates, and Similitudes," written about the middle of the second Christian century, which was long accepted in certain quarters as a part of the Christian canon but was relegated, at the end of the fifth century, through the action of a council of the Roman Church, to a non-canonical status. This book has always been found rather puzzling. Though a son of God figures in it, he is never referred to as Jesus or Christ, and neither he nor a Holy Spirit who is also occasionally mentioned behaves as one would expect them to do in conformity with Christian theology. Pere Audet now rereads the *Shepherd* in the light of these recent discoveries. It has always, he says, been hard to account for it precisely because scholars have approached it from the point of view of what it is *not*— that is, in relation to Christianity. If one looks at it from the point of view of what it *is*, one sees that it is perfectly in order as a product of the doctrines of the brotherhood. The God, the Son of God and the Holy Spirit of Hermas do not constitute a Trinity: it is God who dominates the

---

* Père Audet, since this was written, has published a full-length book, in which he deals with this subject, *La Didachē, Introductions des Apôtres* (J. Gabalda et Cie, Paris, 1958). 1969.

*Shepherd;* the son and the spirit are mentioned only in special connections. The "Church" of which Hermas speaks does not owe its establishment to the "Son of God": it had already a long history behind it when the latter was sent to purify it and to recall it to God's commandments; it has not even been founded by men. "Something," says Père Audet, "has dictated in a positive way the unity of Hermas' theological thought, and something must also have determined its quality." This something is a Judaic, not a Christian tradition, but a Judaic tradition of a particular kind that now for the first time becomes recognizable. Hermas mentions the *Didachē,* which is evidently one of the sources of his "Mandates"; and you find again in the *Shepherd* the Way of Darkness and the Way of Light that lead to salvation or perdition, and, again, the two angels assigned to them. You find the atonement by baptism, and this is the only kind of atonement mentioned. As for the Holy Spirit, we have seen, in the passage just quoted from the Manual, that a Holy Spirit was associated with the ritual of cleansing by baptism, and this seems to be the same Holy Spirit that twice figures in the Zadokite fragments as something that must not be defiled. Now, Hermas tells us that he lived in Rome, and that he had been at one time a slave. The guess has been hazarded by Père Audet that his father had been a Jew who belonged to the Dead Sea sect, and that, after the descent of the Romans in 70 A.D. (when the monastery was probably destroyed), he brought the boy to Rome and sold him. ("He who brought me up," writes Hermas, "sold me to a certain Rhoda at Rome.") The son would eventually have become a Christian, but would already have been so deeply imbued with the doctrine in its older form that he would never have really assimilated the theology elaborated by the Christians.

# V

# WHAT WOULD RENAN HAVE SAID?

As soon as one sets out to study the controversies provoked by the Dead Sea scrolls, one becomes aware of a certain "tension." "During the past three years," wrote Dr. Albright in 1951, "there has been a debate about the chronology of the scrolls which has at times attained the status of a veritable *guerre des savants*. It is an astounding chapter in the history of learning, in some ways without parallel." But the tension does not all arise from the at first much disputed problems of dating, and the contention about the dating itself had, perhaps, behind it other anxieties than the purely scholarly ones.

The elements of the situation, of which I was already though vaguely aware, were pointed up for me in a piquant manner by an evening I spent in Israeli Jerusalem with a distinguished Jewish scholar from Prague, Mr. David Flusser. I had just read, in the *Israel Exploration Journal*, an interesting paper by Flusser, connecting still another apocryphal book, the so-called *Ascension of Isaiah*, with the Dead Sea literature. In examining the section of this book known as *The Martyrdom of Isaiah*, which is supposed to be pre-Christian, Dr. Flusser was led to suspect that the Old Testament prophet had here been made to stand for the Teacher of Righteousness. The opponent of Isaiah here is Belial, the Angel of Lawlessness, whom—since Belial, as we have seen, is the characteristic name

given, in this group of writings, to the ruler of the forces
of evil—Flusser identifies with the Angel of Darkness,
ruler of "all the sons of lawlessness," who figures in the
Manual of Discipline; as well as with the Angel of Darkness and Evil of the Two Ways of the *Didachē*. This
Isaiah is sawed in two by the human agents of Belial for
saying that he has seen God—which Moses had expressly
said it was impossible to do and live—and that he now
knows more than Moses. (The Habakkuk Commentary
asserts that God had made known to the Teacher of Righteousness "all the secrets of the words of his servants the
prophets.") But just before Isaiah's martyrdom, he has
spoken to his followers and told them to "flee away" to
the region of Tyre and Sidon: "For me only has God
mixed the cup." There is no mention in the Bible or elsewhere of a flight to Tyre and Sidon; but Flusser calls attention to the following passage in the Zadokite fragments: "All those who turned back were delivered to the
sword, and those who held fast escaped into the land of
the north." Damascus and Tyre and Sidon were all to the
north of Jerusalem, and all, in both Seleucid and Roman
times, belonged to the same department of imperial administration. It is Flusser's conjecture that the author of
*The Marytrdom of Isaiah* "took part in the controversy
over this departure" and "tried to prove by the authority
of the prophet Isaiah that the departure was prefigured
according to the Divine Will."

This theory, though not implausible, is hardly supported by such evidence as seems to be quite conclusive
in tying together the other documents. But Flusser is a
learned and intelligent man, who is very much worth
listening to on the subject of the scrolls, with which,
though this is not his field, he has recently been occupying himself. I had met him in the library of the University
and asked him to come to see me, and he arrived at the

King David Hotel, precipitately, abruptly, hatless, with
his briefcase in his hand, and the moment we sat down in
the lobby, quite without a conventional opening—since he
knew that I was looking for light on the subject—he began
to talk about the scrolls. He was dynamic, imaginative,
passionately interested. I had heard about his absorption
in ancient texts—which he seems always to carry about
him—while waiting in queues for his marketing. The important thing, he said at once, was not the polemics about
the dates, but what was implied by the contents of the
manuscripts. He started in English but asked if he could
speak French. His English was bad, he said; and few people understood Czech. (I had the impression that German
was not often spoken in Israel.) Hebrew he had learned,
he added, rather late in life; "My best language here is
really medieval Latin." I knew that he was primarily a
student of medieval subjects, but asked him with whom
he spoke Latin. "With the Jesuits," he replied. I had been
told that if you asked him a question, it would take him
three hours to answer, and I could see now what people
meant, but he was neither a bore nor garrulous. On the
contrary, I have rarely known a scholar who expressed
himself—with all his material at his fingertips—so brilliantly and so much to the point. He would give me, to
each of my questions, a full and closely reasoned answer,
and stop when he had covered the ground. All the texts
that were needed he had brought in his briefcase, and he
handed me a Greek Testament for me to follow the Pauline Epistles while he held before me the Hebrew texts
and translated them fluently into Greek, demonstrating
that not only the doctrine but the language itself was exactly the same. I do not remember now the passages he
read, but one of them must have been the description of
baptism from the Manual of Discipline, quoted above,
which might well have been juxtaposed to the Epistle to

Titus, 3.5: "Not by works of righteousness which we have done, but according to his mercy he saved us, by the washing of regeneration, and renewal in the Holy Spirit." On the doctrine of Election, of salvation by grace, that is implied in such a statement and that dominates the Pauline Epistles, Mr. Flusser talked with much animation. "For the doctrine of Election," he said, "we have now a new genealogy: the Teacher of Righteousness, Paul, Spinoza, Calvin, Hegel, Marx—one of the most disastrous of human ideas, the doctrine of predestination!" Such were the pressure and tempo of Mr. Flusser's talk that he was carried at one point to lengths that had no precedent in my experience of even the most enthusiastic talkers. Not only did he raise his voice, when some insight had taken possession of him, quite oblivious of the people sitting near us and as if he were lecturing in a classroom, but when, at the climax of one of his arguments—though we had tried to get away from the orchestra by going to the farthest corner— the music impinged on our conversation, my companion, caught up by a familiar tune, actually sang a few bars of his exposition, as if it were part of an opera; then pulled himself up and returned to prose, as he put his text back in the briefcase.

I was already beginning to realize the explosive possibilities of the subject, and I now heard these described with candor. "*Les chrétiens sont dérangés,*" Mr. Flusser declared. "*Les juifs sont dérangés aussi. Moi, je ne suis pas dérangé!*" I had already heard it positively stated at the Hebrew University that the sect had "grown up inside Judaism, but had nothing to do with Judaism," and I had seemed to note, also, on the Christian side, a certain reluctance to recognize that the characteristic doctrines of Christianity must have been developed gradually and naturally, in the course of a couple of hundred years, out of a dissident branch of Judaism. This was what was upset-

ting to the scholars, who were mostly, on the Christian
side, either Anglican divines, Roman Catholic priests or
Presbyterian or Methodist ministers, and, on the Jewish
side, if not Orthodox Jews, at least specialists in the literature of Judaism, who approached it with a certain piety.
An independent scholar like Flusser, not committed to
any religion, had no reason for being upset. *"C'est très
désagréable pour tout le monde,"* he said to me on another
occasion,—*"sauf pour ceux qui s'occupent des apocalypses
—ils sont contents."* He seemed even to regard it as a little
risky to come to grips publicly and boldly with the implications of the scrolls; but he enjoyed his informed detach-
ment, and there were moments when I almost felt that the
Devil had sent him to Jerusalem to make the most of the
situation. Mr. Flusser is a short stocky man, with sharp
little cold green eyes that glint behind round-rimmed
glasses, under modestly Mephistophelian eyebrows, and
red hair that stands straight up from his forehead. And he
delights in deadpan humor, which, if one does not show
signs at once of appreciating his ironic intent, he under-
lines with a harsh dry laugh. I have seen him disconcert
other scholars by insisting that the errors in sacred texts
and the ignorant misreadings of them were really the con-
structive element in the history of civilization, since the
religious ideas that have had most success have mainly
been founded upon them. Yet Flusser is much respected,
and his scholarly work is quite sober; nor has he anything
of the polymath's *blasement.* I joined him, when we later
removed to the bar, in a toast to what he called *"le vrai
saint esprit"*—the πνεῦμα ἅγιον and רוח הקדש had been
flitting about our corner of the lobby—that humanity carries with it. And he talked to me with admiration of the
character of the Teacher of Righteousness, of which he
felt he had been able to form some idea through reading
the whole of the text of the then still unpublished *Thanks-*

*giving Hymns*: a courageous man, he believed, who had lived his defeat with dignity. There was nothing of Jesus, said Flusser, in the morality of the Teacher of Righteousness, for Jesus had taught people to love their enemies, and the Teacher felt nothing but hatred for his and expected the Lord to avenge him. Nor was there anything, he pointed out, in the doctrine of the Teacher's followers, of the Christian idea that salvation is to be gained by believing in Jesus, who will take all our sins away.

I later attended with Flusser and two younger Israeli scholars an evening session of lectures devoted to the Dead Sea scrolls. At dinner, he provoked a protest by announcing that, since the function of apologetics was fundamental to science, he did not object to apologetics. He went on, disregarding objections, to explain that, in spite of this, he always distrusted people, who, like one of the speakers on the program, invariably began by explaining that his opinions were quite objective and did not represent special pleading. This session on the scrolls was interesting. The speeches, which were all in Hebrew, were translated to me by one of my other companions. The inhibitions of the Jews in regard to the scrolls were brought out by a well-known Israeli scholar, Mr. A. M. Habermann, who said that the Jewish scholars had sometimes been shy of these documents, for fear of their destroying the authority of the Masoretic text of the Bible, and that they sometimes took the attitude—which the speaker regretted—that the subject was of less interest to Jews than to Christians. Yet the large auditorium was packed. It was the Passover holidays, and this evening session was merely one feature of a week of lectures especially given for teachers, many of them from out of town, who seemed to attend these sessions in preference to other entertainment. They began at, I think, half past eight in the morning and went on till eleven at night. All were on Biblical subjects.

I had the impression that these talks on the scrolls were of special interest to the audiences; and when Flusser, who had also spoken, came back at the end to join us, he exclaimed, in a terrific pun—*megillot* is the Hebrew word for *scrolls: "Tout le monde est mégillotmane!"*

The next morning I crossed over to Jordan, where I stayed, in Old Jerusalem, at the American School of Oriental Research. Dr. Frank M. Cross, Jr., of the McCormick Theological Seminary in Chicago, who was working on the new material, was Annual Professor at the School; and the resident director was Dr. James Muilenburg of Union Theological Seminary, who had been studying some new fragments of Ecclesiastes, and had come to the conclusion that this pessimistic and rather sophisticated book cannot have been written so late as has been supposed by some, but must belong to the third or fourth, rather than to the second, pre-Christian century. These last years—with their findings of Egyptian tombs, the excavations of Paestum, Pompeii and Athens, the plumbing of the millenial layers of Jericho and the deciphering at last of the Minoan script—have been a heyday for archaeologists; and the excavation of the monastery, the reading of the Dead Sea manuscripts, have been followed with intense eagerness. It seemed to me very regrettable that the barrier between Israel and Jordan should be cutting off from one another the two groups of Semitic scholars who —in the Jordan Museum in Old Jerusalem and at the Hebrew University in New—have been working on, respectively, the new harvest of fragments and the three Sukenik manuscripts. The people at the University know nothing of De Vaux's discoveries except what they learn at long intervals from the reports in the *Revue Biblique* (a quarterly published in Paris, but edited by De Vaux from Jerusalem), and they must wait for the texts to be brought out in instalments—which will mean a matter of years—by the Clarendon Press, Oxford. At the same time, until the recent publication of the Hebrew University texts, the Christian scholar had no access to them. In Israel, at the session the night before, I had listened to an expert in rabbinics, a tall, lean, black-bearded man, who wore a black flat-topped cap and looked like a rabbi himself, explaining—from a study of the photographs of the complete Isaiah scroll, then still in the United States—that it showed every evidence of having been executed in strict conformity with rabbinical rules. But no scholar with this kind of competence can examine the newly found manuscripts, for no Jew is admitted to Jordan and no Jew known to be such is left there. Thus the enmity between Jew and Arab is contributing to the obstacles and touchiness of this curious situation, which has also been a little affected by the rivalry between Jews and Christians. You sometimes find Jewish scholars implying that their Gentile opponents do not really know Hebrew well enough to arrive at a sound opinion, and, on the other side, non-Jewish Hebraists taking a lofty and offhand tone on the value of rabbinical studies.

The moment of maximum strain in the discussion of the Dead Sea documents may, perhaps, be fixed on the day—May 26, 1950—when M. Dupont-Sommer, Professor of Semitic Languages and Civilizations at the Sorbonne and Director of Studies at the École des Hautes Études, read before the French Académie des Inscriptions et Belles-Lettres a paper on the Habakkuk Commentary. Dr. W. H. Brownlee, writing of this in the *Bulletin of the American Schools of Oriental Research* of December, 1953, refers to Dupont-Sommer as "the very original French orientalist," calls the paper "dramatic," and says that it "caused a sensation." "What evoked the most astonishment," Dr. Brownlee continued, "was his disclosure that the Teacher of Righteousness, founder of the sect of the scrolls, was in some respects an exact prototype of Jesus, particularly as a martyred prophet, revered by his followers as the suffering Servant of the Lord in Deutero-Isaiah" (Second Isaiah, the unknown author of the later chapters of the Book of Isaiah).

Let us turn to Dupont-Sommer's own statement of his views in his book *Aperçus Préliminaires sur les Manuscrits de la Mer Morte* (translated under the title *The Dead Sea Scrolls: A Preliminary Survey*), published the same year that the paper was read.

"Everything in the Jewish New Covenant," says M. Dupont-Sommer, "heralds and prepares the way for the Christian New Covenant. The Galilean Master, as He is presented to us in the writings of the New Testament, appears in many respects as an astonishing reincarnation of the Teacher of Righteousness. Like the latter, He preached penitence, poverty, humility, love of one's neighbor, chastity. Like him, He prescribed the observance of the Law of Moses, the whole Law, but the Law finished and perfected, thanks to His own revelations. Like him, He was the Elect and the Messiah of God, the Messiah redeemer of the world. Like him, He was the object of the hostility of the priests, the party of the Sadducees. Like him, He was condemned and put to death. Like him, He pronounced judgement on Jerusalem, which was taken and destroyed by the Romans for having put Him to death. Like him, at the end of time, He will be the supreme judge. Like him, He founded a Church whose adherents fervently awaited His glorious return. In the Christian Church, just as in the Essene Church, the essential rite is the sacred meal, which is presided over by the priests. Here and there, at the head of each community, there is the overseer, the 'bishop.' And the ideal of both Churches is essentially that of unity, communion in love—even going so far as the sharing of common property.

"All these similarities—and here I only touch upon the subject—taken together, constitute a very impressive whole. The question at once arises, to which of the two sects, the Jewish or the Christian, does the priority belong? Which of the two was able to influence the other? The reply leaves no room for doubt. The Teacher of Righteousness died about 65-53 B.C.; Jesus the Nazarene died about 30 A.D. In every case in which the resemblance compels or invites us to think of a borrowing, this was on the part of Christianity. But on the other hand, the appearance of the faith in Jesus—the foundation of the New Church—can scarcely be explained without the real historic activity of a new Prophet, a new Messiah, who has rekindled the flame and concentrated on himself the adoration of men."

These conclusions, Dr. Brownlee continued, "aroused much opposition, partly inspired by the fear that the uniqueness of Christ was at stake, but securely grounded upon a careful study of the texts adduced by Dupont-Sommer himself and proving the tenuousness (if not impossibility) of the constructions that he had placed upon them."

Indeed, if one examines the two passages of the Habakkuk Commentary upon which M. Dupont-Sommer mainly bases his theory that the Teacher of Righteousness was martyred—I have given them, in the section above, in Dupont-Sommer's own translation—one finds that they do not necessarily imply this interpretation. In the one case, Habakkuk 2.7, there is a gap of two lines, where the bottom of the manuscript has been broken off, and it is the translator who has filled this in with, "he [the Wicked Priest] persecuted the Teacher of Righteousness." The context seems to make it more probable that—as other translators have assumed—it is the Wicked Priest himself upon the "body" of whose "flesh" the "odious profaners committed horrors and vengeance." (It should be noted, however, that one of the leading British Biblical scholars, Professor H. H. Rowley of Manchester University, believes that "the language" here "seems to favor" Dupont-Sommer's view.) In the case of the other passage, Habakkuk 2.15, the words that Dupont-Sommer translates, "Thou hast dared to strip him of his clothing" may mean also "intended him to go into exile" (Brownlee) or "desired his exile" ( de Vaux). These points were immediately made by Père de Vaux in the *Revue Biblique,* in a review dated Jerusalem, March, 1951; and de Vaux believes also that the words of the Commentary translated by Dupont-Sommer as "he appeared to them all resplendent" do not imply a transfiguration on the part of the Teacher of Righteousness, but that the subject of the verb is the Wicked Priest, and he shows that the verb itself has also been found in a sense—that of merely revealing oneself—quite remote from its original meaning of causing oneself to shine.

It would seem that Dupont-Sommer has here overplayed his hand. Yet the Teacher of Righteousness *was* persecuted, he does seem to have been regarded as a Messiah; and the French scholar, in his second volume, *Nouveaux Aperçus sur les Manuscrits de la Mer Morte,* published in 1953 (and now translated as *The Jewish Sect of Qumrân and the Essenes*), is able to support his thesis by pointing to the following passage from *The Testaments of the Twelve Patriarchs,* a late apocryphal work which has already been mentioned above as connected with the doctrine of the sect and fragments of which have been found in the caves: "And now I have learnt that for seventy weeks ye shall go astray, and profane the priesthood, and pollute the sacrifices. And ye shall make void the law, and set at nought the words of the prophets by evil perverseness. And ye shall persecute righteous men, and hate the godly; the words of the faithful shall ye abhor. [And a man who reneweth the law in the power of the Most High, ye shall call a deceiver; and at last ye shall rush (upon him) to slay him, not knowing his dignity, taking innocent blood through wickedness upon your heads.] And your holy places shall be laid waste even to the ground because of him. And ye shall have no place that is clean; but ye shall be among the Gentiles a curse and a dispersion until he shall again visit you, and in pity shall receive you [through faith and water]." When R. H. Charles edited the *Testaments*, he regarded this part of it as "unintelligible," and in his translation he put certain passages in brackets, as I have left them in the extract above, in order to indicate that he assumed them to be Christian interpolations. But there is now no need thus to exclude them, and the passage seems perfectly appropriate if one applies it to the Teacher of Righteousness. The "Christos" of the Greek text, who figures also in other passages, is translated by Charles as "Christ"; but since "Christ" is merely the Greek for the Hebrew word "Messiah," both meaning "Anointed One," this does not imply that the references are not to the Teacher of Righteousness; and, if they are, it would appear that the Teacher did actually die at the hands of his enemies. *The Testaments of the Twelve Patriarchs* is, besides this, full of ideas and language that are similar, on the one hand, to the literature of the sect and, on the other, to that of Christianity. *The Two Ways* here turns up again; and Dr. Charles, writing forty years ago, clearly showed that "many passages of the Gospels exhibit traces" of the *Testaments*, and that "St. Paul seems to have used the book as a *vade mecum*." "There are over seventy words," it seems, "which are common to the *Testaments* and the

Pauline Epistles, but which are not found in the rest of the New Testament." The most striking parallel, perhaps, is that between Matthew 25.35-36 and a passage from the Testament of Joseph, I. 5-6. It is impossible to doubt that the former is an imitation of the latter or that both were derived from a common source.

> I was sold into slavery, and the Lord of all made
>     me free:
> I was taken into captivity, and His strong hand
>     succored me.
> I was beset with hunger, and the Lord Himself
>     nourished me.
> I was alone, and God comforted me:
> I was sick, and the Lord visited me:
> I was in prison, and my Lord showed favor to
>     me;
> In bonds, and he released me. . . .
>
>                                          TESTAMENTS

> For I was hungry and you gave me food,
> I was thirsty and you gave me drink,
> I was a stranger and you welcomed me,
> I was naked and you clothed me,
> I was sick and you visited me,
> I was in prison, and you came to me. . . .
>
>                                          MATTHEW

And the promises of the Sermon on the Mount are anticipated in several places: "And they who have died in grief shall arise in joy; and they who were poor for the Lord's sake shall be made rich; and they who are put to death for the Lord's sake shall awake to life." The gospel of forgiveness is all through the *Testaments;* and there occurs here the first known conjunction—which was to be repeated in Mark 12.19-31—of the precept of Deuteron-

omy 6.5 to "love the Lord thy God with all thine heart,"
etc. and that of Leviticus 19.18 to "love thy neighbor as
thyself." (The injunction to love one's "neighbor" or
"brother" turns up also in *The Book of Jubilees* and the
Zadokite fragments; and the great rabbi Hillel of the
Talmud, who flourished in the first century B.C. and thus
belongs to the same general period, is supposed to have
said to a Gentile who had come to him and challenged
him to convert him by teaching him the whole of the
Torah during the time that he, the Gentile, could stand
on one foot: "What is hateful to thee, do not unto thy
fellow; this is the whole law." The conversation reported
by Mark has a certain resemblance to this.)

Dr. Brownlee, in the paper already quoted, still maintained, that though Dupont-Sommer had succeeded in his
second book in "laying the foundation of his view somewhat more securely," he had "failed to bring it to rest
safely upon incontrovertible proof texts." But he goes on
to say that "Dupont-Sommer often has an uncanny knack
for being ultimately right (or nearly so), even when his
views are initially based on the wrong texts! So also in the
present case there is a doctrine of a suffering Messiah in
the scrolls, but not (so I believe) where Dupont-Sommer
found it. This is found in a passage of the Manual of
Discipline not then published, and in a passage not yet
discussed in this connection." Now, one of the most impressive pieces of evidence that can be adduced from the
Old Testament in support of the claim of the Christian
that the advent of Jesus as Messiah had been prophesied
in the ancient text is, of course, the chapter (53) of Second Isaiah which speaks of a Suffering Servant, "despised
and rejected of men, a man of sorrows," who has been
"wounded for our transgressions," and yet by whose
"stripes we are healed." If this is not Jesus, the Christians
have asked, who can it possibly be? The scholars have

proposed Israel, the unknown Second Isaiah himself, the real Isaiah and Jeremiah. None of these seems satisfactory; and Dupont-Sommer had suggested that Second Isaiah may date from a period as late as that which is dealt with in the literature of the sect. These later chapters of Isaiah had long been assigned to the Babylonian Exile, two hundred years later than the original Isaiah, and it had already been admitted that still later additions were possible. Why, now asks Dupont-Sommer, could these passages not have been written after the death of the Teacher of Righteousness? And "now that the alert has been sounded," he says, "many passages of the Old Testament must be examined with a fresh eye. Wherever it is more or less explicitly a question of an Anointed One or of a Prophet carried off by a violent death, how is it possible to avoid asking whether the person indicated is not precisely our Teacher of Righteousness?" He mentions certain passages from Daniel, Zechariah and Psalms; and he says of the passages in Second Isaiah called "Songs of the Servant of Yahweh," "For twenty centuries people have been asking who was this gentle and humble Prophet, this suffering righteous man whose agony has saved multitudes; the truth is that, apart from Jesus, the Christian Messiah, only one such is known in the whole of Jewish history—and this one has only been known for a very short time. It is the pious Master who was martyred by Aristobulus II. It is not a *single* revolution in the study of Biblical exegesis that the Dead Sea documents have brought about; they will mean, one begins to foresee, a whole torrent of revolutions."

It is impossible for the layman to estimate the value of this hypothesis. Let us simply return to Brownlee, who has been working, in connection with Second Isaiah, on an interesting line of his own. What Brownlee calls "a startling new reading" of Isaiah 52.14 has been found in the complete Isaiah scroll discovered in the first cave. The addition in this text of a single letter changes the accepted meaning from "his appearance [that of the 'Servant'] was so marred beyond semblance," to "I so anointed his appearance beyond anyone (else)," and this for the first time makes plausible the beginning of the following verse, a passage over which editors have always stumbled. The new Revised Standard Version makes this, "So that he startled many nations," but the more obvious meaning of the verb would be, "so shall he *sprinkle* many nations" (it is so translated in the King James Version). But if the Suffering Servant of the Lord was *anointed* instead of *marred*, it would be natural that he should, in turn, have the mission of sprinkling the nations. Whoever was responsible for this variant, it seems plain that a definite Messiah is meant by the scribe of the Dead Sea scroll, and Dr. Brownlee, like Dupont-Sommer, associates this passage with the Messianic references in Zechariah and Daniel (9.24-27: the "Anointed One," who is to be "cut off"). Dr. Brownlee does not commit himself to the theory that this Messiah is the Teacher of Righteousness; but he does try to connect the *refining* and *sprinkling* referred to in the Manual of Discipline and associated with giving the adepts an "insight into the knowledge of the Most High," as well as the statement in the Manual that "God has chosen them to be an eternal covenant," with the language of Second Isaiah in the chapters on the Suffering Messiah. This would seem to make it probable that Jesus "intended to give his life [as] a ransom for many in fulfilment of Old Testament prophecy"—prophecy which, if it did not derive from, was cherished and elaborated in the literature of the sect. It would appear, in other words, that Jesus may well have found prepared for him, by the teaching of the Dead Sea sect, a special Messianic role, the pattern of a martyr's career, which he accepted, to which he aspired.

When the Manual of Discipline was first discovered, the purgations by sprinkling that appear in it made the scholars at once think of John the Baptist, and there was even, at first, some idea that he might be the Teacher of Righteousness. John the Baptist is supposed to have been born—perhaps in Hebron—not very far away from the monastery; "the word of God" came to him, says Luke, "in the wilderness," which must have meant the bald and sub-sea-level mountains that stand between the monastery and civilization; and his ministry, according to Luke, was in "all the regions about the Jordan." He not only had the practice of baptism in common with the members of the sect, but he seems to be following their principles (Luke 3.11) when he preaches to "the multitudes" who have come to be baptized by him: "He who has two coats, let him share with him who has none; and he who has food, let him do likewise." Like the sect, he expects the Messiah, and like the sect—as Mr. Brownlee reminds us—he invokes, in this connection, the Second Isaiah: "The voice of one crying in the wilderness: Prepare the way of the Lord." But the sect lived together in this wilderness, whereas John, in the Gospels and Josephus, always appears as a lonely ascetic, like Bannus, the desert saint at whose feet Josephus had sat. What, then, was John the Baptist's relation to the sect? Dr. Brownlee suggests that John may have been one of those "other men's children" that Josephus says the Essenes adopted and "molded in accordance with their own principles." "And the child grew," says Luke (1:80), "and became strong in spirit, and he was in the wilderness till the day of his manifestation to Israel." This would give us an explanation of the otherwise rather unaccountable circumstance that John's childhood was spent in the desert. I have nowhere seen it suggested that John was at odds with the sect; but, in connection with his desert diet of locusts and wild honey, one remembers the expelled Essenes, who resorted to living on grass because they had sworn an oath never to eat any food not prepared by the brotherhood.

But what was the relation of Jesus to the ritual and doctrine of the sect, which the Gospels so persistently echo? Could he have been actually a member of the sect during those early years of his life when we know nothing about him—where he was or how he occupied himself —or was his contact with it, as Albright believes, chiefly by way of John the Baptist? We must remember that Bethlehem itself is not very far from the monastery. The Bedouins were on their way there when they found the scrolls in the cave. Now, John and Jesus, according to Luke, were relatives on their mother's side. Jesus, in his late twenties and hardly younger than John, came down, we are told, from Galilee in order to be baptized by John, and fasted forty days in the wilderness. Not very long afterwards, apparently, John was arrested by Herod, and then the ministry of Jesus began. We know very little, of course, about the first thirty years of Jesus' life—what he had read or by whom he had been influenced. We can feel behind the pages of his followers the fire and dynamic force, the power to melt and to magnetize, of an extraordinary personality. But we know also that the rites and the precepts of the Gospels and Epistles both are to be found on every other page of the literature of the sect. Some scholars believe, in the light of the scrolls, that the Gospel according to John, which hitherto was thought to have been written late and under the influence of the movement—part Persian, part Platonic—that goes by the name of Gnosticism, must actually have come out of the sect and be the most, instead of the least, Jewish of all the Gospels. You have, at the very beginning of John, the conflict between Light and Darkness, and thereafter many such phrases as "the spirit of truth," "the light of life," "walking in the darkness," "children of light," and "eternal life," which occur in the Manual of Discipline. And you have also, in the Manual, a passage that parallels almost exactly the description of the Logos ("Word") which stands at the beginning of John and which has hitherto been thought to derive from the Gnostics. Manual 11.11 reads, "And by his knowledge everything has been brought into being. And everything that is, he established by his purpose; and apart from him, nothing is done." John 1.2-3: "He was in the beginning with God; and all things were made through him, and without him was not anything made that was made."

What, finally, is the evolution that leads from the morality of the sect—which imposes fraternal forbearance among the members of the order itself and which insists upon charity to the poor, yet condemns and declares war on an enemy who is trying to crush it—to the later morality of Jesus, which is marked by occasional flashes of pugnacity ("I have come not to bring peace, but a sword") yet is dominated by the principle of forgiveness? How reconcile *The War of the Children of Light*, which is full of soldierly weapons, with Philo's first-century statement that the Essenes do not produce these?

The answer is, no doubt, that we are dealing here with the successive phases of a movement. Did the return of the sect from its exile—which the earliest of the coins of the second long sequence found by de Vaux in the monastery seem to date about 4 B.C.—begin a new phase of its life, of which Jesus and John, with their itinerant ministries, are somehow symptomatic or characteristic? One can, in any case, plausibly explain the defiance of the Teacher of Righteousness, the pacifism of Philo's Essenes, and the turning of the other cheek of Jesus as marking successive stages of the adjustment of the Jews to defeat. We can see clearly in the Bible how the Jewish God has been modulated from the savage and revengeful Jehovah, who is feared and propitiated in the Pentateuch, to the God of mercy and love who begins to be conceived by the later prophets. In *The Testaments of the Twelve Patriarchs*—assigned by Charles to the end of the second pre-Christian century—meekness and mercy are emphasized almost to the same degree that they are in the Gospels themselves. Is it that here the resentment of defeat is already giving way to resignation, the resignation of political helplessness; that neither Jews nor sectarians can hope to prevail, and that he who believes himself to be, or is believed by his followers to be, the desperately expected Messiah can preach only a moral salvation through faith in a non-militant God, and the righteousness of the individual? The sword that Jesus is bringing, in the quotation from Matthew 10.34 above, is the zeal for his own gospel, which will set the son against the father and make "a man's foes those of his own household." Yet in all this there seems still some conflict between, on the one hand, forgiveness and renunciation of the world and, on the other, combativeness and worldly ambition. In the language of the Sermon on the Mount, there is what seems a strange vacillation between promising, on the one hand, to "the poor in spirit" "the kingdom of *heaven*," and, on the other, to "the meek" that "they shall inherit the *earth*." In the supposedly much earlier *Testaments*—in the passage already quoted, which seems obviously a prototype of the Sermon on the Mount—the "poor" are to be made "rich."*

* It should be mentioned that Dr. J. L. Teicher of Cambridge believes that the sect were Ebionites, "Poor Ones"—that is, Jews, who had been converted to Jesus, but who continued Judaistic

If, in any case, we look now at Jesus in the perspective
supplied by the scrolls, we can trace a new continuity and,
at last, get some sense of the drama that culminated in
Christianity. We can see how the movement represented
by the Essenes stood up for perhaps two centuries to the
coercion by the Greeks and the Romans, and how it resisted not merely the methods of Rome but also the Roman ideals. We can guess how, about a half century before its refuge was burned together with the Temple of
the Jewish God, this movement had nourished a leader
who was to transcend both Judaism and Essenism, and
whose followers would found a church that was to outlive
the Roman Empire and ultimately be identified with
Rome herself. Under the goading of these agonizing centuries, the spirit of the Essene brotherhood, even before its
expulsion from its sunken base, had already thus made
itself free to range through the whole ancient world,
touching souls with that gospel of purity and light to
which the brotherhood had consecrated itself, and incul-
cating the contempt for those eagles which they had noted
—with evident astonishment—that the army of their enemy worshipped. The monastery, this structure of stone
that endures, between the bitter waters and precipitous
cliffs, with its oven and its inkwells, its mill and its sump,
its constellation of sacred fonts and the unadorned graves
of its dead, is perhaps, more than Bethlehem or Nazareth,
the cradle of Christianity.

---

practices. The Teacher of Righteousness would then be Jesus, and
the Man of Untruth, Paul, who has extended the cult to the
Gentiles. One difficulty with this theory is that the dating of the
departure from the monastery is too early to make this possible;
and another that the literature of the sect contains no obvious
mention of Jesus or any direct reference to his teaching. Dr.
Teicher has tried to discover some, but the few resemblances he
points to seem farfetched or very faint. The words of Jesus
should have left plainer marks on even still Judaizing adherents.

One would like to see these problems discussed; and, in the meantime, one cannot but ask oneself whether the scholars who have been working on the scrolls—so many of whom have taken Christian orders or been trained in the rabbinical tradition—may not have been somewhat inhibited in dealing with such questions as these by their various religious commitments. It is surprising to the layman, and inspires respect, to find that the ablest of these scholars have been bringing to what a couple of centuries ago must have been for such men of the church almost a domain of pure myth, a keenness and a coolness that seem quite objective. On almost any aspect of the scrolls that demands special learning and special research you may find, by one of these churchmen, an acute and exhaustive study; and yet one feels also, a nervousness, a reluctance to take hold of the subject and to place it in historical perspective. On the Jewish side, as A. M. Habermann has said, it is a fear of impairing the authority of the Masoretic text, and also, one gathers, a resistance to admitting that the religion of Jesus could have grown in an organic way, the product of a traceable sequence of pressures and inspirations, out of one branch of Judaism; on the Christian side, it is, of course, as Dr. Brownlee says, the fear "that the uniqueness of Christ is at stake," as well as a reciprocal resistance to admitting that the morality and mysticism of the Gospels may perfectly well be explained as the creation of several generations of Jews working by and for themselves, in their own religious tradition, and that one need not assume the miracle of a special magnanimous act of God to allow the salvation of the human race. Do these prejudices and preconceptions play some role in certain stubborn attempts—apparently, against all the evidence—of such scholars as Solomon Zeitlin of Dropsie College in Philadelphia and G. R. Driver of Oxford to date the scrolls very late? Dr. Zeitlin, who believes that the Karaites did not merely derive their doctrine from the Zadokites but wrote the Zadokite documents themselves, wants to put them in the eighth century; Mr. Driver inclines toward the sixth. In either case, their teachings could have played no role in the early development of Christianity. Do such considerations have anything to do with the persistence—not untinged, one fears, with acrimony—with which Dr. Joseph Reider, also of Dropsie College, has attempted to explain away the text of the Dead Sea Isaiah, in which Brownlee has found evidence of the Messianism either of Second Isaiah himself or of the scribe who made the Dead Sea copy.

New Testament scholars, it seems, have almost without exception boycotted the whole subject of the scrolls. The situation in this field is peculiar. It is precisely the more "liberal" scholars in Britain and the United States who have been most reluctant to deal with the scrolls, for the reason that these liberals tend to assume that the doctrines known as Christian were not really formulated till several generations after Jesus' death, and especially, as I have said, that the Gospel of John came late and was influenced by Gnostic thought. Professor Albright believes that the doctrine of John was "already either explicit or implicit before the Crucifixion," that the material relating to Jesus—though it was not written down till later—must go back to before 70 A.D. (by which date, according to the evidence of the coins, the Romans would have driven out the sect), and that it represents authentic memories and correctly reflects Jesus' teaching.

These new documents have thus loomed as a menace to a variety of rooted assumptions, from matters of tradition and dogma to hypotheses that are exploits of scholarship. How gingerly, in many quarters, the approach to the scrolls long remained has been shown in a striking way by the disturbing but air-clearing effects of the writings of Dupont-Sommer.

Professor A. Dupont-Sommer occupies a unique position in the controversy of the scrolls. I had noticed, in reading his books, that (so far as my experience went) he was the only one of all these scholars who invoked the authority of Renan. The author of the *Histoire du Peuple d'Israël* and the *Origines du Christianisme* calls attention to the first emergence in the "intertestamental" apocrypha of certain characteristic Christian themes, and M. Dupont-Sommer refers to this. I was, therefore, not surprised, when I met him, to find that he is conscious of carrying on what may be called the Renanian tradition. Renan now is *"vieux,"* he told me, in the sense that he now dates, but his ideal for writing history is valid. M. Dupont-Sommer himself occupies the chair of Hebrew at the Sorbonne, whereas Renan was professor at the Collège de France, but their roles are somewhat similar, and Dupont-Sommer is the present director of the project over which Renan presided and of which he sometimes said that he regarded it as the most important work of his life, the *Corpus Inscriptionum Semiticarum*. M. Dupont-Sommer, when one meets him, presents a remarkable example of a phenomenon encountered so often that it cannot be due wholly to coincidence. Just as biographers sometimes look like their subjects and ornithologists are often birdlike, so M. Dupont-Sommer in person astonishingly resembles Renan. He is round-faced, short and rotund, bland and urbane and smiling. Though brought up in the Catholic faith, he is now, he says, *"un pur savant,"* without any religious affiliations; and to an inquirer in the same situation, it is pleasant and reassuring to find that the great secular seekers for truth as well as the Teachers of Righteousness may establish their lasting disciplines. Such an inquirer comes finally to ask himself whether anyone but a secular scholar is really quite free to grapple with the problems of the Dead Sea discoveries. There may have been just a shade of the sensational in the manner in which Dupont-Sommer originally propounded his thesis in connection with the Habakkuk Commentary. Other scholars were certainly shocked, and a reference to the broken text will show, as I have said, that he has filled in the gap with a somewhat highhanded conjecture. Yet the fact, after all, remains that this independent French scholar has made so far the only attempt on any considerable scale to recover the lost chapter of history and to put it before the public. You can buy his two admirably written books—in the series *L'Orient Ancien Illustré*—at any first-rate bookstore in Paris. They have till now been the only source—aside from a few mostly perfunctory articles in newspapers and magazines—from which it was possible for the world at large to form any idea of the interest and scope of the writings contained in the scrolls. The whole subject, though the first announcements made news in 1948-49, has largely since been hidden from general knowledge in monographs and periodicals. In order to acquaint yourself, for example, with Dr. Brownlee's undoubtedly important ideas about the Suffering Servant of Isaiah, you must combine a technical paper of his on the language of the text in the *Bulletin of the American Schools of Oriental Research* with another paper by him which, chopped up into very short lengths, appeared in no less than five issues of the *United Presbyterian,* a church weekly published in Pittsburg. And it is impossible to explore this literature without becoming aware that the impact of Dupont-Sommer has not merely been to rouse resistance. It is evident that two of the ablest men who have concerned themselves with the scrolls—H. H. Rowley and Père de Vaux—in spite of their strong criticisms and their reservations, have in some respects been led to revise their views more nearly in conformity with his.

It must, however, be left to the scholars to criticize scholarly theories. The layman can but try to calculate whether a scholar committed to the Christian faith has anything really at stake in dealing with the possible debt of the morality and practice of Christianity to those of the Dead Sea sect. For anyone who believes that the Son of God was born into the family of a carpenter of Nazareth in northern Palestine, that he preached by the Lake of Tiberias and that he was questioned in Jerusalem by Pilate, should it really be any more difficult to admit that he had been trained in the discipline and influenced by the special doctrine—against which he seems to have reacted—of a certain Jewish sect, and that he had learned from it the role that he afterwards lived of teacher, Messiah and martyr? Or will the explanation of Jesus—as well as of Paul—in terms or preëxistent factors, the placing him and visualizing him in a definite historical setting, inevitably have the effect of weakening the claims of divinity that have been made for him by the Church? Anyone who goes to the Gospels from the literature of the intertestamental apocrypha and the literature of the Dead Sea sect must feel at once the peculiar genius of Jesus and be struck by the impossibility of falling in with one of the worst tendencies of insensitive modern scholarship and accounting for everything in the Gospels in terms of analogies and precedents. The writings of these pre-Christian prophets and saints are often, though not always, insipid. Properly to judge them, however, one would have to know them in the Hebrew, which, in the case of the apocryphal writings, has usually not survived; and one must pay attention to General Yadin when he says of the *Thanksgiving Hymns* that he "doubts that any language other than the original Hebrew can convey the depth of emotion and the spiritual beauty of these verses." Yet even in their non-classical Greek, the Gospels still convey an electrical power; they can move and excite and convert. I have spoken before of the moral audacity, the sense of spiritual freedom, that one gets from certain scenes in the Gospels; and such a passage of high drama as that of John 18-19: Jesus arraigned before Pilate, must surely have been inspired—like Plato's account of the trial and death of Socrates—(whether literally true or not) by a noble and commanding personality. Neither Hillel nor the author of the *Testaments* nor, apparently, the Teacher of Righteousness ever stirred and drew people as Jesus did. And yet, as Albright has said, it is now for the first time possible to "elucidate the New Testament historically in the light of the immediate background of John the Baptist and Jesus." Will or will not this process of elucidation inevitably have the effect of making Jesus seem less superhuman till he has come to appear miraculous only in the sense, say, that Shakespeare is miraculous: in relation to his predecessors? Professor Albright himself evidently does not think so, for he elsewhere declares that "the historian cannot control the details of Jesus' birth and resurrection and thus has no right to pass judgment on their historicity. . . . The decision must be left to the Church and to the individual believer, who are historically warranted in accepting the whole of the Messianic framework of the Gospels or in regarding it as partly true literally and as partly true spiritually—which is far more important in the region of spirit with which the Christian faith must primarily deal."

Yes: only the believer can answer this. But, for one who is not concerned with the theological problem, the implications of the scrolls are reassuring. The point of fundamental importance was put to the present writer in a precise and conservative way by Professor Millar Burrows of Yale. "We now realize," he said, "that there was much more variety and flexibility in Judaism than had ever been supposed." To anyone who has given thought to the peculiar and strained relations that for centuries prevailed between Jews and Christians, and that in some quarters still continue, it must be plain that behind these antagonisms lies an ancient deep-seated fear on the part of each of these groups of the other. Almost everyone must have noted some instance of an involuntary irrational suspicion, in cases where it is quite unjustified, cropping up, if only for a moment, to trouble normal relations. I was told, when in Israel, an anecdote that is typical of this kind of situation. At the time of the last war, an Englishwoman in England had felt very strongly that enough was not being done for the Jewish refugees from Hitler. One of her neighbors in the country was Jewish, and one day when she was passing his house at the time he was watering his garden, she somehow got sprayed with his hose. "Do you think he did it on purpose?," she appealed to a Jewish friend. This reaction—the result of instinctive fear combined with a feeling of guilt—may be matched, from the other direction, by instances in which Jewish critics have sometimes found anti-Semitic implications in books where there was certainly no question of anything of the kind. This nervousness has recently been mainly due to the atmosphere created by the Nazi persecutions; and these persecutions, of course, were not carried on in the name of the ancient religious issues. Hitler preached the innate inferiority of the Poles as well as of the Jews, and he had repudiated Christianity as a Jewish religion for mollycoddles; the Nazi leaders, indubitably, in making a scapegoat of the Jews, were playing on something in the German mind so primitive as to seem pre-Christian. Yet such persecutions could hardly have been possible if there

had not been the opportunity to revive the traditional restrictions against Jews in medieval Germany—restrictions
which had been the product of bigotry and superstition.
The Christians, brought up on the Gospels, have never
been able to forget that the Jews rejected Jesus and demanded his death. For centuries—as I learn from a Jewish
historian, Dr. Cecil Roth—they could not imagine that the
Jews believed in good faith that their Judaic theology,
their ritual and their law, were the true ones, given them
through Moses by God; the Christians were convinced
that the Jews knew better, and that their failure to accept
the Christian faith was due to a stubborn perversity that
must have the Devil behind it. It was for centuries a
Christian objective to convert the Jews to Christ, and
since they almost invariably failed in this, the Christians
became very bitter against them. Even—as in Spain and
Portugal—when they extorted the forms of conversion, the
Jews would go on practising Judaism, and to the Christians it seemed that their counter-religionists were still in
the same state of mind that had led them to crucify Jesus,
that they would willingly crucify him again. This gave
rise to the legend of the ritual murder of Christian children at Passover, a symbolic perpetuation of the Crucifixion. The reciprocal Jewish legends connected with ritual murder—such as those about Rabbi Loew of Prague
—show that as late as the sixteenth century the dwellers
in the European ghettos lived in continual terror of being
framed for this crime by the Christians: the great rabbi is
always rescuing them; and trials for ritual murder were
still occurring in Central Europe through the turn of the
nineteenth century. In the meantime, the assumption of
Jewish depravity had been giving the followers of Christ
carte blanche—not merely with a quiet conscience but
with fervor and exaltation—to penalize, tax, torture and
slaughter the Jews, under the sign of the crucified Jesus.

On the Jewish side, the moral sense was outraged, and the resentment to some extent still lingers, that the communicants of a religion whose Deity is a God of Love and whose Savior brings salvation through mercy, should, for example, inaugurate a crusade to the Holy Land for the purpose of rescuing the tomb of this Savior by massacers of their Jewish compatriots. If the Christian has never ceased to be horrified by the callousness of the Jews toward Jesus, the Jew has never ceased to be shocked by what seems to him the hypocrisy of the Christians. A Jew, on occasion, in a position of power, may become as fanatical and ruthless as any other kind of man; but, though he may do it in the name of Justice, like certain of the Jewish Communists, he does not do it in the name of a religion which talks about forgiving everybody and turning the other cheek. Yet the bitterness of the Jew toward the Christian may have had other sources, too. I have sometimes imagined that the Jew has resented the success of Jesus, that he has been troubled by an uneasy sense that, in its day, the religion of Jesus was a beneficent, a "progressive" movement, and that the Christians have stolen his Messiah and attempted to appropriate his Bible. Of the two post-Christian Messiahs that have most raised the hopes of the Jews, one, Sabbatai Zevi, let them down, under pressure, by confessing Muhammedanism, and the other, Jacob Frank, by succumbing to Christianity. The Orthodox Jew was left with a discipline of difficult observances, an anxious devotion to the letter of Scripture, which in time did perhaps as much as the malignity of Christian prejudice to keep him locked in his special compartment.

The rigors and repressions of this old Jewish world may be gauged by the attitude of the strongest spirits who have liberated themselves from it. I remember a conversation with the late Professor Morris Cohen—a man who gave the impression, as Mr. Alvin Johnson once said of him, of an alabaster lamp inside of which burned a bright flame. He told me—to my astonishment and rather to my horror—that, though he had loved the *Divine Comedy* in youth and known a good deal of it by heart, he had never been able to bear it from the time that he broke with Judaism: it reminded him too claustrophobically of the tight medieval system in which he had himself grown up. As he talked, I became aware that this had actually distorted his conception of Dante, for whom Thomism was not really a prison, since he had his premonitions of the Renaissance and even some affinity with the Reformation. How close Morris Cohen remained, none the less, to this closed-in Orthodox world was shown me by a curious incident. In my then capacity as an editor of a weekly magazine, I persuaded him, sometime in the middle twenties, to contribute an article on a current documentary film that attempted to demonstrate the Einstein theory. One day, some fifteen years later, I happened to meet him on a train. "You know," he said, "it was you who induced me to go to a movie—you paid me fifty dollars. It was the only movie I have ever seen." It was thus Morris Cohen who gave me the first memorable glimpse I had had of the conditions under which the Jewish intellect had survived through the Middle Ages, and I have had it in mind in the present connection. It is as cramping to creative thought to accept the Judaic restrictions as it is misleading and warping to imagine that respect for suffering, consideration for other people and the light of the Holy Spirit were invented by Christianity. All these antiquated prejudices and limitations sound crude enough when thus stated baldly, but the present is hardly the moment to take lightly the baleful power of fanaticisms and superstitions; and it would seem an immense advantage for cultural and social intercourse—that is, for civilization—that the rise of Christianity should, at last, be generally understood as simply an episode of human history rather than propagated as dogma and divine revelation. The study of the Dead Sea scrolls—with the direction it is now taking—cannot fail, one would think, to conduce to this.

In the meantime, it is going forward at what is evidently a vigorous pace. In the handsome modern museum in Old Jerusalem, built with Rockefeller money, which has so admirably been designed to fit into the architectural landscape of blunt yellow towers and blank old walls, yet which makes you feel, once inside, that you are luxuriously back in New York, in a new wing of the Metropolitan, the fragments of the Dead Sea documents have been gathered and are being examined. Père de Vaux presides over this; and there are only three scholars authorized to decipher and report on the manuscripts: J. T. Milik, a Polish Roman Catholic priest; Dr. John Allegro of Manchester; and one American expert: last year Professor Cross of Chicago, at the present time Monsignor Patrick W. Skehan of the Catholic University of America. The tens of thousands of fragments—there has been no attempt to count them—have been put away in boxes. The utmost pains, of course, have been taken to keep separate the contents of the different caves and the pieces found in groups together. These range in size from morsels as large as your hand, which may include a whole column, to crumbs with a single letter. Some believe that it will take fifty years to sort them all out and decipher them, but the energetic de Vaux is more hopeful and thinks they may get through it in ten. The fragments selected for study are set out on long tables in a large white-walled room. They are mostly of leather but a few are papyrus. In color, they range from the darkest brown to an almost paper-like

paleness, so that they give the impression of autumn
leaves that have lain in the forest all winter. The ones
that are being studied have been flattened under plates
of glass; but before they can be thus smoothed out, they
have to be rendered less brittle by being put into a "hu-
midifier," a bell-glass containing moist sponges. When
they are taken out of this, they are cleaned with a camel's
hair brush, dipped in alcohol or castor-oil. Sometimes the
ink comes off along with the marly clay of the caves.
Sometimes they flake at the touch of the brush and have
to be backed with tape. Sometimes they have turned quite
black, in which case they are photographed with infra-
red rays and examined through a magnifying glass. The
first problem is to bring together—through a study of the
various hands of the scribes and the substances on which
they have written—the pieces that belong together. The
scholars work on this in a small inner room, equipped
with concordances, dictionaries and all the relevant texts.
The concordance may place a fragment as coming from a
Biblical book or a known non-canonical work, and others
may be found to fit it.

The whole harvest of the fragments is not yet in; there
are still hundreds in the hands of the Arabs, who have
been making things more difficult by cutting the large
pieces into strips and selling them one after the other at
successive interviews—raising the price for the second
piece, asking still more for the third, etc. To put a stop to
this, it has been necessary to offer special baksheesh in
proportion to the size of the pieces. It is estimated by Père
de Vaux that $15,000 is still needed to buy the rest of
these fragments. It has been harder than one might suppose to raise the money required to purchase the mass of
material that was carried away by the Arabs. A hard and
fast rule has been made that the fragments must not be
dispersed till everything has been classed and deciphered

under Père de Vaux's supervision. Of course this is very wise: it is important to keep them together for comparison and coördination; but the effect has been somewhat to discourage institutions of learning from acquiring sets of these fragments, since any institution that buys them, as Manchester and McGill Universities have done, will not get them till they have already been read and published.

As one bends over the tables with the fragments under glass, one recognizes here and there—it is astonishing how beautifully clear much of the writing remains—the inextinguishable "tetragrammaton," the unutterable name of God. (The awe with which this name was treated is carried to a further remove in the Habakkuk Commentary, where it is written in archaic Hebrew characters; and it should also be mentioned that fragments of various Biblical books among the later finds have added to the very few specimens known of manuscripts in this script.) Here are most of the books of the Bible, though sometimes in an unfamiliar text or a text that corresponds with the Greek of the Septuagint but not with the Masoretic Hebrew; and there are also non-canonical books, unknown as well as known. One wonders what new revelations may still come to light from these tatters. With what eagerness the scholars must hover over these layers of old leaf-mold spread out here!—an eagerness perhaps not unmixed, at moments, with apprehension.

The finds that, among these materials, are, I gather, causing most excitement, stimulating most expectation, are two as yet unread rolls of copper. Strips of copper like these, it seems, have hitherto not been known. They were found in one of the Qumrân caves that otherwise proved rather disappointing, one on top of the other, resting against the wall. It is supposed that they were hastily hidden there, and that access to the cave was soon afterwards made impossible by an earthquake. These copper strips have been rolled with the writing on the inner side, but the stylus has incised so deeply—it must have been pounded in—that the text can be partly made out in relief. The difficulty is to unroll these strips. They are green with oxidization and would crumble if subjected to pressure. Bits of them have been sent to Johns Hopkins in the hope of discovering some method by which they may be made more flexible. If this fails, they must be cut into sections. It has been calculated that, if put end to end, the two rolls would be eight feet long.

It was suggested at first that these strips were inscriptions from the walls of the monastery, and some have even imagined that they might come from the walls of the Temple, in which case they would have been taken down just before it was burned by the Romans in 70 A.D., and hidden away in a cave, about a mile and a quarter north of the monastery, when the monastery, too, was in danger. But Professor K. G. Kuhn of Göttingen,* who has recently visited Jerusalem and studied the rolls in the museum, has come to a different conclusion. Deciphering as much of the text as can be read in reverse on the outside layers, he has found a succession of numerals accompanied by the word for cubits and a word that may mean either *buried* or a place—such as a ditch or a cave—in which something might be buried, as well as phrases such as "above," "on this side," "in the room," that seem to refer to locations. He believes that the strips are a list of the treasures of the monastery, with directions for finding the places in which they have been hidden from the Romans. They cannot, he thinks, have been plaques on the walls, since there are no signs of rivets or nails, nor does the text leave wide enough margins to make it possible that they may have been framed. One of the rolls consists of two separate pieces which can be seen to be fastened together,

* Now Heidelberg. 1969.

just as the strips of leather are in the scrolls, and this has led Dr. Kuhn to suppose that, like the scrolls themselves, they were meant to be unrolled and read. The members of the brotherhood, about to flee, would have written out their inventory on copper and put it in a cave by itself in the hope that it might survive, as leather scrolls might not do, the systematic wrecking of the Romans. If this turns out to be true, the archaeologists may have before them a veritable Gold-Bug treasure hunt.

# VI

## GENERAL YADIN

AND NOW let us return at last to the Metropolitan Samuel, who bought the first lot of scrolls and persisted in believing in their antiquity, who allowed them to be photographed by the scholars of the American School in Jerusalem and was encouraged by these Americans to come to the United States in January, 1949. The Metropolitan Samuel was hoping then to sell the scrolls to some institution of learning, but this turned out to be more difficult than the Americans had led him to believe. The publication of the texts by the School did not have the effect that had been predicted of exciting an interest in buying the manuscripts; on the contrary, it diminished their market value. Since the texts were available to scholars, there was no need to have the manuscripts in the library. The Metropolitan Samuel had signed an agreement that the American School should publish within three years the texts that had been photographed, and that he should receive, in return, fifty per cent of the profits from the published texts. But the process of publishing Hebrew texts along with photographic facsimiles is a very expensive one. The first volume of the Dead Sea manuscripts cost the American School $8000, and, though it has now gone into a second edition, it has been only in the last year that the Metropolitan Samuel has been able to collect any royalties: about $300. Before this, the only revenue he was able to derive from the scrolls consisted of a few small fees that had been paid him for exhibitions in museums.

In the meantime, an outcry had been raised by the Department of Antiquities of Jordan, whose director is the British Harding, that the Metropolitan Samuel had had no right to take the scrolls out of the country, and that the Americans had no right to publish them and had connived with the Metropolitan in committing an illegal act. It was intimated that steps would be taken if he ever came back to Jerusalem. The American reply to this declares that it was precisely the men at the School who had explained to the Metropolitan the antiquity laws of Palestine, with which he was not familiar; that they themselves had reported the scrolls to the Department, and that, even before this, the Metropolitan himself, at the time he was looking for an expert opinion, had had them shown to the people of the Museum; that in neither case had anybody connected with the Department exhibited the slightest interest;* and, finally, that when the Metropolitan at last took his scrolls abroad, his monastery was being bombarded by the crossfire of Jews and Arabs (the latter under the British Brigadier Glubb), and that, in the general chaos which the English had left, there was no safety for priest or manuscript, and no government, and hence no law, for antiquities or anything else. One recognizes at

---

* It should be noted that these statements have just been denied by Mr. G. Lankester Harding: "During the whole of this time [between the finding of the scrolls and the departure of the Metropolitan for America], if anyone seriously thought of reporting the matter to the Government Department of Antiquities the idea was apparently dismissed as sheer folly, for it was never done. The Archbishop's claim to have done so because he consulted a member of his flock who was assistant librarian at the Palestine Archaeological Museum can be discounted, as the person in question had no competence to give a judgment on antiquities of any kind, and even he did not report the matter to his superiors." *Discoveries in the Judaean Desert. I,* Clarendon Press, 1955.

once in Jerusalem, whenever this subject is broached, the familiar Anglo-American feud that one has run into so often in Europe where the two nationalities have come together. The Yankees, the British imply, have as usual been guilty of sharp practice; the Americans retort that it was they, after all, who first realized the importance of the Metropolitan's manuscripts, and that they advised him to come to the United States in order to be sure of saving them. I might add, in support of the American side, that I was told by Professor Dupont-Sommer that European scholars are grateful to the men of the American School for so promptly making the texts available.

Dr. Burrows, of the Yale Divinity School, has been active in connection with the scrolls, and the Library of Yale University at one time considered acquiring the manuscripts, but finally decided not to. Those interested in the scrolls have complained—not without a certain justified bitterness—that the Library has had no difficulty in raising a sum that has been quoted at $450,000 in order to buy the Boswell papers but could not produce the probably smaller sum that would have bought what were undoubtedly the most precious discoveries of their kind since the texts of the Greek and Latin classics brought to light in the Renaissance. This was all the more unfortunate because everything had not yet been published. There was a group of fragments of Daniel which the Metropolitan had not released, as well as a whole manuscript which had not even been read.

It was this manuscript, the smallest of his lot, that the Metropolitan had taken home with him, the day of the photographing, when the layers turned out to be so tightly stuck together that it could not be easily unrolled. It has not been unrolled yet; but from two fragments detached from the back, it has been found to be written in Aramaic in "a very neat and fine script." These pieces have been deciphered by Dr. John C. Trever, who identified the word BT'NWŠ* with the feminine name Betenos in the Ethiopic text of *The Book of Jubilees*. Betenos was the wife of Lamech, one of the patriarchs in the early part of Genesis, and the identification seems established by a passage that reads, "then I, Lamech, hastened to go in unto Betenos." Now, in an ancient list of apocryphal works, a *Book of Lamech* is mentioned, and it has been thought that this must have been embedded in the later *Book of Enoch*—since Enoch was an ancestor of Lamech. But the reading of the manuscript stopped there. The Metropolitan took it to the Fogg Museum in Cambridge, and the Museum authorities told him that the scroll was gummed together by a gluey substance like tar, which presented a problem in organic chemistry. In view of the objections raised by the Jordanians to the Metropolitan's title to the scrolls, the museum insisted on insuring them against possible suits on this ground, and the money to cover the premium was found by Dr. C. H. Kraeling of the Chicago Oriental Institute. The situation was, of course, unusual, and since Lloyd's would not undertake a policy, it was some time before the Fogg was able to arrange for one. The Metropolitan was asked, also, to sign a waiver that he would not hold the museum responsible in the event of damage to the scrolls. In the meantime, he had taken them back, and he must have become discouraged about getting the work done by the Fogg, for he eventually dropped the whole matter. He complains that whereas in the Middle East arrangements are made by word of mouth and usually lived up to by the parties, he has found that in the United States you are always being asked to sign papers,

* Hebrew, up to about the tenth century A.D., was written mainly without vowels, so, in the case of a previously unknown name, it is possible to print only the consonants without what are called "pointings."

which turn out not to guarantee anything. He has, for example, always had to sign agreements in connection with exhibiting his scrolls, and he has made a point of stipulating that no photographs of them should be taken. Such an agreement was, however, violated when the scrolls were shown in Chicago at the Oriental Institute. A scholar who wanted to check on a disputed passage managed to photograph a word that was blurred, with infra-red rays. The Metropolitan discovered this later when he came upon a learned paper based on this photograph.

In the meantime, the scrolls were not sold, and the scholars were becoming impatient and worrying for fear the manuscripts might be deteriorating. The Metropolitan, when he brought them to the United States, had put them in a safety deposit vault, and he had made them the charge of a trust, the Trustees of which were Syrians of the Metropolitan's own church. All business connected with them was to be transacted in the name of the trust, the proceeds from selling them were to be handled by it, and the money was to be devoted to churchwork and education. By this time, the Metropolitan had announced that he would not sell the Lamech roll separately. Since the value of the other manuscripts had fallen with their publication, he would now have less chance of disposing of them without the inducement of the unread scroll. He had decided to sell them in a lot, but not to set a definite price on them. He offered to have them appraised by experts. That he should have had to wait in vain for an American buyer throws into relief the false values of the market for rare books in this country. One remembers the $150,000 paid by Dr. Rosenbach for a copy of the Bay Psalm Book, the $106,000 paid by him for a Gutenberg Bible, the $50,000 for the first version of *Alice in Wonderland*. The difficulties about the Metropolitan's title may possibly have had something to do with the reluctance of

learned institutions; but undoubtedly the principal obsta-
cle was the relative poverty of such institutions—divinity
schools and seminaries—as are interested in Biblical manuscripts, and the high susceptibility of rich collectors, cultivated by the book dealers through decades, to first editions
of classics that are perfectly accessible to everyone.

Last summer, General Yigael Yadin—the son of Professor Sukenik—visited the United States. He remained from
the middle of May to the end of the first week in July. He
and Albright discussed the scrolls, and Yadin then decided
to try to raise the money from Israel. He wrote the Metropolitan a letter, to which he received no reply, and he concluded that it would not be possible for the Syrians, under
the circumstances, to sell the scrolls openly to Israel. There
was always the possibility that the Jordanians would appeal to the authorities and try to prevent their being sent
out of the country or that Jordan would bring a suit in the
United Nations. The General's attention, however, was
drawn to an ad in the *Wall Street Journal* that appeared
during the first three days of June under the heading
"Miscellaneous For Sale":

### The Four Dead Sea Scrolls

Biblical Manuscripts dating back to at least 2000
B.C. are for sale. This would be an ideal gift to an
educational or religious institution by an individual
or group.

The Syrians, becoming anxious, had resorted to this
device. Yadin, without letting his name appear, applied
to purchase the scrolls, employing as intermediary a lawyer
not associated with Israeli business, who negotiated the sale
through a New York bank. The Syrians were never told
that the manuscripts were going to Israel, and so ought to
be held by the Jordanians quite innocent of selling them
to their enemies. The price was $250,000. There hap-

pened to be $100,000 available in the treasury of an organization called the American Fund for Israeli Institutions, and Yadin persuaded his government to lend the remaining $150,000. An American millionaire in the paper business, Mr. D. Samuel Gottesman of New York, offered to repay the money to the fund and the Israeli government. The whole matter was kept a secret until the scrolls had been transported to Israel. This, of course, took place some time ago, but the purchase of the scrolls for Israel was not announced till February 13, 1955, when Premier Sharett explained that they would be housed, with other ancient documents, in a museum to be built for the purpose and to be called the Shrine of the Book. The first manuscripts found in the Qumrân cave are thus at last united in New Jerusalem. The Lamech scroll will now be opened, and the Hebrew University will publish its text. This will be of great interest to scholars, since it is the only known specimen of literary Aramaic from the period of four hundred years between the Aramaic of the Book of Daniel in the early third century B.C. and that of the Scroll of Fasting, a document of the second century A.D.

The Metropolitan Samuel has been living in Hackensack, New Jersey. There are in the United States four churches of his confession—one of them in West New York, not far away—and a single one in Canada. He has been travelling around among them, but his position has been rather difficult, for there has never been a metropolitan of the Syrian Jacobite Church in this part of the world before, and there is really no see for one. Exiled from the pomp and antiquity of his monastery in Old Jerusalem, he has taken a little cottage in a suburban section of Hackensack, where, supported by the Syrian congregation of the town, he has been living in modest comfort. I went to call on him in the May of 1954. The white woodwork and neat brick of his new Colonial house stood out among the family residences, rather gloomy and sometimes shabby, of the older New Jersey suburbs. One crossed a small, well-tended front lawn of glaring New Jersey grass to find his name and his rank, in the ancient Syrian lettering called estrangelo, spanning in wrought iron an ornamental glass outer door. He seemed an exotic figure with his dark and magnetic eyes, his Assyrian beard and enveloping robes, the sober black of which was set off by a lining of brilliant puce. He told me that a good many of the Russian priests now in the United States have, except when officiating, discarded their priestly robes and taken to business suits, but that he has kept on wearing his. The furniture was modern American; two bookends had heads of Lincoln. But on the mantelpiece was a Syrian prayer book underneath a painting of Christ, and on one side of the fireplace hung a glowing ruby-studded crosier. He has made of this mantelpiece an altar, and he holds before it Sunday services for his congregation. He was planning at that time to have built for himself a small cathedral in Hackensack.

I called on him again last February. I did not know that the scrolls had been sold. He greeted me with radiant good humor and explained that he had disposed of the manuscripts to a buyer who, for unknown reasons, would not allow his name to be revealed. The Metropolitan himself had seen only the vice-president of a bank. He entertained me with a sumptuous Syrian lunch of vegetables, salads, fruits and cheeses. The principal dish was fish, and the Metropolitan explained to me that in his Syrian Jacobite Church three days in February were appointed as a special Lent, to commemorate the fasting of the Ninevites when Jonah had preached to them and caused them to repent. This fast is a unique institution of the dissident Eastern churches. He told me that the money from the scrolls would be spent on education and church work for the Syrian Church in the Middle East. He was not clear, has perhaps not decided, what he himself will do now. There is no question, in any case, that he will still be performing his archiepiscopal duties, untroubled by the controversies provoked by the scrolls.

1955-1967

# INTRODUCTION

THE FOLLOWING chapters are intended as a supplement to *The Scrolls from the Dead Sea,* published in 1955. In view of the fact that a number of new manuscripts, then unknown, have been discovered, that some manuscripts already discovered have for the first time been unrolled and read, and that several new and interesting theories in connection with these documents have been advanced, I have thought it worth while to bring my book up to date by describing what, so far as I am able to judge, are the most important of these events. It ought clearly to be understood that I am no Semitic scholar and that I can only give my own account of what others have established or conjectured. My position in regard to this field is rather like that of Hemingway in relation to bullfighting—also an occupation which requires thorough training, strict self-discipline, and a willingness to take certain risks. Without being qualified to participate in any professional way, I am an attentive and enthusiastic onlooker who has learned in the course of time to know something of the matadors and their managers. I am aware of the towering authority of the Dominican Roland de Vaux, the adroit and polished cape-work of André Dupont-Sommer, the rapidity and panache of Yigael Yadin, the bumbling tactics of G. R. Driver, who is likely to look for the bull in the wrong direction, and the showy performances of John Allegro, which make one nervous because one cannot depend on them to finish as well as they have seemed to start. And I can distinguish between the different schools: the Jewish scholars who tend to complain that the Gentiles do not know enough Hebrew, and that they may labor for years on a text that one steeped in Hebrew learning could edit in months—which is countered by the Gentile complaint that when the Jewish scholars work too rapidly they may read back later rabbinical ideas into this pre-Talmudic literature. And then there are the Jewish and other Orientalists who declare that the Paris scholars, in the rationalizing tradition of Renan, look for too much precision and logic in the writings of Eastern authors who, not possessing our idea of time, write confusingly of past, present and future, who have had so little Western sense of individual personality that it is mistaken to trust a detection of modern French *romans à clef* in cloudy accounts of happenings that have been given apocalyptic form; and the dissensions between the archaeologists, who are obliged to base their speculations on the evidence found in the field, and the purely academic scholars, who have never set foot on a site but who can satisfy themselves with theories elaborated entirely in their studies. To these last I shall revert later.

I should acknowledge to several of these scroll scholars debts of gratitude not only for their writings but also for their having been kind enough to see me or correspond with me or provide me with materials, and, in many cases, to check my proofs for errors: Professor W. F. Albright of Johns Hopkins; Professor John M. Allegro of the University of Manchester; Professor W. H. Brownlee of Claremont Graduate School; Professor Frank M. Cross, Jr., of Harvard; Père Roland de Vaux of l'École Biblique et Archéologique of what was till lately Jordanian Jerusalem; Professor André Dupont-Sommer, formerly of the Sorbonne, now of the Collège de France; Professor David Flusser of the Hebrew University; Dr. Malachi B. Martin, former professor at the Pontifical Institute of Rome; Professor Menahem Mansoor of the University of Wisconsin; Professor J. A. Sanders of Union Theological Seminary; and Professor Yigael Yadin of the Hebrew University.

# I

# POLEMICS

THE RECEPTION by the clerical world of my book published in 1955 became for me an educational experience: I gained from it more understanding than I had ever had before—since I have no affiliation with any Church—of the doctrines and the attitudes of the various religious bodies. The religious group that was least disturbed by the implications of the scrolls was the American Unitarians, who were then having a controversy among themselves as to whether or not they were Christians and who welcomed with something like glee anything that might seem to weaken the pretensions of the more fundamentalist Churches. The groups that were most disturbed were the Orthodox Jews, the Catholics and the "Establishment" of the Church of England.

In the case of those Jewish scholars—such as Solomon Zeitlin of Dropsie College and Yitzhak Baer, now retired, of the Hebrew University—who have refused to recognize the antiquity of the documents, I believe that this reluctance has been due either to their presenting so many variants from the Masoretic text of the Bible, which was established at an unknown date by a committee of rabbinical scholars who did their best to suppress any other text, and which has since been accepted by the Orthodox Synagogue as unalterable and unquestionable, or to the natural conservatism of learned men who have arranged to their

satisfaction the available materials of their subject and
who recoil from any fresh evidence that adds new un-
accounted-for matter. To the Gentile, this may seem surprising. We know that both the Greek Septuagint and St.
Jerome's Latin Vulgate were translated from texts different from the Masoretic one, and that the Samaritans have
always claimed that their differing version of the Torah—
that is, what Christians call the Pentateuch—is more authentic than the Jewish one. But for the strictly Orthodox
Jew the Masoretic text of the Bible is a kind of sacred object that is almost worshipped and that cannot be tampered with. Every word—even every known error—is unalterable except, safely, in the margin. The Orthodox
world of Judaism is tightly closed and not easily invaded,
and when early Hebrew texts turn up that correspond
with the Greek or Samaritan ones or contain entirely new
readings, they have to be pushed away; they cannot belong
to that system. From the point of view of history as well,
for the traditionalist Christian scholar as well as for the
Jew, the evidence is supposed to be all in: it consists of the
Bible, the Talmud, Josephus, the various kinds of apocrypha, and the hitherto accepted historians and patristic or
rabbinical writings.

The behavior of the Roman Catholics exposed to me for
the first time a phenomenon of which I had hardly been
aware: the extent to which the Catholic Church operates
on several levels. I have been told by a Catholic scholar
that at first, in regard to the scrolls, a kind of official policy
tended to bias Catholic scholarship in the direction of
minimizing their importance. The priesthood had shown
an unnecessary alarm which prevented them from dealing
with the subject. He said that for a time he had complied
with this policy but had later departed from it. The outsider may ask of the Catholic why, if Christ had a human
identity as Jesus of Nazareth, who at a definite time and

place got into trouble with the Jewish Establishment and
the Roman occupation both, it should be shocking to conjecture that He might have acquired certain of His theological ideas from the teachers of the Dead Sea Sect, now
usually identified with the Essenes, as He had presumably
learned carpentry in Joseph's shop, or that certain of His
sayings and actions may be interpreted as representing a
repudiation of these teachers. An intelligent and well-
educated Catholic will not, of course, be disturbed—since
he knows that his Christ appeared at a certain moment, in
a special historical situation—to find that certain elements
of this background are now becoming more distinct. But
many Catholics—like many of the members of any other
religious group—are not intelligent and not well educated.
To attempt to fill in with more historical facts the human
context of Christ's career is to risk impairing the legend
which is cherished by the ignorant populace and which,
if the Church is to maintain its authority, this populace
must not be allowed to question. What have the political
and military and even doctrinal happenings of ancient
Jewish history got to do with the halos and the sacred
hearts, the blue robe of the Virgin, the white robe of the
risen Jesus, the angel chorus that heralds His birth and
the angels "in shining garments" that announce His resurrection? The most learned and enlightened of priests will
answer that these efforts at concrete depiction, whether
the masterpieces of Fra Angelico and Raphael or the taw-
dry statuettes and amulets of the cheapest seller of images,
that even those legends whose literal truth these priests
may not themselves accept are symbols and reminders to
the simple of a divine salvation and passion, and thus may
share in the sacredness of the Faith. But the simple do not
know, cannot know, and ought not to be encouraged to
know what the Catholic scholars are writing. Perhaps the
most important service that has been rendered in connec-

tion with the scrolls has been the work of Père Roland
de Vaux, the enterprising and accomplished archaeologist,
who has found or bought from the Bedouins much of the
literature of the Dead Sea caves and who has revealed the
reason for their presence in this out-of-the-way place,
Qumrân, by excavating the ruin of what was presumably
the Essene monastery in the neighborhood of these caves,
of which the scrolls must have composed the library, hidden away in the caves in order to protect them from the
Romans. Père de Vaux was till recently the editor of a
quarterly published in Paris, the *Revue Biblique*, which
has at the present time a circulation of twenty-eight hundred, yet this far from widely read periodical has been the
vehicle for most of the important announcements in connection with the Qumrân discoveries; and the findings of
other scholars—with the exception of those of Dupont-
Sommer, whose accessibly lucid books began coming out in
1950—were appearing for ten years or so after the first discoveries only in learned journals as little read as the *Revue
Biblique*.

The first two books by Dupont-Sommer, which were
soon translated in England, excited the antagonism of the
Catholic clergy but were not very widely discussed. My
own little book, however, a merely journalistic attempt to
explain to the ordinary reader the contents and significance of the scrolls and what had been happening in connection with them, which first appeared in a popular magazine, seemed to demand, on the part of the Catholic
world, a popular antidote. This took the form, among
other protestations, of a book, published a year later and
dated Rome (the jacket wreathed with Christian fishes),
by the Marist Father Geoffrey Graystone, with the title
*The Dead Sea Scrolls and the Originality of Christ*. This
seemed to be a pamphlet aimed at me, since I was the only
writer on the subject who was dealt with at any length. It

is a simple piece of Catholic apologetics, of no scholarly value whatever, intended for a literate but not learned public, and it goes about its task, without acrimony, in a tone of patient good will. But in other such attempts at correction, Anglican as well as Catholic, one is surprised by the lofty tone, combined with complete lack of scruple, which the apologists sometimes adopt. When reviewing a book on the scrolls for a non-specialist publication, they assume that the people who will read the review know nothing about Biblical scholarship and that any statement of the reviewer will be believed if he pretends to be speaking with authority. And of course this assumption is in general correct. Even the serious non-clerical reviewer to whom the subject is new is not aware when he is misreporting, as was demonstrated by the fact that none of the reviews of my book, with the exception of those by superior professional scholars such as Arnold Toynbee and W. F. Albright, failed to make misrepresentations in summarizing what I had said. My clerical opponents knew well how easy it was in this field to lead the layman astray. The devices to which they resorted sometimes took the line of declaring that it was much too early to come to conclusions, by which was meant, to form any hypotheses, or that the really sound Biblical scholars were dismissing the flights of the superficial or, as they are often called, "sensational," ones—the assumption being, of course, that the reviewer was quite competent to pronounce as to which scholars were sound and which were superficial—or that the falsity of certain conjectures had already long ago been proved, as when a Reverend Hugh William Montefiore, now Vicar of Great Saint Mary's, Cambridge, and once lecturer on the New Testament at Cambridge, asserted, in the *Spectator* of May 18, 1956, that the Anglican scholar J. B. Lightfoot had irrefutably demonstrated that Jesus could never have been an Essene. Now, Lightfoot,

though a serious scholar, was at the same time a spokesman for his Church. He was Honorary Chaplain in Ordinary to the Queen and became, successively, Canon of
St. Paul's and Bishop of Durham, and his aim was to defend the sanctity of the Scriptures against the current
German attacks on their authenticity. The small treatise
in which he deals with the Essenes is contained in a volume of commentary called *St. Paul's Epistles to the Colossians and to Philemon*, first published in 1875. Lightfoot
felt, at that date, that it was of special importance to show
that Jesus was not and had never been an Essene. He says
that, for the secular scholars, "wherever some external
power is needed to solve a perplexity, here is the *deus ex
machina* whose aid they most readily invoke." And, on the
basis of the descriptions of the Essenes by Philo, Josephus
and the elder Pliny, who supplied the only testimony then
available, he goes into the subject quite thoroughly. The
two principal arguments of those who believe in the Es-
senian derivation of Christianity are, he says, "first, that
there is direct historical evidence of close intercourse between the two; and, secondly, that the resemblances of
doctrine and practice are so striking as to oblige, or at least
warrant, the belief in such a connexion. If both these lines
of argument fail, the case must be considered to have
broken down." In refutation of the first of these points,
Lightfoot urges that John the Baptist, though an ascetic
who baptized his followers, as the Essenes were ascetics
who baptized, was an independent preacher, whereas the
Essenes constituted a brotherhood of which baptism was
one of the rites, and that Jesus and his disciples, so far
from inhabiting a monastery, were always moving around;
and that, furthermore, Jesus disregarded observances which
the members of the order held sacred, showing disrespect
for the Sabbath, eating with unwashed hands, uncon-
strainedly dining with sinners such as the Essenes re-

garded as untouchable, allowing himself to be anointed
with oil, assisting at an ordinary wedding, and referring
to weddings "as symbols of the highest theological truths,"
when most of the Essenes were supposed to be celibates,
and failing to eschew, as the Essenes did, the conventional
sacrifices in the Temple. Lightfoot believed that there was
nothing significant in the fact that, though Josephus asserts that the three chief Jewish sects of his time were the
Pharisees, the Sadducees and the Essenes, there is nothing
about the last of these in the Gospels, and nothing that is
direct and certain in rabbinical literature. It has been suggested that the first of these omissions was due to some
special relation of John and Jesus to the Essene Sect—perhaps to John's having seceded from the Sect, though he
continued to echo its language; that Jesus may have deliberately been flouting their code. But Lightfoot explains
all this as due simply to the relative unimportance of the
Essenes and the remoteness of their monasteries. Some of
Lightfoot's conclusions are not incompatible with those
that have lately been drawn: "The Essenes were extreme
sufferers in the Roman war of extermination. . . . After
the destruction of Jerusalem, the Christian body was
largely reinforced from their ranks. The Judaizing tendencies among the Hebrew Christians, which hitherto had
been wholly Pharisaic, are henceforth largely Essene." But
the important point here is that Lightfoot had none of the
information now supplied by the Qumrân library. "As
preachers of righteousness," he says, not having any evidence to the contrary, "as heralds of the kingdom, they
had no claim to the title [of prophets]. Throughout the
notices in Josephus and Philo, we cannot trace the faintest
indication of Messianic hopes." Yet we know now that the
personality who chiefly figures in the Essene documents
is the leader called the Teacher of Righteousness, and that
the Sect had a prophetic literature of much of which he

may have been the author. We know also that this literature abounds in Messianic references and is charged with
Messianic hopes. For the Reverend Hugh Montefiore to
declare that the last definitive word on the relation of
Christianity to the Essenes was laid down by J. B. Lightfoot in 1875 is like telling a modern physicist that the
atom cannot be split.

Another example of this clerical bluffing—which illustrates, also, clearly the different levels of Catholic approach—is to be found in the issue of February 4, 1956,
of the Jesuit weekly *America*. When my article came out
in the *New Yorker*, I had a courteous and appreciative
letter from a Father Frederick L. Moriarty, S. J., Professor
of Old Testament at Weston College in Massachusetts,
expressing the hope that the article would eventually be
published in a book, "without the distraction of bathing-
suit ads!" When it did come out in a book, he sent me
proofs of a review he had written for *America*, in which
he spoke of it as he had in his letter. But when the review
appeared, I saw that it was offset by another article, featured on the cover as the review was not, by the Very Reverend John J. Dougherty, Professor of Sacred Scripture at
the Immaculate Conception Seminary of Darlington, New
Jersey, and Regent of the Institute of Judaeo-Christian
Studies of Seton Hall University in Newark. This article
seemed designed to counteract the possible effect of Father
Moriarty's friendly review, and certainly, in any case, to
put the readers of *America* on guard against my insidious
book. It contained the following statement:

"He [Mr. Wilson] has taken *one* hypothetical interpretation, that of the French scholar André Dupont-Sommer
of the Sorbonne, and presented it, dressed up in exciting
diction, to the circle of those who can read but not eval-
uate. That is mischief. Dupont-Sommer's sensational and
unproved thesis, adopted by Wilson, was that the Qumrân

documents revealed an anticipation of Christianity in the sect of the Essenes. Allow me to give one example of Dupont-Sommer's interpretation to bring out my point and to pull this discussion together. Column eight of the [Habakkuk] Commentary ends in the middle of a sentence; part of the text is missing. [I have spoken of this commentary above.] Column nine begins in the middle of a sentence. The opening words of column nine speak of *someone* who suffered 'vengeance in the body of his flesh.' M. Dupont-Sommer *conjecturally* supplied the missing words at the bottom of column eight to make the one suffering in column nine 'the Teacher of Righteousness' [who is constantly referred to as the head of the sect], and from the words 'body of his flesh' *inferred* that he was a divine being. *Sic.* True, in his later work he abandoned this and much of his theory, but Mr. Wilson has written just one article, which gives unmerited life to a hypothesis already discarded by its author."

Now, first of all, Dupont-Sommer was by no means the only scholar who had advanced the "sensational and unproved thesis . . . that the Qumrân documents reveal an anticipation of Christianity in the sect of the Essenes." There had been also W. F. Albright, W. H. Brownlee, K. G. Kuhn, and a number of others. If Monsignor Dougherty had written a year later, he would have had to come to terms with the Catholic scholar Père Jean Daniélou, who, writing in *L'Express* of February 1, 1957, listed twenty-seven reasons for believing that the early Christians were influenced by the Essenes. Furthermore, it is not true that I took only *"one hypothetical interpretation"* —that of Dupont-Sommer. Actually, I gave three. Nor is it true that I did not explain that the hiatus at the bottom of column eight had been filled in by Dupont-Sommer. I suggested, in fact, that he had "overplayed his hand." It is true that Dupont-Sommer, in the first of his books on the scrolls, asserts that the passages mentioned above in the Habakkuk Commentary are "evidently an allusion to the Passion of the Master of Justice; he was judged, condemned, and tortured. He suffered 'in the body of his flesh'; he was doubtless a divine being, who had become incarnate to live and die as a man." But I had made nothing at all of an inference that the Teacher of Righteousness was "a divine being," etc., because, like Monsignor Dougherty, I was aware of Dupont-Sommer's second book, in which he is at pains to make it clear that he does not identify the Teacher with Jesus and shows that, though their situations would appear to have had certain features in common, "the resemblance was far from total." Aside from correcting this impression that had been drawn by some readers from the first of his books, he has certainly not, as the Monsignor asserts, "abandoned much of his theory," but, on the contrary, has vigorously defended it.

I can think of only two explanations for Monsignor Dougherty's misrepresentations. Either he had not really read either my book or those of Dupont-Sommer, or, counting on the unfamiliarity of his readers with the literature of the scrolls, he had deliberately set out to mislead them by faking a superior scholarship.

An insistence on postdating the scrolls, in defiance of the archaeological evidence, has been manifested not merely by conservative Jewish scholars but also by Professor G. R. Driver of Oxford, who published in 1965, with the purpose of propounding such a theory, a long and elaborate work called *The Judaean Scrolls: The Problem and a Solution*. But before going on to this theory, I shall continue to grind my own axe—which is also to defend those scholars whom Driver is out to discredit. In a remarkably cavalier prologue, Mr. Driver, in quoting from my book, refers, but without naming him, to Professor David Flusser of the Hebrew University as "a Jewish jour-

nalist who learned Hebrew 'rather late in life.'" I am sorry
to have misled Professor Driver. When I said that Professor Flusser had learned Hebrew rather late in life, I
meant, as I depended on the context to show, that he had
learned only relatively late, when he came to live in Israel,
to speak Hebrew as a living language. For the rest, it
seems strange for Driver to have assumed that Flusser was
a journalist. He has always been a scholar. Flusser was a
lecturer in Hebrew in Prague from 1947 to 1950, and at
the time of my conversation with him, he was a lecturer
at the Hebrew University, from which, very soon afterwards, he received a Doctor's degree. I am mentioned in
the same sentence, after a semicolon—also, without being
named—as "another" [Jewish journalist] who has also expressed what are to Driver abhorrent views. I am myself,
if you like, a journalist, but to treat David Flusser as one
when he had never, so far as I know, written anything but
papers for learned periodicals is a piece of impertinence
quite shocking in a scholar of Driver's supposed standing
—as is, even more inexcusably, his snubbing of Dupont-
Sommer, who now occupies at the Collège de France the
Chair of Hebrew and Aramaic, by not mentioning this
distinction and, again, not calling him by name but referring to him merely as "a French professor." Mr. Driver,
himself an English professor, asserts, like Monsignor
Dougherty, that this French professor refers to the Teacher
of Righteousness as obviously "a divine being," and he
quotes a passage belittling Jesus from a certainly rather
absurd French journalist whom I cannot identify.

The main purpose of Mr. Driver's book is to refute the
generally accepted theory, best stated in Père de Vaux's
book *L'Archéologie et les Manuscrits de la Mer Morte*,
that the building first excavated by him and by the Jordanian Department of Antiquities was a monastery of the
Essene order, the sect described by Philo and Josephus and

located in the region by Pliny, which it occupied—with at one point, apparently, an absence of thirty years—from some date at the end of the second century B.C. up to 68 A.D., when, at the time of the first Jewish revolt, the Romans besieged it and held it; and that the scrolls were put away in the caves to keep them out of the hands of the Romans. (It was Professor Dupont-Sommer who first suggested that the Qumrân library must have belonged to and at least partly have been written by the Essenes—which may account for Mr. Driver's snubbing him.) Mr. Driver's objections to this theory consist of farfetched suppositions which are quite incompatible with the evidence on which the theory is based. The Sect in the monastery, according to Mr. Driver, were not Essenes—it is true that in the documents we have they never speak of themselves by that name—but some other Jewish group; Mr. Driver calls them "the Covenanters." Pliny's Latin, he says, does not mean what it seems to mean—it may not indicate the site of the monastery—and the Essenes, who "abjured war," would not have required "such substantial buildings." The manuscripts found in the caves may not have had any connection with the monastery. He admits that the jars in which they were stored are the same as those found in the monastery; "the coincidence, however, may be a pure matter of chance." The smallness of the room which has been called the *scriptorium* and the fewness of the inkwells found in it "make it an unlikely place for the copying of many hundreds of manuscripts." Mr. Driver develops a complicated and extremely implausible theory, for which he presents no real evidence. This theory is arrived at by the negative method of first, on principal, rejecting the evidence that has hitherto been accepted. The upshot of all this is an attempt to date the scrolls so late—between the middle of the first century A.D. and the first half of the second century—that the doctrines and

practices of the people who wrote them could not possibly
have had any influence on the origins of Christianity.
Père de Vaux, in an article in the *Revue Biblique* of April
12, 1966, and in a somewhat abridged English version in
*New Testament Studies* of October 13, 1966, reviewed
Professor Driver's book and, after expressions of personal
esteem and regret that he is forced to oppose him, proceeds to make mincemeat of his theory. He begins, in the
original French version, by devoting no less than six pages
to the unscholarly inaccuracy and confusion of Mr.
Driver's references and to the defects of his bibliography.
He then goes on to show that Driver's attempts to disprove
the archaeological evidence are due to his not really having grasped what it is. The Qumrân ruins, according to
Driver, cannot be the remains of the monastery of the
Essenes because his reinterpretation of Pliny puts the
monastery somewhere else, and he believes that in the
latter place there have turned up remains contemporary
with those of Qumrân. De Vaux answers that these remains represent the headquarters of the Romans, and that
the Essenes, since Pliny makes it plain that they were isolated, could not possibly have lived near them. The buildings, according to Driver, cannot have been attacked by
the Romans because the arrows found at Qumrân and
assumed to have been shot by the invaders were "collected
together in certain rooms," so probably belonged to the
occupants, whom Driver believes to have been, or to have
had some connection with, the belligerent party of Zealots. This is not the case, says de Vaux: some of the arrows
were found in the courtyards, "and I think that we may
be pardoned for not having dug up the whole hillside outside the walls in search of others," etc. Mr. Driver, de
Vaux continues, "seems not to have understood" the evidence of the coins in the monastery, which establish the
dates of certain events as well as a *terminus ad quem*,

June, 68 A.D., for the composition of the documents, and
he totally fails to mention, though he shows that he has
read an article which tells about it, the discovery on
Masada of a document—the so-called "Angelic Liturgies"
or "Songs of the Sabbath Sacrifices," four other fragments
from four copies of which had been found in the Qumrân
library—a document which identifies itself as belonging to
the Qumrâ.ı Sect because the sequence of dates of the
Sabbaths is given in terms of its peculiar calendar. Since
Masada, where the Jews made their last stand at the time
of their first revolt, was taken by the Romans in 73 A.D.,
when its defenders committed suicide rather than fall into
their hands, it is impossible that the literature of Qumrân
can, as Driver is trying to show, have been written at a
later date.

"It is a sad thing," remarks de Vaux, "to find here once
more this conflict of method and mentality between the
textual critic and the archaeologist, the man at his desk
and the man in the field." This is a case of the disagreement mentioned above, which ought to be borne in mind
in connection with the controversies about the scrolls.
"The man at his desk," through textual detective work
and historical imagination, will try to reconstruct what has
happened—I shall later give a striking example of the reconstruction by Dupont-Sommer of the events behind the
Nahum Commentary—but he will sometimes fail to take
into account the archaeological data. The archaeologist, on
the other hand, is occupied primarily with approximating
to an accurate chronology, and he will note with a certain
skepticism that the events, for example, of the Nahum
Commentary have been reconstructed quite differently by
other scholars equally competent.

It may be well to mention here another reason for disagreement among those who study the scrolls: the opposition between those who by faith or affiliation are com-

mitted to some orthodox Christian creed and those who are "freethinkers" or very liberal theologians. The former, who instinctively shrink from anything that would seem to conflict with the divine ascription of the Gospels, are likely to make an effort to dissociate the scrolls from the New Testament by emphasizing the differences between them; the latter find it exciting to discover their similarities. Now, no responsible writer has ever denied the differences between, on the one hand, the views attributed to Jesus in the Gospels, with their acceptance of the poor and proscribed, their preaching of love and forgiveness, as well as Paul's opening the Faith to the Gentiles, and, on the other hand, the theology of a narrow Jewish sect who regarded themselves as an élite—though they sometimes speak cordially of "the simple"—and the apparently fierce bellicosity of their Teacher of Righteousness. Though the Messianic literature of the Sect does seem to prepare the way for the appearance of some such figure as Jesus—it must always be remembered that Christ is simply the Greek for "Messiah," that is, the Anointed One—and though some of its words and conceptions are to be found in the literature of Christianity, the divergences are still so plain between the scrolls and the sayings of Jesus, with no unmistakable bridge from one to the other, that no evidence has yet been produced which should shake the belief of many that Jesus was the son of God in a special, a literal sense, and that the tremendous power of the Gospels is explicable only by this.

"My faith," Père de Vaux once said to me, "has nothing to fear from my scholarship." And although he has shown himself in the past on occasion rather harshly severe to non-believing scholars, I get the impression that in general the inhibitions imposed by religious commitments and by the taboos of superstition are now tending to disappear in connection with the study of the scrolls. The young man who began in a seminary may come to disregard theology and go in for archaeological or palaeographical research, or he may find that he can make a living teaching Hebrew or ancient Oriental history in a seminary or university where his orthodoxy will not be questioned.

# II

# THE GENESIS APOCRYPHON

THE ONLY one of the scrolls from Cave One which had not been read and published when these had all been acquired by the Israeli government was originally referred to, on the basis of two detached fragments, as the Book of Lamech, a work mentioned in an ancient list of apocrypha. It was in much worse condition than the others of this group. The layers were so stuck together by some gluey substance exuded during the decomposition of the leather that it was difficult to unroll it, and the leather was now so dry that it was difficult to keep it from crumbling. The ink in which the scroll was written, which seemed different from that of the other scrolls and sometimes either ate away the leather or gave the effect of ink on blotting paper, made it also very hard to read, so that recourse had to be made to infra-red rays. The lower parts of the columns were covered by a sheet of some thin white material, and this had to be removed. Part of the scroll has been rotted away, so that the tops or bottoms of columns are missing. The Hebrew University published in 1956 five more or less legible columns of this document, edited by Professors Yigael Yadin and Nahman Avigad, and announced that work was going forward on the rest. It now turns out that only at the beginning is this apocryphon concerned with Lamech; it is an Aramaic version of Genesis. In patches, it follows Genesis quite closely, and in others it corresponds with the intertestamental books of Enoch and Jubilees, which were perhaps partly derived from this text. The tentative date assigned to this copy is the end of the first century B.C. or the first half of the first century A.D.

This document is, in several ways, interesting to Semitic and Biblical scholars: it adds to the knowledge of Aramaic, the lingua franca of the Middle East which superseded Hebrew; it makes more specific than Genesis the geography of Abraham's wanderings; it identifies the "Red Sea" as the Indian Ocean; it attempts to fill in and explain some of the gaps and inconsistencies in the Biblical narrative. But for the ordinary reader of the Bible, the most interesting feature of this Aramaic Genesis is probably the account of the beauty of Sarah, and its version, supposed to be told by Abraham himself, of his and Sarah's experiences in Egypt. (They are here called Abram and Sarai, as they are at first in the Bible, before they have been renamed by God to signalize the high destiny for which He has chosen them.) Now, in Genesis there are two episodes (12.10-20 and 20.1-18) in which a ruler—first the Pharaoh of Egypt, then Abimelech, King of Gerar—becomes enamored of Sarah, and a similar one (26.6-11) in which the king is again Abimelech but the couple are Isaac and Rebecca. The unknown scribe or scribes who put together Genesis from earlier narratives made no effort to produce a consistent story, as the Peisistratean editors of the Homeric lays presumably did for Homer. He or they simply included everything that was thought to have the authority of antiquity. So we are told that when Abram and Sarai have been driven by the famine to Egypt, the Pharaoh becomes so smitten with Sarai, on account of her wonderful beauty, that he takes her away from Abram. Abram has foreseen this and pretended that Sarai is his sister, so that the Pharaoh will refrain from killing him. (From now on I follow the new account, in which it is Sarai herself who tells the king this.) He now appeals to God to intervene so that the king will not defile his wife, and God sends an evil pestilential wind—or spirit, רוה —which, with other plagues, afflicts him for two years, making him so ill that he cannot take advantage of Sarai. All the physicians and wizards and wise men of Egypt who are summoned by the Pharaoh are powerless to restore him: "The wind—or spirit—smote them all and they fled." One of the princes comes to Abram and begs him to pray for the Pharaoh, but his nephew Lot explains that Abram and Sarai are husband and wife and that his uncle cannot pray for the Pharaoh while the Pharaoh is holding his aunt. The prince explains this to the King, and the latter immediately releases her. Abram prays for him, and the plagues depart.

Later on, at Gerar, in the Negev—according to the Biblical account: the published columns of the apocryphon do not include this story—Abimelech, a local king, is also attracted by Sarah. Abraham tries the same ruse, but God warns the King in a dream before he has even touched her. Now, if we trust the account of Genesis, Sarah was sixty-five when she was found irresistible by the Pharaoh, and even older when she roused Abimelech. We wonder about her beauty. We tend to imagine her, I think, as the matron, a patriarch's consort, who laughed when she heard God announce that, hitherto sterile and at ninety, she was at last to give birth to a son. But this apocryphon furnishes for the first time a description of Sarai in her bloom, as reported to the Pharaoh by a courtier: "How . . . beautiful the look of her face . . . and how . . . fine is the hair of her head, how fair indeed are her eyes and how pleasing her nose and all the radiance of her face . . . how beautiful her breast and how lovely all her whiteness. Her arms goodly to look upon, and her hands how perfect . . . all the appearance of her hands. How fair her palms and how long and fine all the fingers of her hands. Her legs how beautiful and how without blemish her thighs. And all maidens and all brides that go beneath the wedding canopy are not more fair than she. And above all women is she lovely and higher is her beauty than that of them all, and with all her beauty there is much wisdom in her. And the tip of her hands is comely."

Another interesting point is that Abram, in healing the Pharaoh, not only prays for him but lays hands on his head. Professor David Flusser has commented on this in the *Israel Exploration Journal*, Volume 7, No. 2, 1957. This laying-on of hands is often mentioned in the New Testament as a feature of the healing of Jesus, but it does not occur in the Old Testament or, so far as is known, in rabbinical literature. Yet its occurrence in the Genesis apocryphon, this copy of which is supposed to have been made either during the lifetime of Jesus or a little earlier, would seem to indicate that the practice was not peculiar to Jesus but was a recognized method of effecting cures.

# III

# THE PSALMS

A NEW MANUSCRIPT of the Psalms was published in 1965
in the regular series of *Discoveries in the Judaean Desert
of Jordan*—that is, of the Dead Sea manuscripts not owned
by the Hebrew University but supervised by Père de
Vaux and brought out by the Clarendon Press. It has been
edited by Dr. J. A. Sanders, of the New York Union Theological Seminary, who has also published a more informal
and very readable book on the subject, *The Dead Sea
Psalms Scroll* (Cornell). This scroll, says Mr. Sanders,
when found, was covered with bat dung and partly de-
composed, but it contains forty-one psalms, either fragmentary or complete. The tetragrammaton, the unpronounceable name of God, for which, in reading the Bible
aloud, *Adonai* must be substituted, is here made even
more remote by being always written in Old Hebrew characters as 𐤉𐤄𐤅𐤄. (This is usual in the literature of the
Sect, but not in its Bible texts.) There are variants here
from the Masoretic Bible—that is, from the official Hebrew
text, as there are in fragments of the Psalms that have
been found in one of the other caves—but the most interesting feature of this manuscript is the inclusion of eight
apocryphal compositions. (Scraps of such uncanonical
psalms have also been found elsewhere.) Four of these
pieces were already known in Greek, Latin or Syriac
translations. One has been identified as a Hebrew version

of a canticle at the end of the Book of Sirach (known in
the apocrypha as Ecclesiasticus): one of the curious eulo-
gies of the pursuit of Wisdom as a woman, which approaches the erotic so closely that Mr. Sanders is led to
suggest that it was used for encouragement to "sublima-
tion" by the celibate community in the monastery. But
three of the non-Biblical Psalms had never before been
seen: a paean of praise to God for having saved the psalm-
ist from sins that had brought him near to death; a paean
of praise to Zion; and a glorification of God as the creator
of the world. There is also a short prose passage, hitherto
unknown, which speaks of the high qualities of David
and asserts that he wrote thirty-six hundred psalms (the
Hebrew word *tehillim* means "songs of praise") and four
hundred and fifty songs of other kinds.

The most interesting of these uncanonic pieces is probably the somewhat mysterious 151st Psalm. (There are
only a hundred and fifty in the Masoretic Bible.) This
had already been known in Greek as well as in Syriac,
because it occurs in the Septuagint, the Greek translation
of the Old Testament made in Alexandria, which does not
always correspond with the Masoretic Bible and was obviously done from a different text. This 151st Psalm of
the Septuagint now turns up in the new text as two separate pieces, which have evidently been combined in the
Greek and Syriac versions and to some extent censored.
This censoring is thought to be significant, because in this
new Hebrew version the flocks and the trees are made to
respond to the music of David's lyre as they are not in the
other versions. Now, the influence of the Greek cult of
Orpheus, whose music was supposed to have enchanted its
animal and vegetable hearers, is clearly traceable both in
Jewish and Christian art, in the former of which Orpheus
merges with David and in the latter of which with Christ.
The animals and trees charmed by Orpheus are trans-

formed into the sheep watched by David and the flock of
that other good shepherd, Christ. Among the frescoes of
a third-century synagogue discovered at Dura-Europus on
the upper Euphrates, is one of Orpheus in a Phrygian cap
playing his cithern to a monkey and a lion. An Orpheus
was also discovered in a Jewish catacomb near Rome, and
it was remembered that certain Byzantine psalters had
somewhat similar miniatures of David playing to his flock.
The most striking of these representations is a second-
century mosaic in a Christian church in Jerusalem, which
shows a male figure with a lyre, also in a Phrygian cap,
surrounded by four animals, two birds and some plants
and trees. What is most surprising is that below him stand
a horned and goat-footed satyr and a centaur with a leop-
ard skin and club. Eusebius, the Church historian of the
early fourth century, has compared the magic of the music
of Orpheus to the magic of the words of Jesus.

The scholars who have translated this psalm have differed from one another in emphasizing or minimizing
the supposed Orphic influence to be seen in it. Almost all
of them, like Mr. Sanders, translate the words that precede the statement that the trees and the flocks respond
to David's music as a statement that the mountains do *not*
bear witness to the Lord nor do the hills proclaim Him.
The Hebrew negative is certainly there, but M. Dupont-
Sommer, in a paper called *David et Orphée,* avoids
these apparently contradictory statements by interpreting
these lines as questions: "Do the mountains not bear witness?," etc. He regards the lines that follow as also betraying Greek influence—in this case, Pythagoreanism, a conception of the harmony of the world, the music of the
spheres, which the pious musician imitates and repro-
duces on his lyre in homage to the supreme God. "For
who will proclaim and who will celebrate and who will re-
count the works of the Lord? God sees the universe; God

hears the universe, and He gives ear." The Hebrew phrase
for *the all* Sanders simply renders as *everything*; Dupont-
Sommer translates *"l'univers"* as I have left it above. God
gives ear, Dupont-Sommer goes on, "as if to taste as a
connoisseur both the smooth harmony of the world which
he has created and the accents that rise from the inspired
cords and mingle in the same mystic concert with the
music of the universe." The Jews, in their reaction against
the Greeks, would have eliminated any trace of Orphism
or Pythagoreanism, hence the abridged version in the Septuagint and the Syriac texts of this Hellenistic psalm.

Dupont-Sommer further believes that this piece was
composed by some poet belonging to the Sect. What seem
his most persuasive arguments are based on the promi-
nence given to music in the Dead Sea literature and the
fact that Josephus says that the life of the Essenes had a
good deal in common with the life of the Pythagoreans.
The Orphean hymn, furthermore, ends with the statement by David that God "made me prince of His people
and ruler over the sons of His covenant." The phrase
"sons of His covenant" is also found in another of the
Qumrân scrolls, but, like the Orphean phrases, it does
not occur in the Septuagint version. The inference would
be, then, that an attempt had been made here to weed
out any traces of the Sect, who had introduced the
"David-Orpheus" into their Psalter and referred to themselves as "the sons of the covenant."

A word should be said at this point about the scrolls
from Cave Eleven, which were discovered only as recently as 1956. Among these were this manuscript of the
Psalms, some fragments of Leviticus, a gelatinized scroll
of Ezekiel, an Aramaic targum of Job (that is, a version to
be read in synagogues in the period when Biblical Hebrew was no longer widely understood), and some frag-

ments on the Sect's "New Jerusalem," a subject not yet expounded by the scholars in spite of the fact that other fragments relating to it had already been found. The Palestine Museum, in purchasing these scrolls, had been obliged to pay forty-eight thousand pounds to Kando, a Syrian dealer in Bethlehem, who has been acting as a go-between between the Bedouins and the buyers. This made such inroads on the museum's trust funds, supplied by Rockefeller money, that the museum now refused to release any of these manuscripts for publication unless someone came forward with sums on a scale to repair this expense. The result was that only in 1964, eight years after the acquisition of the scrolls, when a wealthy American donor had put up for it twenty-five thousand pounds, was the first of this lot published. The Job has been financed by the Dutch government and has been in the hands of J. van der Ploeg, the Dutch Dominican scholar, who has been taking a very long time over it.

A certain dissatisfaction has been felt by some Protestant and Jewish and uncommitted scholars at the slowness with which, even before this special situation at the Palestine Museum arose, the contents of the Jordanian scrolls have been made public. Three of the original lot from Cave One were almost immediately published by the American Schools of Oriental Research through the Yale University Press, and the remaining four as promptly by the Hebrew University as soon as they came into its possession and could be read as a printable text. This was done with very little editing. The text was reproduced, with a decipherment in modern Hebrew characters and a tentative translation. The scrolls were in this way put at the disposition of scholars all over the world. Yadin's idea was that any scholar who chose to study them would thus be able to have the benefit of other people's interpretations. But the scrolls from the Palestine Museum have been issued only at long intervals and many years after being discovered, with heavy editorial equipment, textual and archaeological, and at prices that few can afford, in the Clarendon Press series mentioned at the beginning of this section. This has all been controlled by the École Biblique, and consequently by Catholic authority, and it has been intimated that something has been found prejudicial to the dogma of the Catholic Church which on that account is being kept concealed. But although it is no doubt true, as has been reported above, that the Catholics have felt reluctant to attract special attention to the scrolls, I have found no reason to believe that any of these documents has been or is likely to be suppressed—or that anything, in fact, is likely to be found which will cast any doubt on the Catholic faith. There has not as yet turned up any reference to either Jesus or John the Baptist in any of the Qumrân writings, and since the Sect would surely never have accepted these prophets, it is difficult to see why they should not have been ignored. Why, in any case, should a Christian be shaken by anything that the Sect might have said about them? Aside from a possible intention of retarding and muffling the publication of the scrolls in order to prevent their implications coming out with too forceful an impact, the delay is partly to be explained by the difficulty of fitting together those manuscripts which were found in fragments, and partly by the laggardness of certain scholars. Add to this, perhaps, the very natural and familiar scholarly instinct for establishing priority and proprietorship which would impel such a man as  de Vaux to desire to direct the handling and make sure of the proper presentation of materials which, after all, he himself had brought to light and for which he feels a personal responsibility. He has, in any case, recently responded to the complaints of the hungry scholars by bringing pressure on the various editors to get on with the tasks assigned them.

# IV

# THE NAHUM PESHER

ONE OF THE fascinating features of the Qumrân library
has been a series of ostensible commentaries on certain of
the Psalms and the Prophets, evidently written by a member or members of the Sect, which are actually half-
disguised records of events in the history of the Sect itself.
These commentaries are known as *pesharim,* because after
each verse the special interpretation begins with *"Pishro
al . . ."* ("Its interpretation relates to . . ."). At the
time I first wrote on this subject, the most extensive of
these was the commentary on Habakkuk which had
been found in Cave One among the first batch of manuscripts. This stimulated a great deal of interest because it
seemed to throw some light on the historical background
of the documents. There appear certain unnamed figures
who are mentioned in others of the scrolls: the Teacher
of Righteousness, the Wicked Priest, the Prophet or Man
of Untruth, and the enemy the Essenes are opposing, who
are referred to as the Kittim. The last of these, who are
said to worship their eagles and who seem to be identified
in other ways, were believed to be the Romans, who invaded Palestine in 63 B.C. The Teacher of Righteousness
had been evidently the leader of the Sect; the Wicked
Priest and the Man of Untruth were perhaps the same
hated person, and he was eventually identified by Dupont-
Sommer as the Hasmonean Hyrcanus II, who was at once

High Priest of Jerusalem (78-40 B.C.) and King of the
Jews in that dynasty—a descendant, that is, of the Maccabees, the pugnacious Jewish family who put up such a
fight against the Seleucids, the successors, in possession of
Palestine, of Alexander the Great, after he had conquered
Judea. But it was tantalizing not to know exactly who
these persons were or precisely what had taken place.

Then more scrolls were recovered from other caves,
among them a *pesher* on Nahum, in which, it was
rumored among Biblical scholars, though they were
otherwise pledged to silence, that historically known
names were mentioned and that important revelations
were looming. These names turned out, when one of the
columns of the text was published in 1956, to be those of
an Antiochus and a Demetrius, though of the latter only
three characters survived. John Allegro, a young English
scholar attached to the University of Manchester, to
whom this manuscript had been entrusted, announced
before its publication that the Wicked Priest was not
Hyrcanus II but his father, Alexander Jannaeus, also
High Priest and King, whose cruelty to his own people
has been recorded by Josephus. Jannaeus, believed Allegro, had been persecuting the Sect and had "stormed
down" on the Dead Sea monastery, "dragged forth the
Teacher [of Righteousness], and, as now seems probable,
gave him into the hands of the Gentile troops to be
crucified. . . . But when the Jewish King had left, and
peace descended once more on Qumrân, the scattered
community returned, and took down the broken body of
their Master, to stand guard over it until the Judgment
Day." It had already been suggested—from the practices
of the Sect, their writings, and their presence in that locality, where John the Baptist had preached as "a voice
crying in the wilderness" and where he had baptized
Jesus in the Jordan—that John and Jesus had had some

connection with the Sect, and the inference had already
been drawn that the Teacher might have been a pre-
cursor of that Jesus who, by his disciples, had been accepted as the Christ—that is, as the Messiah. The Sect had
been expecting a Messiah, and there is a theory that they
were looking forward to the return of the dead leader in
this role. If it turned out that the Teacher of Righteousness was crucified, there would seem to be an obvious
parallel between Jesus's career and his as well as—what
the texts do undoubtedly establish—a good deal in common between Christian doctrine and the doctrine of the
Dead Sea Sect. Mr. Allegro called attention to this. "For
most of us," he said, "these events will associate themselves automatically with the betrayal and crucifixion of
another Master, living a century later."

Mr. Allegro, however, had been unwise in broadcasting, on the basis of the *pesher*, conclusions that were entirely conjectural before he had published this text so
that anyone could check on his accuracy. Alexander Jannaeus, actually, is never mentioned by name in the text,
and although in a very scrappy passage there is a mention
of someone who was crucified, there is no indication whatever that this was the Teacher of Righteousness, and none
at all that "the scattered community returned and took
down the body of their Master." Mr. Allegro's contribution to this subject consists of three radio broadcasts with
an article based on these, and of an interview with a reporter from *Time* that Mr. Allegro declares was so mis-
quoted and garbled that he can really not be held responsible for anything reported in it, as well as of his later
fuller version of his argument in a book called *The Dead
Sea Scrolls*. In this book, Mr. Allegro does not repeat his
statement that the scattered Sect took down the body of
their Master, and he here tells his story in such a way as
to make it perfectly clear that his earlier account of the

content of the scroll was mainly a matter of conjecture. It is probable, however, that even here he ought to have been a little more explicit in indicating, clue by clue, the steps by which the episode had been reconstructed. What he gave was a connected narrative which he allowed himself to animate and color. He indulged himself, for example, in inventing a rather melodramatic confrontation of the Teacher of Righteousness and the Wicked Priest: "The scene as these two priests faced one another must have been dramatic enough. The one haughty and proud, scarred by the wounds of many battles, and the ravaging of a lifetime of greed and lechery, the other, white-robed and saintly, gazing scornfully on his enemy, secure in his simple trust in God and the hope of resurrection to eternal life." But it is true that it may be supposed from one interpretation of a passage in the Habakkuk Commentary that the Wicked Priest at some point appeared to the Teacher of Righteousness and his followers, "to confound them and to make them stumble on the day of fasting." There is also a reference to "the house of his exile." The residence of the Sect in the monastery is dated by the coins that have been found in it, and this date is exactly right for the identification of the Wicked Priest with Alexander Jannaeus. The Demetrius named in the commentary, who is said to have attempted to enter Jerusalem "by the counsel of the Seekers after Smooth Things" (presumably the Pharisees), was Demetrius III, the current Seleucid king, who is known to have been called in by the Pharisees, at the time they were contending against Jannaeus; and the Antiochus can be identified with Antiochus Epiphanes, an earlier Seleucid, who had been King of Syria and an enemy of the Jews.

The next event of importance in connection with the Nahum *pesher* is a paper—written after the publication

by Allegro of the three columns of the document's text—
by M. Dupont-Sommer in the issue of the *Journal des
Savants* of October-December, 1963, which seems to me
one of the most masterly reconstructions on the basis of
scrappy and scattered evidence that I remember ever to
have read. M. Dupont-Sommer agrees with Allegro's iden-
tifications of a "Lion of Wrath" as Jannaeus, the Demetrius as the Greek king, and the Seekers after Smooth
Things (Dupont-Sommer makes it Flattering Things
using another meaning of חלקת) as the Pharisees. The
Nineveh which Nahum denounces is made to stand
here, Dupont-Sommer believes, for the official Jerusalem
"Establishment," from which the Sect had dissociated
themselves. The Seekers of Flattering Things (by which
they were trying to win over the people), who had
previously figured in certain Dead Sea fragments, we
now know to be the Pharisees—I am giving here Dupont-Sommer's argument—since it was the Pharisees who
called in Demetrius. It should be grasped that the Pharisees made a popular appeal—that is, they tried to win
over by flattery—while the Sadducees, who supported
Jannaeus, were conservative and aristocratic; and that the
Sect, who had escaped from Jerusalem and now inhabited
a monastery on the Dead Sea, were equally antagonistic
to both of them. The commentator says that the Lion of
Wrath—that is, Alexander Jannaeus—"will smite by his
nobles and the men of his counsel." We know from
Josephus that Jannaeus, after Demetrius had been driven
out, crucified eight hundred of the Jews who had fought
against him: "He brought them to Jerusalem, and did one
of the most barbarous actions in the world to them; for as
he was feasting with his concubines, in the sight of all
the city, he ordered the throats of their children and wives
to be cut before their eyes." It is evidently to this that the
commentator refers when he says that the Lion of Wrath

worked his vengeance on the Seekers of Flattering
Things, who had backed Demetrius, by "hanging them
alive." The text at this point is much broken. Both Allegro and Dupont-Sommer fill in a defective passage to
read, "which had never been done before in Israel," and
there follows an unfinished sentence which speaks of
someone "hanged alive on a tree" (or "on wood"—עץ
has both meanings), and this was the usual way of referring to crucifixion. It was this phrase which had stimulated Allegro to imagine that Alexander Jannaeus had
crucified the Teacher of Righteousness. The passage contains two incomplete words, which Allegro and Dupont-
Sommer restore in different ways. Allegro makes it, "For
the man hanged alive upon a tree is [cal]led . . ." Dupont-Sommer translates it, "But he who was hanged alive
upon [the] wood," and, as Allegro does, fills in the word
that follows, of which the only surviving characters are a
*resh* and an *aleph* with a form of the verb קרא, *call*, but
makes it read "They will [c]all (upon him)." He adds,
"If the word is completed in this way, the phrase refers
to someone who suffered punishment on the cross and
became an object of invocation. Who can this extraordinary person be? By whom could he have been crucified?
There is nothing to lead us to conclude that he was executed by Jannaeus: his death may have been ordered by
a successor of Jannaeus. The phrase may spring from an
association of ideas: although crucifixion is a scandal,
there is one crucified man who will, on the contrary, become for some an object of prayer."

Let us go on to Dupont-Sommer's reconstruction of the
historical events involved. When Alexander Jannaeus
died, his widow, Alexandra, reigned. She had two sons,
Hyrcanus II and Aristobulus II. Since Hyrcanus was the
elder, she made him High Priest. She established the

Pharisees as the ruling party, and these plagued Alexandra to put to death those who had persuaded her husband to crucify the eight hundred. They cut the throats of several of her councillors. Her younger son, Aristobulus, came to her with a delegation of Jannaeus' party, the Sadducees, and begged her to call off the Pharisees and to allow the Sadducean followers of Aristobulus to live safely in the national fortresses. Eventually, when Alexandra was old and ill, Aristobulus got control of twenty-two of these fortresses and made Hyrcanus, who had no taste for government and only wanted a quiet life, acknowledge his brother's accession to the kingship. Josephus says that "the Pharisees have delivered to the people a great many observances, by succession from their fathers, which are not written in the law of Moses; and for that reason it is that the Sadducees reject them, and say that we are to esteem those observances to be obligatory which are in the written word, but are not to observe those that are [merely] derived from the tradition of our forefathers; and concerning these things it is that great disputes and differences have arisen among them, while the Sadducees are able to persuade none but the rich, and have not the populace obsequious to them, but the Pharisees have the multitude on their side." Dupont-Sommer points out that if the Seekers of Flattering Things are the Pharisees, the Essenes were just as much opposed to them as they were to the Sadducees. These seducers of the people are thus named and denounced in two other Qumrân documents: the so-called Thanksgiving Hymns and the Zadokite or Damascus Document. The Wicked Priest, who figures here and also in the Habakkuk Commentary, would then be Hyrcanus II (so not the same as the Lion of Wrath). Dupont-Sommer reminds us of the denunciation by Jesus (Matthew 23.15) of the scribes and Pharisees, which he suggests may be a continuation—

on the assumption that Jesus had at some time been influenced by the Sect—of the attitude toward them of the Essenes.

In the *pesher*, an Ephraim and a Manasseh are mentioned. Who are they? In Genesis 41.51, two sons are born to Joseph who are given these names. Manasseh is the older. Later on (48.13-20), their grandfather Jacob (now called Israel) blesses them, but he puts his right hand on Ephraim's head and his left hand on Manasseh's. Joseph attempts to correct him, but Jacob replies that the younger brother will be greater than the elder, "and his seed shall become a multitude of nations." Then the Ephraim and Manasseh of the *pesher* must be the brothers Hyrcanus and Aristobulus. Of these latter, to be sure, Hyrcanus was the older, but since Jacob, in his blessings, interchanged the order of birth, Hyrcanus must be Ephraim, whose name is associated with the Pharisees, those "who by their false teaching and their lying tongue and lip of deceit will lead many astray." Manasseh is associated with "the nobles, the honored ones"—that is, the aristocratic Sadducees—and is also a leader of "warriors," as Aristobulus so conspicuously was. We are told that Manasseh will lose his royalty, that his women and children will go into captivity and his warriors and nobles be slaughtered— which was precisely what happened to Aristobulus when he fell into the hands of the Romans. In a fragment of a *pesher* on the Thirty-seventh Psalm, we learn of "the wicked of Ephraim and Manasseh, who will seek to lay hands on the Priest," meaning, presumably, the Teacher of Righteousness. We hear also, in the Nahum *pesher*, of "the wicked ones of its [army], of the House of Peleg," those who joined Manasseh. Now, Peleg suggests a Hebrew verb, *palag*, which means *divide*, and this is played on in Genesis 10.25, where the name Peleg is given to the son of a patriarch who was destined to "divide the earth."

May this not refer to the Hasmonean dynasty, who are always so extremely divided?

M. Dupont-Sommer, unlike certain other scholars, who believe that the Teacher of Righteousness flourished at the beginning of the Hasmonean era—that is to say, perhaps, between 160 and 135 B.C.—has become convinced, on the evidence of the passage cited above from the commentary on Psalm 37, that he lived during the period of Hyrcanus and Aristobulus, who, contending against one another, were united in hostility to the Essenes, themselves equally hostile to both parties of the Jerusalem "Establishment," as their supporters, the Pharisees and the Sadducees, were later to unite against Jesus. Both Josephus and Diodorus Siculus, M. Dupont-Sommer has noted, have accounts of a suggestive incident that took place when Pompey was moving against Jerusalem. Hyrcanus and Aristobulus came to him and urged their conflicting claims, but there was also a delegation that represented a third group of the Jews, who said that they did not want any king at all, that their tradition was to be ruled by "the priests of that God whom they worshipped," that though Hyrcanus and Aristobulus were the descendants of a priestly family they were actually, in their role of kings, now turning into tyrants. M. Dupont-Sommer believes that this group could only have been the Essenes—which would account both for their resistance to official Jerusalem and for Hyrcanus' having killed their leader.

I hope that this brief account may not be confusing to the reader. It can certainly give no idea of the elegance, lucidity and logic of Dupont-Sommer's demonstration.

# V

# JOHN ALLEGRO

THE ATTEMPTS to trace the relations of these Biblical commentaries found among the Dead Sea scrolls to events in the history of the Dead Sea Sect are already in themselves so complicated that I have forborne to complicate them further by describing the personal relations of the scholars who have been working on them. The occasion for the most acrimonious of the controversies about the scrolls has been the opinions and exploits of Mr. John Allegro of Manchester University, and in summarizing the work in this field it is important to explain his role. Though his credentials as a scholar have been sound enough to win him his present chair as Lecturer in Old Testament and Intertestamental Studies and his membership in the international committee appointed to work on the Jordanian scrolls, he could hardly contrast more strongly with the typical Biblical scholar or the traditional English don. He is irreverent and rather brash. When I first met him, twelve years ago, he seemed to me, in fact, to belong to the species of what was then called the Angry Young Men —a member of this generation who had landed, by some strange accident, in the field of Semitic scholarship. The explanation of his occupying his present position is that he prepared himself in youth for the Methodist ministry, that he excelled in Hebrew studies and got a scholarship for advanced work at Oxford, was recommended by H. H.

Rowley, the head of the Semitic department of Manchester University, for a place on the Jordan team, and went on to a chair at Manchester in Comparative Semitic Philology. He has been assigned for editing and publication in the series of *Discoveries in the Judaean Desert of Jordan* a group of mostly non-Biblical fragments which includes the Nahum *pesher*. In the meantime—quite early, I imagine—Allegro had lost his faith, had now no commitment to any Church, and was thus in a unique position among the Protestant, Anglican and Catholic scholars who made up the rest of the interdenominational commission. It has been partly, it seems to me, an inevitable result of this that he and his colleagues should not always have agreed, but it also cannot be denied that his having so much annoyed them—as well as having come to be on rather uneasy terms with some of the Jewish scholars and Arab officials—has been due to a certain element of bad judgment and indiscretion on his own part. It ought to be explained in advance, before giving specific examples, that his quarrels with other scholars have usually been provoked by his making through the press or radio sensational-sounding statements about unheard-of and disturbing revelations supposed to have been found in the scrolls, before publication of the documents on which these statements were based and which, when the texts were published, did not necessarily prove what he had given the impression they did. Allegro may thus at moments have misled the public. He has certainly been at cross purposes with his colleagues.

I have already noted his conclusions or "conjectures" in connection with the commentary on Nahum, and the objections to them afterwards urged when he had published the three extant columns of the document. But in the meantime his opinions had been expressed in a positive, rather jaunty way in his three B.B.C. broadcasts and had been somewhat distorted in the article in *Time* put together from these and from an interview. This article had the result of arousing Père Roland de Vaux to write a letter to the London *Times* declaring that there was nothing whatever in any of the documents so far deciphered which would indicate that the Teacher of Righteousness had been crucified or to warrant other statements of Allegro's. This letter was signed also by four other members of the team, three of them Catholic priests. Later on, there appeared in the Catholic *Tablet* three articles by another Catholic priest, the Marist Father Geoffrey Graystone, of whose vapid little book on the scrolls I have already spoken and who here also gave somewhat the impression of having entered the controversy as an official spokesman for the Vatican. The line Father Graystone took was, as usual, to pooh-pooh the parallels between the doctrines and practices of the Sect and those of the early Christians and to emphasize the many divergences. One of these articles, called "The Mind of Mr. Allegro," seemed intended—though it dealt only with the B.B.C. broadcasts —to discredit his forthcoming book before its publication. Father Graystone accepted as authoritative the *Times* letter of Père de Vaux and a protest by one of the latter's colleagues, the American Monsignor Patrick Skehan of the Catholic University in Washington, D.C., who had recently been added to the team, and he reassured his Catholic readers by telling them that at least half of the team now working on the scrolls were Catholics and that the Vatican had just contributed five thousand pounds to the enterprise of deciphering them—which meant that five thousand pounds' worth of the manuscripts would go to the Vatican library. I have already explained that, in his book which followed, Mr. Allegro made it plain that his previous statements had been mainly based on conjectures, though it did not cease to be true that, in elaborating these, he had indulged certain fictional fantasies. It is said that his superior at the university, the Baptist Professor Rowley, admonished him on one occasion, "Allegro, *adagio, adagio!*"

I ought to note here, in regard to Mr. Allegro's behavior in general, that, although he is professionally functioning in a very much restricted academic field, he has some of the talents and instincts of a dramatically minded journalist which prompt him to make sallies outside it. In doing so, in issuing his astonishing statements, which the public may take for scholarly truth, he is trading as much on its ignorance—with the intent of influencing them in the opposite direction—as the orthodox bluffing clerics of whose practices I have complained. But his position as a freethinker in a department to which, in Britain, few such candidates are likely to aspire or in which, without some at least nominal religious affiliation, they are unlikely to get posts is bound to be somewhat precarious. How many such chairs in Britain are available to an openly uncommitted and independent scholar? Mr. Allegro was at one time unsure of his tenure and, with a family to support, it was obviously to his interest to write as many articles, deliver as many broadcasts and publish as many popular books as possible. And we should be wrong to be quick to discredit the man of historical imagination, though he may sometimes be carried away to imagine beyond the evidence, in favor of the scholar with none.

Mr. Allegro's later adventures in connection with the copper scrolls I shall treat in the next section. But I shall go beyond that here to give some account of his most recent "conjectures," which seem to me quite fantastic. In articles in *Harper's* of August, 1966, and in the Sunday color supplement of the London *Observer* of November 13, 1966, he has been advancing a theory that the Gospels are actually an Essene document, that the names of Jesus

and all the Apostles, including Judas, are disguises for the
titles of Essene officials, and that the Gospel personalities
are probably "myths." He says that the members of the
Sect were "diviners" as well as healers, and calls the Gospels a "handbook of witchcraft." He arrives at these opinions by an extremely far-fetched method of searching for
Hebrew or Aramaic words that can be made to bear some
relation to the names of the New Testament and to allow
such an interpretation. Allegro makes much of the fact
that the Greek word for carpenter, τέκτων, which in Matthew is applied to Joseph and in Mark to Jesus himself,
must have as its Hebrew equivalent חרש, which may
also mean *magician*. Professor J. A. Sanders, whom I have
mentioned as the editor of the new Psalms manuscript, protested, in a letter to *Harper's*, that this word could mean
also *engraver*, *ploughing*, *potsherd*, and *hillock of trees*, and
he discredited another claim that the name Jesus must
mean *magician*. When I first read Allegro on this subject,
I was strongly reminded of the people who manage to find
in Shakespeare hidden ciphers that show that the works
which have been credited to him were actually written by
Bacon or Marlowe or the Earl of Oxford, and it seemed to
me that by using such methods I should have little difficulty in proving that the Pentateuch was written by Ben-
Gurion. Later on, when I went the rounds of the scholars
most interested in the scrolls, I did not find one, even
among those who had no stake in the divinity of Jesus,
who took Allegro's theories seriously. At a conversation
tape-recorded in December, 1966, in the office of the London *Observer*, Mr. Allegro was confronted by Professor
Yigael Yadin of the Hebrew University; Professor Géza
Vermès of Oxford; and Canon E. F. Carpenter of Westminster, who challenged him to defend his thesis—which
he constantly refers to as a "break-through." Allegro, for

example, had made a good deal of what he calls "a little document" in which, he says, occurs a Semitic word which must underlie the significant name Cephas given by Jesus to Simon Peter. (*Kefa*, the Aramaic for *stone*, is translated into Greek as πέτρος .) "The Essenes," says Allegro, "deemed it a rather 'special' word, since it signifies one having the ability to read men's minds through their faces." Therefore, Peter is an Essene "overseer," and he is the first to recognize Jesus as the Messiah. Therefore, he "speaks with tongues"—how does this follow?—"relating the wonderful works of God, supervising the admittance of new members into the community, handling the common fund," etc. Here again Allegro is arguing from a text that has not been published, and Professors Yadin and Vermès keep asking him what it is. Professor Vermès reminds him that it has been the habit of that other unorthodox but scrupulous scrollsman M. Dupont-Sommer always first to publish scholarly papers that can be read and judged by other scholars before making any public statement that is directed to a wider audience. But they do not get Allegro to answer them till the very end of the conference, and then, though he has formerly suggested that he has been working on the document in question, he explains that he has not got it:

"YADIN: Can we have the text? What is it?

"ALLEGRO: Why don't you ask Milik [another of the scrolls editors]? It's part of his documents.

"VERMÈS: How is it spelled? [the word that Allegro connects with Cephas]

"ALLEGRO: In the document? It's spelled in two ways—where you've got a signature at the end and where you've got the abbreviation—and at the beginning you've got the letters *kaph, 'ayin, pe, samekh*.

"CROSS [not Dr. Frank M. Cross, Jr., of Harvard, to

whom I have already referred, but a person of that name who was presiding over the conversation]: What is the document?

"ALLEGRO: It's this little clinical record.

"CROSS: On that basis Cephas means Essene overseer?

"ALLEGRO: No, no: it's more complicated than that.

"VERMÈS: Very complicated.

"ALLEGRO: It seems to be a special title within the community. The Hebrew equivalent would be *paqid, overseer.* . . .

"YADIN: I don't find your argument on the word convincing at all.

"ALLEGRO: Fine, fine—work it out for yourself."

It would be unfair to deal with Allegro's theories on the basis of anything but considered and well-documented texts if it were not for the fact that his utterances are coming to sound more and more fanciful. The following report of an interview appeared in the London *Daily Mail* of October 13, 1967, and that professionally sensational paper can surely not entirely be blamed for either the language or the content of Allegro's remarks. Allegro, the reporter says, "is shortly to publish new findings which will trace the roots of Christianity to 'a phallic, drug-taking mystery cult we none of us would want anything to do with.'" "What?" the reporter inquires. "The prophets on LSD?" "'Yes, indeed,' says Allegro, 'or something very like it. They *had* visions. They went on a trip.' . . . Allegro believes he has established a common fund of religious vocabulary between the pre-Christian literatures and the Bible stories—between the mysteries of the earlier cults and what he calls the 'readable, merry tales of this rabbi, Jesus, and his Mum and Dad. . . . [The New Testament is] no more than a cover document. . . . The origins of Christianity can be seen against the pattern of this vegetation cult, which involved the use of drugs. Its priest and prophets were dope-pushers, if you like, but only within their own groups. They were seeking the release of the soul from the body, as something which could fly into the future and then come back. Either with drugs or through fasting—which gives much the same effect—they went off on a trip and then came back. Here is your speaking with tongues. The Church's misunderstanding of the origins of its cult began when it took the New Testament at its face value. Once you break it down into its Semitic substratum, you get close to the mystery, fertility cult, which is much more significant than we have ever given it credit for. There is no Jesus or Joseph or Mary left. You are dealing with myths. If there is any one personality involved, it is possibly some shadowy figure from the Essene sect, about a century earlier.'" The only thing that seems to me plausible here—and it has sometimes been suggested before—is that the cult of Jesus, with its spring resurrection, has taken on something of the aspect of the ancient fertility cults. Otherwise, the theory reminded me of that of the late Benjamin Smith, a very learned scholar, nonetheless, who also believed that Jesus may not have been an actual historical character and that the whole of the Gospels is an allegory, in which Jesus is made to figure as the Jewish people.

# VI

## THE COPPER SCROLLS

IN MARCH, 1952, two mysterious scrolls of copper were found, one on top of the other, in one of the Dead Sea caves. They were evidently so brittle with oxidation that it was thought undesirable to try to unroll them. But the characters had been incised so deeply that it was possible, in reverse, to make out the outermost layer. Professor K. G. Kuhn of Göttingen, having studied them, came to the conclusion that they contained instructions for finding the buried treasure of the Essene monastery. Later on, one of these scrolls was sent to the Manchester College of Science and Technology in the hope that it might be possible to devise some method of opening them. This was managed in 1955-56 by Dr. H. Wright Baker, Professor of Mechanical Engineering, who contrived a small circular saw which, cutting between the characters, sliced the scroll into strips that could be laid side by side and read. The second scroll was now sent on, and the pair proved to be two sections of the same document. This was deciphered by Mr. Allegro and turned out to be, indeed, directions for discovering a hidden treasure. These directions were rather crudely written, as if in haste, and it could not have been easy to use a stylus on copper, but it was probably thought safer to leave the message on copper rather than parchment, since the chances of preservation were better. Yet was it really the treasure of the monastery, whose inmates were supposed to have led so austere a life? There was a good deal of money involved, and vessels of gold and silver. These scrolls were found at some distance from fragments of broken jars, which suggested that they might have been deposited separately. Allegro came to believe that the Essenes had nothing to do with these scrolls except, no doubt, to allow them to be hidden in a cave near the monastery, and that the treasure was that of the Temple in Jerusalem, which the priests there had taken the precaution of putting out of the reach of the plundering Roman invaders, just as the Essenes had hidden their library.

We must now return to the rather painful subject of Allegro's relations with his colleagues. He gave out to a Manchester paper a statement about the cutting of the scrolls, and at once received from Jerusalem an order to say nothing more about them. He was also reprimanded by Dr. Baker for having photographed the process of cutting open the first scroll. Allegro had not made and did not make any public announcement of the contents of the scrolls, but six months after they had been opened, Dr. Baker relayed to the press a statement from de Vaux and his colleagues that the hidden treasure listed in them was almost certainly imaginary. This became a kind of official view. Though Allegro, as a professor at Manchester, had been the first to decipher the scrolls, it was made clear to him that they had been assigned for editing to J. T. Milik, a Polish priest and scholar, who, as Allegro is ready to admit, "is perhaps the most brilliant of our little team of scroll editors. . . . He developed an extraordinary facility for reading Semitic scripts of a cursive character never before seen, and for recognizing the work of individual scribes from the tiniest fragments, which is the basis of our work of piecing together the torn scrolls into their original documents." But Allegro had made a translation,

and he published it in 1960, before Milik's text and translation came out in the third section of the official series of
*Discoveries in the Judaean Desert of Jordan.* This evoked
a blast from de Vaux in an article on Allegro's book in
his *Revue Biblique* of January, 1961. Allegro had asserted
that three successive directors of the Department of Antiquities of Jordan had given him permission to publish
the scrolls, but Père de Vaux says they had had no right to
do so. The right to publish belonged to those who had
actually discovered the scrolls, and Allegro does not even
mention by name the American School of Oriental Research or L'École Archéologique Française de Jérusalem,
of which de Vaux was the head, or the Palestine Archaeological Museum, which was the true custodian of the
scrolls. In dudgeon or under orders, Father Milik refuses,
in his volume, even to mention the work of Allegro until
the very end: "I have added in the proofs a certain number of references to studies which have appeared after the
manuscript was sent to the publisher. I do not, however,
take notice of the book of J. M. Allegro, *The Treasure of
the Copper Scrolls,* London, 1960, and this is due to the
reasons one may guess in reading the remarks of R. de
Vaux" in his *Revue Biblique* article. Allegro had in the
meantime succeeded in raising money in Manchester to
take an expedition into Jordan in the hope of finding the
sites of the hidden treasure, and de Vaux, in his article,
had asserted that "these expeditions, with no serious archaeological authority, have eviscerated the soil and the
walls of Khirbet Qumrân and the approaches to the great
Jewish tombs of the Valley of Kedron" and "have only
been prevented at the last moment from extending their
depredations to the esplanade of the Mosque of Omar."
Milik is content to quote this statement. Allegro says in
*Search in the Desert,* a book about his expedition, that he
had the permission of the custodian of the mosque to tun-

nel under the pavement of its terrace without doing any damage to it. But I gathered when I was in Jerusalem that his action had immediately excited alarm. The mosque is on the site of the ancient Jewish Temple and contains the rough rock which is venerated doubly as that on which Abraham was to have sacrificed Isaac and that on which Muhammed descended in his flight through the air from Mecca. The soldiery had been called out to prevent Allegro's explorations. Allegro explains that he is not the first Englishman to poke into the Dome of the Rock, as the Mosque of Omar is also called. In regard to the directions in the copper scrolls, Father Milik adheres firmly to what Allegro calls the "party line," with which other scholars are inclined to disagree: that the treasure is imaginary, and that the scrolls are an attempt to add documentation to an oriental fantasy. He cites a work of "popular literature," written in Egypt in Arabic, *The Book of Buried Pearls and Precious Mysteries,* which gives directions for locating these and which he says is typical of a genre, but he admits that the author of the Dead Sea directions "has succeeded in creating a strong illusion of the real, thanks to the principles that he has adopted: the elimination of 'historical' details and explanations of the origin of the caches, reduction of the information to the strict minimum of topographical and numerical data." But Milik, like Allegro, makes an effort to exactly determine these sites. This is difficult because there are only a few place names—Mount Gerizim, the Vale of Achor—that are recognizable today; about the Tomb of Absalom, the Tomb and Garden of Zadok, and the Valley of Secacah, which is so often mentioned, one can only speculate. The descriptions of the sites may be purposely puzzling, so as to be understood only by initiates. I agree with Allegro that this list is too terse and particularized—in its way, too businesslike—not to indicate genuine treasures. Allegro de-

fends his conviction by reminding us of the three jugs
containing five hundred silver coins that were found
under the floor of the monastery, and the accusation
brought by de Vaux of "eviscerating its soil and walls" refers to Allegro's attempt there to excavate further and find
something more—an attempt which, as can easily be understood, very much distressed the archaeologist when, on
visiting the ruins he had excavated, he discovered that,
without his permission, someone else had been tampering
with them. Milik tries to insist that the value of the treasure is so enormous as to be incredible, but Allegro replies
that we do not know how the talent was then valued. The
values assigned in the Old Testament and the later rabbinical literature would indeed give fantastic weights, and
if the unjust steward of Matthew was dealing in Old
Testament values, "he could have held his own quite com-
fortably on Wall Street," and the "good and faithful servant" of the same gospel "who speculated so successfully
with his five talents would have needed a fair-sized wheel-
barrow to bring his master the resultant four hundred-
weights of silver."

The translations by Allegro and by Milik of the text of
the copper scrolls differ considerably from one another,
and the former, in a second edition of his work, acknowl-
edges Milik's contribution and defers to it to some extent
in making revisions in his own. He regrets that the recent
controversy should have destroyed a pleasant relationship,
which had been based partly on a common enthusiasm for
the writings of P. G. Wodehouse. Allegro's self-defense
for publishing the text without permission of his colleagues is based on the complaint that I have already
noted on the part of several scholars: that de Vaux had
taken an unconscionably long time in publishing the other
documents. To this the team in Old Jerusalem reply that
Allegro, as a member of the team, has violated the ethics

of scholarship. He justifies the expedition undertaken on his own initiative on the ground that the official group, since they regarded the treasure as imaginary, were not trying to do anything about it. I was told in Jordanian Jerusalem that the official authorities of Jordan, who had undoubtedly given some authorization to Allegro's expedition, had become rather cold, as he reports in his book, when he had failed to find anything of importance—a few coins merely and pieces of pottery.

# VII

## THE TEXTS

I HAVE mentioned the consternation among Orthodox Jewish scholars which was caused by the discovery of ancient Hebrew texts of the Bible that differ from the Masoretic version, and of the nuisance to Christian scholars of the turning-up of unknown documents that throw new light on the emergence of Christianity. The ordinary non-scholarly Jew knows simply that the Torah and the Prophets and the Writings, the three sections of his Bible, are sacred; the ordinary non-scholarly Gentile that *his* Bible, of which the first section is differently arranged from the Hebrew "Tanakh" (a word made from the initial consonants of the three sections) and which has been translated in several different ways, is a work of Divine revelation, consisting of two solid units called the Old and the New Testaments. He nowadays rarely reads it, and if he goes to church he hears it read in a few selected verses at a time, often very much detached from their contexts. I have been surprised to find, by inquiry, how many literate Gentiles do not know in what languages the Bible was written. The author of a grammar of New Testament Greek, D. F. Hudson, of Serampore College in Bengal, tells of an English lady who is reported to have said to a missionary engaged in translating the New Testament out of Greek into one of the Central African languages, "But why do that? If English was good enough for St. Paul, why isn't it good enough for them?" F. F. Bruce of the University of Manchester, in his book *The English Bible: A History of Translations*, has some equally amusing stories of the reaction to the Revised Standard Version of 1952—revised, of course, in the interests of accuracy: there could be no question at that date of recapturing the style of the King James translation. Some people had objected to the inclusion in the committee who prepared the Revised Version of a distinguished Jewish scholar, an authority on the Septuagint. And when it was published, "one American preacher was reported to have burned a copy . . . with a blowlamp in his pulpit, remarking that it was like the Devil because it was hard to burn." Pamphlets appeared bearing such titles as "The Bible of Antichrist," "The New Blasphemous Bible," and "Whose Unclean Fingers Have Been Tampering with the Holy Bible, God's Pure, Infallible, Verbally Inspired Word?"—the last of which opens with the sentence "Every informed and intelligent person knows that our government is crawling with Communists, or those who sanction and encourage Communism." Such people, of course, are even further from understanding what sort of problems are presented by any serious effort to establish what was actually written in the Bible and what it meant to those who wrote it. The King James Version of the Bible, in its poetic seventeenth-century language, is such a fine piece of literature that it has been difficult for anyone familiar with it not to imagine, like the English lady or the author of the anti-Communist pamphlet, that it fixes the Word of God in plain print. We not only remember, from First Corinthians, "For now we see through a glass, darkly," and do not recognize—probably have not read—James Moffatt's "At present we only see the baffling reflections in a mirror" or Ronald Knox's "At present we are looking at a confused reflection in a mirror," but we even imagine the young

Joseph of Genesis in a kind of harlequin costume, the "coat of many colors," though we have been told by Moffatt and the Revised Standard Version that this was really a robe or tunic with long sleeves (Knox tries to make the old interpretation more presentable by calling it "a coat that was all embroidery"). Yet every teacher of beginners' Hebrew has to commence by contending with this influence, by explaining that in many cases we now know better than the seventeenth-century translators. A professor at Union Seminary told me that he passed out to his students mimeographed copies of Professor Walter Raleigh's essay on the beauties of the King James translation, telling them that everything Raleigh said was true: they were to read this, but then bear in mind that it was quite irrelevant to what they were going to study. A professor at the Princeton Seminary used to issue a similar warning, referring to the old cliché that the greatest treasures of English literature are Shakespeare and the King James Bible, and thereafter, when he recognized in a class translation any echo of the latter, which had been obviously used as a trot, would interrupt it with "Never mind about Shakespeare!"

The student who pursues any further the question of what the Bible says and the reasons for the many variations between its different versions—in Hebrew, Greek and Latin, Samaritan and the other Semitic languages—will find himself, especially since the Dead Sea caves have presented so many new texts, faced with a challenge to pore endlessly over something in the nature of jigsaw puzzles that rarely come out quite right because so many of the pieces are missing. The monographs written on these subjects are extremely hard to grasp for the layman: Why is it that fragments of another Greek text seem to differ from that of the Septuagint? Does a fragment which has just been found in Hebrew represent an anterior version of the text of the Samaritan Pentateuch, which, though written in the characters and dialect of the alienated Samaritans, the latter have always claimed to be older and more authentic than that of their Jewish distant cousins? Are not certain new readings from the scrolls really a good deal more satisfactory than those that have been so sedulously guarded in the sacred Masoretic Bible? A remarkable example of this last is the text of the columns of Samuel discovered in Cave Four, the importance of which was first grasped by Dr. Cross. It is amusing to contrast his way of dealing with this, perfectly dry and impersonal, in his book *The Ancient Library of Qumrân and Modern Biblical Studies*, with Mr. Allegro's characteristically more exciting one in *The Dead Sea Scrolls: A Reappraisal*. If Mr. Cross will not dramatize his discovery, Mr. Allegro will do it for him. "Whilst engaged one day," he writes, "in cleaning and assembling some fragile leather pieces of the book of Samuel from the Fourth Cave, Frank Cross noticed that at one place the text seemed to run completely contrary to MT [the Masoretic text]. He checked again, and there was no doubt. He carried on brushing very gently until the next line came into view. Again the text showed marked variations, and the next few lines included a whole paragraph which was not represented in the standard Hebrew. His excitement mounting, Cross began to refer to the principal versions, and almost immediately saw that his text corresponded word for word with the Greek translation. The precious pieces joined to others," etc. Mr. Allegro prints in three parallel columns his translations of the same passages from this new text, from that of the Septuagint, and from that of the current Revised Standard Version translation, and this can give the ordinary reader perhaps the clearest idea of the variations in these texts. (This book is now readily available in a Pelican paperback.) The new manuscript of

Samuel, says Dr. Cross, agrees more often with the Greek
Septuagint than it does with the "traditional" text, but has
many new readings that agree with neither. It is closer
than the Masoretic text to that used by the author of
Chronicles, who is telling more or less the same story.
Thanks to a backing of papyrus, this Samuel is much the
best of the Biblical texts found in Cave Four. An older
text of Samuel has survived only in seven fragments. Dr.
Cross believes that it is the oldest of the manuscripts from
the Dead Sea caves and can hardly date later than 200 B.C.
From this Fourth Cave alone have come fragments of
what are estimated to be three hundred and eighty-two
manuscripts, Biblical and Sectarian. Among the whole
body of scrolls are versions—never complete except in the
case of Isaiah—of all of the canonical books except Esther.

   Dr. Cross delivered, for a scholarly audience, at the
dedication of the Shrine of the Book, the special museum
in Israeli Jerusalem for the display of the Hebrew University's scrolls, an address on "The Contribution of the
Qumrân Discoveries to the Study of the Biblical Text,"
which was afterwards published in Volume XVI, Number
2, 1966, of the *Israel Exploration Journal*. This paper
will give the layman an idea of the extreme complexity of
the problem of unravelling the relations between the different Biblical texts, but it is worthwhile to quote at this
point some of Cross's more general conclusions. There
are, he says, three main "families" of texts: Palestinian,
Egyptian and Babylonian, each of which exhibits special
features from having grown up in a different locality.
Among the Qumrân manuscripts, Mr. Cross can find no
indications that a standard Biblical text existed at the time
they were written and collected. "There is no exemplar,"
he says, "of the Masoretic text, and no evidence of its influence." This Masoretic text—that is, for the Jews, the
"traditional" and today official one—was compounded out

of the Palestinian and Babylonian versions and the Septuagint, the version in Greek translated in Alexandria
from the one then current in Egypt, which accounts for
the differences between them. The "Rabbinic recension,"
says Cross, must have "come into being between the era of
Hillel"—that is, the later part of the last B.C. century—
"and the first Jewish revolt." Though not the established
version for the library at Qumrân, it "appears to have
been the accepted text in other circles by 70 A.D., and, in
the interval between the Jewish revolts against Rome, became the reigning text in all surviving Jewish communities. Its victory was complete, and rival textual traditions
shortly died out, except as they were preserved frozen in
ancient translations or survived in the text of an isolated
sect such as the Samaritans."

It will be better, having reached this point, to continue
the discussion of the Biblical texts in connection with the
so-called Testimonia.

# VIII

# THE TESTIMONIA

THE PASSAGES from the Old Testament which are adduced in the New Testament as prophecies of the coming of Jesus Christ—that is, of Jesus of Nazareth as the Messiah expected by the Jews—and of other events in the Gospels have always been an embarrassment to scholarship, because they either do not occur in the Hebrew Bible as we have it or occur in a different form. As early, it is estimated, as the beginning of the ninth century—I have spoken of this above—a Patriarch of Seleucia wrote to a Metropolitan of Elam inquiring about some writings which were said to have been found in a cave near Jericho. The Patriarch, he explains, had asked of a scholar who had seen them whether any texts had turned up that contained these passages, which did not appear in either the Masoretic text or the Septuagint. The scholar replied that such passages had indeed been found in texts from this cave, and that there had also been found among them more than two hundred Psalms of David. (As has been seen, Psalms additional to the canonical hundred and fifty, though not so many as this, have recently turned up at Qumrân.) Further inquiries brought no reply, and the Patriarch was left in frustration. "This is as fire in my heart," he writes in his letter to the Metropolitan, "burning and blazing in my bones." We do not know how his letter was answered. But the puzzle as to whence the

Christians had derived what have come to be called their
"proof texts" continued to worry the students of the
Bible. Not only the Bible itself but the apocryphal Epistle
of Barnabas and certain of the Church Fathers seem to
reflect in their quotations the Septuagint text—they could
have read the Bible only in Greek—but in certain ways
they differ from it. The theory was first suggested in 1838
by a German scholar, K. A. Credner, and clearly formulated, fifty years later, by an English scholar, Edwin
Hatch, that anthologies of prophetic quotations existed—
first, however, compiled by the Jews themselves—which
were used also by the authors of the New Testament and
the Fathers of the Christian Church. By the end of the
last century, F. C. Burkitt and J. R. Harris had arrived
at the hypothesis of the Testimonia—that is, of collecions
of prophetic texts intended exclusively for Christian use
in the arguments of the Christians with the Jews, to show
that the Jews' own sacred books predicted the coming of
Jesus as the Christ. The contentions to which this claim
gave rise are dramatically illustrated by the "Dialogue of
Justin, Philosopher and Martyr, with Trypho, a Jew,"
written by Justin himself in the second century. Justin,
who is waiting for a ship at Ephesus, falls in with the
Rabbi Trypho, who has escaped from Palestine, now occupied by the Romans, at the time of Bar-Kochba's rebellion against them. In the course of a very long argument, which apparently went on for two days and in
which Justin rather browbeats the Rabbi, he makes the
charges that the Jews have tampered with the text of their
Scripture in order to eliminate such passages as properly
lend themselves to Christian interpretation as prophecies
of the miraculous origin and divine mission of Jesus. In
one still much-mooted case, it is merely a question of
translation, where the Jew can reasonably plead that the
Hebrew has been wrongly rendered. In Isaiah 7.14, the

Christian Bible has this version: "Therefore the Lord himself shall give you a sign; Behold, a virgin shall conceive, and bear a son, and shall call his name Immanuel [God with us]," evidently following the Septuagint, where the Hebrew word for Immanuel's mother has been translated ἡ παρθένος; whereas Trypho objects that *ha-almah* does not necessarily mean a virgin but merely a young woman, and that the prophecy, which was fulfilled, applies not to Jesus but to Hezekaiah, to whose father, Ahaz, Isaiah is addressing it. The Rabbi further remarks that this story of the birth of Jesus is on a level with the Greek myth that Zeus begot Perseus on Danaë by descending in the guise of a shower of gold, and that the Christians ought to be ashamed to make such absurd assertions. (How much this has remained an issue may be seen from the recent translation of the Bible by Monsignor Ronald Knox, who seems rather amusingly to compromise a little by translating the word as *maid*—like *almah*, not necessarily, he evidently believes, a virgin—"since it refers rather to a time than to a state of life"; "but in view of the event," he adds, "we cannot doubt that this prophecy looks forward to the Virgin Birth.") It is evident, however, that Trypho and Justin have been arguing from different texts, and it is now thought that the three Greek translations, apart from the Septuagint, which were made in about Trypho's time by the early Jewish scholars Theodotion, Aquila and Symmachus, do show an anti-Christian bias or a non-Christian anti-anthropomorphic emphasis in competition with the kind of thing that lent itself to the uses of the Testimonia.

Then where did the Christians get their "proof texts"? Did these occur in other versions that are lost, or were they sometimes deliberately concocted? The people they were proselytizing were unlikely to be familiar with the Septuagint, still less the Masoretic Hebrew. But the matter of unravelling these mysteries has always been a delicate one because it verges on calling into question the veracity of the New Testament. Mr. Albert C. Sundberg, Jr., begins the introduction to his recent book, *The Old Testament of the Early Church* by explaining that "the Old Testament of the early church, as a problem in canon, has received somewhat the treatment of a stepchild in Biblical studies. Treated as an adjunct to Old Testament canon, New Testament canon, and studies in the Literature of the Apocrypha and Pseudepigrapha, it remains unsettled as to which discipline is properly responsible for the treatment of this problem."

The kind of stumbling-blocks here involved may be illustrated by two conspicuous examples, in Matthew 27.9 and 2.23. The first of these, in telling the story of Judas, says that his turning back to the chief priests and elders the thirty pieces of silver he had been paid for betraying Jesus and their refusing to put the money in their treasury because it was the price of blood, but employing it to buy "the potter's field, as a burial place for strangers," was foretold by the prophet Jeremiah. Now, there is nothing like this in Jeremiah, but Zechariah (11.12-13) does contain the following passage, which has never been understood and which had perhaps slipped in from somewhere else: "And I said unto them, If ye think good, give me my price; and if not, forbear. So they weighed for my price thirty pieces of silver. And the Lord said unto me, Cast it unto the potter: a goodly price that I was prized at of them. And I took the thirty pieces of silver, and cast them to the potter, in the house of the Lord." There is a difference of opinion as to whether the word יוצר stands for the potters' quarter, where there was a court into which were thrown the broken vessels from the Temple, or whether it is a misspelling of a word for *treasurer* which appears in Aramaic and Syrian texts. This is in any

case quite different from Matthew's version, and it has
been suggested by Knox that this passage may have resulted from a combination of the verses in Zechariah with
Jeremiah 32.7-9, which tells of the buying of a field for
"seventeen shekels of silver." The second of these references in Matthew—which had particularly worried the
Seleucian Patriarch when he wrote to the Elam Metropolitan about the newly discovered manuscripts—is "And
he [Jesus] came and dwelt in a city called Nazareth: that
it might be fulfilled which was spoken by the prophets,
He shall be called a Nazarene." But there is no such prediction in the Prophets as we have them. My old English
Bible, printed toward the end of the nineteenth century,
refers us to Judges 13.5 and I Samuel 1.11, but these deal
with not Nazarenes but Nazarites, a special group first
mentioned in Genesis, a part of whose cult it was not to
shave the heads of their children but to allow their hair
to grow long. The Angel of the Lord, in the first of these
passages, is prophesying to the mother of Samson, "For,
lo, thou shalt conceive and bear a son; and no razor shall
come on his head: for the child shall be a Nazarite unto
God from the womb: and he shall begin to deliver Israel
out of the hands of the Philistines." This plainly does not
apply to Jesus. The provenience of this verse in Matthew
has provided a great subject for controversy, and I am
told that in the course of this there have been proposed almost as many explanations as there have been Biblical
scholars who addressed themselves to the problem.

There have been no actual known Testimonia to show
from where the author of Matthew had produced his so
pat citations, and the existence of any such collections was
still entirely hypothetical. But it is one of the more striking features of the discoveries in the Dead Sea caves that
something of the kind has come to light. This is known as
Document IV from Cave Four, and it has been published

by Mr. Allegro in the issue of September, 1956, of the *Journal of Biblical Literature* (later, without his critical comment, in Volume V of *Discoveries in the Judaean Desert*). There is nothing about Nazareth or Jesus or thirty pieces of silver. Here it is merely a Messiah who is being predicted. But the compiler, for his special purposes, has slightly altered his Biblical quotations, as has been done by the New Testament writers, or, as has also been done by these, has run two separate texts together in such a way as to give them a meaning different from that which they had had in their respective contexts. Thus, Deuteronomy 5.28-9 is immediately followed by Deuteronomy 18.18, so as to compound the following passage: "I have heard the voice of the words of this people, which they have spoken unto thee: they have well said all that they have spoken. Oh that there were such a heart in them, that they would fear me, and keep my commandments always, that it might be well with them, and with their children for ever! I will raise them up a Prophet from among their brethren, like unto thee; and I will put my words in his mouth, and he shall speak unto them all that I shall command him." The first text, ending "children for ever," applies in Deuteronomy to Moses, but in the second, which begins "I will raise them up a Prophet," the text that had referred to Moses is made to seem to apply to an unnamed prophet who is coming. It should be noted, also, that, in Acts 3.22 and 7.37, in the course of speeches by Peter and Stephen, the second of these texts is applied to Jesus. What makes the problem even more complicated is that the combination of these two passages occurs in Exodus 20 of the Samaritan Pentateuch, so that it must have been already in existence before the Masoretic text.

What has actually happened here is that the early Christians made use of the Prophets for predictions and authentications of the origins of their own group just as the Qumrân Sect had done—as I have explained in connection with the Nahum *pesher*—for the events of their own history.

# IX

# THE EPISTLE TO THE HEBREWS

IT WILL BE SEEN from the above discussions how sharply every word of these documents has been scrutinized and what far-reaching inferences may be drawn from the slightest allusion or suggestion. The existence of the remnants of this library, which are constantly being augmented, this sudden flooding in of only partially understood evidence, have had the result more and more of extending speculation in every direction—on the history of the documents of what we call the Old Testament, on the documents already known of what is called the intertestamental period, and on the beginnings of Christianity. In the last case, certain resemblances have been obvious from the first: the influence of the Dead Sea Sect seemed traceable in some of the language of the Gospel according to St. John and in the doctrine of the Pauline Epistles; the behavior of Jesus at the Last Supper appeared to be explicable as a challenging of the protocol laid down for the Essenes in the prescriptions for their sacred banquet. And attempts are still being made—sometimes with extremely implausible results—to link what we know of the literature of early Christianity with the last that we know of the literature of the Sect. One of the most interesting of these is the theory of Yigael Yadin in regard to the New Testament Epistle to the Hebrews.

This document, which is now printed as the last of the

epistles attributed to Paul, has always been suspect, not merely to what used to be called the "Higher Criticism" of the nineteenth century but from the very beginning of the Christian canon. In one of three early codices, the Epistle to the Hebrews is omitted; in another, it is given only in Latin; in a third, it is included as a sort of appendix. The early Fathers of the Church had varying opinions about it. It was variously attributed to St. Luke, to Barnabas, who, though not of the Twelve, came early to rank as an apostle, to an early Alexandrian convert of Paul's called Apollos, and to the first-century Bishop Clement of Rome. Modern scholarship seems more and more to be favoring an attribution to Apollos. The conviction that it was written by Paul became stronger toward the middle of the third century, though still, at the end of the fourth, both Augustine and Jerome were doubtful. There is, then, it seems, a certain mystery as to how, in the first place, this epistle got into the New Testament canon and became embedded there. The reasons for believing it not the work of Paul are, among others, that, unlike his other epistles, it bears no salutation, no indication of authorship or locality, and that it is written in much better Greek than Paul was apparently capable of and in a style quite unlike his. The author sounds Alexandrian—hence the preference given Apollos—and he argues from the Greek Septuagint, the Alexandrian translation of the Bible, in such a way as to seem to indicate that he does not know the Hebrew original.

And who exactly are these "Hebrews" to whom this epistle is so vaguely addressed? Who were they and where were they living? We are given as little data by which to identify them as we are to the identity of the author. Professor Yadin, who has discussed the problem with Professors W. F. Albright and David Flusser, has now attempted an answer which has hitherto by others only been dimly approached. He begins a paper on the subject—"The Dead Sea Scrolls and the Epistle to the Hebrews," in the fourth volume of the *Scripta Hierosolymitana*, published by the Hebrew University—by quoting some of the opinions put on record by previous scholars, which show their general disagreement with one another. Were these Hebrews Orthodox Jews or were they Christianized Jews or were they actually Christianized Gentiles? There is now, Professor Yadin believes, another explanation possible: these Hebrews may have been members of the Dead Sea Sect. The writer of this epistle is engaged in warning those to whom it is addressed against certain very special errors which do not seem to have much in common with the opinions and prejudices that Paul is generally trying to discredit. Professor Yadin has had the ingenious idea of turning around this negative doctrine in order to ascertain what the positive side would be, and in the picture produced by the positive side he recognizes some of the doctrines characteristic of the Dead Sea Sect—especially those against which an advocate of Jesus as Messiah would be obliged to contend. "At the outset, it should be emphasized," says Yadin, "that the main part of Hebrews is concerned with proving the superiority of Jesus over several persons and heavenly creatures of Messianic or eschatological character, who—according to the beliefs of the readers—are either superior to Jesus, as a lay Messiah, or were appointed to perform some functions at the End of Days which—according to the writer—are reserved for Jesus the [divine] Messiah. Thus the author of the Epistle discusses the following subjects: Jesus and the prophets; Jesus and the angels; Jesus and Moses; and finally Jesus and Aaron."

To follow this order of presentation: At the very beginning of Hebrews (1.1-2), the Prophets are rather disregarded, pushed into the background as obsolete, since "now at last in these times [God] has spoken to us with a

Son to speak for him; a Son, whom he has appointed to inherit all things, just as it was through him that he created this world of time." (I here and from now on use Father Knox's translation, which, although it respects the Vulgate, is closer to the Greek original than the King James or the Revised Standard Version.) The Prophets, so much invoked in the Dead Sea documents, are, as I say, in these opening two verses downgraded, and the next step is to try to downgrade the angels, since these were of such immense importance to the Sect, who seem to give them—sometimes referring to them as "saints," "gods" or "sons of heaven"—the supreme power under God, with Michael, the Angel of Light, at their head. (Josephus also speaks of this in writing about the Essenes.) Now, the author of the Epistle to the Hebrews devotes most of his first two chapters to emphasizing, in relation to Jesus Christ, the inferiority of the angels: "Did God ever say to one of the angels, Thou art my son, I have begotten thee this day? . . . Why, when the time comes for bringing his first-born into the world anew [no one knows the meaning of this "anew"], then, He says, Let all the angels of God worship before Him. . . . Did he ever say to one of the angels, Sit on my right hand, while I make thy enemies a footstool under thy feet? What are they, all of them, but spirits apt for service, whom He sends out when the destined heirs of eternal salvation have need of them." Jesus, who has been constituted, in his human role, "a little lower than the angels . . . after all, he does not make himself the angels' champion, no sign of that; it is the sons of Abraham that he champions." That is, the angels are the servants of the Son, yet Jesus, insofar as he is human, partakes of the nature of man, who is "a little lower than the angels."

It may be noted here, as Yadin mentions, that Colossians 2.18 also contains a warning against "a false humility which addresses its worship to angels." J. B. Lightfoot, writing on Colossians in 1875, had spoken of this warning against angelology, and from this and other indications concluded that the influence of the Essenes—who, he thought, had themselves been inspired by the Gnostics— was traceable in the same negative way in Paul's attempt to advise the Colossians against what Lightfoot calls "the Colossian heresy." They must not regard themselves as élite and the possessors of esoteric wisdom, because Christ has come to "warn *every* man and teach *every* man in every wisdom, that he may present *every* man perfect in Christ Jesus" (translation and italics Lightfoot's). They must not, as the Essenes did, observe strict regulations about what they drank and ate. "So no one must be allowed to take you to task over what you eat or drink, or in the matter of observing feasts, and new moons, and sabbath days; all these were but shadows cast by future events, the reality is found in Christ" (Knox). Lightfoot, not having the Sectarian literature, could not have known that this last warning would have borne out his theory that the Colossians to whom it was addressed were imbued with the doctrines of the Essenes, who, as we now know, had a solar calendar which made their feasts come on days that differed from those of the other Jews.

To return to the author of Hebrews, he goes on to a special argument that takes up almost half his Epistle, by which he aims to show that Jesus is a real priest in a line that must be accepted by those he is addressing. "Of Christ as priest we have much to say, and it is hard to make ourselves understood in the saying of it, now that you have grown so dull of hearing." The Sect were expecting, at the End of Days, a Messiah who would be a priest in the line of Aaron—that is, a Levite—but this could not be claimed for Jesus, who was definitely in the line of Juda, "and Moses, in speaking of this tribe, said nothing about priests." But God has declared to Jesus; "Thou art a priest for ever, in the line of Melchizedek," who was both a high priest and a king, as was expected by the Sect of its Messiah. Had Melchizedek not "met Abraham and blessed him on his way home, after the defeat of the kings [those of Sodom and Gomorrah and their allies]; and to him Abraham gave a tenth of his spoils. Observe, in the first place, that his name means the King of Justice; and further that he is King of Salem, that is, of peace [*shalem* is evidently taken here as the same as *shalom*]." Melchizedek actually far outranks Aaron. One of the Psalms has said of David, "The Lord has sworn an oath there is no retracting, Thou art a priest for ever in the line of Melchizedek." And we know that Melchizedek held the ranks of both high priest and king long before Levi was born—from the latter of whom the Sect were expecting their double Messiah, so that it did not matter that Jesus was not descended from Levi. (David Flusser, however, believes, on the basis of a fragment from Cave Eleven—*Melchizedek and the Son of Man,* in *Christian News from Israel,* April, 1966—that "at least some members of the Sect believed that the priestly Messiah of the Latter Days would be Melchizedek. How they harmonized this view with the commonly accepted belief in an Aaronic Messiah we do not know. One conclusion, however, seems to impose itself: the reference in Hebrews would be not an expression of opposition to the Aaronic ideology of the Sect but a view already held in certain circles of the Sect.")

Furthermore, it had been stipulated in the War Scroll of the Sect that eventually, after the liberation of Jerusalem, the sacrifices in the Temple should be resumed in accordance with the Mosaic Law: these sacrifices should be made "for the pleasure of God, to atone for all His congregation." The author of Hebrews describes the blood-letting of the Mosaic sacrifices, then explains that it is not necessary for Christ to "make a repeated offering of himself, as the high priest, when he enters the sanctuary, makes a yearly offering of the blood that is not his own. If that were so, he must have suffered again and again, ever since the world was created; as it is, he has been revealed once for all, at the moment when history reached its fulfillment, annulling our sin by his sacrifice."

Every one of these admonitions has thus its very special application to the doctrines of the Dead Sea Sect. Ernest Renan has dated the Epistle to the Hebrews between 65 and 70 A.D.—that is, in the last years of the Sect, just before the destruction of the monastery. Was the converted Jewish author attempting to proselyte its inmates?

It should be noted that a Dutch scholar, J. De Waard, in *A Comparative Study of the Old Testament Text in the Dead Sea Scrolls and in the New Testament* (E. J. Brill, Leiden, 1965), a purely textual work, which has nothing to say about Yadin's theory, has independently come to the conclusion that the author of the Epistle to the Hebrews must have been acquainted with the literature of Qumrân.

# X

# MASADA

MASADA is a huge, butte-like rock that, thirty miles south of Qumrân, rears itself a sheer thirteen hundred feet from the west shore of the Dead Sea. It has a flat top, shaped rather like a ship, that measures nineteen hundred feet from north to south and six hundred and fifty from east to west. Here Herod, in his paranoid suspicion, built one of the several citadels in which he sought to fortify himself against the forces that he felt were threatening him: the Jews who were discontented with a king set up by the Romans and of Edomite, that is, of non-Jewish blood—the hostile feeling between the Jews and their neighbors goes back a very long way—and who might try to bring their Hasmonean dynasty back; and the ambitions of Cleopatra, who had begged Antony to kill Herod and get for her the throne of Judea. He constructed on Masada, we are told by Josephus, our sole ancient authority on the subject, a palace and a casemate wall, surmounted by thirty-eight towers. This stronghold, after Herod's death, was taken over by the Romans, but later it was retaken and their legionaries were killed by Menahem, the leader of the Jewish revolt against them, in 66 A.D. Thereafter it was occupied by the militant Jewish group variously known as the Zealots and the Sicarii (Daggermen), who held it for seven years. It was accessible from below only by two paths, one a zigzagging trail which Josephus says was called "the snake": "For its course is broken in skirting the jutting crags and, returning frequently upon itself and gradually lengthening out again, it makes painful headway. One traversing this route must firmly plant each foot alternately. Destruction faces him; for on either side yawn chasms so terrific as to daunt the hardiest. After following this perilous track for thirty furlongs, one reaches the summit, which, instead of tapering to a sharp peak, expands into a plain." But the Jews were able to bring up provisions, and the top of the rock was so relatively fertile that it had always been possible to grow vegetables there; the climate, Josephus says, was so preservative that the Jews found supplies still edible and drinkable that had been there almost a century. He declares that the Zealots were a nuisance, that they preyed on the country below in a brutal and unscrupulous way. Josephus shows evidence of a certain bias all through his *History of the Jewish War*. He had at first taken part in the Galilee campaign, but had later surrendered to Vespasian, the Roman general in Palestine, and had advised Vespasian's son Titus during the siege of Jerusalem. Jerusalem had been destroyed in 70 A.D., at the time of which Josephus is here writing, and nothing could be more bitter than the feeling between those Jews who had submitted to the invaders—as had earlier been the case with those who had submitted to the Greeks—and those who had continued to fight them. Josephus likes to flatter Titus for his relative magnanimity and—himself a descendant of a noble priestly family, who had visited Rome in his youth and had evidently been impressed by Roman power and civilization—tends to emphasize the barbarities of his countrymen. He was, in fact, writing his book in Rome as a protégé of the Emperor.

Now, we know, of course, that the Jews were capable, on occasion, of being almost as cruel as their Roman en-

emies, and we can understand that Josephus had an interest in trying to show how abominably the defenders of
Judea had behaved and how much better it would have
been for the Jews to give in earlier to the Roman invaders.
Yet it is hard for us to sympathize with the Romans.
Why, we ask, should the Romans have felt that, having
occupied Judea, having destroyed Jerusalem and burnt
the Temple, they had to hunt down the less than one
thousand intransigents who were holding out on Masada,
and why could they not feel easy as long as they had not
slaughtered the men, raped the women, and made slaves
of the children? We can find the reason plainly expressed
in the *Histories* of the Roman Tacitus (Book V). It was
the simple, ungovernable, insatiable greed of the all-en-
gulfing power organism, accompanied by the necessary
conviction that there is something inferior or wicked about
the "way of life" of one's intended victims. The indictment
of Tacitus against the Jews may serve as a comic and
tragic model of all such absurd indictments, up to the
present day, of one group against another. "Moses," declares Tacitus, "in order to assert for the future his authority over his people, introduced a cult that was quite
novel and opposed to that of other mortals—according to
which all things that *we* hold sacred are considered *by
them* profane, and, conversely, they tolerate practices that
we consider unclean. They consecrated in a holy place an
image of the animal by whose guidance they had put an
end to their wandering and thirst [this refers to the ancient legend, often repeated by classical writers, that the
Jews worshipped an ass's head; this cult is here explained
by Tacitus as inspired by gratitude to a herd of wild asses
which, in the wanderings of the Jews in their Exodus, had
led them to the waters of a spring], having already killed a
ram as an insult to Ammon [the chief god of the Pha-
raohs]. They also sacrificed a bull, which the Egyptians

worship as Apis." He goes on to their dietary restrictions
and their fasts and observance of the Sabbath, to which
he gives invidious implications. They are obstinately loyal
among themselves and prompt to show compassion to one
another, but toward everyone else they are hostile. Their
sex life is quite abominable: they are extremely given to
lechery but will not have intercourse with foreigners,
though among themselves nothing is forbidden. They
have established circumcision in order to distinguish
themselves from other people. They bury their dead instead of cremating them, and they consider it an impious
act to kill any of their late-born children (that is, born
after their father's will has been made). The Egyptians
worship many images of animals and men combined, but
the Jews can only conceive of one Deity, and then only in
their minds. (He seems at this point to have forgotten his
objection to the alleged Jewish cult of the ass.) "Profane"
they declare "those who make images of gods out of per-
ishable materials in the likeness of men: their God is supreme and eternal, unchangeable and indestructible, and
so they will not allow images of him in their cities, not
even in their temples. They pay no such honor to their
kings nor to Caesar. Since their priests, however, are
wreathed with ivy and play upon flutes and cymbals, and
since a golden vine has been seen in their Temple, some
think that they worship Bacchus, who has come so to
dominate the East, but Bacchic rites are quite out of character for the Jews: they are full of festivity and gaiety,
whereas the Jewish rites are rude and unseemly." The
point was, of course, that the Jews took their religion seriously in a way that the Romans could not understand.
Tacitus could not see why the Egyptian animals and the
deified Roman emperors were not more acceptable as divinities than a single invisible God insusceptible of repre-
sentation, any more than Antiochus Epiphanes had been

able to see why they could not be reconciled to the instal-
lation of Zeus in the Temple—which they called "the
Abomination of Desolation"—and the demand that they
should sacrifice to him. Their civil wars, the historian goes
on to say, diverted the Romans for a time from the East,
but when matters at home had been settled, they began
to think about it again. *"Augebat iras,"* he writes *"quod
soli Judaei non cessissent."* ("It aroused their indignation
that only the Jews would not give in.") He goes on to
complain of their stubbornness and to describe the prepa-
rations for the seige of Jerusalem. These duties were assigned to the Roman legions, and the fighting did not
begin till everything had been arranged for taking the
city by the "old and new devices" at which the Romans
had become so adept. But Tacitus now switches to their
war with the Germans, and the later books of the *Histories* are lost.

Josephus, however, continues the story. He had been
present at the fall of Jerusalem, and he goes on to the
siege of Masada. The Roman general, Flavius Silva, in
charge of this operation, went at it with the advanced
engineering techniques and the systematic deliberation
characteristic of Roman methods. He first built a wall
around the rock so that none of the besieged should escape; then he started constructing a ramp at the only
place where a wide jutting ledge provided a step to approach the top. He built up an embankment on this and
on it a stone platform as a base for the machines of war.
These included an iron tower, which commanded the top
of the rock and made it possible to assail the defenders
with volleys of spiked missiles and rocks flung by cata-
pults, and a huge battering ram, with which the soldiers
made a breach in the wall. The Zealots, however, foreseeing this, had built another wall inside it: two parallel
piles of beams, with a filling of earth between them,

which impeded the force of the blows. This inner wall the enemy now attacked with showers of burning torches and succeeded in setting it afire. At first, a north wind blew the flames back into their faces; but then the wind shifted and blew them against the wall.

The governor at that time of Masada, a man named Eleazar Ben Ya'ir, seeing now that its defenders were doomed, called together his stoutest companions and, according to the account of Josephus, who follows the practice of the ancient historians, made them speeches of an eloquence and length which can only be the products of his own invention. Eleazar first tells them that they have now no hope. It is plain that, for their past misdeeds, God is now implacably against them, since, although they have been equipped with ample provisions and weapons and an apparently impregnable fortress, He has changed the direction of the wind and driven back the flames to destroy them. "Let us then save our wives from dishonor and our children from the shame of slavery. Let us not pay the Romans the price of our sins; let us pay it directly to God. He has granted us at least this favor: to die by our own hands. And let us, before we die, burn everything in the fortress so that the Romans will get nothing—with the single exception of the food, which we shall leave so that the enemy will know that we have not been reduced by hunger but that we chose death rather than servitude."

Eleazar, however, saw that some of his companions, unwilling to die or unwilling to kill their wives and children, were hesitant about following his recommendations and that some were shedding tears, and he was obliged to renew his appeal, which, in Josephus's version of it, seems closer to Greek philosophy than to traditional Jewish teaching. Josephus's point of view seems a mixture of Jewish and European thought. He had already decided in Jerusalem that the Jews had been condemned by God, who seems, in

Josephus's conception, to have operated somewhat like the
Sophoclean Fate that cuts down the protagonist of a
tragedy, and he had attempted to persuade its inhabitants
to submit to the rule of the Romans. He now makes his
Eleazar preach this, but though he regards these Jewish
rebels as wrongheaded, he cannot help imparting to this
episode a strong character of tragic nobility. "Does not
death," he makes his Hellenizing leader ask, "liberate the
soul from the body, which is subject to so many ills, and
allow it to depart to its pure abode?" He invokes also the
Indian philosophers, who recognize, brave men that they
are, that life must be at best a misfortune and who destroy
themselves by fire in order to free their spirits. "Even if
we had been taught the opposite—that is, that life is the
greatest good for man and that death must be a misfortune—we must still with a stout heart face the situation in
which we now find ourselves. God has long ago decreed
that the whole Jewish people must quit this life, since
they have not cared to make good use of it. Not merely
the Egyptians and Syrians have massacered the Jews in
their midst but even the Jews on their own soil have had
to contend with the Romans, and those who have been
only slain in battle are to be felicitated, for of the others
some have died on the rack, some have been tortured by
flogging and fire, some have been half-eaten by wild beasts
and then, for the laughter and sport of their foes, kept
alive to be eaten again. But most miserable of all are those
who are still alive and who have often prayed for death
but have not had their prayer answered. Have they not
seen their mother-city Jerusalem, who was believed to
have had God as her founder—though she was armed and
entrenched and by myriads defended—uprooted and swept
away, and the only memorial left that of the camp of
those who destroyed her, which still stands among her
ruins? Miserable old men sit in the dust of her shrine,

with a few women reserved by the enemy to be victims of their shameless outrage! They had hoped to retrieve themselves and to avenge themselves on their enemies, but now that that hope is gone, let us hasten to die with honor! Let us hasten to take pity, while still it is possible, on ourselves and our children and wives! How the Romans will hate us for having resisted! Is a man to see his wife led away to be violated, to hear the voice of his child, with bound hands, crying out to his father? If the Romans have their way, not one of us will die before we are captured. Let us hasten to cheat their hope and leave for them amazement at our death and wonder at our fortitude!"

At this point, Eleazar's speech was interrupted. His hearers had now been persuaded. As if eager to act quickly and not to be left among the last, they embraced and kissed their families and almost at the same moment killed them. Then they chose by lot ten who were to kill the rest. They lay down beside their wives and children, and presented their own throats. When all these had been dispatched, one of the ten was chosen by lot to slaughter the nine others. When he had done this, he looked carefully to make sure that none was still alive; then he set the palace on fire and drove his sword with all his force through his own body. One old woman and another woman with five children had hidden themselves in the underground aqueducts, and their absence had not been noticed. They came out when the soldiers had broken through, and told the Romans, who were incredulous, what had happened. It was presumably by way of these women that the story later reached Josephus.

The rock called by the Arabs es-Sebbeh was identified as Masada by two American scholars, Eli Smith and Edward Robinson, on their travels, in 1838. But it was such a hard nut to crack that the archaeologists seldom attempted it. An English painter and an American missionary, W. Tipping and S. W. Wolcott, were stimulated by the suggestion of Smith and Robinson to examine the site more carefully. They succeeded in climbing the rock on the side where the Roman ramp had been and recognized certain features: the Roman encampment itself, the wall, the great tower, and the water tanks which had been described by Josephus, the outlines of long parallel rooms that had evidently been storehouses or barracks. "The language of that historian [Josephus]," wrote Wolcott, "respecting the loftiness of the site is not very extravagant. It requires firm nerves to stand upon the verge of its steepest sides, and look directly down." Tipping did some impressive engravings of it, which are reproduced in a book on Masada by Mr. Yadin. These explorers were followed by an American naval officer who explored the Dead Sea in 1848, and by a French and a Dutch scholar.

The most serious expedition up to the recent ones was that of the German Adolf Schulten, who, in 1932, spent the whole of a month on the site, though only two mornings on top of the rock. In 1955-56, two expeditions of ten days each were made by the Israel Exploration Society, which discovered much of Herod's pleasure palace, exactly as described by Josephus, on the beak of the great ship-shaped rock. Members of Israeli youth movements had already been climbing the cliffs. The "snake path" mentioned by Josephus had already been made out by two of them, Shmaryahu Guttman and his companion, Micha Livne, who restored it and dug out its gate, and they had also discovered the layout of one of the Roman camps. The definitive Israeli expedition, directed by Professor Yadin, was carried on during eleven full months—"less a short interruption for Passover"—from October, 1963, to May, 1964, and from November, 1964, to April, 1965. I

owe everything that follows here to two volumes by Mr.
Yadin: *Masada: Herod's Fortress and the Zealots' Last
Stand*, a book intended for the ordinary reader, with a
more scholarly *Preliminary Report*," brought out in English in Jerusalem by the Israel Exploration Society; and to
*The Zealots of Masada: Story of a Dig*, by Moshe Pearlman. I almost feel that it is a pity to be summarizing the
first of these books, the dramatic discoveries of which have
been translated into such vivid English by Mr. Moshe
Pearlman and illustrated by such amazing photographs,
many of them colored—from below, from the air, and on
the site. I can only assure the reader that if he is interested
in the subject, he will find these books quite enthralling.

Before going on to the discoveries made by this expedition, it is worthwhile to give some account of the remarkable way in which it was manned. Mr. Yadin sent out an
announcement of his project and invited applications to
take part in it, explaining that, although the accepted
volunteers would be supplied with such food and shelter
as would be possible at the site, they would not be paid
any salary or expenses of transportation. This recruited a
good many volunteers, mostly young but some middle-
aged, and not by any means all Jewish. There were quite
a number of Scandinavians. One English married lady
explained that she had chosen to spend a vacation on
Masada. Under the baking Palestinian sun, the women
worked in bikinis. They all slept in khaki tents. Mr.
Yadin says that he had sometimes unsuccessfully to try
to curb his recruits from tasks to which they seemed un-
equal, and that in only two cases did he have to dismiss a
worker. It seems to me that Masada demonstrates that any
appeal to the young for a project which combines idealism
with adventure is likely to meet with a ready response.
Our Peace Corps has attracted many, though now, with
the Vietnam war, its name makes it look so ridiculous that

the kind of challenge it offered seems to have been supplanted by that of burning or returning one's draft card
or going to prison or Canada.

The palace of Herod described by Josephus has turned
out to be rather in the nature of what Yadin calls a
"palace-villa." The administrative palace, with its throne
room, is a larger building, on the western side of the rock.
Herod put his workers to a lot of trouble and must himself have been put to a lot of expense to hang his three
pleasure terraces on the prow of the sheer cliff. It has been
only by great ingenuity and at a very considerable risk
that the Israeli Army engineers have built a set of wooden
steps which makes it possible to reach these terraces from
the foot of the precipice, and the modern workers on its
edge, thirteen hundred feet above the level of the Dead
Sea, had to be tied, like mountain climbers, with ropes.
In the lowest of the terraces were Corinthian columns and
wall paintings. Josephus had put on record that this palace
was panelled in marble and that the columns were each
cut from a single stone, but it turns out that the panels
are plaster merely painted over with veins intended to give
a marblelike effect, and that the columns are made of
drums of soft stone, grooved and plastered to look like
marble. One capital showed remains of gold paint. On
this terrace was also a bathhouse, with a cold pool and a
tepid room and a hot room. Underneath the debris of
these chambers, there was a heavy layer of ashes—presumably left by the fire lighted by the last of the Zealots—in
which were date and olive pits and coins with such inscriptions as "The Freedom of Zion." On the floor of the
bathhouse were found scales of armor, iron arrows, the
scraps of a prayer shawl, a potsherd inked with Hebrew
letters, and the skeletons of a man about twenty and of a
woman and a child, which, it seemed, could only have
belonged to one of those Zealot families who had given

themselves up to be killed. The woman's scalp and her dark-brown braids had been preserved in the dry air, and there were a pair of woman's sandals. The plaster of the steps on which she was found was stained with what looked like blood.

The terrace in the middle was filled with large rocks, which had fallen from the terrace above it and were extremely difficult to move. This contained a circular pavilion, and Mr. Yadin believes that it, too, had been intended by Herod for "leisure and relaxation" but had eventually been taken over by the Zealots, who had collected in order to burn them—some of these objects were charred—a heap of animal bones and remains of other food, fragments of glass and pottery, and fourteen arrow heads. The upper terrace contained the living quarters, which consisted, in Herod's time, of only four rooms, but had been further partitioned by the Byzantine monks who lived on Masada in the fifth century, so as to provide more cells for themselves. There was a semicircular porch, with a tremendous view of the Dead Sea, and a simple mosaic floor, which is, together with a few more elaborate ones, among the earliest known in Palestine.

Other buildings were a large Roman bathhouse, the mechanics of which were still quite plain: an oven produced hot air that went into a space between two floors and from there into clay pipes in the wall; storehouses provided for an armory and for vegetables, fruit and grain; and a kind of apartment house which may also have been used for offices. Each unit of this last consisted of one large room, two small rooms, and a small closed-in court. In one of these larger rooms was found, with the shreds of a bag, a quantity of silver shekels and half-shekels. Two other lots of shekels turned up elsewhere, and all the years of the Revolt were represented by these. In the room in which the first of the lots was found, there was

a potsherd with the name "Hillel," and Yadin suggests
that this may have been a priest who collected the contributions for the Temple. The largest building on Masada was the western palace. There seems here to have
been a throne room, with rich furniture, four hollows in
the floor for the legs of the throne, and a handsome mosaic
in colors, which complies with the Mosaic prescription, as
Herod was bound to do, by not representing men or animals but having been limited to olive branches and vine
leaves and other examples of plant life. There is a kitchen
with enormous stoves, more storehouses, and apartments
for the palace staff. There are many signs of a fire, and
that this must have occurred at the end of the Revolt is
shown by the finding in the ashes of a coin of 72-73. Near
the palace were several small villas and a Byzantine chapel
with later mosaics. A strange circular building had walls
with square niches like a waffle iron. This was thought at
first to be a dovecote, but it was found, on experimenting,
that doves would not fit into the openings, and it was
concluded that it must have been intended for the disposal
of the ashes from cremations when non-Jewish officials or
servants had died. The specifically Jewish structures were
ritual immersion baths and the ruins of a synagogue, with
small remnants of Biblical scrolls.

The casemate wall, with it many chambers, turned out
to be of the greatest interest. The Zealots had split up
these rooms in order to make more lodgings possible. Everything seemed much as they had left it, and one could
easily imagine their domestic life: bronze pans and jugs,
clay lamps, perfume phials, eyeshadow sticks, a wooden
comb, a cosmetic palette made from a Red Sea shell, rings
and buckles and keys. Where the Romans had attacked
the wall, there were hundreds of catapult stones the size
of grapefruit, and at a strategic point just above the snake
path were over a dozen hundred-pound stones which the

Zealots had doubtless assembled to roll down on the Roman attackers. Twenty-five more skeletons were discovered in caves, where the Romans had probably flung them: men from twenty-two to seventy; women from fifteen to twenty-two; children from eight to twelve; and the skeleton of an embryo. In another place were found "eleven small strange ostraca [that is, potsherds used to write upon], different from any others which had come to light in Masada. Upon each was inscribed a single name, different from the others, though all appeared to have been written by the same hand. The names themselves were also odd, rather like nicknames." Were these the names of the men who had been chosen by lot to cut the throats of the others? One of them reads "Ben Ya'ir," which was Eleazar's patronymic.

A number of fragments of scrolls have turned up on Masada in various places, written on leather or parchment —notably from Leviticus, Deuteronomy, Ezekiel and the Psalms, and hardly differing from the Masoretic text. Some of these, like some of the scrolls from Qumrân, seem to have been deliberately torn up by the Romans. And there are almost seven hundred inscriptions on pottery, some of them merely the names—all Hebrew—of the people to whom the pots had belonged; also, fragments of many documents, of which little can be made, in Hebrew, Aramaic, Greek and Latin. An important discovery for scholarship, though of less interest to the ordinary reader, was a part of a Hebrew manuscript of the Book of the Wisdom of Ben Sirach, an apocryphal work which in the Vulgate is known as Ecclesiasticus (not to be confused with Ecclesiastes). Though this book was often quoted in Hebrew, the Hebrew original had disappeared by the beginning of the eleventh century, and for centuries it was known only in translations, until almost two-thirds of a Hebrew text turned up in 1896, in the *genizah*—that is,

storeroom for old discarded manuscripts—of the medieval
Cairo synagogue in which had also been found the so-
called Zadokite document that later was to be identified
as part of the literature of the Dead Sea Sect. There was a
controversy—which need not detain us—as to whether this
represented the original text or was a translation back from
Greek. The new scroll seems to settle this controversy: it
is plainly the same text, and this must date from before
73 A.D. But what is today of more interest is another and
shorter fragment, which must also date before 73, and
thus settles a more important question. Among the other
scrolls from the Qumrân caves were four fragments of
four different manuscripts of what was evidently, for the
Dead Sea Sect, a basic ritualistic document. This has come
to be variously known as the Angelic Liturgies and the
Songs of the Sabbath Sacrifices. The Essene Sect had a
special calendar which differed from the traditional Jewish
one. This was solar, and based on a year of twelve months
of thirty days each, with an extra day at the end of every
quarter. Each Sabbath had its own sacrificial hymn, supposed to be recited in rotation by seven "chief princes,"
who are thought to have been archangels of the kind that
the Essenes so prominently featured. Now, a fragment
has been found at Masada, in one of the compartments of
the casemate wall, which belongs to the same document.
It must have been brought there by someone from the
Sect, who, alienated from the Temple—by that time, perhaps, destroyed—wanted to keep to his sectarian schedule, and so it would have to have been brought during the
occupancy of the rock by the Zealots—that is, not later
than 73. There has been a persistent attempt on the part of
Mr. G. R. Driver and Mr. Cecil Roth, both of Oxford, as
well as of one or two other scholars, too old or inflexible, it
seems, to assimilate new material, to show that the Qumrân scrolls must date from the "middle or late first century

A.D." (in this case I quote Mr. Driver) "or very early in the second century A.D.," and that the inhabitants of the monastery (here I cite Driver and Roth) had never been the Essenes but were, in fact, the Zealots. The Essenes, it is true, were said to be men of peace, but the War Scroll shows that at the End of Days they were expecting a hard-fought showdown between the Children of Darkness and the Children of Light. They may, Mr. Yadin suggests—instead of following the progress of events with the realistic eye of Josephus—have supposed that this showdown had come when the Jews were pitted against the Romans in what seemed to them a final struggle, and it is evident from Josephus that when things had got to this point other Jews had made common cause with the Zealots. Josephus, as Yadin points out, speaks twice of John the Essene as one of the generals in the war with the Romans. And is it not possible that some of the Essenes, still clinging to the schedule of their dissident calendar, had come up from the vulnerable Qumrân on the shore to the formidable heights of Masada? If the document containing their calendar must have been written long before 73, must not the rest of the Sectarian literature, too, have been written well before that date?

From even before the excavations, the administering of the oath of allegiance to the groups of new recruits to the armored units of the Israeli Army has taken place on top of Masada. In a speech at the ceremony of June 19, 1963, Mr. Yadin addressed these soldiers as follows: "When Napoleon stood among his men, against the background of the Pyramids of Egypt, he declared, 'Four thousand years of human history look down upon you!' But what would he not have given to be able to say to his men, 'Four thousand years of *your own* history look down upon you!'" He told them briefly the story of the Zealots and concluded, "Masada has become for us a symbol. The poet's words, 'Masada shall not fall again,' have become a rallying cry for the younger generation and, indeed, for the whole nation. It is no exaggeration to say that it is thanks to the heroism of the warriors of Masada, as to those other links in the long chain of Jewish valor, that we stand here today as soldiers of the Army of a youthful yet ancient people, while all about us are vestiges of the armed encampments of those who wish to destroy us. We stand here today, no longer helpless against the might of our foes, no longer putting up a last desperate stand in a war already lost, but firm, proud and with quiet assurance, knowing that our fate lies in our own hands, in the strength of our spirit, which is the reawakened spirit of age-old Israel. The echo of our oath this evening will be heard among the armies of our foes. In it lies our strength no less than in our armaments. And we, the offspring of those heroes of a distant past, stand here today ready to restore our whole nation. Happy are we to merit this."

# XI

# DUBIOUS DOCUMENTS

In 1868, a German missionary discovered, among the ruins in the Biblical land of Moab on the east side of the Dead Sea, and at the site of the ancient city of Dion, almost directly opposite En-Gedi, a stele made of black basalt, three and a half feet tall and two feet thick, with an inscription in the Moabite dialect that differed very little from Old Hebrew. An impression of it was taken by a young French archaeologist, Charles-Simon Clermont-Ganneau, who was attached to the Jerusalem consulate. It proved to be an account, in the name of the Moabite King Mesha, of his war, in the ninth century, with the Israelites east of the Jordan, which is recounted in II Kings 3. When the Arabs of that locality found the foreigners taking such an interest in the stone, they concluded, as the modern Bedouins have done in connection with the Dead Sea scrolls, that there must be treasure involved. They broke the stele open, but Clermont-Ganneau collected the fragments and put it together again. It is now to be seen in the Louvre and is generally known as the Moabite Stone. It presumably dates from the time of Mesha.

At that time, there was living in Jerusalem a dealer in souvenirs and antiques named Moses Wilhelm Shapira. He and his wife, although Jewish, had been converted to Christianity, but he had a certain competence in Hebrew, and his traffic in rare books and scrolls, Muhammedan,

Jewish and Christian, which he kept in the back of his
shop and sold to museums and libraries, was far more important than his sale to tourists of prayer books and Bibles
with olivewood covers. After the discovery of the Moabite
Stone, he sent men to make excavations at the place where
the stone had been found, and they brought him little pottery figures, with inscriptions in the ancient characters,
which were supposed to be Moabite gods. These he sold
to the Prussian government, but they were exposed by
Clermont-Ganneau as forgeries manufactured in Jerusalem by an employee of Shapira's. Shapira now explained
that he had always had doubts about the authenticity of
these potteries but was not himself responsible for the forgeries. Later on, he produced fifteen fragments of a manuscript written on skins and so blackened as to be almost
illegible, which included the Ten Commandments and
the Shema ("Hear, O Israel, the Lord our God is one
Lord," etc.) from Deuteronomy 6—the speech of Moses on
receiving the Law, which is of special importance to the
Jews in both their private and their synagogue ritual and
which is worn against the skin in their phylacteries and
inscribed on the mezuzahs of their doors. These, too, had
been written in the archaic Hebrew characters, and they
differed very much from the Masoretic text. Shapira, in
1883, went to London and offered to sell them to the British Museum at the price of a million pounds. The manuscripts were at first taken seriously by English and German scholars as contemporary with, if not older than, the
Moabite Stone, but Clermont-Ganneau came to London
and intervened with his positive opinion that Shapira was
peddling forgeries. It had already been objected by an
Oxford professor that the climate of Palestine was much
too damp for a sheepskin to be preserved in it nearly three
thousand years. But the manuscript had been found in a
cave by an Arab, as the scrolls of Qumrân had been, on

the opposite side of the Dead Sea, and so might have been kept dry in the same way. Now Clermont-Ganneau pointed out that the Commandments and the Shema appeared to have been written on margins cut from the bottoms of a scroll only two or three hundred years old, in characters copied from the Moabite Stone and then blackened by some chemical process. The scroll had had a dry-point ruling and the forger had not noticed this. The French scholar mockingly added that he himself would undertake to reproduce a similar text of Leviticus, which would have the advantage of not costing so much. Shapira had by that time been counting on selling the fragments for a very good sum; his family in Jerusalem had moved into a larger house, had bought horses and were running up bills. The news of Shapira's great coup had made them important persons. A Dr. C. D. Ginsburg, who had written on the Moabite Stone, had been consulted by the British Museum and had pronounced no adverse opinion; it was believed that the Museum would buy the fragments. But the advent of Clermont-Ganneau and a letter he wrote to the London *Times* declaring the text a forgery perhaps decided Ginsburg the other way, for he seconded Clermont-Ganneau, alleging more or less the same reasons. The fraudulent Moabite gods, of course, remained in everyone's mind.

Shapira left London for the Continent, and his family heard nothing from him. The bad news from London reached Jerusalem, and the credit of the Shapiras declined; they found themselves, in fact, in disgrace. It was not until the spring of the following year, 1884, that they learned that Shapira, after drifting about and writing letters to his wife which he never mailed, had shot himself in a hotel in Rotterdam.

No one knows whether Shapira had forged the fragments or whether somebody else had forged them. There is not even any agreement as to whether they were forged at all. The manuscripts themselves have disappeared. They were sold in 1885 by Sotheby's—some of them were bought by Ginsburg—but it has so far been impossible to trace them. There are only illegible photographs and deciphered transcriptions available. But recently, in 1959, Professor Menahem Mansoor of the University of Wisconsin has revived the whole question in a paper in Volume XLVII of the *Transactions of the Wisconsin Academy of Sciences, Arts and Letters,* which was afterwards, with the addition of supplementary material, reprinted as a booklet, and in 1965 Professor John Allegro published a small book on the same subject, called *The Shapira Affair.* Both of these scholars—to whom I am indebted for most of my information here—are disposed to accept the Deuteronomy as genuine. I cannot recapitulate their arguments, which, in the case of Professor Mansoor, involve technical discussions of language, and I am not qualified to judge them. The situation is a little confused, in Mr. Allegro's account, by the existence of another document which makes its way to one's attention. The Shapira family left Jerusalem, and Shapira's younger daughter wrote a number of French novels under the name of Myriam Harry. One of these—*Une Petite Fille de Jérusalem,* published in *La Petite Illustration* in instalments in 1914, with many winsome illustrations of the period—is an autobiographical narrative with only thinly disguised names. Miss Shapira had been obviously devoted to her father, and she tells the whole story of his exploits and his tragic death in such a way as to compel us to sympathize with him and to pity his misfortunes. Clermont-Ganneau appears as a bugaboo, who has, however, for the little girl, a strange kind of evil fascination. (There is a legend that she tried to shoot him.) A good deal of this fictionalized story has got into Mr. Allegro's account and perhaps a little into mine. But it ought not to be taken as reliable evidence. There is, for example, in the novel, a scene in which the daughter, when a very young girl, comes to her father in a state of excitement to tell him that she is engaged, but finds him so engrossed in working on the Deuteronomy fragments, which he has only just acquired, that he pays no attention to her, and a comic conversation ensues: "Papa, his name is Casimir Kra." "It will be my glory and your fortune!" "He's still a Jew but is going to be converted." "Siona, it's Deuteronomy. . . . I bought it for a trifle in Arabia," etc. Mr. Allegro quotes this scene, though explaining its source. But did it ever really take place? If it did, it shows either that Shapira, on studying the scroll with care—he is described as, piece by piece, soaking the blackened leather to soften it—became gradually convinced of its authenticity, or that he was putting on a most elaborate act in order to convince his family. It has also been suggested that what he was actually doing was intently working on his forgery. Apart, however, from this, Professors Allegro and Mansoor between them would persuade me that the Shapira fragments were genuine if it were not that Professor Frank Cross, an authority on Hebrew palaeography, assures me that the fragments are forgeries, not merely for the reasons alleged by Clermont-Ganneau but because the "stance" of the characters is impossible, which the forger could not have known, and because the writing of the manuscript cannot be made to fit in with the writing of any known period but mixes the usages of several centuries. Professor W. F. Albright of Johns Hopkins also regards them as forgeries, as he has noted in his book *The Archaeology of Palestine*.

This question, of course, has been raised again on account of the discovery of the Qumrân scrolls—Shapira himself had suggested that his own fragments of Deuteronomy might have belonged to some Dead Sea sect—

they were at first, in the same way, rejected by competent but prejudiced scholars. Certain special features of the Shapira texts, which have been used to discredit their authenticity, have, according to Professor Mansoor, now been found in the Qumrân documents. It does seem a little unlikely that a forger should have produced a text that differs so widely from the accepted one as the Shapira Deuteronomy does: the sixth and seventh commandments interchanged; elements from the old second, third and ninth combined in a new seventh; and the first prohibition of Leviticus 19.17—"Thou shalt not hate thy brother in thy heart"—appearing as a new tenth, etc. But Albright says that such a version would have been impossible for the pious Jews of the period when this text is supposed to have been written.

The discovery of the Dead Sea scrolls, like the Moabite Stone in its day, has now, with the prices that such things have come to bring, been stimulating a whole series of forgeries. Some strips of silver inscribed with nonsense in characters derived from archaic Greek were offered to Dr. Cross and immediately rejected by him. A group of papyri supposed to be in late Hebrew, on which the German Professor K. G. Kuhn paid for an option, also turned out to be fakes. Professor William H. Brownlee, one of the original editors of the Habakkuk *pesher*, has written me that "in the spring of 1962 I was working on the Ezekiel scroll from the 11 Q Cave in Jerusalem. . . . I was surprised by a caller from Bethlehem reporting that the Ta'âmireh Bedouins [who had brought in the first lot of scrolls and have been hunting scrolls ever since] were excavating again and here were some things they found. One was readily identifiable as a portion of a modern scroll of Esther [the only Biblical book that had not yet turned up at Qumrân]. The other was an irregularly shaped limestone slab ... with Aramaic (or Hebrew) letters scratched on it. I sent back word that the one piece was modern and that the limestone slab was a forgery, but that the shapes of letters on the slab were more ancient than the Dead Sea scrolls." These characters turned out to have been copied from a mass of crumbled Samaritan papyri which the Bedouins had stumbled on in a cave, "located," Dr. Cross explains, "in a remote and terrible country fourteen kilometers north of old Jericho . . . about twelve kilometers west of the Jordan in the tortured hills that mark the western line of the faulting which created the Jordan Valley." This faked slab, Dr. Brownlee believes, was the Bedouins' devious way of feeling out the interest of the scholars in characters such as this. Kando of Bethlehem, the middleman for the Bedouins, showed a fragment of papyrus, with Aramaic on both sides, to the director of the American School, and he and Père Roland de Vaux and the director of the Palestine Museum made their way, with considerable difficulty—they first thought they needed helicopters, then found they could climb on donkeys—to the almost inaccessible cave, nearly three hundred and twenty-five feet above sea level, where they discovered, amid clouds of bat dung, the remnants of some forty documents which evidently dated from the fourth century B.C. They were "relatively banal" in themselves, says Professor Cross, who has been working on them—records of "dealings in slaves, sales or conveyances and documents of manumission . . . real-estate transactions, settlements of broken contracts including divorce, and loan agreements," but historically and palaeographically not without interest in regard to a period in Palestine about which little is known. There were also coins and signet rings and an extraordinary quantity of human skeletons—men, women and children: further gruesome evidence of the massacre of the natives by their Western, this time Greek, invaders. These Samaritans had apparently fled to the hills, taking their records with them, to escape from Alexander the Great. It is recorded that Alexander destroyed the city of Samaria and settled upon its site a colony of his Macedonians. Dr. Cross believes that the great gluttonous dominator must have hurried on to Babylon. These refugees would have been the leaders of those who stood up to the Greeks but who "were discovered in their hiding place by the Macedonians, either by assiduous search, or, more likely, by betrayal on the part of their fellows who remained in Samaria, and were mercilessly slaughtered to a man."

Dr. Cross has said that he sometimes shudders at the thought that some well-equipped ingenious forger might produce, like John Collier and the late Thomas Wise in the field of English literature, a masterpiece in this very much more lucrative field.

# "ON THE EVE"
1967

# I

# TATTOO

THIS IS a word which the Israelis have borrowed from the English. It means primarily the beating of a drum at night to recall the soldiers to their quarters, but as it is defined by the Concise Oxford Dictionary it may be extended to mean an "elaboration of this with music and marching as entertainment."

The tattoo which in Israeli Jerusalem, on the night of May 14th, 1967, preceded the next day's parade that celebrated the nineteenth anniversary of Israel's Independence Day took place, beginning at seven-thirty, in the big new Jerusalem stadium. Seventeen thousand people in the stadium seats and many more watching from windows and roofs. A terrific demonstration: feverish, high-keyed, a little sinister. Fast-paced, nasal Jewish music—popular songs and marches—assaulted us from loudspeakers. A military rally with elements of circus: the arena illuminated or darkened to dramatize special events.

The units marched in one by one, representing all branches of the service. But the only weapons permitted were such comparatively light ones as drill rifles and anti-aircraft guns. By the terms of the armistice of 1949, heavy armaments were supposed to be banned from Jerusalem, so no tanks, big guns or planes were paraded. The Jordanians, regarding the demonstration as an act of hostile defiance, had demanded of the Armistice Commission that

the rally and parade be forbidden, but the Commission
came to the decision that if the armistice regulations were
observed, they had no jurisdiction to prevent it. The majority of the diplomatic corps—it is said under pressure
from Britain, which is already in trouble with the Arabs—
did not attend the ceremonies, and the Israelis, I think,
were miffed that almost the only foreign representatives
present were those of the minor South American countries
and the newly established African republics to which Israel has been sending advisers to help them in establishing
their new regimes. Ben-Gurion so disapproved of this deference to foreign opinion that he boycotted the whole celebration. It was thought that he would have brought out
the tanks in contempt of the terms of the armistice, which,
intended to guarantee Jerusalem as an international city,
had become a complete dead letter. The more important
Israeli Arabs, in their black gowns and white headdresses,
were occupying some of the more prestigious seats, and
Jordanian Legionnaires were seen to be watching the pro-
ceedings with binoculars and periscopes from the top of
the Old City wall.

There was, however, no mistaking, in any case, the militant character of this occasion. The performance had begun with the tattoo proper—the drumming. But it was not
merely the name and the nature of the ritual that had
been learned from the English military. The whole style
of the troops on parade was British: the exaggerated
swinging in rhythm of the arms, the long strides with the
legs wide apart, the emphasized stamping in coming to
place. The various commanders and officials made individual entrances, preceded by motorcycles. They were driven
around the arena and escorted to the official stand. This
culminated in the advent of the President, with a motor-
cycle guard in front and outriders on beautiful white
horses behind. (In going back through the gate, one of

these horses slipped and fell and broke the rider's leg—no doubt to the malicious satisfaction of the Arabs, who pride themselves on horsemanship.) Everybody now stood and sang the national anthem—composed by a Palestinian Zionist years before the foundation of the Israeli State. A poem by Natan Alterman was read. It had originally been written at the time of the Sinai campaign and, when it had been tried out at rehearsal, was considered too bellicose for the present occasion; some passages had been cut in the Prime Minister's office. Then the lights were turned out, and, in the dark, pairs of big glowing dots were seen coming down the aisles. These were soldiers wearing bulbs on their shoulders—white, bluish and pink—who, gradually filling the platform, performed interweaving evolutions. Everybody specially clapped. Spotlighted choirs sang in the frames of a high stand and one of the gates.

When the lights went on again, the President made a speech in which he carefully refrained from any show of pugnacity but regretted that "the harmony in which we wish to live with our neighbors is very slow in coming. All our attempts to coöperate and to communicate, even in the slightest, with them have not yet borne fruit, and if hatred against us no longer assures them of unity among themselves, it is still far from weakening." He spoke of the economic difficulties which Israel had lately been having—the unemployment, the lessening of immigration, the dangers of "spiritual relapse"—and the hopeful indications that might be taken to offset these: the narrowing of the gap between imports and exports, improvements in agriculture and advanced mechanization. I did not understand Shazar's speech, but I was close enough to see the repercussions of his back at every emphatic statement, and he seemed to me very forceful. Hebrew is a peculiarly positive language; it packs most of the meanings which we relegate to adverbs into its varied and pregnant verb forms.

I spoke of this afterwards to an Israeli friend, saying that
in contrast to the Russians, who, even when they are making speeches that are intended to be strongly assertive, can
never seem to get away from a complaining lugubrious
tone, a speech in Hebrew always sounds dynamic. (This
is partly due, I believe, to the long, trailing cadence of
Russian words as contrasted with the short words of Hebrew.) He said that if I had understood Shazar's speech
I would not have had this impression. Why not? "Because
he makes everything sound pathetic. If he spoke about
that table, he would make it sound pathetic." But why?
"Because he's a Russian." Shazar was only forceful, he
said, "phonetically." And, indeed, when I came to read the
speech, I saw that the sentiments were actually, as has
been indicated above, quite moderate. This seemed to
me a striking example of the transformative powers of
language.

The maneuvers were now continued. These included a
contingent of men and women veterans from Eastern Upper Galilee, in white shirts and blue trousers or skirts, and
there was a reading of an appropriate passage from Josephus, in which the valor of the Galileans in their war
against the Romans was commended: "These two Gali-
lees, of such a size and encompassed by so many nations
of foreigners, have always been able to make a strong resistance on all occasions of war; for the Galileans are in-
ured to war from their infancy, and have always been very
numerous; nor hath the country been ever destitute of
men of courage, or wanted a numerous host of them."
Nineteen caldrons in which gas was burned were set blazing by a torch which had first been lighted at the tomb of
Theodor Herzl—one for each year of independence—and
went on burning through the rest of the evening. Children
brought flowers in pots and set them on the edge of the
platform, while the band played "Happy Days Are Here

Again." As each unit passed the reviewing stand, a shattering cannon shot was fired. I had not been warned about this, and thought at first it might be the Jordanians bombarding from across the line, as the tension in the air when I came into the stadium had made me fear that a siren which was suddenly heard and which was followed by sudden silence might herald an air raid from Syria. It was explained that this was simply a signal of the ending of the Day of Remembrance of the men who had died for Israel, which had preceded the celebration. The evening performance concluded with a crackling display of fireworks, the most splendid and explosive I have ever seen. The rockets and other starbursts were fired off from both sides of the stadium and so low over the heads of the audience that the sparks just fell short of peppering us. I was told that this display had been very expensive, since the fireworks had been bought in Paris.

It was not till the next day that I learned that Egyptian troops were being moved out of Cairo along the Nile.

# II

## PALESTINIANS

THE KING DAVID HOTEL, in which I stayed, was crowded with visitors who had booked their rooms for the Independence Day festival, and I had to move out for a night. I was invited to stay with a young lawyer and his family, and I was glad to make their acquaintance and to see how such young people lived. Their apartment seemed to be typical of the newer apartment houses—modest, comfortable and with plenty of light and space. (I do not remember, however, seeing one with an elevator.) Since the wife as well as the husband had to be away during the day, they had managed to have a maid—which seemed easier than at home—who came in to do the housework and to be with their little girl. Both husband and wife were old Palestinians, whose families had been there for seven generations. They had found, on comparing notes, that her forebears had been there two years longer than his. Her great-grandfather had been the founder of the first Hebrew-language paper published in Palestine, as well as of the first Jewish settlement established outside Old Jerusalem. I was becoming more aware of these old Palestinians than I had been on my previous visit to Israel. I met quite a number of them, including a handsome Sephardic lady who told me that her family had come straight from Spain to Palestine in the sixteenth century. When a Palestinian has told you about his lineage, he sometimes adds—though she did not—"Mayflower." These natives, I felt,

338

were the bottom rock on which the new state had been based. They are quite self-assured and as indigenous to their country as are the people of any other. They have never had to adapt themselves to another culture. They do not seem to have been influenced by the Arabs, and although the British let them down and have not been especially beloved, they learned from them, in the days of the Mandate, a competence in English and in military training. They speak foreign languages with a Hebrew accent, which is not at all the same as a Yiddish one. I remembered that Frances Gunther (the former wife of John Gunther)—who I was sorry to find had died since my earlier visit—had believed herself to be descended from David, and when I mentioned this I was told that there were even Israeli royalists who also thought themselves the descendants of David and asserted, like all royalists, that the problems of the country could be much more easily solved by a monarchy.

The lawyer and his wife who were good enough to put me up were examples of the kind of young people whose prime aim, apart from their family life, is to work for the new state. The wife was kept busy all day attending to the foreign visitors. She dressed simply, like many of the women, in one of the straight-falling waistless gowns that are circled by green-and-orange or pink-and-blue stripes. Her husband said he drank very little aside from the sweet Carmel wine which they have on Friday night with the Sabbath supper. There was some card-playing, but it was thought rather "decadent." He was worried about the Syrians, who were constantly mining the roads, so one hardly dared nowadays to take one's family out for a drive. Even the road to Tel Aviv had been mined, though this had been now cleaned up. The possibility of five Arab states' combining against Israel was a very disturbing prospect: "They want to drive us into the sea!"

The visitors at the King David Hotel present an unattractive contrast not only to these native Palestinians but also to the Israelis in general, who are active industrious people, with skins that have been darkened by the Eastern sun. The visitors, on the other hand, are Jewish bourgeois from all over, usually pale and fat and amorphous —all bulges and bay windows and thick ankles and necks— and, though evidently prosperous, dowdily dressed. Occasionally there are a lean old couple, who are touching in having, at the end of their lives, taken the trouble to journey to Israel to see what their fellow-Jews have accomplished. They have almost all come for the celebration, and most of them leave the next day. I saw only one old gentleman who wore his black cap in the dining room. All these visitors, I was reminded, belonged to an income level that enabled them to afford the King David prices. The young people who had made it on a shoestring were only to be seen in the hostels. At any rate, it was strange and striking to go from the hotel lobby to the offices of Air France next door and find a beautiful young Israeli girl, as dark as any Arab, with black and high-powered eyes, her slim figure completely hidden by one of those sacklike dresses. She made no play with her beauty, and, when I looked at her, dropped her eyes.

# III

## THE TWO JERUSALEMS

I HAD COME over to Israel from Jordan, where I stayed, as
I had on my earlier trip, at the American School of Oriental Research. I have always found the atmosphere there
friendly and the conversation interesting. I had come to
the Middle East in order to bring up to date this book on
the Dead Sea scrolls and I had found that I could learn a
good deal at the School, whose inmates are mostly archaeologists, historians or Biblical scholars. I was impressed by
the passion for archaeology which had developed during
the last few decades. The excavations of Jericho by Miss
Kathleen Kenyon, of the Qumrân monastery by Père de
Vaux, and of Masada by Professor Yadin are the Palestinian feats that have been most in the news, but Jordan
has been full of foreign excavators—the Arabs seem to take
little interest in their past—and the Israelis have been
equally busy, with the result that the world of the Bible,
its palaces, temples and tombs, and all the textiles and
food and utensils and ornaments of its daily life, is being
brought thus before us in these terms of the concrete objects that have been disinterred in their ancient settings
and that disengage this ancient past from the language of
the King James Bible and the atmosphere of legend which
it inevitably creates. Among the archaeologists at the

School were a Dominican, a Jesuit and a nun—all, I should say, in their thirties. Most of the time they were away at "digs," and came back only on weekends or when the scrambling and exposure had made them ill. They were very agreeable company. When I had been at the School thirteen years ago, no one, I believe, except the Director, in his house, had ever offered me a drink, but now these youngish scholars would invite me to their common room, where I found them fortifying themselves against facing the dreary dinner—monotonous rice and lamb, accompanied by leathery Arab bread—with a couple of shots of whiskey. Sister Marie was in ordinary clothes, and her pretty brown hair was unshaved. She and the Jesuit told me that the cropping of nuns was in the United States today "a myth."

But the School is referred to as a "compound." The foreigners keep to themselves, and complain that at the cocktail parties they see always the same people. I met only two educated Arabs. My happiest impression of an uneducated native—ninety per cent of the Arab world is illiterate—was the night watchman at the School, whom they called "the Hajj," because he had made the pilgrimage to Mecca. He wore a turban, a white robe and a beard, and was shaped like a huge hogshead, with, apparently, the consistency of a bolster. He was posted on the little porch at the top of the steps to the door, either curled up in sleep or praying. He did not know a word of English, but invariably shook hands and blessed one with an air of extreme benevolence. The permanent residents of the School he sometimes embraced and kissed. One has to remember that Muhammedanism, in spite of the fierceness attributed to the Arabs, inculcates, aside from its ritual, gentle virtues like the Christian ones.

The Muslims outside were not always so attractive. A whole little Arab Rue de la Paix—in the windows of the women's-wear shops, half-Europeanized dummies, with miniskirts but slanting Arab eyes—has grown up, since my previous visit, on one of the principal streets outside the old wall, where the School and the chief government building stand, and here you are continually leaped at by bootblacks, antique dealers, pimps and people who want to drive you to Petra for at first an exorbitant price, which they will very quickly reduce to a half or quarter but which still remains excessive. The unwary are subjected to colossal swindles. An American girl warned me—she has lived for some time in the Middle East—"There's no right or wrong about it. They're out for all they can get." I was told that even the post office cheated in selling stamps and that the old Oriental tradition of doing nothing without a bribe had made it difficult for the people at the School even to collect a consignment of books which had been ordered to stock its library. Not that I did not find—in bookstores, for example—quite sober and dignified men, but to walk through that street was annoying. Of course, this kind of thing is found in any city that mainly attracts tourists, but Jordanian Jerusalem is worse than anything I remember in Italy. If you say no, they will not accept it but will follow you for any distance. I was advised to throw back my head and make a clicking sound with my tongue, and I found that this was effective. On the street, people saunter along, with no system for sharing the pavements. There is no system, either, of traffic control, and although there are few cars, they so recklessly hurtle about, with a constant and insolent honking, that they make crossing a street seem dangerous.

I had seen most of the sights when I was there before, and I went only once into the Old City. My reactions to it were no doubt influenced by my ailments and advancing years—it is hard for me now to go up and down steps, and the ancient Damascus Gate lets you in for a good many—but I am not very fond of Old Jerusalem. When I first saw it, years ago, it aroused my imagination; now it only fatigues and disgusts me. When you go in by the Damascus Gate, you find yourself in narrow, bad-smelling tunnels—market arcades called *suqs*, full of all kinds of little booths and shops selling butcher's meat, pastries, sweets, clothing, jewelry, postcards and all sorts of ornamental brass objects—which bazaar the amateurs of Old Jerusalem pretend to find fascinating but which only seemed to me repellent. It makes it, for me, only a little more interesting, but not very much more easily tolerable, to know that this has been for two thousand years the principal market of Jerusalem. I was glad to get out into the open air, but the ancient monuments themselves, with the exception of the Mosque of Omar, are not of remarkable beauty. The Wailing Wall, so important to the Jews as the last remnant of the Second Temple, is not in itself impressive. The Church of the Holy Sepulcher is, as everyone says, "a mess," and was, as usual, surrounded with scaffolding to fend off an abject collapse. At the doorway, you are confronted with what are surely two of the worst sacred murals in the world and with the women leaning down and kissing the unsanitary cover of the stone on which the body of Jesus is supposed to have been laid. I invaded the interior twilight, which is not so much somber as turbid, in order to get out of the sun for a rest, and, avoiding the claustrophobic sepulcher itself, went on to a room where there were benches and read "Dick Tracy" in the Paris *Herald Tribune*. The whole atmosphere here is uncomfortable. No well-informed person believes that these "holy places" are authentic, and the monks of the various rites are always quarrelling among themselves. This year, at the ceremony of the Holy Fire—at which people have been crushed to death and from which a number of women had been carried out unconscious—these monks were, I was told, making the spectators uneasy, in the courtyard in front of the entrance, by throwing rocks at one another.

I was driven to Pella one day with a party of archaeologists. The Christians, in their early years, are supposed to have gone out to Pella in order to get away from the Romans, and it became in the course of time a considerable Christian settlement. There was a Byzantine cathedral there, the stone foundations of which are now being eagerly excavated. The Director of the School, when we started off, told our consul, with whom I was driving, that the road was "not very good." Before we had gone far, the consul said, "I see what he means about the road's not being very good." It was the very worst road I have ever seen—full of great holes and gaping fractures that had to be jolted over, and never quite wide enough so that meeting a truck or a bus did not create a problem. The countryside, I suppose, was typical: Bedouins in black tents; family dwellings that consisted of one or two cooplike cells —a primitive and miserable standard of living. Though they grow things where the soil makes it possible, these people are mainly occupied in attending to their sheep and goats. Burdens are carried by donkeys or by women who balance them on their heads. A few women wear long black veils that cover them from head to foot. (They are even rarer in the cities.) Neither the beasts nor the people pay very much attention to the cars. The most the men, women and children will do is slowly move out of the way when a car is right at their backs. The donkeys, unless somebody pushes them, will stubbornly stand in the middle of the road. If one passes what appears to be, in comparison with the rest, an integrated and soundly built community, it turns out to be a refugee settlement subsidized by the United Nations. These settlements have been equipped with clinics and schools, which are otherwise un-known in this countryside. In the background, the hills are great barren folds. In the stony fields stalk a few camels. The Jordan runs narrow and muddy.

It takes only about fifteen minutes to drive from the School in Jordanian Jerusalem to the King David Hotel on the other side. At the frontier, on the Jordan side, one sees, still in ruins, the old Mandelbaum house, which was bombed in the first Arab war. The contrast, when one has crossed, is, in atmosphere and tempo, abrupt. Jordan is retarded and static, but Israel dynamic and purposeful. This produces an equally dangerous traffic: there are more cars, and the drivers are equally reckless. But they are subject to some traffic control, and at the time I was in Jerusalem a conference was being held in Tel Aviv for the purpose of eliminating accidents. Medals are given to the bus drivers who have had the fewest crashes. Yet this fragment of the prewar Jerusalem is developing into a solid town. I was impressed by the good taste that has been shown in the construction of the new office buildings and apartment houses as well as of the Museum and the University, and I learned that the expansion of the city is directed by a planning board. It is illegal to build houses of any material other than the pale local rough-finished stone. Unfortunately, for reasons of expense, the houses can no longed be roofed with the attractive red tiling that relieved the monotony of this. I noticed, on King David Street, that a vacant lot I remembered as littered and partly bare had now been cleaned up and planted.

Yet, stimulating though the new Jerusalem in so many ways is, one sometimes feels an emptiness and bleakness— that the Jews who have come here from other countries, in which they had become partly assimilated, must have found themselves half in a vacuum. And there has always been an element of uncertainty, of dependence on outside support. The Israelis at the present time are going through a difficult period. The German reparations have come to an end, and they are no longer sustained from this source by seventy million dollars a year; it has besides, it seems, become more difficult to obtain American loans. There is supposed to be ten-per-cent unemployment, and an attempt to freeze wages has already resulted in strikes. Emigration has been increasing and immigration falling off. The presence of Oriental Jews and of Jews from northern Africa has also created problems. The literacy and the standard of living of many of these people are very low. It is the Westernizers who run the country, and the newcomers do not yet really merge with them. I was shown new blocks of apartment houses on the edge of the no man's land that separates the two Jerusalems, which I was told were intended for "slum dwellers." My chambermaid, good-looking and very active, of a dark and African appearance, was a Moroccan who spoke French but said that she now spoke Hebrew better than French. She had travelled to some extent in France—I gathered, on some mission for, or on some bourse provided by, the government. I thought that she must represent the better breed of the North African immigrants.

When I look out at night from my hotel window on the prolongation of King David Street, I see the long road, jewelled with street lamps, and the other thoroughfares of the city's fringe stretching away toward the quiet hills. There is no obliterating blur such as glows in the night sky of a large modern city; a swift rush and hum of motorcars, but none of the nagging of constant horns. It is a feature of the city planning that these streets can be easily joined to the roads on the Jordanian side. (I could not foresee at that time how soon this would become convenient.)

I learn from the paper that fourteen people—including several tourists and policemen—have been killed by explosives in a Syrian car which had been driven into Jordan by Syrians. This was evidently the work of the Syrian Left: the country, where changes of government are frequent, is now supposed to be socialist and, in consequence, anti-monarchist and inimical to King Hussein, whom they accuse of being too "soft" on the Israelis. (The Syrian and Jordanian governments broke off relations in the later crisis and were only persuaded to resume them by the pressure of Nasser for Arab unity.)

A story that circulates in the Middle East and has even reached a column in the Boston *Globe*—I should think an Arab fable brought up to date—tells of a Scorpion who comes to a river and asks a Frog to carry him across. "But you'll sting me," protests the Frog. "Oh, no, I won't," says the Scorpion. "I want to get over to the other side." So the Frog undertakes to ferry him, but when they are only halfway over the Scorpion does sting the Frog. "Oh, why did you do that when you'd promised? Now I'll die and you'll drown!" Hisses the Scorpion, "This is the Middle East!"

# IV

## THE NEW ISRAEL NATIONAL MUSEUM

IT SEEMED to me that the Israel Museum, which had been built since I had last been in Jerusalem, was one of the best-designed I had ever seen. It is relatively low and makes a rambling impression, since the different departments are segments which are adapted to the configuration of the hillside on which it stands, so that you go up and down a few steps in passing from one to another. There is so much space in the rooms that the presentation of exhibits is never confused or crowded: gold and silver and copper menorahs and scroll cases and spice boxes and other rich and curious objects collected from wealthy synagogues; folk pictures illustrating the Bible that include a delightful series on the ideal housewife described in Proverbs, and modern paintings that include one of those gruesome Francis Bacons, more distorted than any folk painting, which are as far as possible from referring to a well-ordered and pious society; Latin inscriptions and pseudo-Greek fauns from the Roman occupation; the mosaic floor from a synagogue and the whole of a Venetian synagogue, transported and reconstructed—all of these side by side with the old bones and stones and fabrics that take us back to the age of Solomon and even to the age of Abraham. Behind the museum is an esplanade park, with a widely spaced display of sculpture—much of it bequeathed by Billy Rose, the American theatrical producer—

349

which ranges from Rodin and Maillol, through a collection of Epstein busts, also left by the sculptor to Israel, to the mechanical contraptions and outlandish objects of which one may now see specimens in the "far-out" collections of New York museums. Jerusalem is quite austere—not merely, I think, from necessity but also, I believe, in submission to the traditional Mosaic ban against making "graven images," which, in spite of the splendor of the sacred objects that have been gathered from these richer synagogues, extends to the visual amenities in general. It has been only in our own day that it seems to have become possible for a Jew to indulge in such artistic exploits as the blazing and gorgeous windows created by Marc Chagall for the embellishment of the Hadassah hospital. (Yet Chagall is said to be dissatisfied with the dreary little box of a chapel which makes such an inadequate setting for them.)

A more imaginative construction is the special museum, designed by two non-Israeli architects, F. J. Kiesler and A. P. Bartos, to house the seven Dead Sea scrolls from the first-discovered of the caves, which were acquired by the Israeli government. This building, called the Shrine of the Book, has been made to dramatize its contents in various symbolic ways. The entrance to the shrine is screened by a section of black basalt wall, the purpose of which seems purely decorative. It is explained that its sheer black is meant to balance the sheer white of the dome of the shrine, thus representing the contrast between the forces of darkness and the forces of light that play such a part in the literature of the scrolls. The approach to the shrine is along a walk which—in order to give the impression of entering a cave—is narrowly confined by walls of rough stone that are tilted so as to lean in toward it. This leads to a cavelike tunnel of symmetrically irregular shape, along the walls of which are set rows of glassed and lighted cases, each with a box of crystals in a corner to protect the exhibits from humidity. These exhibits are the contents of caves explored by teams led by Yadin and other scholars of the Hebrew University from the precarious ledge of a cliffside between Masada and En-Gedi. This was a hideout of Bar-Kochba, the leader, in 132-35 A.D., of the last Jewish revolt against the Romans. There are the toilet appurtenances of the women who accompanied Bar-Kochba's followers: jewel boxes, copper mirrors, combs, objects connected with cosmetics; the sandals of the women and children, not much different from the sandals of today; a glass plate and a large glass bowl, knives, cooking pots, and a basket with coarse grains of salt; remnants of well-dyed and woven shawls; decorated bronze bowls and jugs intended for ritual use, most of which, evidently made in southern Italy, are similar to such vessels found at Pompeii (they must have been loot from the Roman army); human bones and several skulls, one of them still with some hair. What is perhaps most extraordinary—although two such letters had already turned up in one of the caves on the other side of the Jordan-Israel line—is the finding of papyri of fifteen letters in Hebrew, Aramaic and Greek, composed if not written by Bar-Kochba himself, giving orders about supplies and mobilization. There is also a bundle of thirty-five documents carefully docketed, folded and tied, which concern the affairs of a twice-married matron, evidently well-to-do, who owned property in the vicinity: marriage contracts and deeds, papers connected with lawsuits. Nearby was found a property deed in Aramaic made out "on the first day of Iyar in the first year of the redemption of Israel by Shim'on Bar-Kosiba, Prince of Israel." (Bar-Kosiba is thought to have been the leader's real name; Bar-Kochba, Son of the Star, an honorific nick-

name.) The deed included "water rights as proper and fit"—
which meant the right to channel the streams from the hillside springs in such a way that they would run down to
water the gardens. The Israelis like to point out that it was
only after almost a thousand years that En-Gedi was again
to be irrigated. Bar-Kochba, after fifty-two battles, was defeated and killed by the Romans, but after centuries the
Jews of our time have taken possession again.

This tunnel brings you into a kind of rotunda, where
the scrolls are displayed behind glass. The manuscript of
the Thanksgiving Hymns is very dark brown, almost black
in spots; the Manual of Discipline of the Sect beautifully
written and very clear; a Leviticus fragment from Masada
so blackened as to seem unreadable, but a photograph
shows that it is perfectly clear when photographed by
infra-red rays; the tantalizing Habakkuk Commentary,
with the bottoms of its columns gone, which can only be
read in snatches, and the equally deteriorated War Scroll;
the Genesis Apocryphon, partly tattered in lacy shreds like
a sea fan. In the middle of the round room, which makes
a great inverted bowl with a corrugated interior, is a round
platform to which one ascends by steps, and in the center
of this is a large round hole, from which rises a kind of
pedestal. This pedestal is belted by a circular glass case
of dimensions exactly adapted to the length of the complete Isaiah, which one can follow by walking around it.
On top of this showcase, in turn, stands what looks like
a huge old-fashioned office stamp, the clublike brass handle of which gives the impression of a phallic prong,
though it is said to be meant to harmonize with the shape
of the jars in which the scrolls had been hidden. Above
it, like a narrower neck of one of these jars, is an opening
to the sky. This and the blunt stamp-handle were originally intended for a fountain, which would send a jet

up through the roof so that the water would fall on the dome and run off into a trench below, but this was thought not a good idea, since the moisture might damage the exhibits. The prong thus remains rather meaningless, unless it can be taken to represent an upthrusting will to persist.

The effect of this shrine is a little bizarre but dramatically quite impressive.

# V

# CONVERSATIONS WITH YADIN
# AND FLUSSER

I HAD several conversations about the Dead Sea scrolls with Professor Yigael Yadin. Yadin is the son of the late E. L. Sukenik, the former head of the Archaeology Department of the Hebrew University, who was the first, amid the confusion of the Arab war in 1947, to recognize the antiquity of the scrolls and who bought some of the first batch from a Bethlehem dealer. Yadin (he has taken a Hebrew name), also an archaeologist, played a leading role in this first Arab war when, at thirty, he became Chief of Operations of the Israel Defense Forces and, later, Chief of the General Staff. He has an extraordinary combination of high intelligence, informed authority and almost hypnotic persuasive charm. One understands how it was recently possible for him to direct, as described above, the staff of three hundred volunteer workers who succeded in two seasons in excavating the rock fortress of Masada. He combines the scholar with the man of action in a very unusual way.

We discussed the possible relation of the Sect of the Dead Sea scrolls to early Christianity. He thought that the influence of the Sect on John the Baptist and Paul was obvious in their utterances, and he suggested that the importance of Damascus both to the Sect, who, according to one of their documents, at one time retreated there, and to Paul, who is supposed to have been suddenly converted on his way there to persecute the Christians, was a subject that might be looked into. It is assumed that these sectarians afterwards returned to their monastery on the Dead Sea; but what if some had remained in Damascus and communicated their doctrines to Paul? Yadin said he was not aware of anything in the sayings attributed to Jesus which could be credited to Essene doctrine. He suspected that the presence of the Romans in the subjugated Palestine of Jesus was more important in the Gospels than is usually made explicit. People must have come to Jesus and said, "Rabbi, what attitude should we have toward the Romans?," and Jesus would have told them to submit for the time being—"render unto Caesar," etc.—but that eventually they would fight and conquer when the moment to strike came. Yadin reminded me of the passages in the Gospels in which Jesus appears to give evidence of a covertly militant spirit—"I came not to send peace but a sword" (Matthew 10.34) and "He that hath no sword, let him sell his garment and buy one" (Luke 22.36), adding afterwards, however, when two swords are produced, that these will be enough. Then there is Simon the Zealot, who is named among Jesus's disciples (Luke 6.15). The Zealots were the fiercely resistant group who made their last stand at Masada. And then, one of the disciples of Jesus disregards the Master's admonition about turning the other cheek, when the enemies of Jesus have come out with swords and staves "to take him," to the extent of cutting off the ear of the servant of the High Priest. I was ready to agree with Yadin that the non-resistant precepts of Jesus are sometimes inconsistent with his bidding his disciples to stand up to their enemies and the retaliatory gestures of these disciples. Yadin thought that emphasis on forgiveness and self-surrender to authority might have been imposed on Jesus's teaching after his death, at some later phase, but I have no difficulty in imagining that though Jesus, after the triumph of the Romans, found it best to preach resignation, he might occasionally have had flare-ups of the fighting spirit. In any case, in the Gospel accounts of the cutting off of the ear, the four evangelists have curiously different ways of reconciling this act of violence with the supposed gentle spirit of Jesus. In Matthew (26.52-3), Jesus says, "Put up again thy sword in his place: for all they that take the sword shall perish with the sword"—that is, he preaches non-resistance—yet he tells them that he can summon superhuman protection: "Thinkest thou that I cannot now pray to my Father, and he shall presently give me more than twelve legions of angels?" In Mark (14.48), he says simply to his persecutors, as he also does in Matthew and Luke, "Are ye come out, as against a thief, with swords and with staves to take me?"—reminding them, as also in Matthew, that they had listened to him without hostility in the temple. In Luke (22.51)—I use here Ronald Knox's translation, somewhat clearer than the King James Version—his followers ask Jesus, "Lord, shall we strike out with our swords?," and he answers, " 'Let them have their way in this.' And he touched his [the servant's] ear, and healed him." In John (18.10-11)—it is here Simon Peter who cuts off the servant's ear, and the servant is named Malchus—Jesus says to Peter, "Put up thy sword into the sheath: the cup which my Father hath given me, shall I not drink it?"

As I was leaving, I asked Yadin what he thought about the mounting crisis. I had just talked to several people who had not seemed to take it very seriously. I had been wondering whether, after all, the whole thing might not be a comedy. "A strange comedy," he replied, "with their troops massed along the frontier and ours massed on the other side, and seven hundred tanks on each side! If they block our shipping, there'll be war."

The next day, I went to see David Flusser—my friend the incomparable Flusser. He is in every way except scholarly accomplishment the opposite of his colleague Yadin. He had married since I had last seen him and now held a full professorship at the Hebrew University—about both of which events he had written me in the medieval Latin which he had told me, on a previous visit, was then in Israel his best spoken language. Though a professor, he is completely unacademic. He is a scholar who loves scholarship for its own sake, not to secure any kind of advancement. His central interest is comparative religion, but the range of his reading is voraciously immense, and his mind is so teeming with ideas which he feels such an urgency to communicate, and one idea so irresistibly suggests another, that his conversation becomes overwhelming. One of his colleagues once said to me, "The thing about Flusser is that he flusses." And Flusser's *Fluss* may turn into a torrent. He seems to have simultaneously before him, in his mind, open texts for instant reference, both the Old and the New Testaments, the Apocrypha and the Pseudepigrapha (that is, the intertestamental writings), the Talmud and other rabbinical literature and the Fathers of the Church, as well as modern Biblical scholarship and the philosophy and belles-lettres of classical and modern Europe. Though I cannot always follow his leaping and shifting thought and am often left blank by his significant quotations, which he recites or reads in the original tongues, under the impression that I can follow them, I find him fascinating to talk with about the scrolls and kindred topics because his exact memory, his comprehensive learning, and his powers of intuition have led him to make connections and to draw conclusions that nobody else has or would have thought of. Two points that came up in our conversations will give some idea of this. The central figure in the literature of the Dead Sea Sect is the leader referred to as הצדק המורה, which has been variously translated as the Teacher of Righteousness, the Righteous Teacher, the Rightful Teacher, and le Maître de Justice. A Protestant scholar whom I met in Israel at the Hebrew Archaeological School, one of the professional skeptics in regard to the theories about the scrolls, told me with satisfaction that he had found this phrase in the Mishnah in a reference which could not have been to anything Essene, and that he was going to write about it. When I mentioned this to Flusser, he told me that the phrase occurred quite often in the Talmud and that it had been applied to Maimonides. This is a good illustration of the handicap under which a Christian scholar suffers from not having been trained in rabbinics. On another occasion, Flusser showed me an Old Slavonic text of the Book of the Secrets of Enoch—a text unknown to R. H. Charles when he published a translation of this book made from other texts. In one of the Slavonic versions of this work, there is an account of the miraculous birth of the priest-king Melchizedek which has a good deal in common with the Gospel account of the miraculous birth of Jesus. Sophonim, the mother of Melchizedek, had been sterile and was now old. Finding she was pregnant, she hid away; and it was not till her husband summoned her the day she was about to give birth that he became aware of her condition. She protested that she could not imagine how it had happened; but she had had no intercouse with her husband since Methusaleh had anointed him priest, and he made her a terrible scene. The husband was Nir, the brother of Noah, and Methusaleh was his grandfather. He told her to be gone lest he strike her and thus sin in the eyes of the Lord. At this, she fell dead at his feet. Nir was now filled with remorse; and he felt that God had been merciful only because he had restrained himself from striking her. He and Noah secretly prepared a grave, but while they were about this, a child was born of Sophonim's body. He was fully developed and able to speak: when the brothers came back to the house, they found him sitting on the bed and praising the Lord. He had been engendered by God and was appointed to be the high priest Melchizedek. There had already been established, as we learn from the Epistle to the Hebrews, a tradition that Melchizedek had had "no father, no mother, no genealogical line, no beginning of days or end of life; resembling the son of God, he remains a priest forever." But Nir, like his brother Noah, knew that God was contemplating an all but complete purge of mankind, and he made an appeal to Him to know what should be done with the marvellous boy. God answered him in a dream and told him that this problem would be taken care of. The Archangel Michael now appeared to Nir, also in a dream, and said, "Give me back the child that I left with you." Nir, not knowing who his visitor was and knowing how wicked the people had become, was frightened and asked whether the people were intending to kill the divine child. The Angel explained who he was and that he had come to take the child to the Garden of Eden. Nir now felt both joy and grief that he should have this child in place of a son. Melchizedek—his name means King of Jerusalem—was thus preserved from the Flood, eventually to emerge as High Priest.

The Book of the Secrets of Enoch exists only in Slavonic manuscripts, but these are supposed to represent a translation from a Greek original written in Egypt, an outgrowth of that Hebrew Book of Enoch of which Charles says that "without it the history of the develop-

ment of the higher theology during the two centuries before the Christian era could not be written." In this work,
the phrase "Son of Man," as applied to an expected Messiah, "appears for the first time in Jewish literature, and
is, historically, the source of the New Testament designation, and contributes to it some of its most characterestic
contents." The Son of Man in the Book of Enoch is he
"with whom dwelleth righeousness" and "who revealeth
all the treasures of that which is hidden, because the Lord
of Spirits hath chosen him," and who "shall loosen the
reins of the strong and break the teeth of the sinners,"
etc. Those who "deny the Lord of the Spirits . . . persecute the houses of His congregation." Charles puts the
Book of the Secrets—not the Book of Enoch, just quoted,
which must have been written long before—in the first
half of the Christian era and, though he had not seen the
version described above, he noted similarities to the Gospels. The French editor, M. A. Vaillant of the Collège de
France, believes it to be a primitive Christian document.
There is another somewhat similar apocryphal story in an
Ethiopic Book of Adam and Eve, according to which,
when Adam's body, which had been preserved in the Ark,
was brought, after the Flood, to be buried, Melchizedek,
then fifteen, was taken by the Angel from his father,
anointed as a priest and left as a guard at the grave. M.
Vaillant does not suggest—though this seems to me a possibility—that the story of Melchizedek in the Slavonic
Secrets of Enoch—is a typical Russian fairy tale invented
by an imaginative monk. It seems quite different from the
preceding narrative, which tells of Enoch's journey
through the other world. The remorse of Melchizedek's
father and his way of consoling himself, his fear of the
cruelty of the people and his mixture of joy and grief
when he learns that the boy is to escape a dreadful fate
only by being taken away, seem to me, in their psycho-

logical emphasis as well as in a certain realistic detail, quite easy to recognize as Russian. A copyist of this version dropped off the whole story of Melchizedek, feeling, M. Vaillant believes, that it sounded too much like the birth of Christ. The events in either of the Testaments that are left vague or undeveloped gave all sorts of opportunities for invention to the contributors to the Talmud and the composers of Jewish and Christian apocrypha.

I have written of this subject at length not only for its curious interest but because it is typical of the unexpected doors that Flusser is likely to open.

He is full of humorous irony as well as of intellectual excitement, and likes to perpetrate deadpan jokes. He has grown heavier since I last saw him and is thus even more extraordinary in appearance, with his red hair, his sharp little eyes that sometimes look green, sometimes blue, and his rather large pointed ears, which have no lobes and grow directly out from his head. I was not surprised to learn that at some recent scholarly congress in India he was the only one of the delegates whose feet were kissed by the natives and who was regarded, with his genielike appearance, as a semi-supernatural being.

Our conversations about religion were sometimes involved with current events, of which Flusser was very much aware. Before the crisis arose and the Arabs had begun making public statements, he had explained that they were still thinking, as they had been when they were massacring Christians, in terms of a Holy War: every man or woman of Israel that they blew up with dynamite they regarded as a score for Islam. The Jews already, in Talmudic times, had given up the idea of a Holy War. And the Muslims, besides, were still feudal. The countries had quite primitive quarrels with one another, and the groups quarrelled within their own countries. I men-

tioned the Israeli retaliations. I had talked with a driver
for the American School who had spent years in the Jordanian Army and was bitter about the Israeli raid on Jordan last year, when, after driving out the families, they
had blown up forty houses in Jordan. "They resort to reprisals," said Flusser, "because they have come to the conclusion that that's the only language the Arabs can understand. And we don't succeed! We don't really believe in
it!"

I went to see him on May 23rd, the day before I left.
He greeted me with "This is the War of the Children of
Darkness against the Children of Light!"—the title that
has been given to one of the scrolls, which predicts a kind
of Armageddon. "A cloud over Elath! You remember the
cloud that Moses saw over Elath." The Egyptians at the
moment were threatening Elath in their effort to block
Israeli shipping to and from the Gulf of Aqaba. Moses, on
his exodus from Egypt, is supposed to have passed through
Elath, but I have not found the reference to a cloud. It
was very uncomfortable, said Flusser, with a wife and two
small children, to have something like this looming.
"What if this whole thing here should be wiped out! The
prophets are always right! They either say that the disas-
ers have occurred because the Jews have been so sinful or
that the Jews are being so sinful that disasters are going to
occur. And the Jews are always sinful, so the prophet is
always justified!" Whom should we invoke now to intervene? Jeanne d'Arc? No, she might fight for Nasser.
Thomas Aquinas, perhaps. I told him what Yadin had said
about the attitude of Jesus toward the Romans. Yadin had
been a soldier, said Flusser, and he would naturally think
in terms of weapons. The message of the teaching of Jesus
was something entirely different. He then gave me the
most eloquent disquisition on Jesus that I remember ever
to have heard. (He told me that he was just about to write

a book in German on the subject.) The Teacher of Righteousness and Jesus had had completely different ideals and
aims. The former wanted to create, in his isolated Dead
Sea community, a little élite utopia. The members of the
community were to be forbearing toward one another but
to regard everyone else as their enemy; they denounced
both the Romans and Jerusalem. But Jesus was out in the
world, and he instructed his disciples not to resist authority: it would only make the civil authorities worse; they
would very soon put you in prison. "The Kingdom of God
is within you." Yet Jesus was crucified, whereas the
Teacher of Righteousness, as Flusser now believed, on the
evidence of one of the Dead Sea fragments, was not, as
had once been supposed, either executed or murdered by
his enemies. Mrs. Flusser, at the back of the house, had
been listening to the radio news, and her husband now
left the room to find out what was going on. "Eshkol has
appealed to de Gaulle," he reported when he came back.
"Now, if Jesus were here and had heard this, he would
say about Eshkol, 'Poor man!' "—because Eshkol was ap-
pealing to authority. Wouldn't he, I suggested, say the
same thing about Nasser? Flusser was silent a moment.
"Yes, he would say, 'Poor man' about Nasser, too, but he
would not be particularly interested." I did not think to
make the point that Eshkol represented authority, too. I
realized afterwards that Flusser, as a Jew, could put himself in Jesus's place and think he would not have behaved
like Eshkol, but that he took it for granted that Nasser
and de Gaulle belonged to the other side—the authorities
of this world who would want to suppress the Jews. It
seemed to me, too, that Yadin, when he had imagined the
other Jews coming to Jesus and asking what attitude they
should take toward the Romans, must have been interpreting this situation in terms of his own experience when
he had doubtless, in the course of the armistice years, been

consulted by his fellow-Israelis as to what they should do about the Arabs.

[Professor Flusser's book on Jesus has appeared since this was written: *Jesus in Selbstzeugnissen und Bilddokumenten,* in the series Rowohlts Monographien, Rowohlt Taschenbuch Verlag, Reinbeck bei Hamburg.

"This study," Flusser writes, "makes no attempt to establish a bridge between the historical Jesus and the Christian faith. We have sought only, without suppressing ourselves and our own period—it is impossible to write biography otherwise—to bring Jesus here and now before the eyes of the reader. Our period seems an especially appropriate one for understanding him and his preachings. A deep anxiety as to the future and the present has awakened in us a new sensitivity. We are today receptive to Jesus's revaluation of all the other values, and many of us are now becoming aware of the dubiousness of standard morality, from which awareness Jesus starts. We also, like Jesus, are feeling ourselves drawn toward the pariahs and the sinners of society. And if he says that we should *not resist evil,* because we, too, through our going against it, only contribute to the struggle of forces, unimportant in themselves, in society and in the great world, and, in consequence, are at least qualified to understand today. And if we liberate ourselves from the chains of obsolete prejudices, we are surer to respond to his demand for undivided love, not by reason of philanthropic weakness but as a correct psychological conclusion.

"The tremendous achievement of his life appeals to us, also, today: from the call at the time of his baptism, from the breaking of the bonds with his alien family and the finding of a new and more exalted paternity, down amid the pandemonium of the ailing and the insane, and beyond this to his death on the cross. So we come to understand the words which, according to Matthew (28.20), he is to speak at the resurrection, in a new and unchurchly sense: 'And, lo, I am with you always, even unto the end of the world.' "

This book is a significant example of the increasing interest that the Jews have recently been taking in Jesus. The discovery of the Dead Sea scrolls and the new excavations in Palestine have come to fill out some of the obliterations in ancient Jewish history, and this is leading the scholars to ask, Who exactly was Jesus? What impelled him to speak and act as he did? What, in fact, did he say and do? And what was the explanation of the immense extra-Jewish success of his doctrine? 1969.]

# VI

## DEPARTURE

I HAD already made, before I left Boston, the arrangements for my whole itinerary, and I was flying from Tel Aviv the morning of May 24th. On the afternoon of the day before, the American consul called me and said that he had had word from Washington to tell all the Americans to leave.

I did not expect to see again any of my official friends, but late in the afternoon Teddy Kollek, the Mayor of Jerusalem, and Moshe Pearlman, a veteran of the first Arab war, the author of many books and at one time the spokesman for the government, turned up at the King David with a former Israeli ambassador and his wife, whom I had not met before, and, the upstairs bar being closed, which suggested mobilization, we went to the one downstairs. The energetic Kollek, whose family passed through Prague and Vienna, has something of a Germanic toughness and bluntness, but has lived since his teens in Palestine. I was told that he had said of his present office that the trouble with running for mayor was that you risked getting elected. He has not removed his number from the telephone book and has made himself accessible to everybody—with the result that he is likely to be called up at night by someone who complains of being kept awake by the barking of a neighbor's dog. Kollek has a library on the Middle East of the kind that can be acquired only by following catalogues and putting in stand-

366

ing orders, and he has also a carefully chosen collection of ancient utensils and jewelry, which he keeps in glass-doored cupboards. When I first saw him on this visit, he had said, "You're here to talk to people about the scrolls, but I have to worry about garbage disposal." I now asked him if they had a dump. Yes, they had. "And Teddy," cracked Moshe Pearlman, "has a problem to get it back on the streets." The conversation became quite convivial. When I spoke of Eshkol's having appealed to de Gaulle, the wife of the diplomat corrected me quietly: "Reminded him."

I got up at five the next morning and was driven in a car to the airport. Riding along the roads that lead down from Jerusalem, whether in Israel or Jordan, is likely to be rather nerve-racking. The drivers dash around the loops, where one cannot see ahead what is coming, with a sheer unguarded drop at one side, and in Israel the driver, if one talks to him, is likely to gesticulate so wildly that one fears he may lose contact with the steering wheel. The airport gave the impression of a shelter for refugees fleeing from a hostile army. I have never, in a public place, heard such chattering, shrieking, uninhibited howling. The only people who seemed calm and quiet were an occasional old man with a bushy beard or one, shaved, with an open-necked shirt and a Ben Gurion halo of graying hair fluffing out around his head. There were also young Orthodox rabbinical Jews, wearing spectacles and sprouting earlocks, with fringes of black beard underneath their chins and long black coats that reached almost to their ankles. It is charming to read about such people in Agnon, and yet these young neophytes, so spindling and pale, so little adapted to the modern world, I could not help finding queerly incongruous with everything now happening in Israel. The hysteria at the Air France bureau I attributed to Jewish excitement, but I found it much the same at Orly—the same confused officials, the same feverish checking and stamping, the same yelping of some French family whose arrangements were somehow not in order. When you find these two kinds of hysteria combined in the French-speaking officials waiting on French-speaking customers at the airport of Tel Aviv, you have something which makes getting a boarding pass a challenge to a war of nerves.

It was a relief to board the plane. Once in the air, we travellers subsided.

Back at home, I read in the newspapers of my friends of the American School, the Director and his family, getting away from Jordanian Jerusalem just as the shelling of the frontier began, with the dome of the Church of the Dormition smashed and Mount Scopus, once the home of the Hebrew University, so long a useless enclave in Jordan, about to be recovered by Israel; of the refusal of Mrs. Vester, the dowager of the Jordanian American colony and now over eighty, to be persuaded to leave the hotel which had been run for generations by her family; of the Israeli Museum's having been hit by a shell and its contents having been put away for safety; of a shell going off and destroying a tree in front of the King David Hotel, of the inmates' resorting to the downstairs bar, where the windows were now protected by sandbags and where drinks were still being served, of the bartender's losing his nineteen-year-old son, who was knifed in the Old City while trying to rescue a wounded friend (I owe these last details to an article in the *New Yorker* by Miss Flora Lewis); of Teddy Kollek's being driven through the streets of Jerusalem in order to reassure the people, while the shells went off before and behind him, and of his saying of a bullet that had lodged in his car that he would add it to his collection, of his continuing, during the shelling, to joke about garbage disposal, to which now would be added the problem of getting rid of the debris of the war; of Pearlman, a lieutenant colonel, resuming, in Tel Aviv, his old function of military spokesman. As for the Dead Sea scrolls, the nationalization of the Palestine Museum had made them the property of the Jordan government, and I had been trying to get some idea of how they would be handled in the future. I now read that at an early moment the Israelis had occupied the Museum but had so far been able to locate nothing but some fragments of the scrolls, and read later that the Museum had been shot up and the scrolls probably sent to Amman. Before I had left Jordan, Père Roland de Vaux had asked me to give his regards to Yadin and to say to him how much he regretted "the barrier" that had prevented them from meeting anywhere except in Paris or London. I had been told on the Israeli side by the American Director of the Hebrew School of Archaeology that the Americans had had a meeting with the Arab authorities in the neutral house of the United Nations to request permission for foreign scholars to use the library of the Jordanian École Biblique. This request had been denied, but both Israeli and Gentile scholars are, one hopes, for the first time, at last, in a position to examine the whole mass of the scrolls, to confer about them, and to pool their findings.

# THE JUNE WAR AND THE
## TEMPLE SCROLL

WHEN THE Israelis made their way into Old Jerusalem on June 5, 1967, they found that the Palestine Archaeological Museum, in which the later batches of scrolls had been kept and studied, was being used as a fortress by the Jordanian defenders. It was one of the prime objectives of the Israeli forces, and they had little difficulty in capturing it; their blue-and-white flag was flying on it from the noon of June 6th. When Dr. William G. Dever, of the Hebrew Archaeological School in Israeli Jerusalem, got through to it, on June 12th, two days after the ceasefire, he found it, he says, pockmarked by bullets, and its tower, which had been used as a gun position, rather badly damaged. Inside, the showcases and the windows were smashed; the exhibits had been knocked about, and some of them had been broken. The bodies of several Israeli soldiers were lying inside and in the courtyard. There was now a sign at the entrance that announced it was a museum of the State of Israel. The scrolls were not found at first, and it was thought that they had been taken away, but they were later discovered in a safe in the wall, against which a display case had been moved. An inventory was made of the fragments, which had been fitted together by the scholars and fixed between sheets of glass, and everything, apparently, had been collected, with the exception of the strips of the copper scrolls, which had long before been sent to Amman, the capital of Jordan.

This museum had been built with Rockefeller money in 1929. In the days of the British Mandate, it was administered by the Mandate government, but when this came to an end in 1948, as a result of the first Arab-Jewish war and the proclamation of the State of Israel, its management was taken over by an international board of trustees. These trustees, perhaps spurred to emulation by the Shrine of the Book in the new Israel National Museum, proposed, in 1965, having been offered a grant for the purpose, to build a special wing for the scrolls, and asked the Jordanian government to sell them a piece of land behind the museum. The result of this move was that suddenly the Jordanian government, through its chief representative on the museum's board, demanded that the museum be nationalized. The American and British ambassadors made no objection to this, though the foreign scholars were much perturbed, and the nationalization of the museum took place in November, 1966. The Jordanians transferred its securities—which now amounted to less than half a million dollars—from a bank in London to a bank in Amman. The scholars were left embarrassed. The scrolls now belonged to the Jordanians, who were not even able to read them, and it was decided not to allow any of the manuscripts to be published without the foreign scholars' having raised a large sum of money to reimburse the museum for its expenditure in buying from the Bedouins the scrolls found in Cave Eleven. The permission to issue the scroll of the Psalms, the only one from this cave that has yet been published, had to be financed in this way, and the rich lady who had put up the money could not be induced to contribute any more because, now that the Palestine Museum had been taken over by Jordan and was not an American institution as the American School had been, such a donation would no longer be eligible for deduction from her income tax. I had the impression in

Jerusalem that the whole affair was rather in the doldrums. It was known that there were other scrolls yet to be bought, but there was no way of getting at them. If the officials knew where they were, they might simply confiscate them and put the man who had them in jail, so there was no inducement now for the latter to offer them. And it was rumored, perhaps falsely, that exhibits from the museum had recently turned up for sale in antique shops. The scholars could not be sure that new scrolls might not be sold outside Jordan. The capture of the museum puts the scrolls that are already in it safely in the hands of the Israelis, but the bitterness of the Arabs rather increases the danger that the Bedouins will not allow them to buy any not yet acquired.

Neither the École Biblique nor the American School was seriously damaged by the war. On Monday, June 5th, the first day, Père de Vaux was reading in the library when a shell exploded outside and shattered the windows. The personnel all went down to the basement, and the next morning Israeli soldiers arrived and brought them out at the point of a gun. They took all the Jordanians captive but allowed the priests to go to their rooms on condition that two of them, taking turns for an hour, would sit outside in the yard as hostages. They were told they would be executed at once if a single shot came from the building. Machine guns had been mounted on the terrace and the monastery tower. The reason for all this was evidently that the Jordanians on Monday morning had been shelling Israeli Jerusalem from a vacant lot next to the École Biblique. The priests are said to have accepted the situation without protest or agitation, though it came at a peculiarly inconvenient time. The remains of the founder of the School had just been brought back from France to be reburied on the monastery grounds, and, while sitting as hostages in the yard, the priests exchanged stories of its

early days. They decided on Wednesday to distract their
minds by delivering a series of lectures—Père Benoit, the
director, was to give a talk on the Magi, Père de Vaux one
on Abraham—but then the shelling began again and continued for an hour and a half, in the course of which the
grounds and the building—though not the monastery
church itself—were considerably battered and scarred.
When the war was over and the Palestine Museum was
in the possession of the Israelis, there was no longer, in
regard to the scrolls, anything to be feared from the Arabs,
but it might still have been awkward for the foreign scholars who had already done so much work on them for the
Hebrew University to take them over and distribute them
to different editors. Père de Vaux is said to have announced that if this happened, his usefulness in Jerusalem
would be over, and since he had already retired as Director of the School, he would simply go back to France. He
was immediately reassured by a meeting with Professor
Yigael Yadin and the Director of the Department of Antiquities of the Government of Israel. It was agreed that
all the work begun by de Vaux and his colleagues and the
scholars to whom he had assigned the editing of the various unedited scrolls should go on as if nothing had happened. The principal change on which Yadin insisted was
that the general title of the series published by the Clarendon Press should be changed from *Discoveries in the Judaean Desert of Jordan* to *Discoveries in the Judaean
Desert.*

As for the American School, at which I had been stay-
ing in May, when the Director for the year was Dr. John
H. Marks of Princeton, he got away with his family in a
taxi at eleven twenty-five Monday morning, just as the
first shots were being fired. They were caught several
times in crossfire, and saw the dome of the Church of the
Dormition, just over the border in Israel, from which the

body of Mary is supposed to have ascended to Heaven and which the Israelis had been using as a military post, "enveloped," as he says, "by a cloud of debris" when it was hit by a Jordanian shell. They got through to the airport at Amman, but it was closed and the personnel were fleeing. The Israelis were about to dive-bomb it, and several air raids on the city followed, which drove the Markses into a night club that was now being used as a shelter. The party was eventually flown, by way of Teheran, to Athens. The American consulate in Jordanian Jerusalem was shelled, and its inmates took refuge in the School building. This building, at the time I left Jordan, was supposed to have been sold to a sheikh who was acting for the Jordanian government. The Jordanians had resented its being free of taxation and wanted it for government offices, since it stood almost opposite the government headquarters. The price was to have been a million dollars, and Dr. Marks at that time believed that he had nearly completed the deal when—after many unnecessarily secretive meetings and muffled negotiations—he received a postdated check for about a seventh of that sum. The check was sent back by the Amman bank, which said it had no such account. The School's lawyer attached some of the sheikh's property as compensation for the expenses incurred by the School. The School wrote the sheikh a letter expressing indignation over the bad check and received this delightful reply: "Since the United States declared at the United Nations Assembly in May its decision to oppose the United Arab States and stand by Israel, the payment of my check . . . is something in my opinion the outcome of which may not be safe."

In less than two weeks after the Markses had left, the new Director for the year arrived at the School and was admitted by Omar, the chef, who had been working there for years and who had explained to the Israeli soldiers that the School was American property and could not be tampered with. The business of the School then went on as before, and I owe to its Bulletins and Letters the greater part of my information on the happenings recorded above.

Professor Yigael Yadin had known for seven years of the existence of another scroll in the possession of the Syrian Kando, to whom the Bedouins, in 1947, had brought the first batch of scrolls. He was a cobbler, and he bought the old leather because he thought it would be useful for his shoemaking. Since then, as I have already explained, he had been acting as the go-between for the Bedouins with the scholars. Totally ignorant, he is said to be a master of Middle Eastern cunning, and he had been enriching himself by hoarding and selling manuscripts. "I cannot at this stage," says Mr. Yadin, in a paper on the new scroll, "disclose the way this scroll came into our hands, lest I endanger the chances of acquiring further scrolls; it is sufficient perhaps to say that this aspect of the scroll, when told, will seem like a tale from the *Arabian Nights*." All we know from other sources is that Kando was seized by the Israelis and taken to Tel Aviv, where for five days he was put under house arrest and, it is said, "interrogated," and that the scroll was brought to Yadin from the newly invaded territory. Kando had been asking for it a price of $1,300,000, for which he held out in the hope that some rich Westerner would buy it, and Yadin believes that it has suffered more damage from seven years in the damp climate of Bethlehem than from the preceding two thousand years that it had lain in a Dead Sea cave. When it came into his hands, says Yadin, the upper part looked like melted chocolate and the worms had got into the outside layers. Kando is said to be suing the State of Israel for having broken a Jordanian law that gives the Palestine Museum the right to purchase any manuscript found in the country. But the museum is now held by the Israelis, and so is the west bank of the Jordan, where Kando lives. The status of this region has not yet been settled, but one feels that Kando has as little chance of ever getting back his scroll or being compensated on the scale he demanded as the American School had of being compensated for its expenses in negotiating for the sale of its buildings.

This scroll is a singular document. It is the longest that has yet been found; it unrolled to four feet longer than even the complete Isaiah scroll from Cave One, and it is written on the thinnest parchment, Yadin reports, of any of the scrolls yet known to him—less than one tenth of a millimeter. The text is from sixty-five to seventy per cent intact. This was evidently, from its language, written in the latter part of the Second Temple period—that is, in the first B.C. century, and copied perhaps a little later. The author was obviously a member of the Sect, because he reckons by the Sect's special calendar and, in correcting the practice of the Temple, has an emphasis of Sectarian polemics.

The most striking feature of the scroll, which makes it unique among Hebrew religious writings, is that it purports to be a message communicated not through a prophet but directly by God Himself, who speaks in the first person, even changing it thus from the third when He is quoting His past utterances from the Torah, and nonchalantly referring to Himself by His otherwise unpronounceable name, which He makes no attempt to disguise, as is done in other non-Biblical books of the Sect, by putting it into Old Hebrew characters or indicating it simply by *yodhs*. The author appears to believe that God is speaking directly to Moses—in fact, adding a new book to the Torah. He gives rules about cleanness and uncleanness, often quoting the Torah, but with additions to and deletions from the accepted text; He enumerates the sacrifices

and offerings appropriate to the Festivals, as reckoned by
the Essene calendar, and lays down the rules for the services of the Temple. Almost half of the scroll is occupied
—which has led Yadin to call it the Temple Scroll—with
plans for building the Temple, and these descriptions are
at variance in many details with what we know of the
Second Temple as it had been remodelled by Herod. Yet
it is not a visionary temple foreseen for "the End of Days"
but a practical temple to be built by men. Even the problem of the toilets has been thought of. They must not be
set so high as to be in sight, so they cannot be east on the
Mount of Olives, nor west, because the frequent west
winds would be blowing in the direction of the Temple.
The place for them is fifteen hundred yards north of the
sacred building, which would have put them not far from
the site of the now destroyed Mandelbaum Gate and quite
close to the present American School. The Temple is to
comprise three courts, one inside another, and both the
outer and middle courts shall be provided with twelve
gates named for the Twelve Tribes, as in the specifications
given in Ezekiel and the Apocalypse for the gates of Jerusalem. In I Chronicles 28, David is said to have given Solomon the divine plans for building the Temple: "All this,
said David, the Lord made me understand in writing by
His hand upon me, even all the works of this pattern."
Yadin believes that the Temple Scroll is an attempt to
supply this document, not to be found in the Scriptures,
which was given by God to David and handed on by
David to his son, who did actually build the first Temple.
There is, in fact, it seems, a reference to such a scroll in
the Palestinian Talmud.

Another section of the scroll deals with the Statutes of
the King. I had better let Mr. Yadin describe this in his
own words: "Although it begins with a direct quotation
from Deuteronomy 17.14 ff. ['When thou art come unto

the land which the Lord thy God giveth thee, and shalt possess it, and shalt dwell therein, and shalt say, I will set a king over me, like as all the nations that are about me; Thou shalt in any wise set him king over thee whom the Lord thy God shall choose.'] . . . it proceeds immediately to the two main subjects of interest to the author: the King's bodyguard and the mobilization plans—phase by phase—to be taken by the King when the 'land of Israel' is faced with the threat of a war of extermination. On the first subject, God prescribes, according to our author, that the King's bodyguard comprise twelve thousand soldiers— a thousand per tribe. These soldiers must be without blemish—'men of truth, God-fearing, hating unjust gain.' While some of the expressions and principles are borrowed from Exodus 18, our interest is in the additions which reflect the political situation of the period. The main purpose of this guard is to protect the King 'day and night lest he fall into the hands of the Gentiles.' This fear of the danger from the Gentiles is paramount in this section. In another place, the scroll prescribes the death penalty for anyone who betrays the people of Israel and passes information to the enemy. However, the most interesting part—also historically—refers to the mobilization phases. When the King is aware of a danger from an enemy who wants 'to take everything which belongs to Israel,' he should mobilize a tenth of the nation's force. If the enemy force be large, one fifth of the King's force is to be called up. Should the enemy come 'with his king and chariotry and great multitude,' a third of the force should be mobilized; two thirds should remain in the land to protect its frontiers and cities lest 'an enemy band penetrate into the country.' If, however, 'the battle be strong, the King must mobilize half the total fighting strength and 'the other half will remain in the cities' to defend them. Having read these rules immediately after the war,

I could not help commenting at the time that here was an excellent description of the actual phases of mobilization preceding the Six-Day War in Israel. The parallel between the scroll's prescription for mobilization in the face of complete extermination and what actually happened in Israel two weeks before the war is quite fantastic. This is, of course, a strictly personal and subjective reaction; the real importance of this section is that it reflects the true political and historical problems facing ancient Israel at the time the scroll was written. These rules are basically different from those in the scroll of the *War of the Sons of Light against the Sons of Darkness*. The latter deals exclusively with the offensive eschatological war, while here we deal with a defensive war against an attacking unnamed enemy."

Yadin also feels a significance, a symbol of the rebirth of Israel, in the appearance after two thousand years of the apocalyptic Essene War Scroll, in the midst of the first Arab war, when his father got through to Bethlehem and recognized the genuineness of the first set of scrolls. This millennia-spanning mixture in Israel of ancient and modern history makes it, in my opinion, a place of unique interest and of heartening inspiration. The ancient Jews had no real sense of time in the way that we understand it. Their verbs had not tenses but "aspects." Certain of these aspects are now used to indicate time, yet to visit the modern Israel and to see what is going on there is to feel oneself partly released from the narrow constrictions of today's and yesterday's newspaper and to find oneself, thus rising above the years, with their catastrophes and their comings and goings, in touch with one of the greatest human forces for the tenacity and authority of our race.

# GENERAL REFLECTIONS

WHAT IS the fascination that is exercised by this much-damaged Dead Sea library which causes us to grope so intently among the fragments of old manuscripts written almost two thousand years ago, and to speculate on the differences in doctrine among ancient sects whose mode of thinking was strikingly dissimilar to our own, sometimes spinning whole webs of theory out of passages incomplete or blurred, in order to find out who composed them and what situations provoked them? If the Old and the New Testaments represent Divine Revelation, no such investigations are important. If they are of merely human provenience, the investigators are impelled by mere human curiosity as to how they came to be written and what their relation is to a cult of immense prestige. I know that the more liberal churchmen would say that these documents occupied in their time a kind of intermediate position between Judaism and the New Testament; that Jesus and the older prophets were real spokesmen for the word of God, and are susceptible of being studied in their human roles with all the more interest on account of this. But this position raises theological problems which I do not want to go into here. I want merely to indicate the point of view from which I have been writing on this subject. I have discovered that I am by temperament, by congenital cast of mind, a born shrinker of myths. In my books on Marxist socialism and on the Civil War, I was

at first, I suppose, attracted by the dramatic interest of the
historical crises that these involved and by the ameliora-
tive idealism that played such a large part in both, but by
the time I had got done studying them and had actually
written about them, I was aware that, as an inveterate
myth-shrinker, I had to some extent undermined the
idealistic pretensions of both. In my writings on the Dead
Sea Scrolls, I have performed a somewhat similar function for the myth of the origins of Christianity—though I
was not, of course, the first in this field. It was inevitable
that the scholars who had dealt with the scrolls, and on
whom I have depended for my information, should already have performed that function. They did so sometimes unintentionally; but now, although most of these
scholars have still, or had begun by having, some ecclesi-
astical commitment, I have noticed that these commitments
to official faiths appear to be less of an impediment and
that they present their researches more candidly as moti-
vated by an interest in finding out what actually happened in intelligible earthly terms—the desire by which
I, too, who follow their conclusions at second hand, have
been prompted to write about them. Albert Schweitzer, in
*The Quest of the Historical Jesus,* written before the finding of the scrolls, has summarized the various attempts to
reconstruct or account for the life of Jesus only to come
to the conclusion at last that there was no way of knowing the historical Jesus, who "will be to our time a stran-
ger and an enigma," since he is "a Being not subject to
temporal conditions," but comes to us as "an imperious
ruler," "One Unknown, without a name," who "speaks
to us the same word: 'Follow thou me!' and sets us to the
tasks which He has to fulfil for our time," etc. But, with
no such conception of Jesus, one cannot accept this point
of view, and it is becoming, I gather, more difficult, now
that we have so much new evidence on the history of

Jewish prophecy, for even the men of the Churches to accept it.

This does not mean that, as some seem to have thought, I am either, necessarily, "anti-religious" or "anti-clerical." I am aware that, for those of real religious vocation, their religious transcendences and revelations are as real as anything else in their lives, that they may be, in fact, more real than anything else. The printed researches of the scholars into the origins of their religions may seem to them of no significance. The scholars collect human relics of the lives of prophets and saints, but do not catch the great light of God. This vision of God's light I have never had, no moment of exaltation has ever made me feel that I was close to God, but I know that this has been felt by a variety of other human beings in a variety of situations and in a variety of earthly environments, so why may it not be experienced through the words and deeds of Jesus as reported in the New Testament? The cult of "reason," so widely applied in the course of the last three centuries, has come to seem to me in a sense a blind alley. Our thoughts and actions may be controlled by but they do not spring from what we call reason. I am no metaphysician, and I cannot attempt to describe what has happened when the artist or the scientist who has banished some problem from his mind or has not even been thinking about it is aware that he has suddenly been given the answer—that, like Coleridge, he is now in possession of the words that make the harmony of "Kubla Khan" or that, like Descartes, lying in bed, he has had the revelation that was to give the clue to the system of coördinate geometry—that is, that geometrical lines may be represented by algebraic equations. Both such intellectual products may be explained in "rational" terms, but what prompts these creative acts? They derive from some power we do not "understand"; and this power the believer calls

God. I cannot accept the word God, because I feel it involves a myth. Any kind of accepted God must, it seems to
me, wear an anthropomorphic face, and I cannot accept as
an embodiment of God the face of Jesus of which we know
nothing but can only imagine and idealize, nor even his reported words and deeds of which our knowledge is rather
uncertain and which must have been conditioned by the
circumstances of their historical time and place and by
those of the persons who chronicled them. I feel more
nearly at home with Henri Bergson's *élan vital* or A. N.
Whitehead's principle of concretion in the universe. And
yet there are passages in literature based on the Christian
theology which have moved and impressed me as much
as any: the climax at the end of Dante when he says that
he cannot describe the illumination of the Divine Vision,
because it has melted from his mind and can never be
captured again, that it can only be compared to the squar-
ing of the circle and recorded as our human semblance in
some way made one with the Eternal Light; the last poem
of *Dr. Zhivago,* in which Jesus, after the agony of Geth-
semane, betrayed by one of his disciples and with the
forces of society all against him, predicts that he will rise
again to judge the centuries which, like rafts on a river,
"like the barges of a caravan," will float down to him out
of the darkness.

And yet when one comes to realize how ready human
beings have been to accept "charismatic" leaders, one cannot help feeling a certain contempt. When northern New
York State was settled at the end of the eighteenth century,
its population came mostly from New England and, moving into that immense open countryside, they cast off the
cramping theology of the Calvinism of their fathers. But
they nonetheless needed religion, and they soon invented
cults for themselves. There were the Perfectionism of the
Oneida Community founded by John Humphrey Noyes,

who believed that the Second Coming had already taken place; the Shakers of Mother Ann Lee, who believed herself a reincarnation of Christ; and the followers of Jemima Wilkinson, who also set up as Christ's reincarnation and announced she would never die. But the most powerful and the most enduring of these cults was the Mormonism of Joseph Smith, which had its origin in the town of Palmyra, just north of the Finger Lakes. It is strange to read a documented and honest description—I believe the only such that has been written—of the rise of this new religion in the biography of Joseph Smith, with the title *No Man Knows My History,* by Mrs. Fawn M. Brodie, who grew up, in a Mormon village, on the legends of miraculous occurrences and the ministry of Smith the Prophet, and who in later life set herself the task of finding out what had actually happened in all its absurdity and scandal. Here we have had growing up, as it were, right under our noses, in our familiar American West and as lately as the last century, the cult of a swindler, a charlatan and an unscrupulous and insatiable lecher, and the establishment, based upon it, of a solid and respectable church, which now flourishes with huge ugly sacred buildings, a Tabernacle and a Temple, its special educational system and its international missionary service, on the basis of fraudulent and nonsensical scriptures and the legend of Joseph Smith the martyr, as well as of the able management and the inculcation of discipline contributed by his successor Brigham Young.

Joseph Smith, born in 1805, had been brought, at the age of ten, from Vermont to upstate New York. According to non-Mormon documents cited by Mrs. Brodie, he had been known to his neighbors as an untruthful and trouble-making boy, much given to pretended feats of magic and digging for buried treasure. At twenty-one, he was haled into court as a "disorderly person and impostor."

But he was likeable and very imaginative. It was said of him by one of his townsmen who helped set up type for the Book of Mormon, "I never knew so ignorant a man as Joe was to have such a fertile imagination. He could never tell a common occurrence in his daily life without embellishing the story with his imagination; yet I remember that he was grieved one day when old Parson Reed told Joe that he was going to Hell for his lying habits." The young Joseph Smith became interested in the Indian burial mounds and, not knowing that they were simply cemeteries, assumed that there had been a great war in which many had been killed in battle. When Joseph was about twenty-two, he pretended that an angel in "a loose robe of most exquisite whiteness," who said that his name was Moroni, had been sent by God to reveal to him a sacred book of revelation written upon gold plates. Smith asserted that he had found these plates in a stone box along with a sword and a breast plate, to which were fastened the mysterious Urim and Thummim supposed to have been contained in the Ark. He would not at first let anyone see the plates: this would mean, he said, instant death. He declared that this book solved the problem of the origin of the Indians. There had originally been two races in America who fought one another for a thousand years, and these mounds were memorials of their battles. He pretended to have dictated the contents of the book without even unwrapping the plates. Later he put a screen between himself and the person to whom he was dictating and explained that the Angel Moroni had also supplied him with glasses which enabled him to translate the plates from what he called "reformed Egyptian." (Hieroglyphics had not yet been deciphered.) Smith did try to confirm his story by producing what he said were these sacred plates, the text of which a Columbia professor of classics declared to be a nonsensical conglomeration:

"Greek and Hebrew letters, crosses and flourishes, Roman letters inverted or placed sideways, were arranged in perpendicular columns, and the whole ended in a rude delineation of a circle divided into various compartments, decked with various strange marks, and evidently copied after the Mexican calendar by Humboldt, but copied in such a way as not to betray the source from which it was derived." The "translation" is a farrago of balderdash of which the only passages that possess any dignity are borrowings from the King James Bible, carefully doctored to make them seem distinct from it. (When, in an earlier article in the *New Yorker* magazine, I referred to Joseph Smith as having "dictated" the Book of Mormon, some official Mormon bureau to which this statement was shown for checking tried to insist that this should be changed to "translated.") The prophet Lehi, according to the Book of Mormon, sails from Jerusalem to America in barges that contain specimens of all the species of animals which were then to be found on the North American continent, including several—such as horses, pigs and sheep—which had actually been imported by the Europeans. When I asked at the Bureau of Information at the Joseph Smith Memorial in Palmyra where the plates of Smith's revelation were kept at the present time, I was told that they had been taken back to Heaven.

Martin Harris, a well-to-do farmer, who had already passed through several sects, became an enthusiastic Mormon. He testified—I quote Mrs. Brodie—that "he had seen Jesus in the shape of a deer, and had walked with Him two or three miles, talking with Him as familiarly as one man talks with another: the devil, he said, resembled a jackass, with very short, smooth hair similar to that of a mouse. He prophesied that Palmyra would be destroyed by 1836, and that by 1838 Joseph's church would be so large that there would be no need for a president of the

United States." Other visions had occurred in New York State. Three unknown strangers had ploughed a field at night and had spread another field with fertilizer. An old man with a white beard had appeared to a farmwife who was milking and told her that she was tired out and that he had been sent to strengthen her faith.

Joseph Smith himself was supposed to have cast out a devil from a man who had since youth been what we now call a neurotic, and was obsessed, as was common in that period, with morbid fears about his salvation. Smith established in 1830 a church with a congregation of six, which in a month increased to forty. Among those who were not converted, he continued to have a bad reputation. He was mobbed and twice arrested and twice acquitted. He identified himself with the Christian martyrs. He now began to talk, like the authors of certain of the Dead Sea documents, of the building of a new Jerusalem. He sent missionaries to an evangelist in Ohio, who had established at Kirtland, not far from Cleveland, a small communistic colony and who became almost immediately converted to the Gospel of the Book of Mormon. Smith himself now removed to Kirtland, which he told the sixty followers who accompanied him was the eastern frontier of the Promised Land. He made more converts, who flocked to join him, and Mormonism became infused with the current millennianism—an inheritance from Jewish prophecy—which, in the earlier half of that century, had given impetus to so many other American sects. Joseph Smith ordained high priests and appointed twelve disciples. In his pretensions to perform miracles he was found rather unreliable: he was supposed to have effected a cure in the case of a woman with a paralyzed arm; but other attempts at such cures were failures, and, when challenged by a Campbellite preacher, he evaded the test by inquiring whether this skeptic would prefer to have a withered hand or be stricken blind and dumb. He explained that Ohio was not consecrated ground and so not favorable to the accomplishment of miracles, and, as a result of having been tarred and beaten in Ohio, he moved on to the boom town of Independence, Missouri, where he founded a Holy City by laying the cornerstone for a temple. He had persuaded many of his converts to donate their money to the movement and to deed their property to its Church.

The Mormons were everywhere persecuted. They had established in Kirtland a bogus bank, which was supposed to have been sponsored by God and on the credit of which Smith boldly borrowed. The bank vault contained many boxes, each labelled $1000, which actually, under a layer of genuine silver half-dollars, contained nothing but stone, sand and old iron. When creditors became urgently pressing, the bank manufactured new notes which it sometimes exchanged for good money. But when the fraudulence of the bank became unmistakable, the Mormons were overwhelmed with law suits, and there was a warrant out for Smith's arrest. They were always having to move further West, and Smith, in 1844, when he was thirty-nine, was shot and killed in an Illinois jail, to which he had been consigned for burning the press of a hostile paper. All these misfortunes, of course, were turned by legend into martyrdoms. Joseph Smith, it is plain, did have something of the personal magnetism, hypnotic power, which suggests the supernatural and to which his otherwise relentless biographer expresses herself as not entirely insensible. He had a robust undiscourageable vitality, a friendly and plausible warmth. He was particularly persuasive to women, and, according to Mrs. Brodie, it was his desire to go to bed with any who happened to attract him, including the wives of his colleagues, that first inspired the policy of polygamy—a practice which added much to the unpopularity of the Mormons and which in public Smith always disavowed. Joseph Smith must have lived for a large part of the time in a megalomaniac fantasy. Yet he was also a conscious and unhesitating faker who once referred to his followers as "dupes." After his murder in Illinois, his followers were led by Brigham Young into the wilderness of uninhabited Deseret, as Utah was then called, where this shrewder and more practical henchman established the Church of Jesus Christ of Latter-day Saints as a self-contained and stable community.

Near Palmyra, a tall granite shaft has been erected to the revelation of Joseph Smith. This monument is the work of a Norwegian sculptor who was converted to Mormonism in Norway. At its top, a gilt statue of the Angel Moroni uplifts his right arm to Heaven, and under his left arm holds the plates of the Book. The shaft represents the great beam of light that came to Joseph Smith in a nearby wood, and the designs on it symbolize the structure of the administration of the Mormon Church. On three of the sides at the base are plaques which depict Joseph Smith receiving the plates from the Angel; the Three Witnesses who were supposed to have testified that they later, in the company of Smith, had been privileged to behold plates and Angel; and the Eight Witnesses who still later testified that they had seen and handled the plates—though they said that at first when the box was opened, it had seemed to them to be empty till Smith had exhorted them to get down on their knees and pray for more faith. These first three witnesses are made to stand, in deference to the Angel, with their period straw hats in their hands. They were very important to Smith to supply confirmation for his story, and he induced them to sign a statement that he had summoned the Angel in their presence. The ridge of "the Hill Cumorah," as the Mormons Biblically call it, very high and steep above the fields, at the end of the wedge of

which the monument to Moroni stands, commands a magnificent view of the now cultivated plain of the countryside,
and one can see that it might stimulate an imaginative
boy, with little learning and not much more reading than
the Bible, to assume a Sinaitic role and compose a prophetic vision. A Bureau of Information below presents, at
no cost, for visitors, a color film, with recorded lecture, of
Joseph Smith's boyhood and "call," and the covered-
wagon trek of the Mormons. In August, a great pageant
is held on the hillside, with a script adapted from the
Book of Mormon. "So realistic," we are told in a leaflet
advertising this occasion, "is the pantomime acting, the
thunderous sound system and the brilliant lighting that
one critic wrote, of the climactic 'Destruction Scene': 'The
action was so realistic I found myself sitting there, mouth
wide open with awe. When the city was destroyed [the
city of Zarahemla, an invention of the Book of Mormon],
they perfectly reproduced lightning and thunder. Smoke
bombs were set off, colored light split the darkness, and
the actors moved and fell like a crowd in panic.'"

I do not, of course, except as an illustration of the inevitable human need for some kind of superhuman hero,
compare the growth of Mormonism to the progress of
Christianity. The whole story here is unpleasant; Joseph
Smith had no aspect of saintliness. But to a non-believer
like myself, the phenomenon is worthy of attention as an
example of this recurrent need. Miss Alison Lurie, the
novelist, has presented the birth of a fictional religion in
her novel *Imaginary Friends*. It has always been this
writer's special gift to be able to catch the atmosphere, to
blend the various ingredients of any milieu in which she
has been immersed. She has rendered Southern Califor-
nia, a small élite New England college and the Boston of
Harvard and Cambridge with a fidelity to accent and
color, to the all-pervading spirit of place, that is astonish-

ing to anyone who has ever been in contact with the
places about which she has written. Her recent residence
in northwestern New York has resulted in an equally remarkable book which dramatizes the religion-breeding elements that once became so active there. An academic sociologist is attempting to study from a point of view
rigorously scientific an exalted local group who, dominated
by a clairvoyant girl, imagine themselves to have made
contact with beings in outer space. These beings are
inspired and ruled by a divinity who is called Ro of Varna,
and at a moment of intense expectancy when the group
is awaiting the advent of their master from another world,
the university sociologist, who has been entering into their
delusion, comes to believe that he embodies Ro. He is eventually confined to a sanitarium, where he continues to identify himself with this deity and is converting some of the
inmates at the same time that, for the benefit of one of his
old students, he professes, as a sociologist, to be checking
on how easy it is to gain power in such a community.
Miss Lurie has here described in plausible contemporary
terms the metamorphosis of such a leader as Joseph Smith
—and perhaps also of Jesus as the Jewish Messiah, who,
on the basis of the Gospel narratives, would seem also to
have had, at moments, not the questionings of modern
psychology, but certain doubts of his divine mission and
his heavenly sponsorship.

It is possible to imagine that someone who has grown
up in the belief in a Deity may, in a moment of ambition
and inspiration, thus imagine himself the spokesman of
that Deity; but though I always try to understand the reasons for other people's beliefs, to enter into the minds of
others whose ideas are different from my own, and though
I can see from the Dead Sea scrolls that the role of a
Jewish Messiah had been sedulously built up in advance

and that Jesus may well have been assigned and have allowed himself to be assigned to it, I am unable to identify myself imaginatively with the Christian who believes that Jesus was actually the son of God, sent down by the Heavenly Father to provide us with an opportunity of having our sins somehow redeemed by our believing in the myth of his divine-human role. Why should we never doubt that we are governed by a God who loves us and whom it is our duty to love, a God who created mankind so fallible that it slipped at once into Original Sin and committed crimes that could only be forgiven by God's begetting a child on a virgin and then sacrificing this child to save us? How could Jesus, in being crucified, atone for his half-brothers' sins? The idea of propitiating God by animal or human sacrifice is of course a familiar one; and I know that it is possible to trace, by the study of other mythologies, all the elements of Christianity. But how is it possible, at the present time, to persuade human beings to invest in this story? It seems to me as preposterous a fairy tale as it did to the Rabbi Trypho, in his dialogue with Justin Martyr—though Justin did not, of course, intend us to agree with the Rabbi—as the Greek myth that Zeus begat Perseus by descending on Danaë in the guise of a shower of gold. The best I can do is to see that the feelings of guilt aroused by the results of one's imperfect efforts to live up to the practical standards imposed by the requirements of one's particular society in the interests of its viability may spur one to imagine oneself forgiven by the half-human offspring of a Diety, who sees our lives from a higher level—that is, what it seems to me to come down to, by raising ourselves, at moments, to a higher level, to be able to forgive ourselves. For the rest, I can only explain the power of Christianity, like the power of other religions, by the innocent credulity of

the human race. And this is not at all difficult for one who
has seen both Stalin and Hitler exalted as the saviors of societies which they were leading into serfdom or ruin.

Yet one must make a fundamental distinction between
these tyrants like Stalin and Hitler and the founders of
the great religions. They have appealed to quite different
needs; it is impossible to look into the career and the personality of Herod "the Great" without becoming aware of
analogies to the career and personality of Stalin; and it is
suggestive to contrast Herod's role with Jesus's.

Herod, like Stalin, did not belong by blood to the majority of the people over whom he ruled, and since he felt
his situation precarious, he was at pains to play down his
origins—just as Stalin, a Georgian, showed no kindness to
the minority nationalities of the Soviet Union to one of
which he himself belonged. Herod's parents were Edomites, and the Edomites, close neighbors of the Jews, were
among their hereditary enemies. Their king, when Moses
was returning from Egypt, had refused to let the Jews
pass through his territory; and the Edomites had later been
subjugated by David, whose general, Joab, according to
Kings, remained in their country six months in order to
make sure that every male was slaughtered. And then
Herod had been set up by Rome. His father had been
Procurator of Judea, and Herod had been Prefect of Galilee. After the siege and destruction of Jerusalem, defended
by the last Hasmonean Jewish king, he had this Hasmonean executed; and he later persuaded Augustus to install
him as King of Judea. The Galileans, during his absence
from Palestine while he was visiting Rome for this purpose, had risen against and murdered his brother Joseph,
and Herod could never be sure that the people might not
rise against him, too, and restore the Hasmonean dynasty
—just as Stalin, crudely educated and untravelled, had al-

ways hated and feared the cosmopolitan old Bolsheviks, whom he later systematically extinguished. The chronicle, as narrated by Josephus, of palace intrigue, family murder and sexual scandal is too complicated to summarize here. An important element in it is the marriage of Herod to the Hasmonean princess Mariamne. Herod is supposed to have loved her. She was the granddaughter of one of the Jewish kings and taunted Herod's mother and sister for their inferior Edomite birth. When away on an official visit, Herod left her in charge of a brother-in-law called Joseph, with orders to kill her if he did not come back. But Joseph told Mariamne of these orders, and when he returned, this was reported to Herod, and he listened to his sister's story that Joseph had been Mariamne's lover. Joseph was put to death but Mariamne allowed to live—until the King, after another absence, was told by his mother and sister that Mariamne wanted to poison him and, egged on by his sister, though reluctantly, he had her executed at the age of twenty-eight. But after this, he was tortured by remorse and fell ill on a hunting trip in Samaria. Mariamne's formidable Hasmonean mother, hoping that he was going to die, took steps to secure the throne for herself, and Herod, finding out about this when he was well and had got back to the court, had his mother-in-law executed, too. So Stalin became suspicious of the relatives of the wife whom he had driven to suicide, and had them imprisoned or exiled. And Herod, like Stalin, became more and more suspicious, more and more malignantly demented. He had been persuaded by Mariamne's mother to make her sixteen-year-old son high priest, but when he found that this buttressed the morale of the Jews, he had had the boy drowned, on a visit for a feast to Jericho, by having him held under water in a bath. Now Herod's two sons by Mariamne came back from a visit to Rome and, as at least half of Hasmonean blood, became quite popular with the Jews. Their father, however, pushed forward a son by an earlier wife, who, together with Herod's sister, manufactured, by forging letters and extracting confessions from tortured slaves, false evidence that their half-brothers from Rome had sinister designs on their father. Herod had them both strangled. Their surviving half-brother himself now plotted the death of Herod, and his father, finding this out, had him thrown into prison in chains. In the meantime, now firmly established, he had entered upon his period of splendor: he lavished money on public works, rebuilt demolished Samaria, which had been given him by Augustus, and raised handsome temples to Augustus at the same time that he made a point of restoring the Jewish Temple in Jerusalem. But the Jews could not be appeased by his favors to Jewish institutions at the same time that he was forcing upon them the heathen Olympic games and the gladiatorial combats with wild animals. He hired mercenaries from Germany, Galatia and Thrace, and suppressed with much cruelty conspiracies against him. Some young men who were led by two teachers of the Law tried to tear down a Roman eagle from the Temple gate in Jerusalem and were, in consequence, burned alive. Herod himself was now literally rotting away with an illness of which Josephus gives a peculiarly gruesome account. We have only the Gospel of Matthew as an authority for the story that, learning from the Wise Men that the King of the Jews had just now been born in Bethlehem, he ordered the immediate massacer of all the babies there; but this is exactly the sort of thing that Herod at that time was doing. He at one point attempted to kill himself, and his imprisoned son, hearing his lamentations, tried to bribe his jailer to set him free; but this was brought to the ears of the father, who at once had the son executed. In fear lest the Jews might not mourn his own death, he had a group of their most honored men herded into an arena and held there. He gave orders that, when he died, they were all to be put to death, but when he did die, five days after the murder of his son, his sister set them all at liberty.

Is there some law of polarization by which such a life as Herod's, such a period as that in which he flourished, must demand and give rise to its opposite—so that the fear-ridden insolence of the Edomite, with the conquests of Rome behind him, is compensated by the birth at Bethlehem of the Jesus who, with a softened Jewish God behind him, tries to pardon, to declare human brotherhood and to liberate the maddened brothers from the ignominy of murderous competition? I have allowed above for the impulse to combat that may have remained partly latent in the preachments attributed to Jesus; but another message, also, is there, the message that, however mythologized, was to count for so much in the world. The reign of Stalin in Russia, even more exterminatory with its modern equipment for destruction, has produced, although not on the earlier scale, certain results that are somewhat similar. The Jewish poet, Boris Pasternak, reproached the tradition of his fathers for its failure to accept Jesus and he released in *Doctor Zhivago*, to the consternation of Stalin's successors, a great reassertion of what are still for many accepted as Christian principles. Stalin's daughter, Svetlana Alliluyeva, has detached herself from the Soviet Union, repudiating the system that her father maintained and declaring a religious commitment by having herself baptized in the proscribed Greek Orthodox Church. She had never read Pasternak's book till she found it, after leaving Russia, in Switzerland, when, discovering that her own dispositions had been substantially the same as his, she was much moved and fortified by it. This is not, of course, to say that every tyrant, every period of obtuseness and brutality, has engendered the ideal of a Jesus Christ, but it would seem that, in such situations, there is stimulated sometimes a counter-tendency toward harmony, forbearance and peace. The self-contained little communist units of the early years of the nineteenth century aimed at realizing something of this kind. That Communism should now have become the name for a despotic government and an enslaved population, as Christendom came to be the name for fanatic persecutions and internecine wars, only shows that the destructive pole may always be counted upon to reassert itself.

It is striking, at any rate, that, in spite of the many inconsistencies and thaumaturgic marvels in the sectarian accounts of the Gospels, in spite of the obvious signs of the pressure of political events under the Roman occupation and of the rebellion against corrupt practices and antiquated official prescriptions of the Jewish religion itself, at the moment of Jewish history at which Jesus lived, the myth of the all-forgiving, the all-suffering and redeeming demigod, should have taken shape after his death and endured through the subsequent centuries, coëxistent with that name of Jesus in which so many horrors and hatreds have been justified, so many disunions maintained; that it can still stand as something real for certain rather exceptional people—and haunt with its admonishments many more—who attempt to make their thoughts and behavior conform to this obsessive ideal projected by the human imagination.

The uncertainties and the inconsistencies, the dark sayings and the mystical invocations, of course, have been important factors in the success of the New Testament because, as in the more recent cases of the writings of Nietzsche and Marx and Engels, they lend themselves to a variety of interpretations.

# INDEX

Aaron, 45, 301, 303–4
Abel, 12
Abimelech, 16, 254–5
Abraham, 7, 36, 82, 254, 302, 304, 349, 376; in Egypt, 8, 16, 254–6; and Hagar, 20; and Isaac, 20–1, 49, 91, 283; and Jehovah, 17–18, 28; tents of, 49, 152
Abram, *see* Abraham
Absalom, 85, 177, 179; Tomb of, 283
Achor, Vale of, 283
Acre, 78
Acts, 146, 297
Adam, 5, 12–14, 85, 360
*Adonai*, 257
*Affinités Littéraires et Doctrinales du 'Manuel de Discipline'*, 186
Agnon, Shmuel Yosef, 59–67, 104–5, 367
Ahaz, 294
Ain Feshka, 114
Air France, 340, 367–8
Albright, W. F., 111, 229, 236, 241; on dating of scrolls, 128, 165, 188; and Epistle to Hebrews, 300; and Essenes, 137, 205, 245; and John the Baptist, 210, 214; and Manual of Discipline, 171–2; and Shapira fragments, 327–8; on

significance of scrolls, 118–119
Aleph, 81
Alexander the Great, 143, 264, 330
Alexander Jannaeus, 162, 180, 264–9
Alexandra, 268–9
Algerians, and Arabs, 106
*Alice in Wonderland*, 228
Allegro, Dr. John, 235–6; background and personality of, 272–3; and book of Samuel, 289; conjectures of, 274–8; and copper scrolls, 275, 280–285; and deciphering of scrolls, 219; and Document IV, 297; and Shapira fragments, 326–7
Alliluyeva, Svetlana, 401
Alterman, Natan, 335
*America*, 244
American Fund for Israeli Institutions, 230
American School of Oriental Research, 121, 126, 128–9, 131, 194, 224–6, 261, 282, 329, 341–3, 346, 362, 374–380; *Bulletin* of, 195, 212, 378; director of, 44, 50–1, 345, 368, 376–7
American University, Beirut, 120

Perseus, 294, 397
Persia, 146
*Pesharin*, 263
Peter, Simon, 117, 277, 297, 356
*Petite Fille de Jérusalem, Une*, 326
*Petite Illustration, La*, 326
Petra, 343
Petronius, 118
Pharaoh, 8, 16, 27, 41, 254-6, 308
Pharisees, 138, 243, 266-7, 269-71
Philistines, 296
Philo, 136-44, 146, 149-50, 161, 177, 206, 242-3, 247
Pilate, Pontius, 99, 213-14
Plato, 214
Pliny the Elder, 136-7, 137n., 147, 153, 155-7, 242, 247, 249
Ploeg, J. van der, 120, 261
Poland (Poles), 53, 100, 215
Pompeii, 118, 194, 351
Pompey, 99, 177, 271
Prague, 216, 247, 366
*Preliminary Report*, 315
Prophet of Untruth, 176-7, 263
Prophets, 84, 121, 134, 169, 173, 263, 286, 296-7, 301-302
Proust, Marcel, 80
Proverbs, 349
Psalm 37, 270-1
Psalm 51, 169
Psalm 151, 258-9
Psalm of David, 170, 292
Psalms, 170, 180, 202, 257-9, 263, 304; non-Biblical, 257-258, 292
Psalms scroll, 257-62, 276, 319, 374
Pseudepigrapha, 167n., 295, 357
Ptolemies, 174

Pushkin, A. S., 118
Pythagoreans, 139, 259-60

*Quest of the Historical Jesus, The*, 386
Quinet, Edgar, 88
Qumrân, building and ruins at, 161, 163-4, 249, *see also* Essenes, monastery of; Cave I scrolls, 203, 253, 261, 263, 379; Cave IV scrolls, 289-290, 296; Cave XI scrolls, 260, 304, 328, 374; and coins, 161, 163-4; and copper scrolls, 221; excavation at, 341; library, 240, 243, 248, 250, 263, 291; Psalms from 292; Romans and, 163, 249; scrolls, 134-5, 168, 185, 230, 245, 250, 260, 262-4, 305, 320-1, 324, 327-8
Qumrân Sect, *see* Essenes

Rachel, 22-3, 27-8, 41
Raleigh, Walter, 288
Râs Feshka, 163-4, 239
Rebecca, 7, 254
Reed, Parson, 390
Reider, Dr. Joseph, 210
Reformation, 218
Renaissance, 85, 218, 226
Renan, Ernest, 4, 16, 37, 66, 211, 236, 305
Reuben, 27
*Revue Biblique, La*, 137, 186, 194, 198, 240, 249, 282
Rhoda, 187
Ro, 396
Robinson, Edward, 313-14
Rockefellers, 219, 261, 374
Rodin, Auguste, 350
Rodkinson, Michael L., 65-6
Romance languages, 37-8
Romans, 86, 189, 355-6, 362-363; artifacts of, 132-3; clocks, calendars, and language of, 37-8; and Gali-